D1561117

WATER AND THE ENVIRONMENT
IN THE ANGLO-SAXON WORLD

EXETER STUDIES IN MEDIEVAL EUROPE

History, Society and the Arts

SERIES EDITORS
Simon Barton, Anthony Musson,
Yolanda Plumley and Oliver Creighton

Water and the Environment in the Anglo-Saxon World

Volume III of
The Material Culture of Daily Living
in the Anglo-Saxon World

edited by
Maren Clegg Hyer and Della Hooke
with contributions by
Hal Dalwood[†], Jill Frederick, Mark Gardiner, Della Hooke,
Rebecca Reynolds, Stephen Rippon, Martin Watts
and Kelley M. Wickham-Crowley

LIVERPOOL UNIVERSITY PRESS

First published 2017 by
Liverpool University Press
4 Cambridge Street
Liverpool
L69 7ZU

© 2017 Liverpool University Press

The right of Maren Clegg Hyer and Della Hooke to be identified as editors of
this work has been asserted by them in accordance with the Copyright, Designs
and Patents Acts 1988.

British Library Cataloguing-in-Publication Data
A British Library CIP record is available

ISBN 978 1 78694 028 5

Typeset by Carnegie Book Production, Lancaster.
Printed and bound in Cornwall by TJ International Ltd.

For all of the great fishermen in our lives, then and now.

In Memoriam: Hal Dalwood, colleague and friend

Contents

Illustrations

Cover art redrawn by Doug Ellis from Oxford, University College MS 165 (prose copy of Bede's *Life of St Cuthbert*), fol. 14, early twelfth century. The image represents monks being saved from shipwreck by St Cuthbert's prayerful intervention from shore.

Tables

Contributors

Hal Dalwood[†] was an independent professional archaeologist, formerly a field archaeologist at Worcestershire County Council for 25 years. His professional career focused on urban archaeology, in particular excavations in towns with early medieval origins including Aylesbury and Worcester. His publications include *Excavations at Deansway, Worcester, 1988–89* (CBA 2004) and *Excavation at Newport Street, Worcester* (Cotswold Archaeological Trust forthcoming). He directed the extensive urban assessment project for the smaller historic towns of Worcestershire, Herefordshire and Shropshire (reports online at ADS).

Jill Frederick is Professor of English at Minnesota State University. She has presented and published on Anglo-Saxon saints' lives, the Exeter Book riddles and the Bayeux Tapestry. Her most recent article, 'Ships and the Sea in the Exeter Riddles', is forthcoming in a Proceedings volume from the 2010 conference of the Manchester Center for Anglo-Saxon Studies, 'The Anglo-Saxons in their World'.

Mark Gardiner is Senior Lecturer in medieval archaeology at Queen's University Belfast. He was President of the Society for Medieval Archaeology and editor of the *Archaeological Journal*, and is a Vice-President of 'Ruralia', the European body for medieval rural archaeology. He has an interest in coastal and inland transport and trade in both the early and late Middle Ages, and has excavated sites associated with these activities.

Della Hooke, PhD, FSA, is an Associate Member of the School of Geography, Earth and Environmental Sciences in the University of Birmingham, editor of *Landscape History* (the journal of the Society for Landscape Studies) and editor of the *Birmingham and Warwickshire Archaeological Transactions*. She specializes in studies of the development of the historical landscape in England and Wales, especially in the early medieval period. Her recent publications include *England's Landscape: The West Midlands* (English Heritage/HarperCollins 2006) and *Trees in Anglo-Saxon England: Literature, Lore and Landscape* (Boydell 2010).

Maren Clegg Hyer is Associate Professor of English at Valdosta State University (Georgia). She specializes in researching textiles and textile imagery in Anglo-Saxon culture. Some of her recent publications include *The Material Culture of Daily Living in Anglo-Saxon England* (edited with Gale R. Owen-Crocker, Exeter 2011), *The Material Culture of the Built Environment in the Anglo-Saxon World* (edited with Gale R. Owen-Crocker, Liverpool 2015) and *Textiles, Text, Intertext: Essays in Honour of Gale R. Owen-Crocker* (edited with Jill Frederick, Boydell 2016), including a chapter in that volume, 'Text, Textile, Context: Aldhelm and Wordweaving as Metaphor in Old English'.

Rebecca Reynolds finished her PhD at the University of Nottingham on the social dynamics of fishing and fish consumption in Anglo-Saxon England. For her thesis she worked on several assemblages such as Bishopstone, East Sussex, and Lyminge, Kent, the former of which is now published. She is presently concentrating on publishing her thesis and preparing post-doctoral applications to pursue her interest in medieval fishing and fish consumption.

Stephen Rippon is Professor of Landscape Archaeology at the University of Exeter. His research concerns the archaeology and history of wetlands in the past two millennia, and he is the author of *The Transformation of Coastal Wetlands: Exploitation and Management of Marshland Landscapes in North West Europe During the Roman and Medieval Periods* (Oxford University Press for the British Academy 2000) and *Landscape, Community and Colonisation: the North Somerset Levels During the 1st to 2nd Millennia AD* (Council for British Archaeology c.2006).

Martin Watts is a freelance molinologist and researcher who has practical experience in repairing both watermills and windmills, and working with millstones. His particular research interests are the use of water-power and corn-milling technology during the medieval period. He is the author of several books and articles, including *The Archaeology of Mills and Milling* (Tempus 2002), *Water and Wind Power* (Shire 2005) and *Corn Milling* (Shire 2008).

Kelley Wickham-Crowley is Associate Professor of English at Georgetown University, Washington, D.C., and a past Director of Medieval Studies and of Undergraduate Studies in English. She holds degrees in interdisciplinary Medieval Studies from Cornell and a Masters in Anglo-Saxon and Viking Archaeology from the University of Durham. Research interests include Old English and Early Middle English literature; intersections of physical and intellectual cultures; archaeology of the British Isles; feminist and gender theory; Anglo-Saxon architecture; *Laȝamon's Brut*; and J.R.R. Tolkien's writings. Her current book project, *Buried Truths: Fragments of the Anglo-Saxon World*, confronts the gaps in cultural evidence by placing the material and textual in dialogue, putting their contradictions and complements to work.

Introduction

Della Hooke and Maren Clegg Hyer

As one of the essentials of life, water was never far away from early medieval consciousness. In Britain one was rarely far from a supply of water, which had many uses. Rivers and their drainage systems were to influence the territorial divisions of England, as will be shown below, offering inroads to vast areas of countryside. Rivers not only attracted settlement, but many were used for the transport of goods, although their courses may have been altered in subtle ways since this period. In a landscape in which man-made drainage was nowhere near as prevalent as it is today, wetlands and marshes were common and might provide pasture as well as act as habitats for water birds that might be taken as food. It was a regular supply of clean water that was essential for settlement, and although water could be drawn from rivers and streams, springs were particularly important sources. Archaeology sets out the material background of living at this time while the documentary records that survive provide insights as to how the Anglo-Saxons and sometimes, too, their predecessors, viewed the waterscapes in their environment.

The geography of Anglo-Saxon England: rivers and territories

The importance of rivers in the territorial delineation of the early Anglo-Saxon kingdoms has long been recognized. Many river valleys tended to run through the cores of emerging territories forming the hub of early Anglo-Saxon kingdoms and folk regions, although boundaries remained fluid until well into the seventh century. The Severn, for instance, upstream from its estuary in the Bristol Channel, flowing through what was to become Gloucestershire and Worcestershire, was the hub of the late Iron Age tribal kingdom of the Dobunni, a territory which underpinned the Anglo-Saxon kingdom of the Hwicce.[1] What may be termed the northern part of a 'North Sea Province' included

Fig. i.1 Early medieval kingdoms (drawn by Della Hooke). The boundaries of drainage provinces are based upon the drainage systems depicted in Roberts and Wrathmell, *Region and Place: A Study of English Rural Settlement.*

Bernicia and Deira in Northumbria.[2] At its strongest, in the seventh century, Northumbria included not only the earlier units of Bernicia and Deira, but extended both northwards and also westwards across the Pennines, also taking in the former British kingdom of Elmet and extending southwards to include *Lindesfarona* (Lindsey). Bernicia, to the north, appears to have represented a largely Anglian takeover of earlier British territorial groupings, and in the Tweed basin the royal centre of Yeavering was established at an earlier British one known as *Ad Gefrin*, while earlier settlement may also now be emerging beneath the Anglian stronghold of Bamburgh. The Bernician heartland appears, however, to have been in the Tyne/Wear River region (Figure i.1). To the south, Deira was another Anglian kingdom perhaps originally focused on the Derwent river valley, a tributary of the Humber, but extending northwards towards the River Tees and inland from the coast westwards to the western edge of the Vale of York. These units, Bernicia and Deira, are likely at first to have been separated by a fluctuating border.

Rivers and river valleys were also often inroads for settlement. Navigable rivers had offered opportunities for trade and contact with the outside world since prehistoric and Roman times and continued to do so after the Roman withdrawal. Early Anglo-Saxons penetrated along the Thames valley, and there is evidence for co-existence between the first Anglo-Saxon generations and the post-Roman populations in the fifth century, especially at Dorchester. Immigration is, however, clearly indicated by the distinctive funeral rites of the newcomers, which included cremation, and their grave-goods suggest an affiliation with the people of the north German coast around the mouth of the River Weser (also 'West Saxons' according to Bede). Further to the west, in the south of England, in what was to become Hampshire, the Solent offered an entry point for what many have argued were mainly Jutish settlers.[3] The valley regions were to become the heartland of Wessex, the land of the 'West Saxons'. Other groups penetrated along the Trent valley and this river became the focus of the kingdom of Mercia, also said by Bede to form the divide between the North and South Mercians.

As obvious linear and relatively stable features in the landscape, rivers and watercourses were often taken to mark territorial boundaries from an early date. Early Welsh laws regard a major river as one of the 'stays' of a boundary, a 'stay' denoting a limiting feature.[4] Indeed, rivers were to mark the boundaries between the East Saxons of Essex and Surrey/Kent, in this case the River Thames; Deira and Lindsey were separated by the Humber, and, at an early stage, the northern boundary of the *Magonsæte* extended from Herefordshire as far north as the River Severn in Shropshire where that kingdom met the territory of the *Wreocensæte*.[5] As Anglo-Saxon dominance was extended westwards in the South-West Peninsula, the River Tamar was to mark the divide between Cornwall and Devon, the latter eventually taken over by the Anglo-Saxons and incorporated into Wessex. Cornwall maintained its independence until the tenth century when it was finally subdued in the reign of Æthelstan and the Tamar fixed as the eastern boundary. It was then administered as an English shire, but cultural assimilation was a much slower process, as the language and place names clearly indicate.[6] The Tamar maintains a strong role as a cultural divide in the perception of the region today (Figure i.2). The Mersey, *Mærse* C11, too, was probably 'boundary river' and did indeed mark the northern boundary

Fig. i.2 *above and opposite* The River Tamar, which forms the boundary between Cornwall and Devon (photograph by Della Hooke).

of Mercian-controlled territory in the eighth century, marching with lands under Northumbrian control. The River Thames, which had separated the East from the South Saxons, regained prominence as an administrative boundary when Alfred drew up a treaty with the Danish leader Guthrum post-886. The agreed boundary in the south-east began:

... up on Temese, 7 ðonne up on Ligan, 7 andlang Ligan oð hire æwylm, ðonne on gerihte to Bedanforda, ðonne up on Usan oð Wætlingastræt

... up the Thames, and then up the Lea, and along the Lea to its source, then in a straight line to Bedford, and then up the Ouse to Watling Street [which it subsequently followed].[7]

Rivers undoubtedly had a strong role to play in early medieval territorial demarcation.

At a smaller scale, this is also evident in the case of the folk regions that were the building blocks of the Anglo-Saxon kingdoms. There is strong evidence to suggest that some of these may also have had earlier British antecedents although others appear to represent grants of land to groups with at least Anglo-Saxon leaders (especially territories associated with -*ingas* place names).[8] A number of such folk regions

were associated with groups who took their names from the rivers themselves (below). Towards the end of the period under discussion rivers were also often followed by the boundaries of the later county divisions (e.g. the Thames between Surrey/Kent and Middlesex/Essex; the Stour between Essex and Suffolk; the Waveney between Suffolk and Norfolk; the Bristol Avon between Somerset and Gloucestershire; the Humber between Yorkshire East Riding and Lincolnshire; the Tees between Durham and Yorkshire North Riding and the Mersey between Lancashire and Cheshire).

Folk names

Rivers often gave their names to a group of people inhabiting a region, whether this was a major folk group or one of more limited extent. In Herefordshire, in the Welsh Borderland, the British district of Leen was focused upon several rivers and appears to take its name from these.[9] In the kingdom of the Hwicce, the *Arowsætna* were probably a group centred on the Arrow valley, the Arrow a tributary of the Avon; and in Greater Mercia the *Tomsæte* were a group centred on the Tame valley.[10] This is also true elsewhere in the country: in Kent a folk group known as the *Limenwara*, who gave their name to one of the administrative divisions known as lathes, took their name from the River Limen, and another group, the *Weowara*, from the Kentish River Wye. The *Anglo-Saxon Chronicle*, under the years 800, 878, 898 and 955, also refers to a group known as the *Wilsætan/Wilsæte* 'the dwellers by the River Wylye', who gave their name to the estate of Wilton in Wiltshire and to that of the county itself: *Wiltunescire* c.1000, *Wiltescire* 1086.[11] The place name Collingbourne Ducis in Wiltshire (*Colengaburnam*, etc.), may derive from 'the stream of the *Collingas*', 'the folk who live by the River Coll'; the *Dorcingas* in Surrey may have been 'the dwellers on the River Dorce', perhaps the upper Mole, 'clear, bright stream' (see below); the *Lodningas*, referred to in the place name Loddon in Norfolk, are 'the dwellers on the River Loddon'; the Pangbourne in Berkshire is the 'stream of the *Pægingas*, the people called after Pæga'. While the *Muccingas* of Essex may have been 'the people of Mucca', Margaret Gelling has, however, suggested that the name may be a reference to 'the mud place', referring to the great silver mud-banks on either side of Mucking Creek.[12] One folk name in the kingdom of the Hwicce appears to have taken its name from a mere: the *Husmeræ* were a group centred upon the Stour valley in Worcestershire and the mere name, possibly but not certainly, derived from a British word *udso*, pre-Welsh *ws* 'water' with Old English *mere*, survives in that of Ismere in Churchill and Blakedown in a valley that drains into the River Stour. These are examples of groups taking their names from obvious topographical features in their region: some others, such as the *Cilternsætna* and the *Pecsætna*, were named after prominent upland areas, the Chilterns and the Peak, respectively.

The geography of Anglo-Saxon England: wetlands and marshes

The wetlands of Anglo-Saxon England were far more extensive than they are today. Although some drainage had been carried out in Roman times, in the Somerset levels a period of flooding at the end of the Roman/beginning of the early medieval period, due partly to marine transgression, had inundated at least the western parts of these landscapes and the lower reaches of the rivers Yeo, Axe, Brue and Parrett. Drainage recommenced in Anglo-Saxon times (see Stephen Rippon, Chapter 4),[13] but much of the remaining lowland was often used more for seasonal pasture than for continuous crop cultivation for many centuries. There may also have been increasing precipitation levels as the Anglo-Saxon period progressed, although increased flooding along rivers and in marshy areas may also have resulted from the extension of agriculture in this period entailing clearance of the natural vegetation and the ploughing up of new ground.[14]

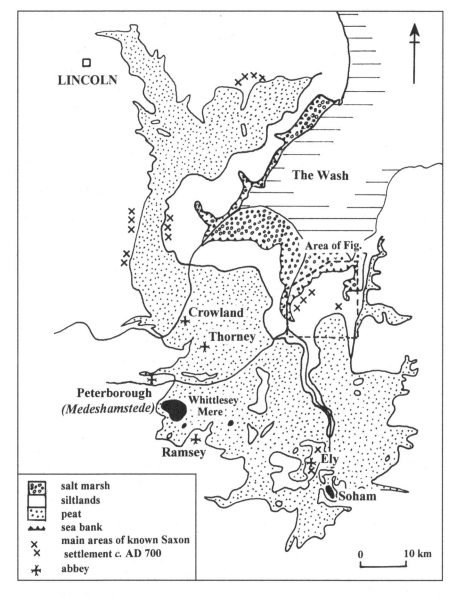

Fig. i.3 The Eastern Fenlands around the Wash (from Hooke, *The Landscape of Anglo-Saxon England*).

LINCOLN

The Wash

Area of Fig.

Crowland

Thorney

Peterborough
(*Medeshamstede*)

Whittlesey Mere

Ramsey

Ely

Soham

salt marsh
siltlands
peat
sea bank
main areas of known Saxon
 settlement *c.* AD 700
abbey

0   10 km

Most change has, however, occurred in eastern England, where whole regions lie at little more than 2 metres above sea level. Here, too, a degree of drainage had been carried out in Roman times, taking advantage of falling water tables, and settlements lay thick along the peat/siltland margin and on the southern islands. However, sea and river floods and a gradually rising water table led to peat formation and again to true fen conditions in many regions in Anglo-Saxon times (Figure i.3). A massive flood defence, the Sea Bank, was constructed all around the Wash towards the end of the period to protect settlements and agriculture on the siltlands, but much of the inland peatlands and coastal salt marsh remained empty areas used only as seasonal pasture.[15] Extensive wetlands thus bordered the Wash, and the abbeys of Thorney, Chatteris and Crowland were established within the marshes and those of Ramsey, Ely, Peterborough and St Ives close to their inland margins. To the south of Peterborough, Whittelsey Mere in Cambridgeshire was one of the most extensive stretches of inland water at this time, noted for its fisheries and wildfowl. The area covered by water was at least 756 hectares (ha) in summer, extending to 1,214 ha in winter, and was but one of a series of shallow lakes in the area. It was to be reduced by silting and peat expansion over time, with attempts at drainage carried out after 1600, but was only finally drained in the nineteenth century, to be replaced by fertile farmland. In the south-east of England, in the early medieval period, the Isle of Thanet was still cut off from mainland Kent by the Wantsum Channel, which was then used for shipping, with the two important ports of Sandwich and Richborough located to the south. On the south coast, Romney Marsh was also an extensive area of wetland at the mouth of the River Rother, again with the port of Rye at the western end of a large lagoon. Much of it belonged to the Priory of Canterbury in the ninth century. Reclamation was being carried out by various landholders in the eighth and ninth centuries when much of the land was being used as sheep pasture.[16] However, despite the construction of earthen embankments and sluices in medieval times, it was to be many centuries before drainage was complete. There were also extensive fenlands in Yorkshire and north Lincolnshire around the River Humber and its tributaries, again noted as a source of peat, fish and fowl, especially for supplying the monastic communities of the area. These, too, were only finally drained by the construction of drainage channels in late historical times.[17]

Inland, too, there is evidence of greater areas of marshy land further inland in the early medieval period. Some areas such as the Weald Moors of Shropshire were used for intercommoning by surrounding estates, but other areas which are farmland today were also once more marshy. In central Worcestershire, for instance, a tract of land, part of it described in charters as *byligan fen*, perhaps 'the bag-shaped fen', lay along headwater streams of the Whitsun Brook.[18] Many such areas were to be drained as agriculture expanded in the later medieval period (when drainage was often also aided by extended use of ridge and furrow cultivation).

Coastline changes were part of a continuous process, as the *Anglo-Saxon Chronicle* for 1014 reveals:

And in this year on St Michael's Eve [28 September], that great sea-flood came widely throughout this country, and ran further inland than it ever did before, and drowned many settlements and a countless number of human beings.[19]

It was the coastal districts bordering on the North Sea that suffered most, but marine erosion was to worsen after this period, with numerous settlements subsequently lost in medieval times, especially in the East Riding of Yorkshire and East Anglia.[20] The widespread nature of these waterscapes makes clear that water would have been a daily feature in the landscape for an Anglo-Saxon of any region, and would play a profound role in both the literal and imaginative landscapes of Anglo-Saxon England.

The location of settlements

All settlements needed access to a pure source of water and this would influence the location of settlement. Romano-British settlements were often strung out along rivers, but with increasing nucleation in the early medieval period, village founders usually sought out the most favourable locations, which were either beside the rivers in question or close to springs of pure water. Certainly, most inland central places, whether royal estates or the sites of early minsters, frequently stood beside rivers, some again with Roman antecedents. Facilities for transport along a river may also have influenced the choice of site (see chapters by Mark Gardiner and Hal Dalwood, this volume). In the Hwiccan kingdom, central places included Worcester (Roman *Vertis*), 'the Roman town of the *Weogoran*' (the folk group centred here), located beside the River Severn, the place which became the seat of the bishopric that served this kingdom in the seventh century, and Gloucester, 'the Roman fort/ city *Glevum*', the latter perhaps a name meaning 'bright' 'either literally referring to the reflection of the setting sun here on the waters of the Severn or transferred in the sense "noble, famous place"'.[21] In Roman Britain, several place names incorporated British river names, among them *Alauna* (Alcester, etc.), *Portus Abonae* (Sea Mills, Bristol)[22] and *Isca* as in *Isca Dumnoniorum*, Exeter. Early minsters were also often established in such riverine locations: in Worcestershire, this included seven of the eight early minsters, with the remaining one at Hanbury located within an Iron Age hillfort also overlooking a tributary of the Bow Brook and the Avon; in Gloucestershire, nine of the twelve known minsters stood beside rivers with the remaining three minsters not far away.

While some have argued that the availability of water in areas of predominantly stagnogley soils (such as clays which can be excessively wet in winter but which become baked dry in summer)[23] may have led to the nucleation of settlement, this is not entirely convincing as so many other factors need to be considered. It is reasonable to expect that founders of such nucleated settlements might choose the best locations well provided with sources of fresh water, but cultural factors need also to be taken into consideration. These included increased population density in more fertile regions and developing towns and monastic centres offering new markets in the eighth century. Such factors indeed affected the main crop-growing regions where new farming practices were coming into use and included changing farming systems such as the greater use of the mould-board plough, the introduction of new crops (including improved grain crops for white bread production), crop rotation and the more efficient centralization of plough teams within an open-field system. There is even conflicting evidence as to when nucleation took place – whether before or after the estate fragmentation that was such a feature of early medieval England.[24]

Many place names, too, contain references to water, and they might help to provide a picture of the landscape and how it was used. In this period, fishing weirs and mills were increasing in number and find mention in both names and documents; some rivers were also valuable lines of water communication offering routes for the transfer of both people and goods. On a smaller scale, the names given to local watercourses might reflect the nature of the rivers and streams themselves or hint at the nature of the countryside around and its local wildlife. They might also express a sense of local identity, but were often coined by travellers and administrators. Some of these aspects will be explored in the chapters that follow.

The chapters

A number of chapters in this volume concentrate upon the documentary evidence relating to the rivers, wetlands and marshes in the Anglo-Saxon landscape. In Chapter 2, Della Hooke looks carefully at the wide range of evidence for waterscapes found in pre-Conquest charters, both the rights stipulated in transfers of land and the names of watercourses revealed in charter-bounds. These include not only major river names well known to travellers and traders, but also minor names likely to have been coined by those living in the locality. The patterns in the naming of watercourses and related settlements tell us much about the ethnic and cultural intersections so characteristic of Anglo-Saxon

England. In Chapter 4, Stephen Rippon focuses our attention on one set of such waterscapes, the wide variety of wetland environments that dotted the Anglo-Saxon landscape. Such landscapes were rich in natural resources and ideal for activities such as pasturing livestock, salt making, growing seasonal crops suited to these unique environments and fishing; indeed, the usefulness of these lands inspired reclamation of wetlands and new patterns of land use as sea levels rose and fell. The rich history of the wetlands reflects the profound impact they had on the life of Anglo-Saxon peoples who inhabited these regions.

Rebecca Reynolds examines the evidence for one of these activities in Chapter 6, assessing the role that fish and fishing played in Anglo-Saxon England. That role is indeed significant, with finds and textual sources documenting a wide array of methods for catching fish, from simple hooks and nets to diverse types of fish traps or weirs suggestive of local fishing industries. Reynolds traces the increasing importance of fish in Anglo-Saxon diets across the period, noting interesting differences in the kinds of fish eaten by elites, including larger marine fish, compared to the flatfish and cod of many communities. She also considers the cultural assumptions that may have influenced the frequent consumption of fish in the Anglo-Saxon world: a handful of religious practices, and perhaps also humoral theory. In Chapter 7, Mark Gardiner turns our attention to the evidence for water transport along the same channels in Anglo-Saxon England. Sedimentation and other factors could make river transport challenging, and resulted in the creation of canals as well as the heavy use of larger and deeper rivers as conduits for trade and transport of goods and building materials, as well as people. The water traffic and the landing places on the coasts and inland rivers in turn have great influence on the eventual development and character of communities built by the water within the period. These developing communities, the surprising paucity of bridges (which might impede travel and transport) and the equally significant siting of churches for sailors at harbour illustrate ways that water transport made a significant impact on the structures and livelihoods along the waterways of Anglo-Saxon England.

In Chapter 8, Martin Watts investigates a slightly different set of structures which, like (and at times in competition with) weirs and landing spaces, are symbolic of the personal and commercial exploitation of waterscapes in the period: watermills. Watts explores the variety of options and technologies available to the Anglo-Saxons as they harnessed the power of water to meet ever-expanding needs. Evidence of mills comes early and persists; by the time of the Domesday survey, over 6,000 mills are documented. Millers and millwrights must have been many, and, alongside their customers, represent the important impact of the development of fresh and seawater mills in Anglo-Saxon England. In Chapter 9, Hal Dalwood takes a closer look at the natural development of these many commercial activities and landing places: water towns. As Dalwood points out, river and sea routes were the principal trade routes in Roman Britain as well as Anglo-Saxon England, and landing and trading spaces developed into towns in both periods. The mid-Saxon *wic*s, for example, were often located on waterways to take advantage of these trade routes. This beneficial location ultimately became a liability, when Viking invaders used the same water routes and preyed upon the growing commercial centres. Later *burh*s were also often built on navigable rivers and experienced similar advantages, with citizens becoming merchants and traders. Dalwood notes an interesting feature in that many *burh*s were sited at river crossings and downstream from major centres. The builders of the *burh*s may thus have been turning a former disadvantage of the *wic*s into a fortified advantage at a later age: such sitings, for an armed and fortified *burh*, might have proven an effective counter against Viking incursions along the same waterways. Dalwood also considers the regional and international trade networks that enriched later Anglo-Saxon England, as well as the waterways within towns so critical to flourishing trades such as textile production, tanning and even ale-brewing. Provision of sufficient water for growing industrial needs must have created tension and competition with water for household needs, and removal of waste water is likewise a clear preoccupation for town dwellers of any age, in the late Anglo-Saxon days, resulting in the building of drains. As Dalwood argues, water must have been a personal and commercial concern for the town-dwelling Anglo-Saxons throughout the period.

These discussions of the important material realities where waterscape and Anglo-Saxon life intersect are complemented by another set of chapters which offer a different perspective: considerations of feeling, impression, belief and thought about these waterscapes that play such a critical role in the Anglo-Saxon world. In Chapter 1, Jill Frederick examines the attitudes of the Anglo-Saxons to the water and waterscapes of their world through a textual lens. Although Bede and other writers mention practical realities of water – the abundant varieties of food it produces for their people, the necessary role it plays in household tasks and first aid – the bulk of the textual references to water and waterscapes, poetic references, in particular, imagine water as a dangerous matter, indeed. Water in these textual environments is depicted through high, dangerous seas and causeways and frightening, unknown waters. These waterscapes are powerful, unpredictable and, at times, malevolent.

Certainly, they are liminal boundary spaces where life meets death. Among these fearful waters, however, Frederick notes a number of instances where water becomes a path to the heavenly worlds, as well as death. The difference in these waters is who controls them – God. Such liminal waters, though fearsome, can be traversed with God's help, becoming a conduit to spiritual life and transformation.

These ambivalent attitudes and feelings towards water are explored in a different way in Chapter 3. In this chapter, Kelley Wickham-Crowley examines more closely one specific waterscape with special resonance for the Anglo-Saxons: the fenland environment. The Fens function as a spatial frontier or boundary between marshy wetland and farmland, a physically liminal space between water and earth. As a spatial boundary, the Fens have a long history of exploitation by Romans, Britons and Anglo-Saxons, all interested in the commercial benefits of the rich resources found there. As Rippon does more generally with wetlands, Wickham-Crowley identifies the resources of the Fens – wool, meat, salt, fish – and also many herbs or plants identified in the Old English lexicon as being native to the 'fens'. The value perceived in the unique resources of the Fens led to efforts at reclamation, settlement and maintenance. At the same time, the Fens continued to symbolize what they had been in the eighth century: a watery, liminal wilderness on the frontier between the good and the known, and the malevolent unknown. It is perhaps no surprise that, as Wickham-Crowley points out, Grendel and Grendel's Mother are identified repeatedly as dwellers of fens. There is clearly physical and emotional danger associated with the Fens. Such associations explain the decision of St Guthlac to enter the Fens: he desires a wilderness where he may fight for Christ against devils, parallel to the wilderness of the early hermitic saints. The devils oblige him; he fights and reclaims a section of the Fens. Thereafter, the Fens are not just spiritually, but spatially reclaimed, resulting in the construction of a full monastic community, Crowland Abbey. Wickham-Crowley notes the similar pattern of Alfred in the marshlands of Somerset, and the later lexical association of 'fen' with 'refuge'. Thus, as Frederick also notes, the ambivalence about waterscapes remains: dangerous wilderness is transformed or reclaimed with divine assistance to fen foundations, or, in the case of Alfred, a royal fortress.

In Chapter 5, Della Hooke looks at another set of waterscapes: the rivers, wells and sacred springs of British, Anglo-Saxon and Anglo-Scandinavian England. Hooke argues that the pre-Christian and later pagan beliefs about water are evident in the structures and monuments located at springs and sources of rivers, as well as the many ritual offerings found in rivers, lakes and bogs: prized goods (often ritually broken), animals and even people. These waterscapes were clearly perceived as a liminal space between the human world and the otherworld, sites of offerings and devotions. As Hooke's analysis demonstrates, it is no great surprise that, in a post-Christian world, such waterscapes would be associated with ungodly things to be conquered by men such as St Guthlac. Other churchmen may have followed suit in interesting ways: Hooke notes the frequency with which the Anglo-Saxons built churches near or over 'holy' springs and wells, perhaps reclaiming them for Christ and the saints. Indeed, 'holy water' may itself be a syncretic notion. The widespread occurrences of place names for 'holy well' only serve to emphasize the extent of belief in water as sacred substance: unholy if associated with nature or pre-Christian belief, but holy when claimed for God.

All of the chapters, while they focus on different aspects of the water landscape, have one message in common: water not only affected Anglo-Saxon life through trade, transport, shelter and food and drink, water and waterscapes inhabited thoughts, attitudes, perceptions and ritual beliefs. Waterscapes in the Anglo-Saxon world were thus material, spatial, intellectual and spiritual features, affecting both the daily lives and the sense of identity of the people who inhabited them.

1

From Whale's Road to Water under the Earth: Water in Anglo-Saxon Poetry

Jill A. Frederick

Dol bið se ðe gæð   on deop wæter,
se ðe sund nafað   ne gesegled scip
ne fugles flyht,   ne he mid fotum ne mæg
grund geræcan;   huru se Godes cunnað
full dyslice,   Dryhtnes meahta[1]

He who goes on deep water is foolish, he who does not have the skill to swim nor a sailed ship nor the flight of a bird, nor can he with his feet touch the ground; he certainly tests the power of God, the Lord, very foolishly.

Introduction

Almost any subject in Old English studies begins with Bede, and the subject of water is no exception. In the very first line of his *Ecclesiastical History of the English People*, Bede writes: 'Britain, once called Albion, is an island of the ocean'. This womb-like image, suggesting that the island is birthed from the sea, defines Britain by virtue of its placement in water. As Bede continues his description, he establishes the importance of water to, its interconnectedness with, the nation's very existence. He seems to emphasize the bounty that the nation reaps from the seas and other sources of water, noting:

[Britain] is remarkable too for its rivers, which abound in fish, particularly salmon and eels, and for copious springs. Seals as well as dolphins are frequently captured and even whales; besides these there are various kinds of shellfish, among which are mussels, and enclosed in these there are often found excellent pearls of every colour, red and purple, violet and green, but mostly white. There is a great abundance of whelks, from which a scarlet-coloured dye is made, a most beautiful red which neither fades through the heat of the sun nor exposure to the rain; indeed the older it is the more beautiful it becomes. The land possesses salt springs and warm springs and from them flow rivers which supply hot baths, suitable for all ages and both sexes, in separate places and adapted to the needs of each.[2]

We see, therefore, that the sustenance of Bede's people, the good fortune of their existence, depends as much on the gifts of water as on those from the land, acknowledging the significance of water to the physical health of the island's inhabitants. Significantly, Bede's language here also emphasizes the aesthetic aspect of these products, ascribing to them a jewelled quality that transforms their utilitarian properties.

In this brief section of Bede's account, too, he begins to categorize the kinds of waters contained on the island as well as their functions. In his description, Bede sketches the practical uses of water available to the inhabitants of the island, practicalities that are attested to by archaeological evidence and any number of Anglo-Saxon prose documents such as wills and charters. With trade crucial to any group's economic well-being, David Wilson notes that in Anglo-Saxon England, 'Whenever possible, merchandise was transported by water' because it 'was quicker, less physically exhausting, and cheaper'.[3] In terms of agriculture, water was vital at all stages; after harvest, grain required milling, and evidence exists for multiple water-wheel processes.[4] Della Hooke observes, 'Rivers and streams were frequently used as boundaries, especially in wooded regions where they were often the only distinctive landmarks. They had the virtue of being clearly visible and relatively stable features'.[5] Water would also have been vital for brewing ale, if not for drinking right out of the river, stream or well.

However, Bede's benign overview of Britain's waters seemingly runs counter to the ways in which water appears most frequently in the poetry of Old English. As has been established in a number of studies, the poetry expresses that nature in general was no friend to the Anglo-Saxons: exile into the wilderness was often equated with both physical and spiritual death, and the power of water was equally frightening.[6] The corpus of Old English poetry contains many passages describing the terrifying qualities of water, especially the ocean, and the potential doom awaiting anyone brave – or foolhardy – enough to venture out onto waters, although the available evidence suggests strongly that ocean-going transport was a commonplace.[7] However, these passages more often than not move beyond simple cautionary advice about travel. They speak profoundly on a metaphorical and symbolic level, representing waters both as figurative boundaries between the natural world and the otherworldly, and channels to the other world. As Jennifer Neville observes, '[The] representation of the natural world is part of a poetic tradition that reflects and participates in [the Anglo-Saxons'] definition of themselves and is a response to issues of particular concern to themselves'.[8] These issues have much to do with survival of both body and soul. While Old English prose offers accounts of how water can function in practical ways, the majority of the poetry emphasizes its role in what might be termed imaginative landscapes, where water provides a means to a different end. Representations of water in Old English poetry create a world that is apart from and that transcends the actual physical conditions of Anglo-Saxon existence. Outside of a handful of very few depictions of how water is used in ordinary daily life, the poetry presents water as an element to be battled, a physical conduit of emotional and spiritual states of being, and ultimately – sometimes simultaneously – a channel passing through liminal space to eternal life.

Water and the everyday in poetry

Conspicuous by their infrequency in poetry are descriptions of more harmless, quotidian uses of water. Very few poems, if any, allude to bathing for instance, to washing clothes, to cleaning, to quenching thirst,[9] no matter how significant water must have been for these activities. There does exist a fragmentary description of mysterious baths in *The Ruin*, although these are remnants of an age lost in time, not facilities known or used by the Anglo-Saxons.[10] They exist in the midst of shattered walls, stained with moss, only memories of the *burnsele monige* 'many bath-halls' (l. 1b) and *beorn monig glædmod ond goldbeorht* 'many men, glad-minded and bright with gold' (l. 33). The poem looks back on *beorhtan burg* 'the bright city' (l. 37a), when

> *Stanhofu stodan,*   *stream hate wearp*
> *widan wylme;*   *weal eall befeng*
> *beorhtan bosme,*   *þær þa baþu wæron,*
> *hat on hreþre.*   *Þæt wæs hyðelic*   (ll. 38–41)

the stone buildings stood, the flowing water rushing with heat
in a wide upwelling; a wall surrounded all in its bright embrace,
there where the baths were, hot at their heart. That was beneficial.

Clearly the Anglo-Saxons must have bathed, but either the activity was
not worthy of notice on its own terms, or other references are lost to us.

Another uncommon reference to the activities of daily life is this
homely observation from *Maxims I*:

> leof wilcuma
> *Frysan wife,   þonne flota stondeð;*
> *biþ his ceol cumen   ond hyre ceorl to ham,*
> *agen ætgeofa,   ond heo hine in laðaþ,*
> *wæsceð his warig hrægl   ond him syleþ wæde niwe*
>
> (ll. 94b–98).[11]

the beloved is welcome to the Frisian wife when the ship is
harbored; the boat has come and her man is home, her own
provider, and she leads him inside, washes his stained garments,
and gives him new clothing.

This tender description of a loving wife who greets, then tends to the
needs of her long-absent husband, fuses the emotional warmth of their
reunion with the inescapable necessity of household tasks. A scene
with equally emotional overtones occurs in *Beowulf*, when the young
warrior Wiglaf attempts to revive the dying Beowulf by bathing his
lord's face:

> He gewergad sæt,
> *feðecempa,   frean eaxlum neah,*
> *wehte hyne wætre,   him wiht ne speow* (ll. 2852b–54).

He sat, weary, the champion, near the shoulder of his lord, tried
to wake him with water. It helped not at all.

This practical, personal use of water (never mind the depth of private
emotion that accompanies it) is rare, if not unique, within what remains
to us of Old English poetry. The remaining poems which discuss water,
however, although offering equally practical advice and observations,
often intensify and transform their pragmatism with an acute awareness
of the various threats, physical and spiritual, that water always seems
to present.

The dangerous waters of Old English poetry

Cautionary notes about water and its dangers, infused with a mindfulness of a more supernatural kind of experience, commonly seem to occur in what is termed sapiential literature.[12] Perhaps the most literal warning against ocean-going travel occurs in *Solomon and Saturn*, wherein Solomon says:

Dol bið se ðe gæð   on deop wæter,
se ðe sund nafað   ne gesegled scip
ne fugles flyht,   ne he mid fotum ne mæg
grund geræcan;   huru se Godes cunnað
full dyslice,   Dryhtnes meahta (ll. 225–29)[13]

He who goes on deep water is foolish, he who does not have the skill to swim nor a sailed ship nor the flight of a bird, nor can he with his feet touch the ground; he certainly tests the power of God, the Lord, very foolishly.

These lines assert the dangers of venturing beyond the limits of one's abilities and natural place in the world, but they also extend that awareness. Their sense that life on the water presents, in heightened ways, the human awareness of always-immanent death is emphasized by the passage's acknowledgment that human life rests in God's hands. *The Rune Poem* echoes Solomon's warning about the precariousness of human skills at sea, but does so implicitly, by voicing the state of mind of those who find themselves at sea:

[Lagu] byþ leodum   langsum geþuht,
gif hi sculun neþan   on nacan tealtum,
and hi sæyþa   swyþe bregaþ,
and se brimhengest   bridles ne gymeð. (ll. 63–66)[14]

Water seems never-ending to people if they must embark upon an unsteady ship, and the sea-waves greatly frighten them, and the ocean-horse does not obey the bridle.

The metaphor of the sea as an uncontrollable horse (*brimhengest*) in these lines makes concrete for a horse-dependent people the potentially fatal difficulties of venturing beyond the limitations of land-based abilities. No one, under any circumstances, seems very happy about the prospect of an ocean-voyage.

The real physical fear that such a journey would have raised among those who needed to travel, and a justifiable reluctance, also occurs in the poetic saint's life, *Andreas*. Understandably frightened by God's command to rescue Matthew, the disciple asks a reasonable question about sailing to Mermedonia:

> *Hu mæg ic, Dryhten min,   ofer deop gelad*
> *fore gefremman   on feorne weg*
> *swa hrædlice,   heofona scyppend,*
> *wuldres waldend,   swa ðu worde becwist?* (ll. 190–93)[15]

How may I, my Lord, travel over the deep sea, make the journey on that far way, as quickly, creator of heaven, god of glory, as you have commanded with your words?

As he continues to protest, he names at least one source of his fear, *waroðfaruða gewinn ond wæterbrogan* 'the strife of the wave's shore-surge and the water-terror' (l. 197). In subsequent lines which give physical form to the warning of Solomon, the description of Andrew's journey confirms the aptness of his foreboding:

> *   Þa gedrefed wearð,*
> *onhrered hwælmere.   Hornfisc plegode,*
> *glad geond garsecg,   ond se græga mæw*
> *wælgifre wand.   Wedercandel swearc,*
> *windas weoxon,   wægas grundon,*
> *streamas styredon,   strengas gurron,*
> *wædo gewætte.   Wæteregsa stod*
> *þreata þryðum.* (ll. 369b–76a)

Then the whale's waters became roiled up, disturbed; the sharp-nosed fish gambolled and glided through the rough waves, and the grey gull gyred, slaughter-hungry. The sun darkened, the winds grew stronger, waves crashed, currents swirled, the ropes and wet sails groaned; the dreadful waters held on with the force of troops.

The language used in these lines emphasizes the power and unpredictability of deep water; even its denizens are threatening to devour the men, and given the quality of the verbs attached to the *hornfisc* and the *mæw*, taking some delight in the prospect. These animal allusions suggest a further, more spectral aspect of water's threat: its menacing inhabitants represent the dwelling of the inhuman, the Other. As Sarah Semple has noted about what she terms the pre-Christian sacred landscape, 'Watery places could be dangerous gateways to other worlds, occupied by less than welcoming inhabitants', pointing to the succinct assertion in *Maxims II*, 'The monster must dwell in the fen, alone in his realm' (ll. 42–43).[16]

This maxim also characterizes the malevolent waterscape occurring in *Beowulf*, the body of water termed Grendel's mother's *mere*.[17] With its fearsome, mostly unseen, water-creatures, the *mere* expresses the same real physical dangers manifested by the sea even as it conjures a watery hell-mouth, a channel to potential death. The *Beowulf*-poet describes the *mere* and its surrounding land in language that evokes desolation and monstrosity; the monster-woman lives in *wæteregesan* 'terrible waters' (l. 1260a), *cealde streamas*, 'cold currents' (l. 1261a), images at distinct odds with the warmth and security of the hall. When Hroðgar finally explains to Beowulf that another of the Grendel kin still walks, he describes the territory they inhabit as *dygel lond*, 'a secret land' (l. 1357b), from which

> *fyrgenstream*
> *under næssa genipu   niþer gewiteð,*
> *flod under foldan* (ll. 1359b–61a)

a mountain stream under the darkness of the headlands departs beneath, water under the earth.

Although the *mere* is not far from Heorot in terms of its actual distance, it might as well be in another dimension. Its bleak setting, with overhanging roots and general gloom, exudes dread, but it is the water itself that repels, to the point that a stag in despair for its life will not save itself by plunging into the dark pool (ll. 1368–72b). Whatever this body of water may be, it acts as both a physical limit and a psychological boundary for ordinary men; only the hero Beowulf can penetrate the waters, conquer the *aglaecwif* 'monster-woman' (l. 1259a) and return unscathed.

The connection between water's physical and spiritual dangers implied in the above passages becomes more vivid in another passage from the sapiential text, *Maxims I*. It offers realistic advice about travelling:

> *Styran sceal mon strongum mode.   Storm oft holm gebringeþ,*
> *geofen in grimmum sælum;   onginnað grome fundian*
> *fealwe on feorran to londe,   hwæþer he fæste stonde.*
>
> (ll. 50–52)[18]

A man must journey with a strong mind. A storm often brings the sea, the waves, into a grim state; angry, dark, from afar to the land, they begin to test whether he can stand fast.

There is no doubt that any Anglo-Saxon who sailed would have needed a tough spirit and a keen attention to the ocean's volatility. However, although echoing the advice in *Solomon and Saturn* and *The Rune Poem*, the metaphoric quality of this passage deepens the sense that the storm's grim state transcends the physical experience of the water's darkness, which is a metaphor for the challenges of life itself.

That metaphor is an old one, scripturally based,[19] and it also shapes one of the most haunting elegiac lyrics, *The Wanderer*,[20] which makes clear that the speaker can only negotiate the treacherous waters with God's help. The narrator of *The Wanderer* makes this perspective clear in the poem's opening lines:

> *Oft him anhaga   are gebideð,*
> *metudes miltse,   þeah þe he modcearig*
> *geond lagulade   longe sceolde*
> *hreran mid hondum   hrimcealde sæ,*
> *wadan wræclastas* (ll. 1–5a)

Often one who lives alone waits for grace, the lord's mercy, for himself, although weary in spirit he must, through the water-ways, row with his hands the rime-cold sea, travel the exile-tracks.

These lines express an important dichotomy. While the central point of this poem is the loneliness of the *anhaga*, his profound separation from human community rather than the privations of the ocean itself, it is the sea to which the poet attaches all the sorrow. In using the sea – rather than moors or forest – as a symbol of that isolation and deprivation, the Anglo-Saxon poet seems to delineate a primal fear, a primal distinction between the safety of the land and the Otherness of the ocean. While later in the poem the *anhaga* will enumerate all the losses he has undergone, he paradoxically establishes those lost hall pleasures by means of the cruelty of the ocean's waters. He travelled, he says,

> *... wintercearig   ofer waþema gebind,*
> *sohte sele dreorig   sinces bryttan* (ll. 24–25)

... winter-weary over the waves' fetters, sorrowing for a hall, sought out a giver of treasure.

The poem emphasizes this utter estrangement by situating the *anhaga* in the environment most alien to men and, in a trick of despair, offers a cold shadow of the community for which the *anhaga* longs:

> *wineleas guma,*
> *gesihð him biforan   fealwe wegas,*
> *baþian brimfuglas,   brædan feþra,*
> *hreosan hrim ond snaw,   hagle gemenged* (ll. 45b–48)

The lordless man sees in front of him the dark waves, the seabirds bathing, spreading their wings, the frost and snow falling, mingled with hail.

Here the seabirds mock his memories of hall companions, the wintry weather a dreary contrast to the warmth of a hearth. While the poem closes by acknowledging life's transience and the need to wait steadfastly for God's consolation, it offers cold comfort to the audience, acutely aware that the *anhaga* still drifts, alone. Nevertheless, within this poem, we can perhaps see two sides of a coin: on the one, the struggle with the sea's physical terrors, and, on the other, the potential for that physical struggle to lead to true solace in the Lord. It is the ocean's expanse that allows for such expansive thoughts, the fetters of the waters that paradoxically allow for the freedom that ultimately will move the believer towards the safe harbour of the Lord.

Water: spiritual and emotional, liminal space

Water is also characterized as not simply a physical threat, a barrier or a metaphor for the challenges of life; in Old English poetry, it often acts as a conduit to emotional and spiritual spaces. Water as crossing point between life and death appears subtly, for example, in the conventional fight poem, *The Battle of Maldon*, based on a historical event which occurs on the banks of the river Blackwater (known at the time as the Panta). In this poem, documenting the Anglo-Saxon defeat by the Vikings in 991, the description of the river is negligible, perhaps because the poem is fragmentary, but the riverbank setting is integral to the narrative conflict. The encounter between the Vikings and the Anglo-Saxons occurs in a liminal space between the two armies, the Vikings trapped on the one side of the Panta, the Anglo-Saxons holding the other, as lines 25 and 62–71 show.[21] The river's inherent fluidity mirrors the fluidity of the conflict, as the tide of the battle holds, then turns. While the two sides confront one another across its water, the river presents a boundary that can be and is breached physically by the Vikings, but not overcome emotionally, as the stirring exhortation of the surviving warrior Byrhtwold to the remaining Anglo-Saxon troops in lines 312–19 demonstrates:

> *Hige sceal þe heardra,   heorte þe cenre,*
> *mod sceal þe mare,   þe ure mægen lytlað.*
> *Her lið ure ealdor   eall forheawen,*
> *god on greote.   A mæg gnornian*
> *se ðe nu fram þis wigplegan   wendan þenceð.*
> *Ic eom frod feores;   fram ic ne wille,*
> *ac ic me be healfe   minum hlaforde,*
> *be swa leofan men,   licgan þence.*[22]

Our courage will be the harder, our hearts the keener, our spirit will be greater as our strength wanes. Here our lord lies, all hacked apart, good on the ground. May he always grieve who intends to go from this battle-place. I am old in life, I will not leave it but I by the side of my lord, by such a beloved man, intend to lie.

In this instance the river implicitly carries the same treacherous qualities as other waters, yet (as does Grendel's mother's *mere*) provides a paradoxical means to a psychological victory, and, especially in its Christian framework, a spiritual victory. As Beowulf penetrated the water to face death and returned home to fight another day, the river becomes for Byrhtnoð and his men the channel for facing death and transcending it, returning them to their eternal home. This potential deliverance offered by destructive and dangerous waters seems to characterize the mentality found in Old English poetic texts, at once profoundly cognizant of the threat that ordinary, everyday activities present, while simultaneously looking beyond the threat to the extraordinary possibilities of a life beyond the earthly realm.

Curiously, the idea of water as a liminal space of loss and potential redemption does not appear especially strongly in the Old Testament poetic narratives found in Old English. One might think that the story of *Exodus*, with its vivid picture of the Red Sea's parting – the means to safety for the Israelites and simultaneously the mechanism of Pharaoh's army's destruction – or Noah's Flood in *Genesis*, with its typological implications, would be natural repositories for the ambiguities that appear in other, less overtly scripturally based poems. However, the water-motifs of these two poems do deviate somewhat from the patterns suggested earlier in that both *Exodus* and *Genesis* seem more focused on rendering the images of destruction than their figural associations. The concern of these two Old English biblical narratives with literal description can be seen in the diction they use to describe the scenes of destruction by water: they lack, for the most part, metaphors and kennings for ocean, tropes that appear in many if not most of the poems that incorporate the ocean into their verses. In the Old English *Genesis*'s account of Noah's flood, for example, words that directly refer to the ocean include *flod* (l. 1296a), *wæter* (l. 1300b), *wælstreams* (l. 1301a), *sæstreamas* (l. 1326a), *mereflod* (l. 1341b), *sæ* (l. 1375b), *mere* (l. 1381b), *yþ* (l. 1385a), *sund* (l. 1388b), *holm* (l. 1393a) and *lagu* (l. 1413b), all straightforward and literal. The same pattern occurs in *Exodus*, where references to the sea are also simple lexemes: *saestreamum* (l. 250b), *yþ* (l. 282a), *wæter* (l. 283a), *brim* (l. 290b), *mere* (l. 300b), *sund* (l. 319b), *geofon* (l. 448b) and *holm* (l. 450a). The only kenning for ocean that occurs in this narrative moment in *Exodus* is *garsecg* (ll. 345a, 490b), perhaps because the sea's power participates in the battle. While the nouns in both these poems are frequently modified with adjectives denoting darkness and destruction – *Genesis*'s *sweart wæter* (l. 1300b), *swearte sæstreamas* (l. 1326a) – or simply to add other details – *Exodus*'s *holm gerymed* (l. 284b), *merestream modig* (l. 469) – the lexemes for ocean are literal rather than figurative, unlike the kennings used in *Andreas*, for instance: *swanrad* 'swan's road' (l. 196b), *bæþweg* 'bath way' (l. 223), *hranrad* 'whale's road' (l. 266a), *hwæles eðel* 'whale's kingdom' (l. 274b), *fisces bæð* 'fish's bath' (l. 293b), *garsecges begang* 'spear-man's passage' (l. 530a) and *seolhpæð* 'seal's path' (l. 1769).[23] That these moments in *Genesis* and *Exodus* avoid presenting the sea using metaphoric terms may simply reflect their need to transmit as faithfully as possible the biblical stories, as opposed to a hagiographic narrative like *Andreas* which has more latitude with its apocryphal tale. We cannot be certain about the impetus behind the poets' choices, but it appears to rest on the people involved in the conflicts rather than on water as an agent. Nevertheless, within these narratives, we still see water functioning as a spiritual conduit, moving the wicked towards death and the righteous to life's safe shore.

The layers of spiritual and emotional meaning extant in poetic uses of water likewise exist in those glimpses of daily life not often found elsewhere: the riddles of the *Exeter Book*.[24] Although in *Exeter Book* Riddles 1–3 the literal level clearly presents the physical challenge and terror of the sea, the lines open up the possibility of a more spectral meaning well beyond their surface details. The arrangement and content of the riddles have challenged scholars: these texts may be three separate riddles, or they may be read (as Craig Williamson does) as a single riddle,[25] and no consensus has been reached in terms of their solution(s).[26] Nevertheless, no matter how the texts are divided or solved, their lines contain two descriptions of the ocean every bit as threatening and layered as those found in other poems. In the first, the second riddle presents the sea's terrible force as well beyond the control of the humans who sail on it:

> *hwælmere hlimmeð,* *hlude grimmeð,*
> *streamas staþu beatað,* *stundum weorpaþ*
> *on stealc hleoþa* *stane ond sonde,*
> *ware ond wæge,* *þonne ic winnende,*
> *holmmægne biþeaht,* *hrusan styrge,*
> *side sægrundas.* (ll. 5–10a)[27]

the whale's water resounds, loudly rages, the currents beat the shore, sometimes cast at the steep slopes stones and sand, seaweed and waves, when, raging, I covered the forces of the waves, stirred the earth, the vast seafloors.

But the lines also imply that travelling by sea creates a pathway to the eternal, as the scene shows the traveller immediately caught up in a greater power, in the waves that seem to be almost literal extensions of that power. In the second passage, the third riddle suggests that the sea journey is a metaphor for the chaos of human existence that can only be eased by a greater, quieting force:

>   *Þær bið hlud wudu,*
> *brimgiesta breahtm,* *bidað stille*
> *stealc stanhleoþu* *streamgewinnes,*
> *hopgehnastes,* *þonne heah geþring*
> *on cleofu crydeþ.* *Þær bið ceole wen*
> *sliþre sæcce,* *gif hine sæ byreð*
> *on þa grimman tid,* *gæsta fulne,*
> *þæt he scyle rice* *birofen weorþan,*
> *feore bifohten* *fæmig ridan*
> *yþa hrycgum.* *Þær bið egsa sum*
> *ældum geywed,* *þara þe ic hyran sceal*
> *strong on stiðweg.* *Hwa gestilleð þæt?* (ll. 24b–35)

There is loud wood, the noise of sea-guests, the lofty bluffs wait quietly for the water-turmoil, for the dashing of the waves, when the high commotion crowds onto the cliffs. There is expectation

of savage strife for the ship, if the sea carries it full of guests
onto the grim tide, so that it must be despoiled of its power, the
foamy spirit to ride, surrounded, the ridge of the waves. There is
a certain terror revealed to men, of those whom I, strong on the
rough way, must obey. Who quiets it?

At the very end of this long, bleak description, the question, *Hwa
gestilleð þæt*, cannot be answered easily. On a metaphoric level, however,
the question becomes merely rhetorical: it expresses an implicit and
fundamental acknowledgement of God's power, which can bring a
frightened man across the turbulence of the ocean, even as it quiets the
waves. As in other poetry, here the poetic language embodies water as
a literal and figurative channel to another, supernatural world.

One of the most powerful statements in Old English poetry about
water as a means to an eternal home, or water's spiritual powers, occurs
in the opening lines of *The Metrical Epilogue to the Pastoral Care*:

> *Ðis is nu se wæterscipe   ðe us wereda god*
> *to frofre gehet   foldbuendum.*
> *He cwæð ðæt he wolde   ðæt on worulde forð*
> *of ðæm innoðum   a libbendu*
> *wætru fleowen,   ðe wel on hine*
> *gelifden under lyfte.   Is hit lytel tweo*
> *ðæt ðæs wæterscipes   welsprynge is*
> *on hefonrice ...* (ll. 1–8a) [28]

Now this is the water-source that the God of hosts promised as
a solace for us earth dwellers. He said that he wanted ever-living
waters to flow forth in the world from the very hearts of those
under the sky who fully trusted in him. There is little doubt that
this water-source's well-spring is in the kingdom of heaven.

These lines begin, as Hugh Magennis asserts in his study, *Anglo-Saxon
Appetites*, 'a sophisticated elaboration on the theme of the water of
wisdom',[29] a theme which the poem expands in the remainder of its thirty
lines. The poem's serene tone is at odds with other poetic descriptions of
water, almost always troubled; here, the water can offer comfort to those
living on earth because its source is undeniably the kingdom of heaven.
Perhaps even more importantly, no matter how it flows into the minds
of men, the water needs to lie still and deep inside them. It needs to be
guarded, not allowed to slip away loudly and uselessly, to form shallow
and stagnant pools. The poem exhorts its audience to fill its pitchers from

the pool's depths, and to be careful in the process not to spill *scirost wætra* 'the clearest water' (l. 29b), *lifes drync* 'the drink of life' (l. 30a). While Magennis argues that, in Old English poetry, the act of drinking alcohol is less important than the social values such drinking represents, he notes that the same does not hold true for drinking water.[30] In this instance, it is water's 'life-giving quality',[31] in the larger spiritual sense, which is so significant. Its *welsprynge is/on hefonrice* 'its well-spring is in heaven's kingdom' (ll. 7b–8a); it is *dryhtnes welle* 'the Lord's water' (l. 24b).

In creating the trope so deftly set out by Magennis, the passage works on a dual level, to present not just the image of water for drinking, but water – and its conventional means of travel – as an actual physical passageway to heaven. The word *waterscipe*, in lines 1 and 7, broken down into its component parts, means 'water-patch' or 'water-piece', but the word *scip* also denotes an ocean-going vessel, a ship. On the one hand, the Lord offers the water of wisdom from the pool, but, on the other, the water and the water-ship itself provide the transport for salvation. Such imagery embodies the paradox seen elsewhere in the poetry of water as both a physical and spiritual channel, a space which connects earth to heaven.

The lines of Exeter Book Riddle 84, solved by consensus as 'water',[32] also transform water's worldly beauty and utility into a sacrament. In this riddle, the object – water – is miraculous, both mother and child, in the first instance *wundrum acenned* 'born from wonders' (l. 1b), in the second, *Modor is monigra mærra wihta* 'the mother is of many greater wonders' (l. 4). It is *fæger* 'beautiful' (l. 5a), and, despite its somewhat fragmentary nature, always carries a sense of brilliance and jewelled splendour; it is *wlitig ond wynsum* 'beautiful and joyous':

> *Mægen biþ gemiclad,*   *meaht gesweotlad,*
> *wlite biþ geweorþad*   *wuldornyttingum,*
> *wynsum wuldorgimm*   *wloncum getenge* ... (ll. 24–26)

Power will become great, strength revealed, its splendour will be honoured with glorious service, a joyful glory-jewel presses towards the ... [?]

In fact, the riddle uses the word *wlitig* 'beautiful' or a variant some five times in the course of its extant lines to emphasize water's aesthetic quality. Nevertheless, almost buried in the midst of its description of water's worldly beauty and utility, the riddle suggests another, more refined dimension, that of purification and salvation:

> *worulde wlitigað,   wæstmum tydreð,*
> *firene dwæsceð,*
> *oft utan beweorpeð   anre þecene,*
> *wundrum gewlitegad* (ll. 38–41)

it beautifies, produces offspring for the world, destroys transgressions, often from the outside it surrounds one with a covering, decorated with wonders.

These lines, then, lead to another aspect of Anglo-Saxon mentality: the second side of two opposing visions, the duality or the paradox of the ways Old English poetry seems to configure a cultural understanding of water as a spiritual channel connected to both life and death.

The poem by Cynewulf known as *Christ II*[33] expresses in unmistakable terms how a water journey acts as a metaphor for human life on earth, moving towards unity with God:

> *Nu is þon gelicost   swa we on laguflode*
> *ofer cald wæter   ceolum liðan*
> *geond sidne sæ,   sundhengestum,*
> *flodwudu fergen* (ll. 850–53a)

Now it is just as if we sail in ships on the floodwaters, over cold water, through the wide sea, in water-horses, we guide the water-woods.

This journey, like most journeys, is clearly fraught with danger. The term *sundhengestum* 'water-horses' (l. 852b) uses the image from *The Rune Poem, brimhengest* 'sea-steed' (l. 66, above), but in this instance a horse under control. The waters may be cold and in flood, but humankind has the potential to move along with some safety. The next set of lines, however, reiterates the dangerous quality of the journey, the *drohtað strong* 'powerful plight' (l. 856b) in which we find ourselves. As it does so, the passage emphasizes the particular elements that keep us off-kilter as we make our way through the *wacan woruld* 'the weak world' (l. 855a), *frecne stream/yða* 'the sea's dangerous currents' (ll. 853b–54a), *windge holmas* 'the windy waves' (l. 855b), *deop gelad* 'the deep sea' (l. 856b) into which the unwary traveler will sink.

However, a safe journey – on both literal and metaphorical seas – comes through guidance across that space by the divine:

>   *Þa us help bicwom,*
> *þæt us to hælo*   *hyþe gelædde,*
> *godes gæstsunu,*   *ond us giefe sealde*
> *þæt we oncnawan magun*   *ofer ceoles bord*
> *hwær we sælan sceolon*   *sundhengestas,*
> *ealde yðmearas,*   *ancrum fæste.* (ll. 858b–63b)

Then help came to us, that led us to a safe harbor, God's spirit-son, and gave us a gift that we should know over the ship's boards where we could secure the sound-horses, the old wave-steeds, fast to an anchor.

Suddenly the peril is transformed into a place of safety, as water, the untamed creature of nature, is literally harnessed by God's hand and allows a peaceful haven for the soul as it travels into the eternal. Recognizing the safe harbour after the dangerous voyage, the speaker exhorts the audience as well to make its way to that place of steadfast serenity:

> *Utan us to þære hyðe*   *hyht staþelian,*
> *ða us gerymde*   *rodera waldend,*
> *halge on heahþu,*   *þa he heofonum astag* (ll. 864–66)

Let us to that harbour, establish joy, where for us the ruler of heaven has made room, the holy one on the heights where he ascended to heaven.

This sense of potential and paradoxical freedom finds perhaps its fullest expression in the elegiac text, *The Seafarer*.[34] Although no evidence exists to suggest that the two poems were composed as a pair, *The Seafarer* offers both a complement and a corrective to *The Wanderer*'s bleak outlook. Much of the speaker's meditation echoes the same laments made by The *Wanderer*'s *anhaga*, in that he too describes himself as *merewerges* 'sea-weary' (l. 12a), *winemægum bidroren* 'without a lord or friends' (l. 16a), with only seabirds as his companions and entertainment, *ganetes hleoþor/ond huilpan sweg fore hleahtor wera* 'the gannet's noise and the cry of the curlew, instead of men's laughter' (ll. 20b–21). The ocean waves on which he travels are equally as icy and dangerous as those on which *The Wanderer*'s *anhaga* finds himself. But, as he acknowledges his physical pain – his frozen feet bound by frost and held tightly by the cold (ll. 9b–10) – and considers everything he seems to have lost, he nevertheless transcends the terror of his surroundings by embracing them,

> *... min hyge hweorfeð   ofer hreþerlocan,*
> *min modsefa   mid mereflode*
> *ofer hwæles eþel   hweorfeð wide,*
> *eorþan sceatas,   cymeð eft to me*
> *gifre ond grædig* (ll. 58–62a)

My spirit soars beyond my locked breast, my innermost heart turns widely with the seas' flood, over the whale's realm, the regions of the earth, comes again to me eager and greedy.

The greed noted in this last line is not the rapaciousness of the seabirds, but rather expresses how the speaker's soul covets *Dryhtnes dreamas*, 'the Lord's joys' (l. 65a). The poem offers a kind of meditation on how to achieve those joys, and they are not to be found on the land, amidst *þis deade lif,/læne on londe* 'this dead life, leased on land' (ll. 65b–66a). It is on the sea that the speaker's soul can ascend, turn his gaze towards heaven and move his thoughts towards God:

> *Uton we hycgan   hwær we ham agen,*
> *ond þonne geþencan   hu we þider cumen,*
> *ond we þonne eac tilien,   þæt we to moten*
> *in þa ecan   eadignesse,*
> *þær is life gelong   in lufan Dryhtnes,*
> *hyht in heofonum.* (ll. 117–122a)

Let us consider where we have our home, and think about how we may come there, and then we should also work that we may be allowed in the eternal happiness where life exists in God's love, a joyous expectation in heaven.

This sojourner seems to celebrate the ephemeral movement of the journey, because he understands that the grim realities of the sea are, in fact, the necessary conditions for his entrance into the eternal harbour.

In sum, Old English poetry does not tell us as much about the practical uses of water as it seems to focus on the ominous physical realities, all the dangers that ocean, pool and river might contain. In what appears on the surface to be a contradictory state of affairs, however, the poetry also depicts water as the pathway or conduit to a joyful ending, rather than as a dire fate in itself, indeed, as a significant means of reaching the divine. It is both a literal way to God, that is, by drowning, and a symbolic path, like that provided by baptismal waters, to the eternal home. The poetry of the Anglo-Saxons, then, encompasses a vision of water that speaks first to its utilitarian qualities, but moves beyond pragmatism to consider both sides of its emotional and religious implications, destruction paired with redemption.

2

Water in the Landscape: Charters, Laws and Place Names

Della Hooke

Ærest of pennpoll lannmoren up bi þam broce oð hræt winiau þonne forð 7 lang broces to pen hal þonne to maen wynn þonne to oðrum pen hal þonne adun by þam broce to sæ

First from *penpoll lannmoren* [Cornish for 'Lamorran creek's head'] up by the brook as far as *hræt winiau* ['(the) ?ford']; then onwards along (the) brook to (the) head of the marsh; then to *mæn wynn* ['(the) white stone']; then to the other *pen hal* ['(the) head of the marsh']; then down by the brook to (the) sea. (Boundary clause of Lamorran, Cornwall, AD 969)[1]

Introduction

This chapter looks at how contemporary documents reveal how administrative arrangements valued water and how watercourses were often followed by boundaries. These documents, too, often offer the earliest written evidence for the names by which rivers and lesser watercourses were known in this period and offer material not readily available elsewhere. Some settlements taking their names from rivers might first appear in Domesday Book, which, although it was compiled soon after the Norman Conquest, nevertheless presents a picture of late Anglo-Saxon England. From these early sources, important information can be gleaned about ways that the waters all around them touched the daily life of people in this period in myriad ways.

Rights to rivers and other watercourses in documentary sources

Rights to water frequently find mention in pre-Conquest charter grants or leases, usually as the appurtenances of estates in the Latin preamble. Sometimes they are expressed as rights in *aquarum cursibus* 'running waters' or *diriuatisque aquarum cursibus/dirivatisque cursibus aquarum/ aquis, aquarumque decursibus*, variants of 'running streams of water', or merely as in *aquae* 'in waters', in *flumine, rivulis* or *aquarum riuulis* 'in rivers' or 'in the water of rivers'. Kentish charters, especially, may note rights in other waters and wetlands: *fontanis, paludibus, fluminibus* '(in) springs, marshes and rivers': marshes and rivers were places for the capture of fish and fowl.[2] Sometimes rights in salt marshes, in *marisque salsuginibus*, are specified, and a ninth-century charter granting rights and land to Wulfred, archbishop of Canterbury, includes *piscuosis ac maritimis fretibus* 'sea channels abounding in fish'.[3] Clearly, fishing was a major attribute on the estates concerned.

Examples of rights which included river fisheries – *cum piscariis, fluminalibus piscationibus* 'riverine fisheries' or *captura piscipium/captura piscipum* 'the catching of fish' are noted, for instance, for Ismere and Ripple in Worcestershire, and for Thanet in Kent – the latter in the River Limen, and fisheries are noted in many Kentish charters.[4] Weirs were often constructed not only to direct water to a mill but to aid fishing. A Carolingian capitulary of 802–13 lays down that a good steward on a royal estate should maintain not only mills but *vivaria cum pisces, vennas*, 'fishponds, fish-traps, ponds closed by a weir',[5] and another document known as the *Gerefa*, produced in tenth- or eleventh-century England, also notes the duty of 'the discriminating reeve' to *fiscwer 7 mylne macian* 'construct a fish-weir and a mill'.[6] Some, usually later, charters also note weirs as the places to take fish. Several are noted by name, such as the *fixnað* (for *fiscað* 'fishing' but perhaps confused with *fiscnett* 'a fishing net') at Fenstanton, Cambridgeshire: *æt holanwere. 7 æt deopanwere. 7 æt suon ea. 7 æt niwanwere. 7 æt dinde. 7 æt bicopes were. 7 æt bradan were. 7 æt niwanwere. 7 æt merbece.*[7] Another charter grant of King Athelstan to Milton Abbey in Dorset in 934 included 12 acres *to þan were 7 ðan werhurde* 'for the weir and the keeper' at Christchurch Twyneham on the Avon in Hampshire.[8] In addition to rights in woods and fields, a grant of land at Ombersley in Worcestershire (probably much later in date than that claimed, i.e. tenth or eleventh century) specifies such rights:

> *in captura etiam piscium que terre illi adiacet. ubi sunt scilicet 'duo' quod nostratim dicitur Weres. id est alter ubi fontanus qui*

nominatur Ombreswelle deriuatur in fluuium qui dicitur Saberna.
alter qui est ad uadum qui nuncupatur Leuerford.

in the fishery (or fish-trap) which adjoins the land, namely where
there are two of what amongst us are called weres (weirs), the one,
that is, where the spring which is called *Ombreswelle* flows into
the river which is called Severn, the other which is at the ford
which is called *Leverford*.[9]

Fisheries on the River Darent in Kent were even said to be protected
from unlawful fishing by a curse.[10]

Various kinds of traps are mentioned – from the general *captura
piscium* 'fishery' or 'fish-trap' noted above and elsewhere (in a *stagnum*
at Meare, Somerset), to fishing rights in a *pusting* weir in Kent granted
to one Ealbeorht, probably in the eleventh century, to the *cytwera*
'basket weirs' and *hæcwera* 'hackle weirs' (a wattle barrier set across
the current to produce an eddy in which the fish could be caught from
a boat with a stop-net), the last two types of weirs on the Severn and
Wye at Tidenham. The Tidenham charter notes the kind of fish caught
in river and estuarine fisheries, and probably, too, in coastal waters. It
names valuable 'rare fish' such as sturgeon or porpoises (see Chapter 6
of this volume for additional discussion), and the latter are noted again
in another eleventh-century lease of this estate along with herrings.[11]
A further charter boundary clause of Topsham, Devon, notes breeding
pools on the River Exe, a river later noted for its rich salmon fisheries.[12]

Although literary references to watercourses are discussed in Chapter
5, it may be noted here that a twelfth-century poem about Durham
describes the city as located where 'A strongly running river/Flows past
enclosed by weirs, and therein dwell/All kinds of fishes in the seething
waters'.[13] A genuine pre-Conquest source, however, the *Colloquy of
Ælfric*, describes the role of the fisherman and the type of fish he
caught in both inland and coastal waters (see also Chapter 6).[14] Fishing
rights are also recorded in what was one of the largest Anglo-Saxon
meres: Whittlesey Mere *Witlesmere, Witelesemere* 'Witel's mere' in
the Cambridgeshire fenland, where half of the mere was granted to
Peterborough Abbey in the tenth century and where the abbeys of
Ramsey, Peterborough and Thorney maintained boats and fishermen in
1086 (see Introduction).[15]

Place names also refer to fishing. Fisheries with weirs are suggested at
the two Crewes recorded in Domesday Cheshire, both names deriving
from Primitive Welsh (PrW) **krīw* 'weir, fish-trap': one near Wrexham
is situated on the River Dee, the other (the modern borough) on the

Valley Brook or its tributary. The River Cale in Somerset, *Cawel*, *Wricawel* might be Cornish (Co) *cawal*, Welsh *cawell* 'a basket, a creel, a pannier', so 'creel river' – creels were for trapping fish, for which this river was renowned.[16] Others derive from OE *wer* 'weir', as in a further Cheshire place name Warrington, 'settlement by a river-dam' from OE **wering* with *tūn*, literally '*tūn* of the weir'. Other such names recorded by 1086 include Wargrave, Berkshire, 'grove by the weir'; Warham, Norfolk, 'the weir homestead'; Great Warley, Essex, 'weir wood'; Warwick, Warwickshire, 'the dwellings by the weir'; Laddus Fens, Cambridgeshire, 'the lode weirs or weirs in the watercourse called Lode'; Weare, Somerset; and Weare Giffard, Devon. Yarpole in Herefordshire is OE *yair* 'fish-trap' with *pōl* 'fish-trap pool'. More specific is Drax, North Yorkshire, if this name is derived from OE *dræge* 'drag-net', and a fishery existed here in the eleventh century.[17] While the name Ely in the Fens of Cambridgeshire, *Elge c.*731, does not refer to any specific method of fishing, the name means 'eel district' and Bede explains that it took its name 'from the large number of eels which are caught in the marshes' (see also Chapter 6).[18] A few place names also refer to fishermen: Fiskerton in Lincolnshire close beside the River Witham is 'settlement of the fisherman or fishermen' while a second Fiskerton in Nottinghamshire lies beside the River Trent.

It has been noted above that some charters granted rights in *aucupationibus* 'fowling' and some early place names also refer to this occupation. Fullerton in Hampshire is *Fugelerestune* in 1086 'settlement, estate of the wild fowler(s)'.

Referring to another use of water, to drive the waterwheels of mills, rights to *molendinis* 'mills' are not often encountered in the preamble of Anglo-Saxon charters, but in 822 Ceolwulf of Mercia included such rights in a grant of land at *Mylentun* near Kemsing in Kent to Wulfred, archbishop of Canterbury, and in the tenth century such rights were included in several of King Edgar's grants, such as that of Bemerton, Wiltshire, to Wilton Abbey, and with the restoration of land at Downton, Wiltshire, to the Church of Winchester.[19] A later writ of King Edward in 1053 x 1066 gives the monks of Westminster Abbey land at *Stæingahaga* in London with rights which include those 'in church and mill, in woodland and in open country, in pasture and in heath, in meadows and in aits, in waters and in weirs'.[20] With references to mills in charters increasing in the late ninth and tenth centuries, sometimes as an addition to a grant of land, there are also more references in boundary clauses to *milna*, 'mills'. Often these appear to have been located on side channels or leats (a leat sometimes referred to as a *mylendic* 'mill-dyke') and the mill-pool might also be a source of fish and eels.[21] In the tenth century (964 x 975), a redrawing of boundaries for the New Minster at Winchester and the diversion of a watercourse belonging to the Nunnery led to the destruction of one mill belonging to the nuns for which recompense had to be paid ('120 *mancuses* of red gold').[22] The bequest of a mill at Guist in Norfolk is included in the will of Bishop Ælfric in 1035 x 1040 (plus fenland at Holme).[23] Knowledge of Anglo-Saxon watermills was increased by the excavation of a watermill at the royal centre of Tamworth in 1971 and 1978. This evidence is discussed by Martin Watts in Chapter 8.

Rights to transport along rivers and loading places were of commercial value. As early as AD 743 x 745, King Æthelbald granted Milred, bishop of Worcester, the toll due on two ships at London.[24] In 1023, a grant of the port at Sandwich in Kent by King Cnut to Christchurch, Canterbury (which may, however, be a forgery), shows the river being used for shipment as the monks were allotted *þa gehrihte of ðam ilkan wætere of ægder healue ðas streames age land seðe hit age . fram Pipernæsse to Mærcesfleote . swa þæt ðonne hit bið full flód . 7 þæt scip bið aflote . swa feorr swa mæg an tapersæx beon geworpen ut of ðam scipe up on þæt land þa gereflanges of xp̄es circean underfon ða gerihte* 'the water dues from both sides of the river from Pepperness to *Mærcesfleote*, whoever owns the land, in such wise that when it is high tide and a ship is afloat, the officers of Christchurch shall receive the dues from as far inland as can be reached by a small axe thrown from the ship'.[25] In addition to the details of the weirs associated with the Gloucestershire estate of Tidenham, it is likely that the Welsh sailors who rented land there were working along the estuaries of the Wye and the Severn.[26] Tolls for ships landing at certain ports in Kent might also be the subject of charter grants, such as the toll due on one ship at Fordwich granted to Deneheah, abbot of Reculver, in AD 747, the toll due on two ships at Fordwich and Sarre granted to Sigeburga, abbess, and her *familia* at St Peter's Minster, Thanet, c.AD 761 and the eleventh-century grant which adds *þæt scip 7 si ouerfæreld þare hæuene . 7 si tolne of ealle scipen by þas ðe hit beo 7 cume ðanon þe hit cume to þare ilicare hæuene æt Sandwic cumð* 'the toll of the ship and the ferrying across the haven and the toll of every ship that comes to the said haven at Sandwich' to Christ Church.[27]

River and boundary demarcation

Rivers and other watercourses formed the heartlands of most folk regions and a high proportion of central places lay beside rivers as well as many, if not most, minor estate centres (see Introduction). In the Hwiccan

Fig. 2.1
Worcester
Cathedral beside
the River Severn.
Built on the site
of an earlier
Anglo-Saxon
church, the
present building
is post-Conquest
in date with
later additions
(photograph by
Della Hooke).

kingdom, Worcester, a town established in Roman times, lay beside the River Severn and became the centre of the diocese, its cathedral still occupying a waterside location today (Figure 2.1). Many other early Anglo-Saxon minsters also stood close to rivers (Figure 2.2). But watercourses, as obvious and relatively stable features in the landscape, served as particularly good boundary markers, not only for some kingdoms (see Introduction) but also for lesser units – the Anglo-Saxon estates which became the basis of the ecclesiastical parishes.

In the West Midlands, the rivers Severn, Teme and Avon served as boundaries for the greater parts of their courses through the area, and lesser rivers used as boundaries for considerable distances include the Salwarpe, Leam and Stour (Figure 2.3).[28] It is also in the documents – in the boundary clauses attached to charters – that many river and stream names are first recorded by name (below), although boundary clauses

Fig. 2.2
Stratford-on-
Avon Holy
Trinity Church,
Warwickshire,
on the site of
an early minster
located beside
the River Avon
(photograph by
Della Hooke).

normally had recourse to many other kinds of landmarks, both natural and man-made.

Often a boundary would be described as running *andlang* 'along' a certain *fluvius* or *rivulus* (Latin terms for 'river', 'rivulet, stream'), or along an *ēa* or *strēam* (OE 'river' and 'stream'): the bounds of Evesham holdings in Worcestershire, for instance, run *upp andlang afene streames* 'up along Avon stream' or *iuxta aquam* 'hard by the water'.[29] Others might follow a river *middan streame* 'mid-stream' as in a clause describing the bounds of Cotheridge in Worcestershire.[30] Sometimes the bounds are more precise: in Cornwall the bounds of St Buryan are described as running *contra riuulum* 'against the stream (i.e. upstream)' and others may run *up on stream* 'upstream' or *adun on stream* 'downstream'.[31] In some cases, early medieval estates were almost entirely bounded by rivers or streams. This was the case for an

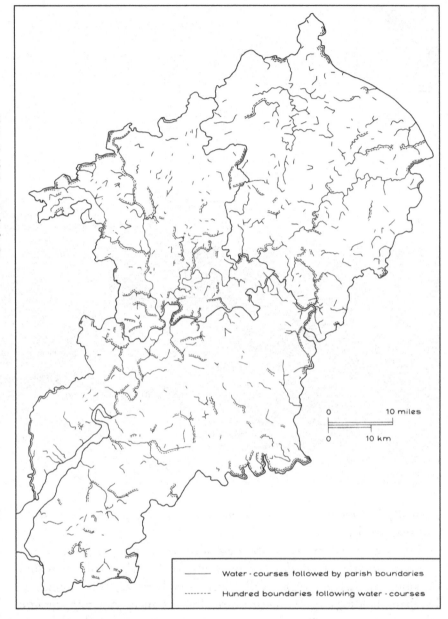

Fig. 2.3 West Midland boundaries following watercourses (from Hooke, *The Anglo-Saxon Landscape: The Kingdom of the Hwicce.*)

estate at Abbots Bromley granted by Wulfric, a Mercian nobleman, to his minister in AD 996, an estate lying between tributary streams of the River Trent (Figure 2.4a).[32] At Lamorran in Cornwall, too, a small estate granted by King Edgar to his man Ælfeah Gerent and his wife in AD 969 lay between streams draining into the Fal estuary (see quotation at the head of this chapter) (Figure 2.4b).[33]

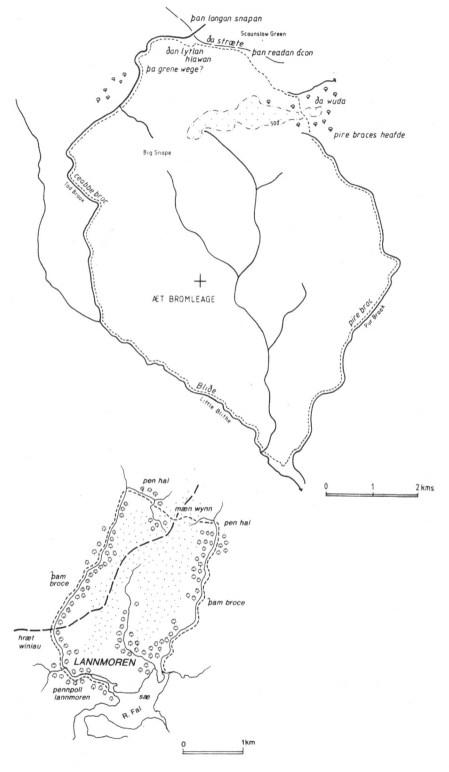

þan longan snapan

Scounslow Green

ða stræte

þan readan ðcon

ðan lytlan hlawan

þa grene wege?

ða wuda

sod

pire broces heafde

Big Snape

ceabbe broc

Tad Brook

+ ÆT BROMLEAGE

pire broc

Pur Brook

Bliðe

Little Blithe

0   1   2 kms

pen hal

mæn wynn

pen hal

þam broce

þam broce

hræt winiau

LANNMOREN

pennpoll lannmoren

sæ

R. Fal

0   1km

Fig. 2.4a *above* Abbots Bromley, Staffordshire, charter-bounds (drawn by Della Hooke).

Fig. 2.4b *below* Lamorran, Cornwall, charter-bounds (drawn by Della Hooke).

The names of rivers and other watercourses

The proper names of rivers and streams

River and stream names have proved to be some of the oldest found in the lexicon of present-day place names.[34] Known to locals and travellers alike, many have survived changes in both language and culture. Some found their way into classical writings, such as those of Tacitus and Ptolemy (the rivers Severn, Thames, Tamar).

Rivers named after divinities

While certain river names appear to be those of goddesses (a feature common in ancient Gaul but which also spread across the Celtic world to include southern Scotland and Ireland), they may alternatively have a rather more prosaic meaning. However, it is possible that this has always been so, the more down-to-earth name even suggesting the mythological one. The most well-known of such names is perhaps that of the River Severn. Tacitus first names the Severn as *Sabrina*, probably the divinity of the river who Anne Ross speculated may have been a Celtic goddess, an interpretation supported by a legend that Geoffrey of Monmouth recounted in the twelfth century in his *History of the Kings of Britain*.[35] Alternatively, Sabrina may be derived from a pre-Indo-European (IE) root *sab-* 'liquid', also found in a lost river name *Saferon* in Bedfordshire and Old Irish *Savara* (C6), *Sabrann*, the river of Cork now known as the Lee.[36] Other contenders for derivations from a goddess include the rivers Dee, Clyde and perhaps the Wharfe, together with the place names Braint in Anglesey and Brent in Middlesex (?after *Brigantiā*).[37] Perhaps the divinity *was* the river, as the name of the Dee 'the goddess, the holy one' appears to suggest. The name of the Trent in Derbyshire is of uncertain meaning but again a British divinity *Sentona* 'goddess of the way' has been suggested (but see below). The name means 'great wanderer' – referring to its great length and its regular flooding; it is also famous for its tidal wave similar to the Severn bore – both 'regarded as a manifestation of the river divinity'. Such a derivation is questioned by Victor Watts, who suggests that the root is Latin *sentina* 'bilge water' < IE *sem-* 'to pour', thus meaning 'flooding strongly, draining thoroughly'.[38]

Pre-English names

Many rivers managed to retain their pre-English names even after language change in the Anglo-Saxon period. Eilert Ekwall notes that while some river names may be Celtic/British in origin, a few others may even pre-date this; however, he concludes: 'I cannot point to any definite name that strikes me as probably pre-Celtic'.[39] Many such names were obviously known by the same name across a wide region of countryside, something that may have helped them to survive language change. It is difficult to say how long the meaning of British names continued to be understood by English-speaking people: it is clear that a language could fall out of use very quickly if it was deemed to have slipped down the social status, as with the use and understanding of Gaelic in parts of Scotland in later historical times.

Despite some names perhaps having links to the names of goddesses, many pre-English names mean little more than 'flowing river' or something similar, many traceable to Indo-European roots. These include ones from *tā-/*tə-* 'to flow': the Thames (*Tamesis* in the works of Caesar and Gildas), Tame, Team, Tavy, Teme, Tone, Taw and Tamar; from *el-*, also 'to flow': the Alne in Warwickshire, which gave its name to the Roman town *Alauna* (Alcester); from *woisā* from a root *weis-/*wis-* 'water': the Wye and Wey rivers, in the Welsh Borderland, Derbyshire, Dorset, Surrey and Kent, and the Wear in Durham; the *Leontan* in King's Norton, Worcestershire, and possibly the River Lyner in Ayshford, Devon (earlier named as the *linor*: the upper reaches of the Spratford Stream), and the Lynher in Cornwall, from *lei- /li-* 'to pour, flow, drip' (with OE *Leon*, *Lion*, Old Welsh *lion*, *lian* on the same IE root appearing as Leen in Herefordshire, derived from rivers which gave their name to several estates including Leominster, Lyonshall, etc.); and the Nadder, Wiltshire, *Nodre*, *Noddre*, from *(s)na-* 'the flowing'. Other pre-English names include the various river Avons, PrW *aβon* 'river' < British (Brit) *abonā* again from an IE base *ab-* 'water, river'; the Dover, Kent, PrW *duβr* (Brit *dubro-*) 'water'; the Nidd, North Yorkshire, PrW *Nið*, Old European *Nidā-*, *Nidi-*, *Nido-* from IE *neid-/*nid-* 'flow'; the Eden in Cumbria, a British river name PrW *Ïdon* from Brit *Itunā*, from roots meaning 'to gush' or simply 'water, river'; and the Rye in North Yorkshire, which gave its name to Ryton, Brit *Rīwā* from the root *rī-* 'flow' or Brit *Reg-iā* from the root *reğ-* 'water, wet'. In time, these seem to have come to be regarded as the proper name of the river and so got passed down through the generations even after language change.

Other pre-English names are more descriptive, some referring to a river as 'swift flowing': the Devon Exe, recorded as *Eaxan* in the eighth century, but already recorded by Ptolemy c.150 as *Ἴσκα*, is a British river name *Iscā* on the IE root *eis-/*is-* 'to move swiftly' and in Roman times had given rise to the name *Isca Dumnoniorum* for Roman Exeter (see above). The Creedy in Devon, the *cridian*, from Brittonic *kridī*, derived from Brit or British-mediated *Kritīo* or *Kridīo* 'winding', is 'the

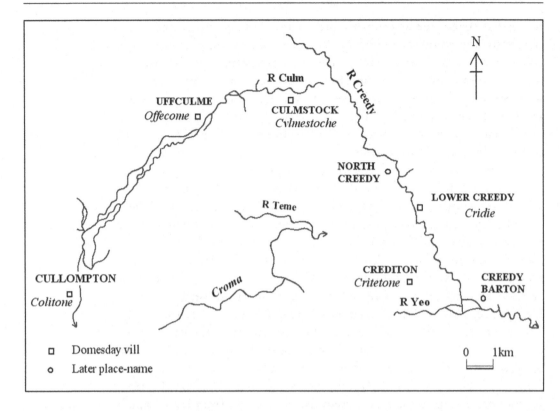

Fig. 2.5 River shapes: (left) the 'looped' River Culm, Devon; (centre) the 'crooked' *Croma*, Worcestershire; (right) the 'winding' River Creedy (Devon) (drawn by Della Hooke).

Fig. 2.6 *opposite* British river names in the West Midlands recorded in early place-names and charters (from Hooke, *The Anglo-Saxon Landscape: The Kingdom of the Hwicce*).

winding or swinging river' (Figure 2.5); the River Kenn in Somerset, from Brit **kantiā* is 'stream of many bends'; the common river name Cocker is derived from Brit **kukrā* 'crooked one'. Several other river names are derived from British or PrW names implying 'turning or twisting', i.e. a river with many bends, among them the Wellow in Hampshire, the Wharfe in North Yorkshire and the *Worfe*, from Brit **werbeiā* incorporating a verb **wer* 'turn, twist', the former the name of the River Ray in Wiltshire, which is preserved in the place name Wroughton.[40] Other names describe the flow of a river: the Tarrant in Dorset, *(to) Terrente, Terente dene*, from Brit **Trisantonā*, PrW **Trihanton*, is 'strongly flooding one', as probably is the name of the River Trent, *Treenta, Treanta, Treontan (stream)* in Derbyshire (noted above): 'strongly flooding one, great wanderer' or 'great flooder'. The Breamish in Northumberland, *Bromic* C11/12, is a British name on the root **brom-*, W *brefu*, with an underlying sense 'rumble, roar', and is a river known in its upper reaches as 'a "brawling torrent" well known for the suddenness with which its spates descend and for its destructive power'.[41] The Torridge *Toric* in Devon is 'violent, rough stream', a British river name related to modern W *terig* 'ardent, severe, harsh'. The Clyst (as in the place name Broadclyst, Devon) is probably 'clear stream'

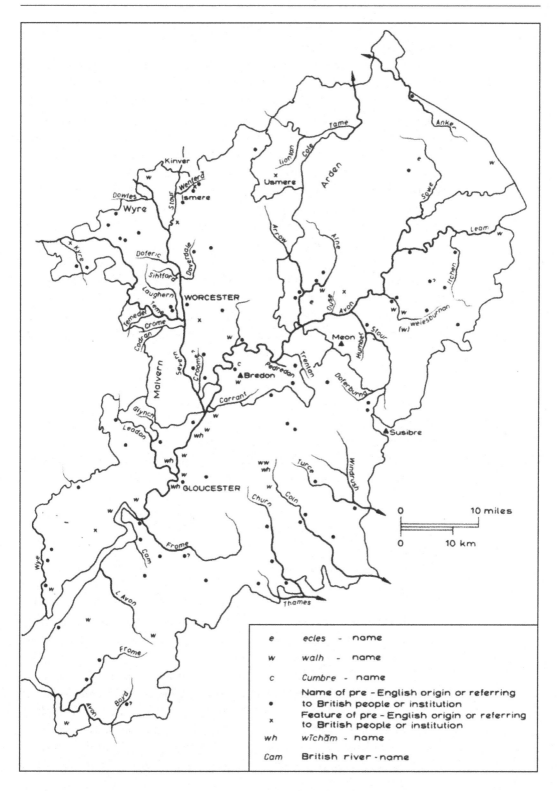

e   ecles - name

w   walh - name

c   Cumbre - name

•   Name of pre-English origin or referring to British people or institution

×   Feature of pre-English origin or referring to British people or institution

wh   wīchām - name

Cam British river-name

deriving its name from Brit *klūst-, *kloust- 'to wash, swill' cognate with Latin *cluo* 'to cleanse'.

Such names are commonest in the western regions of England and Ekwall usefully notes such names by region.[42] Pre-English names are rare in eastern England, an area intensively settled in part by the Anglo-Saxons before 550, and mainly survive for large or medium-sized rivers.[43] However, such names include the rivers Humber, Thames, Ouse and Tyne. Across the midlands the list of such names begins to include more minor rivers but one must also note that documentation in the form of charters also becomes more available in the south and midlands (Figure 2.6). The survival of such pre-English names increases westwards. There is, indeed, a rapid increase in such names in the Welsh Borderland where the British language prevailed longer, and David Parsons has recently been able to show how they are often present in greater numbers in the northern part of the Welsh Borderland than previously thought.[44] It was once believed that the Anglo-Saxons exterminated the British over much of England, a notion encouraged by such writers as Gildas (blaming the invasions on the British lack of Christian faith), but one which is now considered highly unlikely for much of the country where the native British population was simply absorbed into the dominant Anglo-Saxon culture. The names of major rivers were probably best known within any region and are the ones most likely to survive such a change, especially as they were known to and carried by travellers.[45] British names remained common for both major and minor rivers in the West Midlands, but Old English names were making significant inroads even at a local level.

Early medieval terms used to refer to watercourses

Hierarchy of terms

Old English names for rivers are similar in meaning to the pre-English ones, as will be shown below, as are the less frequently recorded Old Norse and Welsh/Cornish names. Although Ekwall argues that individual names for rivers might be unnecessary, even today, in districts where there are few watercourses,[46] in practice the lexicon of such names has been rich and long-lasting.[47]

There was clearly a hierarchy of Old English terms used to describe watercourses. Dictionaries such as those produced by Joseph Bosworth and T. Northcote Toller (with later amendments by Alistair Campbell) offered translations of such terms, but river names were discussed in far greater detail by Eilert Ekwall in 1928.[48] In 1956, A.H. Smith included Old English water terms in his *English Place-Name Elements*,[49] while the volumes produced by Jane Roberts and Christian Kay in 1995,[50] which grouped features and the terms used for them into categories, have also been very useful. Margaret Gelling's work in the 1970s[51] and Barrie Cox's in 1976[52] related such terms to settlement and showed how major centres often bore topographical-type (or archaeological-type) place names, many the names of rivers – a method of naming which seems to have continued from Roman times. Gelling's work, especially her *Place-Names in the Landscape*, published in 1984 and subsequently rewritten as *The Landscape of Place-Names* with Ann Cole,[53] contributed greatly to an understanding of these topographical place name terms, including those for watercourses, and the precise ways in which they were used. Much of this understanding has been incorporated into Victor Watts's *The Cambridge Dictionary of English Place-Names*[54] but other investigations are found in the county volumes of the English Place-Name Society and in specialist journals such as the *Journal of the English Place-Name Society* and *Nomina* (Journal of the Society for Name Studies in Britain and Ireland). Detailed investigations, too, are being carried out for the Toronto Dictionary Project.[55]

Below the river comes *brōc* and *burna*, terms often encountered in different parts of the country. Ann Cole has suggested that 'the Saxon *burna*s usually have very clear water and very few [are] translucent', frequently influenced by geology – the term is common in chalk country or where streams have gravel beds – while 'the *brōc*s show a clear shift towards more sediment-laden water with many being translucent or opaque and very few clear' (cf. German *Bruch* 'bog').[56] The 'winterbournes' also show a periodic change in the flow, meaning 'stream dry in summer', often a characteristic of chalkland regions. Certainly OE *scīr* or 'bright' is found in the early place names Sherborne in Gloucestershire, Sherbourne in Warwickshire and Sherburn in North Yorkshire, in contrast to Fulbrook in Warwickshire and Fulbrook in Oxfordshire, each 'the foul, dirty brook' (OE *fūl*), or the numerous *fūl* or 'dirty' brooks found in West Midland charters. Moving down the scale are terms describing smaller rivulets: *rið* and *riðig* 'small stream'; *lacu*, the latter 'small, slow-moving stream, side-channel' and *læce*, *læcc* 'stream, bog', the latter surviving in dialect form in the north-west midlands for 'a stream (e.g. the Lagbourne in Little Witley, Worcestershire) flowing through boggy land, a muddy hole or ditch, a bog'.[57] OE **spald* 'a trench, a ditch, a fenland river' is met in the name of Spaldington, Yorkshire East Riding, and perhaps Spalding, Lincolnshire. Another term encountered is *bæc*, *bece* 'batch', a term surviving in local dialect for the headwaters of a stream and the small valley it flows in. The term *wella* might also refer not only to a spring but to the headwaters issuing from one (below, and see Chapter 5 in this volume). The OE term *pīpe* or Welsh *pib*, as in the place name Pipe in Herefordshire referring to a small tributary of the Lugg, is 'a pipe, a conduit'. The smallest watercourse is *sīc* 'a small stream, esp. one in flat marshland',[58] in effect one that was little more than a drain. Another rare term is OE **swin²* 'a creek, a channel' as noted on Pershore holdings.[59] It is not clear if this always related to a watercourse, but on the boundary of Pershore estates in Worcestershire a stream is referred to as the *swine*, now known as the Ripple Brook,[60] while another *swinbroch* is recorded in Bradford-on-Avon, Wiltshire. OE *dīc* is a term that could describe either a man-made bank or ditch (often both together) and on a few occasions might refer to huge defensive earthworks such as Grim's Ditch in Wiltshire or the Fleam Dyke in Cambridgeshire: the former is noted as a landmark in the tenth century on the southern boundary of Wylye, the latter in the tenth-century place name Ditton 'ditch settlement'.[61] However, in charter-bounds and early place names the term often indicated an 'artificial watercourse, a drainage channel' and in West Midland and south-western charters many such ditches seem to have been deliberately dug to demarcate stretches of boundary between estates, sometimes linking different streams, and on occasions were indeed named as 'boundary dykes'.[62]

While *pōl* is a 'pool, pond, pool in a river' (as in the case of the *myle pul* 'mill stream or pool' in Stoke Bishop, Bristol,[63] similar terms **pull* or *pyll* may denote 'a tidal creek', one of the meanings given by A.H. Smith.[64] This is used in charters for several streams flowing into the River Severn, such as *lude puylle*, Littleton Pill in Littleton, 'noisy stream' (OE *hlūd*, *(hlyde)*, *pyll*); *ruches pulle* 'Rucche's pill' in Deerhurst (OE *hrycg* 'ridge' + *pull* 'pool'); *miclan pyl* 'great stream or pool' in Aust, all in Gloucestershire, and *sciran pul* 'bright pool or stream' in Upton-on-Severn, Worcestershire. A less common term found is OE **plæsc* 'shallow pool', as in the place name Plaish in Shropshire (*Plesc*, *Plæsc* in the tenth century). Another term is *flēot* 'an estuary, an inlet, a creek' but also 'a river, a stretch of river, a reach'; this was the early name for Seaton in Devon (*Fleote* in 1005), named after the estuary of the River Axe, while Fleet in Lincolnshire (*Fleot* in 1086), the name of a village lying in the heart of the fens but once at the head of an arm of the sea, may have had the sense 'stretch of river with fishing rights' and Fleetham in NorthYorkshire also took its name from an inland stream.[65] Where rivers drained into the sea the term *mūða* 'mouth' is found in a number of early place names such as Sidmouth, Devon (the mouth of the Sid), Weymouth, Dorset (the mouth of the Wey), and Great Yarmouth, Norfolk (the mouth of the Yare).

Other more specialist terms include OE *(ge)mȳðe* 'confluence'. OE *swelgend*, 'a swallowing, a whirlpool, a deep place', is not uncommon in the charter-bounds of the south-west peninsula, noted on three occasions in Devon charters: in Uplyme, the term occurs as a landmark on the East Brook where the valley becomes constricted, 'perhaps suggesting an outpouring of water into a narrow throat', while at Ayshford in the same county the feature lies near the head of the River Lyner where there is also a narrow throat to a wide upper valley which would also have constricted the drainage in much the same way.[66] A similar term *swalwe* 'a whirlpool, rushing water, a swallow', is found in the name Swallow, Lincolnshire (perhaps a stream that rises from an underground source and then disappears again – 'the swallow').[67] OE *wæl*, *wēl* is a deep pool in a river, as found in the place name Thelwall, Cheshire, and Weel on the River Hull in Yorkshire East Riding. Old English *(ge)lād* has generally been interpreted as 'river crossing', but it has been suggested that *lād* alone might mean 'either a road or track, or an artificial waterway or canal' and Cole cites several examples where the term seems to indicate 'a waterway dug through ill-drained land to link a river to nearby rising ground'.[68] Strangely, no reference to a waterfall has been noted in English charter bounds.

As the British tongue evolved into Welsh and Cornish, so other stream names entered the place name lexicon. A Welsh term is *ffryd* or PrW **frud* 'stream, swift-flowing stream', or even 'waterfall', which may also have influenced some in the west of the Hwiccan kingdom such as the *sifhtferð* in Grimley, the *coforet* in *Wican* and the *Wenferð* in Wolverley, all in Worcestershire (but the *Wenferð* may be PrW **winn-frud* 'fair, holy stream'). Cornish terms met in early place names and charter-bounds include *pol* 'pool', *frot* 'stream' and **heyl* 'estuary' (which Ekwall gives as the old name for the Camel estuary: *Hehil*, *Hægelmuða*).[69] Many Welsh terms continue the use of earlier British ones (below) and, in time, Scandinavian terms also become evident in place names, especially in northern England: *á* Old Norse 'river', *lœkr* 'brook', *bekkr* 'stream, beck', *brunnr* 'stream' (as in Burnby, Yorkshire East Riding, *Brunebi* in 1086), and **geysill/*gausli* 'the gusher, the gushing spring' as in Goxhill, Yorkshire East Riding and Lincolnshire.[70]

Old English terms for springs include *ǣwelm*, *ǣwylle* (and dialect forms *ewelm*, *ǣwielm*, *ǣwylm*) 'a river-spring, the source of a river', which Margaret Gelling and Ann Cole suggest was one that was particularly prolific,[71] one such, an affluent of the Cam in Uley, giving its name to the River Ewelme in Gloucestershire and another to Ewelme in Oxfordshire. Smith sees this as a different term to OE *ǣwell*, *ǣwiell* 'a stream' but also frequently 'the source of a stream', as found in the place names Alton, Hampshire, or Alton Priors, Wiltshire.[72] Other OE terms are *spring*, *spryng*, usually with *ēa* 'stream' in such compounds as *ǣ-spring* or *wyll-spring*; *wella* or in its many dialect forms, *wælle*, *wielle*, *wylle*, 'well, spring, stream' (but also sometimes a headwater stream); a rare term *celde*. A landmark on the boundary of Grittleton in Wiltshire is *(to) spring wellen*. *Funta* 'spring' is a loan from late British (PrW) **funtōn*, **font*, **funt*, itself from Latin *fontana* and surviving as Cornish *fenten*. Springs are noted as *wæterwyllas* in the laws of Cnut.[73] Guiting (Power) in Gloucestershire contains another OE term *gyting* < *gyte* 'spring; a pouring forth, a flood', described as *fontanum quod nomintur Gytingbroc* 'the spring of Guiting' in 780.[74] OE *flōde* 'a channel of water, a gutter' is found in some charter boundary clauses especially in the south of England, but in Berkshire and Somerset appears to describe intermittent springs which break forth 'in large volume at intervals of several years' or 'a spring which issues in large volume'.[75] One such is *þa fulan flode* at Avington, Hampshire, perhaps 'the foul channel', but others are described as 'clear', 'great', 'white' or 'red'. In *Nymet* in Down St Mary, Devon, the *readan floda* could therefore be 'red intermittent spring', and this feature occurs close to a large, red-coloured hollow at the source of a stream.[76] Another *readan flodan* refers to a copious spring on the boundary of Stoke St Mary in Somerset,[77] with another noted at Tisted, Hampshire. Another *flōde* occurs as *(on) scyteres flodan* in Privett, Hampshire; OE *scytere* is taken by Jane Roberts and Christian Kay to mean 'torrent',[78] but this is not certain, and *scytere* appears as a stream-name on the Nynehead, Stoke St Mary, Ruishton and Hestercombe estates in Somerset.[79] OE *flōd* is 'flood, tide, a flow of water'[80] as *on flodleah* in the bounds of Withington, Gloucestershire, and *to cleara flode* in the bounds of Withiel Florey, Somerset. OE *lagu* 'sea, flood, water' is usually found only in poetic contexts but occurs in a place name High Laver, Essex.

Lakes and meres, not covered here, are also referred to by a variety of terms, the commonest OE *mere* 'pond, lake, pool', although occasionally *wæter* 'water' is used as an alternative term. OE *fenn* 'fen' describes wetland more generally; *hamm* might be 'land hemmed in by water or marsh', while it has been suggested that *mersc* 'marsh' areas were less infertile than ones described by the term *mōr* ('moor, barren wasteland or barren upland' but also often 'marshland').[81] OE **polra* 'marshy land' is met in the name of Powderham, Devon. Cornish terms met in charter-bounds include *hal* 'moor, marsh'. Old Norse (ON) *mos* 'moss, bog' is a term which is still frequently used in north-west England and *myrr* is another Old Norse term meaning 'swamp'. Welsh *cors*, PrW **cors* 'reeds, bog, swamp' is found as a river name Corse in Somerset (and a place name Corston) and in the Gauze Brook in Wiltshire (and a place name Corsley beside the Rodden Brook in that county) and OW *guern* 'alder swamp' in the place name Llanwarne, Herefordshire. OE *luh* could be 'a lough, a lake, a pool'. OE *sæ* might be used for 'sea' or 'lake', the former giving rise to place names near the coast such as Bursea in Yorkshire East Riding, but Whittlesey Mere in Cambridgeshire (see Introduction), *Witelesmare* 1086, 'Witel's mere' was one of the largest inland stretches of water in the eastern fens, still noted as a breeding ground for wildfowl in the late seventeenth century[82] – it was the last to be drained in the nineteenth century. A smaller muddy place might be described by OE *slōh*, or a *sol(h)*, while *strōd* may have described 'marshy land overgrown with brushwood'.[83] By travelling around the country investigating the use of such terms, Gelling was able to identify OE *wæsse* as 'land by a meandering river which floods and drains quickly' as in the case of Broadwas, Worcestershire, beside the River Teme, Alrewas, Staffordshire, beside the Trent and Buildwas, Shropshire, beside the Severn.

Ekwall notes how rivers may have different names along their courses: he mentions the River Wiley in Wiltshire, whose upper course is known as the Deverill, a change which he attributes to the hill-dwellers on the upper part being isolated from the people of the Wilton district; he further notes that the upper part of the Till in Northumberland is called the Breamish and the upper part of the Windrush in Gloucestershire the Guiting Brook. On occasions, one such name might go out of use over time: thus the Tilnoth in Gloucestershire was an old name for the upper Coln.[84] Yet other rivers like the Thames were known by one name along their entire lengths, something which might be proved by surviving settlement names: Ekwall cites North and South Witham at the source of the Witham, Bruton and Brewham near the source of the Brue and Exton high up on the Exe.[85] Occasionally the early name for a river has been lost, but not before it had given its name to a settlement nearby: the Waver in Warwickshire, *Wavre*, OE *wæfre*, 'wandering', which gave its name to the estate of Churchover, *Wavre*, *Waver(e)* 1086, 'Waver with a church', and later Brownsover, was still recorded as such in the fifteenth century but later became called the Swift. In central Worcestershire, the *hymel broc* (below) gave rise to the estate and settlement name Himbleton, but after the early sixteenth century it became known as the Stone Bow Brook and later simply as the Bow Brook.[86] One of its tributaries, the Erse, *yrse* in the tenth century, carried a name that was lost after the thirteenth century but gave its name to Ersfield Farm in Whittington. Few of the names for streams and lesser watercourses recorded in early medieval documents have survived to the present day: most were only known across a few parishes, but they are of huge interest in that they reveal how the Anglo-Saxons saw their local countryside.

Terms used to describe watercourses: a West Midlands study

The West Midlands is here taken to be the pre-1974 counties of Warwickshire (Wa), Worcestershire (Wo) and Gloucestershire (Gl), an area in Anglo-Saxon times falling mostly within the kingdom of the Hwicce which was focused upon the Severn valley. With the diocesan see established at Worcester with its own monastic scriptorium, the area enjoys good pre-Conquest charter coverage and it is the boundary clauses attached to many such charters that name not only rivers but lesser streams and minor watercourses.

Many names, whether of British or Old English derivation, are descriptive like those noted above, referring to rivers and streams as winding, swift or gushing, gliding, babbling, broad or narrow, little or small, clear and pure or foul and dirty, sometimes merely as 'long'. Thus in the West Midlands the *langan broc* of Whittington is a tributary of the Bow Brook which it does not reach for some 13 kilometres. The Leadon in Gloucestershire, *(in) ledene*, is from Brit **litano-*, PrW **lïdan* 'broad'. Of those described as 'winding' or 'crooked', the Croome in Worcestershire, which gave its name to the estates of Croome D'Abitot, Hill Croombe and Earl's Croome, is derived from Brit **Krumbā* becoming **Crombā* 'crooked stream', or OE *(æt þæm) crumban* 'at the bends' (an alternative interpretation of this name as a district name referring to the great bends here in the River Severn cannot be entirely dismissed).[87] Such a name recurs as *croma*, *crome* in Powick and Leigh, referring to a winding tributary of the Severn draining eastwards from the Malvern Hills (Figure 2.6).[88] The Erse or Yrse on Pershore estates (Wo), *(on) yrse*, may possibly be 'the wandering, winding stream', OE *iersu*, while *(on) swepelan stream* in Stoke Bishop (Gl) may be related to ON *svipall* 'shifty', hence 'the shifty stream'. 'Little' or small streams – presumably narrow – are frequent, including the *lytlan broc* 'the little brook' in Himbleton and Huddington (Wo) and the *litlan broc* in Wormleighton (Wa), *þæt lytle ryðig* in Croome'D'Abitot, *þæt lytle sic* 'the little watercourse' in Pensax and the *smalan broc* 'small brook' in Yardley (all Wo).

Of the river names, the Stour in north Worcestershire, *Stur, (on) Sture*, and the river of the same name in Warwickshire, *(on) Sture, Stuur, Stures stream*, is often explained as meaning 'violent, fierce one', probably an OE river name *Stūre* < adj, **stūr* from a root seen in *storm* 'tumult, onrush'[89] although Smith notes a Germanic name meaning 'fierce, gloomy', accepted by Richard Coates, who sees this as opposed to the name of the Blythe in Warwickshire 'happy river'.[90] In Gloucestershire, the *hrindan broc* in Cutsdean and Rendcomb is from OE *hrindan* 'to thrust, push', perhaps 'thrusting, pushing brook', and the Frome, *(andlang) Frome(s)* is from a PrW *frôm, Brit **frãm-*, the root of Welsh *ffraw* 'fair, brisk'. The Arrow in Warwickshire, *Arwan stream*, and the Arrow in Herefordshire, *Erge*, may be from OE *earu* 'quick, active' (Ekwall suggests a derivation from the Celtic **arg-* '?white' or **arw-* also 'swift'). The noise of the water's flow also gave rise to the name of the *lydeburnan* 'loud stream' running between Offenham and Badsey near Evesham (Wo), the *lhydan* in Upton-on-Severn and in Bredon (Wo) and the *hlidan* in Pucklechurch and South Cerney (Gl), all from OE *hlyde* 'torrent, swift stream' with a derivative *hlūd* 'loud'.[91] Similarly, the *bæle*, or Ball Brook in Grimley (Wo) is OE *bæl 'noisy, babbling stream'. A 'swift' stream is the Roden in Shropshire (Brit *Rutūniā, from the IE root **reu-* 'move swiftly') while, in contrast, the *smitan* of central Worcestershire may be 'to glide, slip'.[92] Others are also described by their individual nature. These include the *pedredan*, a tributary of the Avon (Wo), which as in the Somerset River Parrett may mean 'fourfold ford' (Brit **petrurit-*), the Worcestershire example formed by two arms joining near the efflux,[93] while the *twige* of Cofton Hackett (Wo) may be 'double or branched stream'.

A stream's location might give rise to many names: 'hollow' brooks from OE *hol²* 'lying in a hollow, deep, running in a deep valley' are common, noted three times in Worcestershire, once in Warwickshire and once in Gloucestershire – all but the *hola pyll* 'stream in a hollow' at Olveston, Gloucestershire, are described as brooks. Other batches (a dialect term in this region, OE *bæce* was frequently used to refer to a small brook, as opposed to OE *bæc* 'a back, ridge') and one *rið* are also described as 'deep', presumably referring to their valley, and there is one *denebroc* 'valley brook' with OE *denu* (Withington in Gloucestershire), a more substantial valley. Geology would have given rise to the brooks described as 'chalky' (the *calc broc* of Wolverley), the 'gravelly bourne' (the *cisburne* of Hallow), 'the sandy brook' (the *sandbroc* of Broadway), the 'stony brook' (the *stan broc* of Little Witley), all in Worcestershire, and the 'clay brook' (the *clæg broc* in Tiddington and Alveston in Warwickshire). A sandy stream is also indicated in the settlement name Samborne, *Sandbvrne*, a place situated on the red soils of the Triassic Mercia Mudstone in Warwickshire, while the presence of sandy strata may also explain the colour attributed to the *reade burnan* 'red bourne' of Eldersfield and Chaceley (Wo). However, saltworking may have affected the colour of *salwarpan*, the Salwarpe (from OE *sealu* 'sallow, dirty stuff') downstream from the inland salt-producing centre of Droitwich in Worcestershire, an activity noted for the filth it created. The *feala maeres broc* is 'the brook of the tawny or dark mere' and the *blacan broc* is 'the black brook', both in Oldberrow, now in Warwickshire. 'Cold' watercourses are not uncommon, especially springs or small streamlets such as the *caldes wælle sice* and the *koldes broc*, both in the Pensax (Wo) bounds, the *ceoldryðe bece* of Oldberrow and the *colpuylle* 'cold inlet' of Littleton-upon-Severn (Gl).

Some watercourses in the West Midlands, always brooks, are merely described as 'west, south or north' but not always in relation to the estate being described: the 'west brook' of Elmley Castle (Wo) runs down the eastern boundary of that estate, as does the 'west brook' of an estate at Tiddington and Alveston (Wa); the 'south brook' of Caldicot in Bredon (Wo) runs in the northern part of the estate and the south brook of Bishop's Cleeve (Gl) actually follows the northern boundary of that estate. In some cases such watercourses may have acquired their names before estate fission or in relation to a more important centre in the vicinity. 'Boundary' brooks (*mær broc*, etc. – almost always terms for 'boundary' are associated with *brōc*) are particularly numerous in the charter boundary clauses: an example is *mæra broc*, the Marl Brook, which flows along the boundary between Lindridge and Neen Sollers on the Worcestershire/Shropshire border. In Worcestershire seven such brooks are noted (also once with *wyllan* and with *pul*), plus one *tæcles broc* in Little Witley from OE *tǣcels* 'boundary mark, a boundary' and *brōc*, also found in the name of the Tach Brook (a tributary of the Avon) *tæceles broc*, and a place name Bishops Tachbrook, *Taschebroc*, in Warwickshire. In Warwickshire *mær broc* occurs once and in Gloucestershire five times (plus one possible *mær wille* 'boundary stream or spring'). The various 'salt' watercourses such as the *salt broc* of Lower Wolverton (Wo) (now the Saw Brook) and the *sealter pile* of Maugersbury (Gl) take their names from saltways running past them.[94] (In a post-Conquest perambulation of Icomb the latter is called the 'good spring' and is now called St Edward's Well, a well reputedly beneficial for weak eyes that was turned into a garden feature c.1800).

Some streams were undeniably described as *fūl* or 'dirty', an adjective associated in the West Midlands with 'brook' three times, plus an estate named as Fulbrook recorded in Domesday Book in Warwickshire, twice with *rið*, and once as *hor pyttes riþig* 'the streamlet of the dirty pit'. Others, however, were quite different: *scīr* 'bright' is found with *burna* as *scir burnan* in the name of the Sherbourne in Cofton Hackett (Wo) and in Coundon, Coventry (Wa) (with another *scir burna* recorded in 1310 also forming the north-western boundary of Fulbrook parish in that county) and with *pul* as *sciran pul* 'bright pool or stream' in Upton-on-Severn

(Wo) (as discussed above). Other appreciative terms include 'friendly, pleasant': the Blythe or Blyth in Warwickshire, noted above (but also rivers in Northumberland, Warwickshire, Nottinghamshire and Suffolk), is 'merry, pleasant, gentle one'; in Gloucestershire the Carrant takes its name from Brit *Karantō*, OW, PrW *Kereint* 'white' or 'happy' and the Glynch, *(ondlong) Glences, (ondlong) Glencing*, from Brit *glanīc*, W *glan* 'pure, clean' (it is almost always rivers that have names describing them as 'pure' or 'white'). The numerous 'honey bournes' or 'honey brooks', recorded as both place names and charter boundary landmarks (the latter recorded only once in the West Midlands against three references to 'honey bournes'), incorporate OE *hunig* and *burna* or *brōc* to mean 'sweet water' but several flowed through wooded countryside where bees, their honey an important source of sweetening, may have been plentiful.

Other names refer to the type of countryside the streams were passing through or the plants and animals found along their banks. Thus, the *bærbroc* of Bentley in Holt (Wo) is probably from OE *bǣr²* 'pasture, especially wood-pasture' and is the name of a stream on an estate which is known to have provided this resource;[95] the *winburne* of the Evesham estates (Wo) may be OE *winn, *wynn* with *burna* 'meadow stream' and the *wudewælle sice* in Pensax (Wo) 'the small stream of the woodland spring'. Hunting in the vicinity gave rise to the stream name the *wæðe burnan* (OE *wāð* 'hunting') in Powick and Leigh (Wo) in the Malvern foothills. Marshland, OE *pidele*, 'marsh, marshy stream', is indicated by the name of the Piddle, *Pidele* and *Pidewælla*, in central Worcestershire, and the name of the Leach, too, the *Lec*, in Gloucestershire (giving its name to Northleach, *Lecce, Lec(ch(e)* in 1086), is 'the boggy stream' or 'stream flowing through boggy land' from OE *læcc, lece*.

Plants gave rise to the names of the *gledenun* in Smite, Hindlip (OE *glædene* 'yellow flag'); the *hymel broc* in Himbleton (OE *hymele* 'hop plant'); *heortseges broc* in Upper Arley (OE *heortsecg* 'hart-sedge'); *pyrt broc* in Longdon (probably an error for *wyrt*, hence 'herb, vegetable' brook); the *rixuc* in Cotheridge (OE *rixuc* 'rushbed'); *secg broc* 'sedge brook' in Chaceley estates (OE *secg*); the *beolne* 'Bell' in Belbroughton, perhaps from OE *beolone* 'henbane', hence 'stream where henbane grows' (all in Worcestershire, although Upper Arley was later transferred to Staffordshire); the *hreodburnan* 'reed bourne' in Ladbroke and Radbourne in Warwickshire (OE *hrēod*); and the *bracburne* 'fern ?or bracken bourne' (OE *bracu*) on Deerhurst estates (Gl). Many of these plants may have been collected as flavourings or other uses (the henbane was anciently used in herbal medicine allegedly to induce sleep but fell out of use as it was found to be poisonous). Trees noted in such a context include the ash, associated with a spring, the *æsc wellan* 'ash spring' in Stoke Bishop (Gl), and also a stream in Chaceley (Wo) if the *an burnan* is indeed derived from W *onn* 'ash-tree';[96] the alder, *alre, ælr broc, alr broc* occurring three times in Worcestershire and once in Gloucestershire; the hazel (Latin *corylus*) which gave its name to the River Cole, *(on) Colle*, 'the hazel-tree stream' in Cofton Hackett and Yardley (Wo) from PrW **koll* and W *coll* 'hazel, sapling, twig'; the oak, *ac wyllan* (OE *āc*) in Yardley; the elm in Myton (Wa), *on limenan, on leomene*, the Leam 'elm-tree river', an OE river name *Leomene* from Brit **Lemanā* or **Lemonā, Lemenā*, formations on a root **lem*, cognate with the Latin *ulmus < *lmo-* and English *elm < *elmo-*;[97] and the withy, the *wiði broc* of Tardebigge (Wo): OE *wiði, wiðig*.

Some of these names may recognize the value of particular species of trees or plants.[98] Individual tree species had many kinds of uses: the oak, valued for its strength and durability, was the favoured timber for building and also provided the acorns which were a valuable fodder crop for herds of pigs; the ash is also an excellent timber tree while the alder was a useful wood for items subject to alternate wetting and drying, to which it was resistant; pliant withies were suitable for the manufacture of baskets, fish-traps, chairs and so forth. Reeds had all manner of uses, being particularly valued for thatching, and bracken was historically used as bedding for stock.

Birds frequenting rivers include the crane or heron, OE **cron* 'crane', as in the *corna broc* in Knighton, etc. (Wo), and the *cran meres broc* 'the brook of the crane mere' in Wormleighton (Wa). 'Heron' is an Anglo-Norman word and the birds are not dissimilar; indeed the grey heron is still referred to in some dialects as a 'crane' (West Yorkshire), 'jemmy crane' (Lancashire), or a 'longie crane' (Pembrokeshire).[99] Other birds referred to include the crow, OE *crāwa*, as in the *crawan broc* in Cofton Hackett (Wo); the hen, OE *henn*, as in *hens broc* in Stoke Prior (Wo); the hawk, OE *hafoc*, in the *afoc broc* of Redmarley D'Abitot and *(to) hafoc wylle* in Cold Ashton (both Gl); or birds in general in the *brið broc* 'bird brook' (OE *bridd* 'young bird') of Deerhurst estates (Gl). Animals included the hart or stag, OE *heorot*, in the *hiort burnan* of Bentley in Holt (Wo) and the *heort broc* in Daylesford (Gl) (along with a spring, valley, hill and bridge); the horse, OE *hors*, in the *horsa broc* of Wolverley (Wo), *hengestes broc* in Upper Arley (Wo) which may be from OE *hengest* 'stallion' or may be have been the same word used as a personal name; the otter, OE *otor*, in the *oterburnan* of Tapenhall, North Claines (Wo); and the beaver, OE *befer*, in the *beferburnan* or Barbourne Brook, 'beaver stream' in Barbourne, North Claines, which

also gave rise to the place name, and perhaps too the *beferic* in Little
Witley (Wo). The British beaver was hunted to extinction early in
the medieval period, but such place names show this animal present
there in the early tenth century, although perhaps already in reduced
numbers. The Laughern Brook, which gave its name to small estates
at Laughern *æt Lawern* in St John's in Bedwardine near Worcester and
later to Temple Laughern further to the north in the same parish, may
be derived from a British word for 'a fox', as in the obsolete Welsh word
llywarn, llewyrn (or merely be another name derived from the root in
Latin *lavo* 'to wash' – a possibility for the nearby *lawern*).[100] Geraint
Jones, however, interprets the line *o wythwch a llewyn a llwyuein* in
an ?early seventh-century Welsh rhyme *Pais Dinogad* inserted into *Y
Gododdin* as loosely meaning 'Be it a boar, a wild cat, or a fox' (the 'wild
cat' perhaps the lynx).[101] Shottery in Warwickshire was named from a
stream referred to as *(æt) Scotta rith, Scotriðes gemære*, either 'the Scots'
stream' or a name deriving from OE *sceota* 'trout'.

It might be thought that streams, often flowing for considerable
distances, would acquire few associations with individual personal names
in the same way that trees and similar more localized features might
indicate possession or land ownership. However, streams associated
with individuals are not uncommon, although personal names are far
commoner with *brōc* and *burna*, as, indeed, are most descriptive terms.
In Worcestershire in the case of *ippan burnan*, 'Ippa's bourne' in
Laughern, the stream is indeed a short one flowing along the north-
eastern boundary, which was probably associated with a local person;
nearby *aelles burnan* 'Ælle's bourne', which touched the boundary of
Temple Laughern, is equally short; *luddesbroc* in Norton and Lenchwick,
forming the eastern boundary of Chadbury, is similarly almost restricted
to one estate and *osrices pulle* forms the southern and eastern boundary
of the eastern portion of Pendock; *bæddes wellan* 'Bæddi's streamlet'
flowed through the heart of the estate of Badsey.[102] In Warwickshire,
clæhæma broc, 'the brook of the *clæhæma*' (the inhabitants of Claydon),
formed the boundary between that estate and Wormleighton. In south
Gloucestershire, Duntisbourne Abbots (*Duntedburn(e)*), Duntisbourne
Leer (*Tantesborne*) and Duntisbourne Rous (*Dvntisborne*) all lay along
the *Duntesburne, -borne*, 'Dunt's stream', only to be distinguished
by additional suffixes in the thirteenth century. Thus the majority of
such names were of local significance. However, the *esenburnan*, the
Isbourne, is 'Ēsa's stream' and is a major tributary of the Avon in north
Gloucestershire. The *wixena broc* 'Whitsun Brook' which flows along
the southern boundary of Abberton and Naunton Beauchamp seems to
bear the name of a group known as the *Wixena*, whose home territory

lay in East Anglia, and it seems likely that along with others from the
Fepsætan tribe (noted a little to the north) these indicated small groups
colonizing this woodland area in central Worcestershire.[103] The *fildena
wyllan* of Bickmarsh and Ullington in the Vale of Evesham, on the other
hand, was 'the spring/streamlet of the dwellers in the open country'.

Although so many early names have been subsequently forgotten,
a number were obviously passed down in common speech but thereby
were prone to be reinterpreted. Thus the *mæra broc* 'boundary brook'
separating Lindridge and Neen Sollers in Worcestershire (above) is now
known as the Marl Brook and the *merebroc* of Charlton in the same
county as the Merry Brook. Another Worcestershire example is the
saltbroc 'salt brook' but probably 'salters' brook' of Stoulton which is
now known as the Saw Brook.

Early medieval river names found elsewhere

Similar river names occur across the country. Only major names
recorded by 1086 are discussed here and, even so, those given here
do not form a comprehensive list; names of uncertain meaning are
omitted.[104] 'Non-descriptive' names such as the Avon recur frequently,
as noted above. Other descriptive names referring to the flow of the
river include the Brue, *Briuu, Bru, Briu*, in Somerset, which is 'brisk,
vigorous one', cf. W *bryw* < Celtic **briwo-* 'lively, vigorous, powerful'.
This river has a brisk current, especially in its upper reaches.[105] The
Willett in Somerset, *Willet*, is possibly 'gushing stream' from OE (West
Saxon) *wylle* + **gīete, *gīte*; the Lyn of Lynton, Devon (as in the place
name Lynton), is OE *hlynn* 'torrent' (Watts notes how the west and east
rivers and their affluents sweep down narrow gorges from Exmoor to
form dangerous and sometimes destructive torrents, as in 1952);[106] while
the Webburn in Devon, an affluent of the Dart, takes its name from
OE *wōd* 'mad', *wēdan* 'to rage', i.e. 'the raging stream'. The opposite
meaning is conveyed by the name of the River Idle in Nottinghamshire
and Lincolnshire, the *Idlæ*, possibly 'the idle slow, lazy river' from OE
īdel (although Watts notes a Breton name *Isole, Idol(a)*) and *þa deadan
lace* in Creedy Barton, Devon, which is 'the dead brook', probably a
sluggish backwater stream of the Creedy.[107] The name of the Dacre in
North Yorkshire, *Dacre*, a tributary stream of the River Nidd, derives
from a PrW term **deigr* 'a tear, a drop', perhaps simply implying an
insignificant stream that is little more than a trickle. This may apply,
too, to the Hyle in Surrey, the *hile*, which gave its name to Ilford 'the
ford across the River Hyle', *hil* perhaps representing a Celtic root **sil-*
'trickling stream'. In contrast, the *Wealce* of Walkhampton in Devon
may be 'the rolling one'.

The Trysull in Staffordshire, *Tresel, Treslei*, the old name of the Smestow Brook, is probably a compound of OW *tres* 'uproar, turmoil, commotion' and a stream name forming the suffix *ell*. The Stour rivers in Worcestershire, Dorset, Kent, Wiltshire and Warwickshire may be each 'the violent, fierce one' (but see above). The Lid Brook the *Hlyde*, in Wiltshire, the Lyde Brook in Herefordshire (which gave its name to a district name Lyde and several *Leode/Lude* estates in 1086)[108] and the *Hlyding* in Leicestershire are other rivers taking their name from OE *hlūd* 'loud'. Winding rivers continue to be noted: the Hamble in Hampshire, *homelea, hamalea, (innan) hamele*, is from OE **hamol, *hamel* 'maimed, mutilated, crooked', hence again the 'crooked one', and the *womburnan* of Oborne, Dorset, 'the crooked stream' from OE *wōh* + *burna*, here referring to the winding course of the River Yeo. The Wantsum Channel in Kent, *Uuantsumu, Wantsumo stream, (andlang) Wantsume*, the ancient name for the channel which formerly separated the Isle of Thanet from the mainland, is OE **wændsum* 'the winding river'. The Culm in Devon, *(on) culum* with the place names Cullompton and Culmstock, is 'looped river' from OW *culm* 'knot, tie', and Watts notes how 'the course of the river is a succession of loops and frequently divides into two' (Figure 2.6).[109] The Weaver in Cheshire (with the place name Weaverham) is also 'winding stream' from OE *wēfer(e)* 'wandering', as indeed it still is, while Woore in Shropshire is either that or OE *wæfre* 'unstable, restless, wandering'. More specific is the Toller in Dorset, *tillor*, the old name of the Hooke which rises at Toller Whelme, which is probably PrW **tull* 'a hole' + **duβr* 'water', implying either 'stream with holes in it' or 'stream in the deep valley'.[110] Shalborne, Wiltshire, seems to take its name from a 'shallow' river.

Geology has influenced the name of the Cerne in Dorset, which gave rise to several place names along its course such as Cerne Abbas, *Cernel* in 1086, Up Cerne, *Obcerne*, Dorset in 1086 (with later, also Nether Cerne) and Charminster, *Cerminstre* in 1086 (Figure 2.7); this name is OE **cearn* < PrW **karn*, meaning the 'rocky or stony stream'.[111] This is also the name of a second Devon river which gave its name to Charmouth, *Cernemude* in 1086, 'mouth of the river (Cerne)', close to where it flowed into the sea. The Cary in Somerset, *Kari, Cari*, 'hard, stony stream' is an Old European river name **Karīsa* on the root **kar-* 'hard, stone, stony' (like the River Carey in Devon). Stainburn in North Yorkshire is 'stony bourne', as is Stawell, Somerset. Lumburn Water in Devon, *(of) lamburnan*, and the place name Lamerton, *Lambretone* in 1086, is 'the loam stream' from OE *lām* + *burna* (a derivation from OE *lamb* now considered unlikely).[112] The *Grendling* as in Grindleton, Lancashire, is OE **grendel* + *ing* + *tūn*, 'village beside the *Grendling* or gravelly stream' and the Greet in Nottinghamshire, *(on) greotan*, is from OE *grēot*, also 'the gravelly stream'. The River Coquet in Northumbria, *Coccuveda, Coquedi/cocuedi fluminis*, is 'the red river', and Watts notes that the upper reaches of the river are filled with red porphrytic detritus from the Cheviot.[113] Colours may not always be affected by geology – the various rivers from PrW **duβ* < Brit **dubo-* all 'the dark river', such as the River Dove, *Dufan* C10, in Derbyshire, are stated by Ekwall to have dark beds even if they do not have dark water as they run through deep valleys.[114] The Foulness *(on) Fulanea* in Yorkshire East Riding is 'the foul or filthy river', again from OE *fūl*, while the Granta in Cambridgeshire, *Gronte fluminis, Grantan stream, Grante éa*, is perhaps 'fen' or 'muddy river',[115] the meaning too of the River Loddon in Norfolk, a river name from Brit **Lutnā* 'muddy river'. Also considered unattractive must have been the Meole Brook in Shropshire, from OE *me(o)lu* 'meal, flour', perhaps referring to cloudy water. The Shernborne in Norfolk is from OE *scearn* 'dung', perhaps 'dirty stream', while the place name Skidbrooke in Lincolnshire, *Sc(h)itebroc* in 1086, is from OE *scite* 'dung' with 'brook' and other contendors for such a meaning may include *sciteresford* in Upper Arley (Wo),[116] the *sciterlacu* of Dawlish, Devon, and the *scitere* near Taunton in Somerset.

More appreciative names include the Candover, *Kendefer*, in Hampshire, 'beautiful waters' from PrW **ken*, Brit **kanio-*, with *diβr*; the Cray, *(on) crægean*, in Kent, 'fresh water' from PrW **krei*, W *crai* 'fresh, new'; and the Dorce, *Dorcan*, in Surrey, which may have given its name to the folk known as the *Dorcingas*, 'clear, bright stream' from an IE root **derk-* 'glance' seen in OE *torht* 'bright'. Other 'bright' rivers are suggested by the old name of the River Rother, *(andlang) scire, scyre*, in Hampshire; the Freshwater, *Frescewatre* 1086, on the Isle of Wight, 'river with fresh water' from OE **fresc* + *wæter*; the Glen in Northumberland, *fluvio Gleni, Glene*, 'holy or beautiful river' from PrW **glen*' with the root meaning **glano-* 'clean, holy, beautiful', ModW *glan*;[117] the Glyme in Oxfordshire, *(to) Glim*, perhaps from Brit **glīmo-* 'the bright one'; the Lea in Hertfordshire and Greater London, *(on) Lig(e)an, (on) Lygan* OE *Lyge*, which is cognate with the W river name *Lleu* and ultimately from IE **leug-* 'bright, light' (but an alternative explanation of 'river dedicated to Lug', perhaps Lugus, another deity of the Celtic pantheon, is also noted by Watts);[118] and *(to) fægran broce* in the bounds of Alwalton in Cambridgeshire, 'the fair brook', while the Lugg in Herefordshire, *neah þære Lucge*, giving rise to the place name Lugwardine, is from an IE base **lewk-* 'gleam, light' seen in W *llug* 'radiance, light'. Another river which may have been 'white, fair, holy stream' is the *Wenfre* of Winford in Somerset from PrW **wïnn -frud* (see comments on the Worcestershire stream the *wenferð* above). Other 'white' rivers include the Winster in Cumbria. The Cornish Durra, *(andlang) cendefrion*, seems to be OW *cein* 'beautiful', PrW **ken*, Brit **kanio-*, with Co *dour* 'water'[119] and Pentewan in Cornwall seems to take its name from the River Tewan, the old name of the St Austell river, possibly 'bright river' (cf. W *tywyn* 'radiance').

Locational names continue: another name for 'boundary' is OE **tēo* (gen. sing. **tēon*), found with *burna*, giving rise to the name of the Tyburn in Greater London, *(andlang) teoburnan*, 'the boundary stream'. The Medway, *Medweg, Meduwege*, etc., in Sussex and Kent, is 'middlewater' (IE **medhu* + river name **Waisā* on the root **weis-/*wis* 'water'); Watts notes how this river 'is the main dividing river of Kent and opens a marked gap between the W and E stretches of the North Downs'.[120] Another valley name, OE **corf* 'valley, pass' is transferred to a river name, the Corve, in Shropshire, a river which runs through the long valley between Wenlock Edge and Clee Hill. Another 'meadow stream' is the Wimborne in Dorset, giving the place name *(æt) Winburnan*, from OE **winn, *wynne*, + *burna*. Marshland is again suggested by the Wissey in Norfolk, *Wusan*, 'the marsh river' related to OE **wisse* 'a meadow, a marsh'. Boundary terms recur: the Mersey, *Mærse*, is probably 'boundary river' (see Introduction); the Micheldever, *Mycendefre, Myceldefer*, in Hampshire, is perhaps 'marshy river' from PrW **mïgn*, 'slimy, slippery'+ **diβr* < Brit **dubrī*, here flowing through the marshes of the Test but later reinterpreted as containing OE *micel* 'great'.[121]

Vegetation names continue to refer to plants and trees: the Darent, in Kent, *diorente, De-, Dærentam*, is 'oak-tree river' or 'river where oaks grow abundantly' from PrW **derwint*, a from Brit **derwentjū*, a derivative of **derw-* 'oak-tree' also occurring as the river name Derwent in Cumbria, Derbyshire, Northumberland and North Yorkshire and the Dart in Devon, *(to) dertan*. The yew is again met in the name of the Iwerne 'yew-tree river' in Dorset (Brit **Iuernos* from **iuo* 'yew') in the place name Iwerne Minster, *Evneminstre* in 1086. To these may be added the River Yeo in Devon, *(on) eowan*, if this name is indeed derived from OE *ēow*. Other tree names include the alder as in the *wuern golornan* 'alder-swamp' in Lanow, Cornwall; the *ceacga broc* in Monkton in Shobrooke, Devon, 'broom or furze brook'; the ash as the *æscburne* in *Peadingtun* (an estate on Dartmoor) and the Inny in Cornwall, the *Æni* (Co *enn*, double plural of *onn* 'an ash-tree'); and the withy as the *wyþylake* in Uplyme, Devon. Selborne, Hampshire, is 'sallow-willow bourne', and maples gave their name to the Maplebeck of Nottinghamshire. The Hurstbourne in Hampshire, *(juxta) Hissaburnan*, *(to) Hysseburnan*, and the Husborne in Bedfordshire, *(of) hysseburnan*, are both OE *hysse +burnan*, probably referring to a plant with trailing tendrils such as reed canary grass, which Watts notes fills the former burn.[122] The Rodbourne of Wiltshire is 'the reedy bourne', Sedgebrook, Bedfordshire, 'the sedge brook'.

Among the bird and animal names are further references to cranes, as in the place name Cornwell (*Cornewelle* 1086) in Oxfordshire 'the spring where cranes are seen'; Enborne, Berkshire, is *aneborne -burn(a)*, OE *ened + burna* 'duck stream'. Jackdaws gave their name to the Cabourne *Caburne* of Lincolnshire – almost dried up today – OE *cā + burna*, rooks to Rockbourne, Hampshire. The Lambourn in Berkshire, *(on) lamburnan*, may be 'lamb stream', OE *lamb* with *burna*, and the *scipbroc* of Sandford in Devon 'sheep brook'. Otters gave their name to the Otter, *Otery*, in Ottery St Mary, Devon, and to the Otterborne in North Yorkshire. Although Ekwall believed that OE *lox*, 'lynx', was improbable as an explanation for the Lox Yeo *(on) loxan*, and the Lox *(innan) loxan*, in Somerset, it is now known that the lynx was present in northern Britain until about 1200 and may be referred to in a later Shropshire place name Lostford recorded in 1121 which Gelling translated as 'lynx ford'.[123] *Polmaduc* in St Buryan in Cornwall may be 'fox pool'[124] and *(oþ) wulfwyllan heafod* in Sorley, Churchstow, in Devon is '(from) the head of wolf spring or streamlet'.[125] An investigation of such names in charter-bounds across the country would undoubtedly add to this list.[126] Fishbourne, West Sussex, is 'fish bourne' (OE *fisc*);[127] the Ock, *(on) œoccænen, (on) œoccæn, (on) eocene*, etc., in Oxfordshire, is a PrW *Iogan* < Brit *Esocona*, a formation of the word for 'salmon'; the presence of eels gave rise to the *æl broc* of Meavy in Devon. A name of a type not found in the West Midlands is the *sceoca broces forda*, Shobrook Lake and the place name Shobrooke in Devon: 'goblin's' or 'haunted brook', from OE *sceocca, scucca* 'evil spirit, demon' (also Shocklach, Cheshire, with *læcc, lece* 'boggy stream') (see Chapter 5 in this volume).

Names referring to springs and 'wells' (often head-water streams) have first elements similar to those found in the names for rivers and other kinds of streams, although space does not permit a comprehensive coverage of such names here. Kettlewell, North Yorkshire, is 'bubbling spring or stream' (OE *cetel*); Ledwell, Oxfordshire, again 'noisy one' (OE **hlyde*), while Wherwell, Hampshire, is from OE *hwer* 'cauldron' + *wylle*, where the merging rivers Test and Dever run in multiple channels, giving again the sense 'bubbling stream'. North Greetwell, Lincolnshire, is 'the gravel stream' (OE *grēot + wella*), Radwell, Hertfordshire, 'the red spring' (OE *rēad + wylle*). Cranwell, Lincolnshire, and Cornwell, Oxfordshire, are other references to cranes, Crowell in Oxfordshire to crows, while Titchwell, Norfolk, is 'kid spring' (OE *ticcen*); Harwell, Northamptonshire, 'hart spring'; and Winswell, Devon, 'beetle spring' (OE *wifel*). Snailwell, Cambridgeshire, may be a referance to 'a sluggish stream' or to the snail (OE *snægel*). Plants associated with such features are wild marjoram or mullein in Feltwell, Norfolk, and trees such as the hazel (OE *hæsel*, ON *hesli*) in Heswall, Merseyside. An unusual reference to a spring associated with divination is Fritwell in Oxfordshire (OE **freht* with *welle*, *wylla* 'augury') (see Chapter 5).

Rivers and settlement names

Watercourses taking their names from settlements are rare: *stokkesbroce*, Stock Brook, later 'Stock Well', in Littleton upon Severn in Gloucestershire appears to be from OE *stoc* 'an outlying farmstead' but many more watercourses gave their names to settlements and estates established beside them, as noted, including Ewen in Kemble, Gloucestershire, the source of the Thames (from *ǣwelm* 'spring'), Croome D'Abitot and others). Thus, in Devon, Ottery St Mary, Otterton and Upottery all take their name from the River Otter. An estate named after the River Clyst is referred to as *(æt) Glistune* in the *Anglo-Saxon Chronicle* under the year 1001 and as *Clistone* 'Clyst estate or manor', in Domesday Book, but is later subdivided into Broadclyst (also containing West Clyst), Clyst Honiton, Clyst Hydon, Clyst St George, Clyst St Lawrence and Clyst St Mary in the thirteenth or fourteenth centuries. In Dorset other estates taking their name from a single river are those lying alongside the Piddle, most of them named in Domesday Book simply as *Pidele* or similar: Piddletrenthide (*Pidrie*, with *Uppidelen* the northernmost of several tithings in Piddletrenthide parish), Piddlehinton (*Pidele*), Little Piddle (*Litelpidele*), Waterston (*Pidele*) and Puddletown (*Pi(t)retone*), and, further downstream, Burleston (*Pidele*), Athelhampton (*Pidele*), Tolpuddle (*Pidele*), Affpuddle (*Affapidele*), Briantspuddle (*Pidele*) and Turners Puddle (also *Pidele*), all named after the Piddle (alias the Trent), which flows into Poole Harbour (Figure 2.7). The Cerne, also in Dorset, gave its name to the estates of Cerne Abbas (*Cernel* in 987 and in 1086) and Up Cerne (*æt Upcerl[e]* 1002–12 and *Obcerne* in 1086); later, Nether Cerne, *Nudernecerna*, lying downstream of these is also distinguished as a separate estate by 1206. Much further downstream, where this river flows into the River Frome, lies Charminster (*Cerminstre* in 1086: 'the church on the River Cerne') (also Figure 2.7). Itchington in Warwickshire, an estate on the River Itchen, is divided into Bishop's Itchington and Long Itchington. Old English *ēa* is not a frequent component of place names, but the list includes such names as Ayton, North Yorkshire; Nuneaton, Warwickshire; Yeoford in Devon; Yoevil

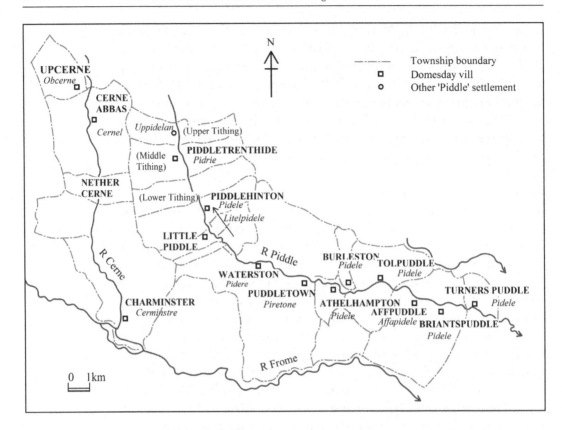

and Yeovilton in Somerset and Twyford in Gloucestershire, the latter '(land) between the rivers', OE *twēonan* + *ēa*, referring to its location between the rivers Severn and Avon. Since northern England is not well-covered by early documentary evidence, this part of England is poorly represented here. An unusual reference to a place lacking water is found in the name Thorton Watlass in North Yorkshire, *Wadles* in 1086 from ON *vatn-lauss* 'waterless' and there is indeed no stream nearby. It was the proper names of rivers which most often gave their names to early medieval settlements and estates.

Apart from place names derived from the proper names of rivers, the Old English terms *burna* and *brōc*, used to describe substantial streams, appear most frequently as early place name generics, the former far more often than the latter. The term 'winterbourne' for a stream with a greater winter flow is particularly outstanding for the frequency of its use. In Wiltshire, three different 'winterbournes' gave their names to such settlements, estates which often only became differentiated by name after the Norman Conquest. In southern Wiltshire, Winterbourne Stoke, *Winterburnestoch* in 1086, Maddington, *Winterburne* in 1086, and Shrewton, *Wintreburne* in 1086, all took their names from a

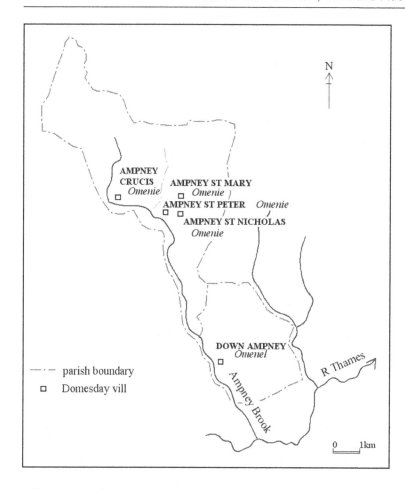

Fig. 2.7 *opposite* 'Cerne' and 'Piddle' estates, Dorset (drawn by Della Hooke).

Fig. 2.8 *left* 'Ampney' estates, Gloucestershire (drawn by Della Hooke).

tributary of the Salisbury Avon which later became known as the Till. Another 'winterbourne', later known simply as the Bourne, a separate tributary of the Salisbury Avon, gave rise to the name of Winterbourne Earls, *Wintrebvrne* in 1086, later possessed by the earls of Salisbury; Winterbourne Dauntsey and Winterbourne Gunner were also named separately in the thirteenth century. In the north of the county another 'winterbourne', a tributary of the River Kennet, gave its name to Winterbourne Bassett and Winterbourne Monkton, *Wintreborne*, *-burne* in 869, 1086, only differentiated as *Wynterburn' Basset* and *Winterburne Monachorum* in 1249. The Nail Bourne in Kent, later the Little Stour, gave its name to several Domesday manors along the stream to the south-east of Canterbury: Littlebourne, *Litebvrne*, Bekesbourne, *Borne*, Bishopsbourne, *Bvrnes*, and Patrixbourne, also *Borne*. The necessity to distinguish between two Domesday 'Bourne' estates is met again elsewhere: Eastbourne and Westbourne, in East Sussex and West Sussex respectively, both *Borne*, *Burne* in 1086, were allotted new qualifiers in the thirteenth and fourteenth centuries to distinguish more easily between the settlements. Another estate later subdivided was Ogbourne in Wiltshire, *Oceburne* in the tenth century and *Ocheburne*, *-borne* in 1086, 'Occa's stream' (a back formation causing the river to become known as the Og), with the thirteenth-century manors named as Ogbourne Maizey, Ogbourne St Andrew and Ogbourne St George. In south Gloucestershire four estates named *Omenie* and *Omenel* in Domesday Book are all named after the Ampney Brook, a tributary of the Thames; they become differentiated as Ampney Crucis, Down Ampney, Ampney St Mary and Ampney St Peter in the thirteenth century (Figure 2.8). Similar developments can be found across the country.

Really small streams (other than those associated with springs) rarely gave their names to settlements. In Watts's dictionary only one *rið* name is noted by 1086 – Sawtry in Cambridgeshire. The terms *lacu*, *lache* and **lacuc* are also rare in place names – Fishlake, South Yorkshire, and Shiplake, Oxfordshire, may be examples of the former while Laycock in Wiltshire is from **lacuc*, 'small stream' and a similar word *lecan* 'to trickle' is found in the place name Leconfield in Yorkshire East Riding 'open land beside the stream'. Coates, however, rejects Beverley in Yorkshire East Riding, *Beferlic*, as being a derivation from a hypothetical OE **licc*, preferring to see this as a form of early Brittonic **beβr-licc*, giving a British **bebro-lecc-* 'beaver lodge'.[128] There may be four examples from *bece*, *bæce* (e.g. Cotesbach, Leicestershire), three from ON *bekkr* and four from ON *brunnr*. There are few, too, for watercourses that were little more than drains: ?*spāld* and **spald* (one in the Fens of Yorkshire East Riding and two others), *luh* (one: Lutton, Lincolnshire) and *pīpe* (one: Pipe and Lyde, Herefordshire).

Of the other 'water' terms, it is those referring to springs and 'wells' that appear most often in place names, with prefixes similar to those for rivers and streams. There are, for instance, a large number of *wi(e)lle* names in Oxfordshire referring to springs or headwater streams found scattered throughout the county: Crowell, Brightwell Baldwin, Cadwell and Mongewell in Crowmarsh are located in the Chilterns; Broadwell, Cornwell, Ledwell in Sandford St Martin; Fritwell and Showell in the Cotswold limestone hills and Epwell in the Ironstone belt. Many more are recorded in charter-bounds, including a *colwullan broc* in Witney, which is 'brook of the charcoal spring' and a reference to the River Cherwell as *cearwyllan* in a charter of Water Eaton.[129]

Conclusion

Pre-Conquest documents referring to rivers and other watercourses offer a wealth of information about the Anglo-Saxon countryside, revealing how it was perceived by travellers and local inhabitants alike, and often what creatures or plants were to be found locally. The value of rivers and streams as sources of water for people, animals and crops is evident and rights to water were jealously protected in law. Rivers, too, were often used to ferry people and goods. Rivers were often the focus of territories or served to mark major territorial boundaries (see above and Introduction) but even minor watercourses might also fulfil this purpose. Probably more than any other topographical features, watercourses have influenced the development of the English countryside.

3

Fens and Frontiers

Kelley M. Wickham-Crowley

[The Peterborough fen] is very valuable to men because there are obtained in abundance all things needful for them that dwell nearby, logs and stubble for kindling, hay for the feeding of their beasts, thatch for the roofing of their houses, and many other things of use and profit, and moreover it is very full of fish and fowl. There are divers rivers and many other waters there, and moreover great fishponds. In all these things the district is very rich. (Hugh Candidus, *The Peterborough Chronicle* 5, mid-twelfth century)[1]

Introduction

A word for 'frontier' did not exist in Old English; writing on fens and frontiers therefore poses a challenge. The nuances of the modern term can be quite wide-ranging: we use it for everything from a place such as America's Wild West to space exploration to finding new treatments on the frontiers of medical research. Here we look at Anglo-Saxon frontiers as both literal and figurative, material and imagined. This approach yields somewhat divergent evidence that suggests settlement of the fens could, on a practical level, increasingly exploit the rich material yields of the environment, seen partly through archaeology and place name study, while, simultaneously, the concept of the fens could evoke layers of interpretation, superstition and belief that grew and evolved in the imagination according to cultural needs and ideologies. Considering how and why fens matter in Anglo-Saxon culture allows an exploration of the impact of fens on the thoughts and perceptions of Anglo-Saxons, showing something of how this particular land- and waterscape shaped its peoples.

In an earlier article, 'Living on the *Ecg*', I attempted to get at habits of mind among the Anglo-Saxons by looking at texts alongside the environmental and archaeological evidence for the interplay of land and water:

> The mutability of the 'edge' between land and water, as recorded in Anglo-Saxon texts and archaeology, fits with a way of thinking that considered land/water intersections as a habit of perception or vision, coloring and marking more than the physical environment … creating something of a cognitive map for how vision translates into thought and perception, and how the physical environment can reveal conceptual boundaries.[2]

For the present chapter, fens narrow my previous considerations of watery environments to one that was highly evocative in Old English literature as well as richly exploited in both secular and religious material contexts. While the Anglo-Saxon referents for what we call 'fen' might have had a broader range than our modern specific and scientific definition, we nevertheless get the word from Old English and Norse *fenn/fen*. It is a type of wetland or mire we now characterize by high mineral content, non-acidic water and particular plant groups of sedges, brown moss and grasses. When the Germanic tribes arrived in Britain, a long history of fen use by native Britons and Romans preceded their advent, as evidenced by a prehistoric site such as Flag Fen, Cambridgeshire, with its wooden roadways and ritual use, and the salt-making evidence at Roman settlements. With water levels rising and probably contributing to the movements of Germanic peoples from their homelands in the early medieval period, fen and marshland would have increased, becoming both more pervasive and more evocative of past histories. The following discussion is therefore divided between the material and literal evidence about the fens – place names and topography, boundaries, and exploitation of resources by settlement, trade and royal sites – followed by the figurative profile of the fens in literary and historical texts, and the impact of their narratives.

Frontiers, literal and littoral

Physical migration made all of Britain a frontier to the arriving Germanic tribes, and the Roman view of Britain as situated on the edge of the world was most likely shared by many continental peoples – German *foederati* would certainly be familiar with that perception when they were part of the Roman occupation of Britain. But given the rising sea levels and inundations in the late Roman period, followed by ever-increasing evidence for Saxon period resettlement of the fens, a seagoing people encountering rising water on the continent would not find fens in Britain an entirely new phenomenon, even if they encountered more variety in the types of marshy landscape. It may well have been the familiarity of such an environment that first stimulated them to occupy Roman and Romano-British siltland sites in the eastern fens, though whether they were aware they were doing so is currently debated.

While the prevailing view holds that Roman sites were sealed with silts deposited by marine incursions, Susan Oosthuizen has recently argued for continuity and for continuous occupation of fenland in the early medieval period (though we might stipulate that does not mean in all areas in all periods). Citing DNA evidence, Oosthuizen accepts 'widespread assimilation of small groups of early medieval north-European migrants into a large late British population' and cites Lucy and Reynolds about a lack of 'highly-distinctive ethnic communities' as shown by fifth- and sixth-century artefacts (that is, chronologically if not culturally, Early Saxon) in eastern Britain. This shared material culture she reads as the continued survival and evolution of late British culture: 'Most people using Anglo-Saxon artefacts in the mid-fifth century were late British by birth and descent'.[3] Elsewhere, however, she seems to contradict this point, asserting that 'not only was it impossible to distinguish between migrants coming from different parts of North-West Europe, but distinctions between "migrant" and "indigenous" populations were as elusive'[4] (see Chapter 4 of this volume for discussion of the coastal wetlands at this time). Whatever the continuity may or may not have been, these locations were nevertheless the preferred ones for Anglo-Saxons as well as earlier groups. Perhaps because before and after the Romans, the native Britons too used the fens, in time they came to be identified with them on a somewhat mythical level in the memories of the later Germanic groups, evoked in associations of fens with devils speaking 'British' in the saint's life written about Guthlac, for example.[5] Prehistoric Britons occupied these areas for centuries if not millennia, followed by Romans, and their barrows, salterns and ritual offerings of weapons and valuables would have been visible and tantalizing reminders of such an association (see Chapter 5 of this volume for details of votive offerings and bog bodies).

Though fens were larger and more extensive in the past, most Anglo-Saxons did not, of course, live in or near fenland, so discussing fens in daily life initially sounds like a limited project: whose daily lives and how many are we discussing? In addition, there are four major areas of wetland in England, each the subject of modern surveys in progress:

the North West Wetlands Survey, the Humber Wetlands Project, the Somerset Levels Project and the best known Fenland Survey.[6] Here, I focus on the eastern Fenlands around the great estuary of the Wash. They were the largest and most likely the earliest wetlands settled in Britain by Anglo-Saxons and are to date the most examined and excavated of the four regions, though all are at risk due to environmental degradation of various types. The Somerset Levels will also feature here somewhat, not least because of how Alfred's association with the famous fen site of Athelney takes hold in the Anglo-Saxon imagination.

Place names and topography

When the Germanic peoples arrived in Britain, the landscape was changing under the influence of rising sea levels and occupied by a variety of British tribes, analogous in some ways to Europeans arriving in a world populated by Native Americans. In the latter case, Europeans had firm ideas about boundaries and ownership, while for many First Nations, the idea that a person could 'own' the land was inconceivable. So we should perhaps not be in a hurry to think that encounters between Britons and Germanic settlers were necessarily confrontational, a point previously noted in discussing Oosthuizen's ideas. We know less than we could wish about what British tribes thought about territorial boundaries, though Roman subjugation caused rebellions early on. While this is not the place to open the continuing debate over invasion versus assimilation, for Britons and Germanic tribes, the frontier between them was initially one of language and culture, and, while its origins are unclear, the practice of intercommoning suggests some co-operation rather than confrontation. Place name research in particular has given us new insights into how those who came to be called Anglo-Saxons perceived and named the land new to them, if nonetheless previously or currently already settled.

In 2000, Margaret Gelling and Ann Cole published *The Landscape of Place-Names*, giving evidence from fieldwork and philology of a major discovery: studying topographical settlement names showed 'a systematic use of specialised terms for identical land-formations' where

> these names represent a system which operated over most of England, from Kent to Northumberland and from the east coast to Offa's Dyke. It is not so apparent in the south-west peninsula, where English speech arrived several centuries later, and this accords with many other indications that the full glory of the topographical naming system belongs to the early part of the Anglo-Saxon period.[7]

The last point had been the main contention of Gelling's earlier *Place-Names in the Landscape* (1984, repr. 1993), and in 2000 she reiterated that topographical settlement-names were 'most likely to have been coined by English-speaking immigrants in the 5th and 6th centuries'.[8] Thus, Anglo-Saxons were giving their own names to places, not adopting any previous native names. References are not simply to hill or pool; they are specific to variations in aspects, such as dry areas in marshy environs or a hill with a hollow in its side: 'The **hōh** [*sic*] of Ivinghoe Beacon in the Chilterns, with its "heel" and instep, is replicated by the end of the ridge on which stands the Northumberland village of Ingoe, and by many others in the country between them'.[9] Asking how such a system emerges in post-Roman Britain, Gelling posits that with Germanic peoples sharing both familiarity with northern European landscapes of 'vast coastal marshes and the great plains and forests' and an inherited vocabulary for describing them, the varied landscapes found in smaller, denser spaces in Britain presented visual and linguistic challenges.[10] Those challenges were met by using a consistent topographical set of terms. She also suggests that travellers had a part in developing and stabilizing the system,[11] an attractive and logical idea. For a landscape without maps, the usefulness of common names for repeated landscape features shows how the names themselves become a kind of map. By rehearsing a list of place names as directions, an Anglo-Saxon would have had a mental image of the contour or types of landscape to look for or prepare to pass through, knowing the shape that each name specified. Thus, even if a previously occupied site had a British name, the Anglo-Saxons would have named the topographical feature for their own use and then derived a place name for it based on specific landscape forms. Gelling argues that geography often dictates where people would choose to live because of innate advantages (high ground, promontories, etc.) regardless of whether they were British or Germanic, and calls landscape terms appearing in names for such places 'quasi-habitative'.[12] Importantly, Gelling stresses that her references are to 'names applied to settlements which for the most part had been long-established when the speakers of English first saw them', though they need not be still occupied when Germanic tribes first arrived. The Anglo-Saxons would have used the topographical features to name both site and settlement for themselves, which makes categorization and comparison for place name work easier and tells us that such shapes or features were part of Anglo-Saxon perception and cognition, their learned experience.[13]

So what does place name evidence tell us about settlements in fens and marshy land? In some senses, it was more of a frontier than we might expect. Despite the later evocative use of fens in Anglo-Saxon literature (discussed later in this chapter and in the figurative aspects for water in Chapter 1 of this volume), *fenn* is rare in place names of eastern England now called The Fens.[14] Gelling suggests limited use of the term in place names in the earliest periods (fifth to sixth centuries), mainly in Essex, with other synonyms dominating instead, such as *mōr*.[15] *Mōr* means both 'marsh' and 'barren upland'. Though the relationship between the two meanings is not established, the latter meaning seems the later one, suggesting early and limited use of *fenn* could have been replaced by *mōr* meaning 'marsh' (as well as similar terms) only to have *fenn* return later when *mōr* mainly referenced 'barren upland'. *Mōr* as wet or boggy land can refer to both low-lying wetlands (in Somerset, Shropshire and Oxfordshire, for example) and to boggy or wet uplands (such as the moors at the boundary of Westmorland and the West Riding of Yorkshire).[16] The East Saxon form *fænn* appears in Essex names as Vange, Fambridge and Bulphan. Showing up also on both sides of the Crouch estuary, it 'was probably the name of the district', and a similar district name may apply to the north bank of London's Thames.[17] Gelling states that enough counties have been surveyed to assert 'confidently ... that *fenn* is rare or absent in place names likely to be of pre-Conquest origin in large areas of England', with Devon as the only southern county with *fenn* in many minor names and three major ones.[18] This accords well with the points previously mentioned: *fenn* is mainly a later (reintroduced) term, used because of the later arrival of English to the south-west peninsula. Thus, the place names suggest evidence that Anglo-Saxons did not settle extensively in eastern Fenland in their earliest period, but they were keen to note the marshy or wetland attributes of places they did settle, and they did choose such places as useful even later in the period (as in Devon). The need for more than one term for the types of marsh found shows the variety and specificity Gelling describes. But the scarcity of 'fen' in early names suggests that Anglo-Saxons were initially disinclined to settle there, for whatever reasons, so that even the absence of fen names constitutes evidence of an uneasy frontier boundary between the settled and the unknown. The next section asks how we can speak of boundaries in fen landscapes.

Pushing boundaries

Rare as the term *fenn* seems in early place names (until we add in other 'marsh' terms such as *mōr*), the eastern fens themselves were apparently well-peopled by Bede's time in the early eighth century (and more broadly in the Middle Saxon period). In his *Ecclesiastical History of the English People* (735), for example, he mentions Bishop Thomas of Dunwich, himself from 'the nation of the Gyrwe',[19] Seaxwulf, the founder of *Medeshamstede* (Peterborough) 'in the land of the Gyrwe'[20] and the ruling family of the South Gyrwas/Girvii, a name meaning 'people of the mud/marsh'. Their prince Tondberht was married to Æthelthryth. After he died, she founded the monastery at Ely in East Anglia (673) on land he gave her at their wedding, surrounded by marshes rich with eels, from which the name derived: 'eel district'.[21] The evidence so far for Anglo-Saxon settlement on the siltlands of eastern England (Norfolk, Lincolnshire, Cambridgeshire) shows some early Saxon and late Saxon use, with most of the settlements found or suspected dating to the Middle Saxon range (see Chapter 4 and its 'larger marshland' section). All sites found were in areas of marine silt and clastic sediments surrounding the Wash, some of which were found to lie over Roman sites which had been sealed by such sediments, as in Lincolnshire, raising the question of whether the Saxon settlements knew of the earlier sites in these cases. Only local memory of previous occupation would have made them aware of it and we are uncertain about contact in the earliest period. Widespread cemetery evidence does not exist, and the relationship of fen settlements to upland settlements remains a work in progress. Notably, in the later Saxon period, when upland Saxon territorial units went from large to small (referred to as fission), the fens saw settlement go in the opposite direction, with later settlers using 'islands' of gravel and building large-scale sea defences to reclaim and expand territory.[22]

Even more detailed if still difficult to know what to do with, the presumed tribute list called *The Tribal Hidage* lists peoples and tribute assessments. Historian David Roffe, who believes they were exclusively Fenland peoples, comments,

> The Middle Anglian section is the most detailed of all. Among others it records the *Spaldas*, North Gyrwe, South Gyrwe, Wigesta, West Wixna, East Wixna, Sweordora, Herefinna/ Hurstingas, Wideringas, and Bilmigas who all held in or close to the fenland. The date and provenance of the document are still a matter of debate, but it must indicate that in the seventh or eighth century the area was organized into communities with recognisable identities. As Stenton has observed, 'The local names of the Fens are very difficult, but they do at least show that this whole country had been explored, and was being exploited, and had been named far back in the Anglo-Saxon period'.[23]

Roffe adds that 'this was not the conquest of uncharted waste. Rather it must be represented as a change in the mode of settlement and exploitation. The environment was a condition rather than a determinant of land use throughout the period'.[24] That last statement implies a conscious choice of this environment for its resources on the part of religious and secular groups alike.

Despite the many separate tribal identifications in *The Tribal Hidage*, David Roffe shows that communal action is clearly evidenced in Fenland in what he terms 'frontier zones' or 'frontiers of interests'.[25] The practice of intercommoning gives us some indications of permeable boundaries, as the sharing of a common space for pasture by two or more groups also made provision for maintaining banks and drains. These groups could be intercommunal or intracommunal, so intercommoning does not necessarily give us boundary zones between different peoples. Roffe argues that while seigneurial rights were asserted in the twelfth and thirteenth centuries, dividing the siltlands, the accompanying responsibilities for maintenance were less attractive to such lords:

> In the Fenland maintenance of the infrastructure of banks and drains devolved upon the communities of the vill, leet, or twelve-carucate hundred (a settlement or groups of settlements that formed a community for the purposes of local government and the management of communal resources in Cambridgeshire, Norfolk, and Lincolnshire respectively). Here was a practice that clearly antedates manorialisation and preserved a vestige of a more ancient communal regulation of resources.[26]

He notes that intercommoning is a well-known characteristic of other early communities, as in Kentish management of the Weald.[27] In contrast, later overlapping claims and disputes may indicate that previously shared resources are subsequently changing from common areas to areas requiring fixed boundaries between groups or districts:

> Frontier zones only become truly so when communities come into contact with each other. It was probably only with the pressures to divide that serious thought was given to boundaries. By the late tenth century Yaxley and Farcet [Cambs.] had both defined their own areas of peat fen in relation to each other and neighbouring communities.[28]

In a sense, the frontier created identity without asserting exclusive rights; instead, a frontier zone can be permeable and arguably thrives on sharing resources and on open exchange, whether material or cultural, but negotiated and vulnerable to shifting placement. By shifting to fixed boundaries, marking the land as separating peoples, a set boundary forms a skin for the body of people who share common perceptions of themselves and lay claim to ownership, identifying in certain particulars as like one another, whether that is in language, genealogy, heritage or political and/or religious goals. But such fixed terms are belied by the reality of a boundary: it is a creation of the mind that can be reified by material 'marks' on the landscape – a boundary cross, a place name recognizing a local resource such as alders, a barrow proclaiming the presence of honoured dead. Creating a boundary is in a real sense the *placing of an idea*, the reification of an abstract concept by tokens or marks of its significance or claims.

Resources and trade

For the local fen economy, settlements are seen as most likely based on stock (sheep and cattle mainly) for wool and meat as well as some probable salt making. Salt itself need not have been traded, though it easily could have been, but it would have been needed to preserve meat if that were a major part of local production.[29] In addition, finds of weaving tools such as spindle whorls and loom weights point unsurprisingly to cloth production, but whether that was a product intended for trade or sale outside of local settlements is unclear. Walpole St Andrew and Terrington St Clement (Norfolk) produced weaving implements such as bone combs, spindle whorls, pin beaters and loom weights, as did Gosberton, Chopdike Drove and Dowsby, Hoe Hills (Lincolnshire).[30] Wool would apparently have been plentiful. Certainly, the amount of sheep bone shows they were the majority of stock kept, with cattle fewer but producing more meat and milk per animal. The fens were important grazing areas, and salt both increased milk production and inhibited liver fluke infestation, so the wet conditions held little threat for herds (see Chapter 4). Excavation has also shown that animals were kept here all year round, not seasonally, as shown by the presence of neonatal and young animals as well as animals killed at all ages. The absence of woodland probably explains the rarity of pig bones. Bird evidence was limited to domestic fowl and wild or domestic geese. Fish included varieties from both salt and fresh water environments, though most were estuarine or marine (see Chapter 6). Some of the latter 'may have been taken inshore, as even large haddock and cod may be found in shallow waters at various times of the year'. Fish caught included haddock, cod, flatfish (plaice, flounder), herring, smelt, eel, cyprinids and pike, and mussels, oysters and cockles were also found.[31]

Vocabulary can also point to and supplement some of the physical resources environmental archaeology can help uncover. We know that fens possessed rich ecologies, and a brief list of terms shows resources that include 'fen' as a qualifier in their names: words for plants and creatures show them to be specific to this environment. *Fenndæc* 'fen thatch' suggests its use for roofing buildings, though it might also serve to make bedding, mats or floor and door coverings, or, when simply cast upon a floor, for a clean or dryer surface. *Fenminte* 'fen mint', and *fencerse* 'fen cress', suggest culinary uses; fen cress may be bog/marsh yellow-cress, a member of the mustard family (*Rorippa palustris* (L.) Besser)[32] or a related type, while the *Dictionary of Old English Plant Names* identifies fen mint as *Mentha aquatica* L.[33] Other plants include *fen fearn* 'fen or water fern' and *fenampre* 'fen sorrel/dock', though no specific types have been identified. Similarly, *merscmealwe* designates the *Althea officinalis* L., a marsh mallow, and *merscmeargealla*, a kind of gentian, possibly *Gentiana pneumonante* L. mentioned in the *Leechdom*, while *merschōfe* refers to ground ivy, *Glechoma hederacea* L.[34] Hunting and fishing are evidenced by the otherwise generic-sounding terms *fenfugol* 'fen fowl', and *fenfisc* 'fen fish'; the word *fenyce* is still a mystery, though suggestions include a fen frog, snail or tortoise. As mentioned earlier, eels would have been found plentifully, as tidal inundation and floods served to introduce them to the waterways of the fens. Their life cycle is well adapted to an area that was shifting from salt to fresh water. Spawning in the salt water of the Sargasso Sea, eel larvae migrate to Europe, changing to glass eels and then elvers as they migrate up estuaries into fresh water. Living surprisingly long lives, they mature into 'yellow eels' and finally 'silver eels' before returning to the Sargasso Sea to spawn.

In terms of manmade material culture, pottery sherds hold great promise for tracking both local frontier identities as well as trade relationships. Paul Blinkhorn asserts that all over Anglo-Saxon England, pottery was part of identity and social cohesion. Considering Middle Saxon Ipswich and Maxey wares, though both were found together in Lincolnshire, Northamptonshire, Cambridgeshire, Buckinghamshire and Bedfordshire, Blinkhorn notes the absence of Maxey ware in Norfolk, and only a single sherd in Wessex, stating 'it seems that Ipswich ware was a necessary part of the East Anglian social/cultural identity'. He continues, 'This suggests that ... artefacts carried with them a sense of social belonging and that, in some areas at least, certain artefact types were regarded as culturally unsuitable, despite any functional superiority'. Such a cultural need to construct an identity through chosen objects will be echoed in the cultural uses of the fens as setting in later texts. In Lincolnshire, he notes evidence that Maxey wares were used 'to make social statements in a similar manner to Ipswich ware'.[35]

Vessel forms also indicate important information about identity and status. East Anglia exported Ipswich ware for two reasons:

> Firstly, the industry was the only English manufactory to produce jug forms which were, in essence, a 'foreign' vessel form. Perhaps these were deemed necessary due to a rise in the popularity of wine-drinking which, socially, may have been viewed as a 'foreign' activity and thus in need of a socially non-local utensil set for its serving and consumption. The second reason was trade; it has been shown that assemblages from outside East Anglia contain a far greater proportion of pitchers and large jars than those from inside the kingdom, indicating that the latter were travelling as containers rather than pots in their own right.[36]

Mark Gardiner examines further the implications of these pottery wares in Chapter 7 of this volume.

In the context of potential trade and transport along waterways, when we review the eastern Fenland place names and settlement evidence the impact of what went into and out of the fens becomes somewhat clearer. Ann Cole documents and discusses the many place names denoting a landing place or hythe (Old English *hȳth*) around the fen edge and on fen islands in early medieval England.[37] Though having different courses today, she notes that the Ouse, Nene and Cam wound through the marshes and made boat travel the best option: 'Accordingly, a series of landing places grew up around the eastern and southern margins of the Fens where the higher, firmer ground of the East Anglian Heights fell away to the marshlands, and where small but navigable streams gave access to the rising ground'.[38] While many names only first appear in documents in the twelfth or thirteenth centuries, enough are attested in Anglo-Saxon times, such as those mentioned in Sawyer charter 595,[39] dated 956: '*Dichyðe, Suðhythe, Færresheafde Hythe*, and *Norðhythe* ... lay beside the old course of the Nene, now Pigs Water, between Yaxley and Farcet' (Cambridgeshire).[40] Despite changes in waterways now, Cole asserts such hythes were beside navigable water in that period and at times also convenient to roads: 'Some would have had quite extensive hinterlands, especially if they were within easy reach of a Roman or other old road. Others served limited areas such as parts of monastic estates. The sites were usually chosen with care, firm ground such as river terrace gravels being preferred'.[41] Some of the place names indicate a resource associated with the site, such as Horseway (Cambridgeshire), which could mean a place for transporting horses, or Aldreth (Cambridgeshire): 'Four miles of fen separate this "alder hithe" from the "gravel hithe" at Earith HNT, and both hithes were surely responsible for the movement of cargoes from fenland channels to dry ground'.[42]

Cole also discusses the significant site of Lakenheath, Suffolk (cited in Domesday Book as *aet Lacingahith*), which

> overlooks the Fens and lies on rising ground about 2 miles south of the Little Ouse, to which it was linked by Lakenheath Old Lode or its predecessor. This waterway must have been in existence by 945 for Lakenheath to have been named after its hythe ('hythe of the dwellers by streams'). It is surrounded by peat on three sides, so it would have been relatively easy to modify an existing stream, or cut a new channel, to link the settlement to the Little Ouse.[43]

Lakenheath is well known now for the substantial early cemetery evidence it produced (late fifth to the seventh centuries), most famously its locally born warrior and horse burial (*c.*500) complete with sword, shield, spear, bucket, horse bridle and cuts of lamb or mutton, now housed in the Mildenhall Museum. (A second man and horse burial, found later, was less richly furnished.) Over 450 burials and cremations were excavated, including rich female burials, pointing to an early and abiding interest in this area by elites who could acquire high-end accoutrements.[44] A few miles away, Mildenhall produced the famous Roman hoard of silver plate, so luxury goods were coming to the area even before the Anglo-Saxon period.

Rulers and resources

Famous secular and religious figures used fens as key strategic sites in defining themselves, and the famous monastery of Jarrow, the Venerable Bede's home, was named *æt Gyrwe*, 'at/in the marsh' (Old English *gyr* = mud, marsh) for 'fen dwellers', though the modern landscape gives little indication of that history after drainage of marshes, dumping of huge amounts of ballast, building of docks, filling Jarrow Slake ('Jarrow's lake') with landfill and increasing industrialization. The 1862 Ordnance Survey map published by historian Ian Woods shows the layout before most of these changes, including a large area of salt marsh south and south-west of the Anglo-Saxon church site and the extent of Jarrow Slake to its east.[45] Jarrow was not alone as a religious house situated near marsh resources, as Ely, Peterborough, Ramsey, Glastonbury and Crowland, among others, were famously situated in the fens on higher ground (islands) to encourage the isolation of monastics from the outside world. That ideal was not necessarily maintained, as the political often allied itself with the religious; such foundations were regularly the gifts of kings and ruled by abbesses and abbots of royal blood. But the value of fens to political foundations is undisputed, and here we turn first to Ecgfrith of Northumbria and Alfred the Great to discuss royals and fens. The reputations of those who settled and used fen resources served ultimately to link the earliest connections with the Britons through to the Saxon resistance to William's Normans.

Jarrow, one half of what came to be known as the twin monastery of Wearmouth and Jarrow, was a royal gift of Northumbria's King Ecgfrith, who continued his interest in the site until his death. It is likely that he kept his fleet in the nearby natural harbour of this place known even after his reign as *Portus Ecgfridi*, and that a month after the dedication in 685, he sailed to disaster at Nechtansmere near Aberlemno, defeated by Picts. The resources of the marshes and the Don and Tyne would have supplied not simply the monastery but also the military expedition. Ian Woods sums up evidence for the region's value:

> It is just worth pausing to emphasise the extent to which the Lower Tyne was a royal centre ... There were monasteries at Jarrow, found on royal land, and Tynemouth, which was at least royal in the sense that Oswine, Eadbert and Osred seem to have been buried there. Tynemouth also seems to have had an association with another royal monastery, Whitby, whose nuns fled there in the late ninth century. In addition there was the nunnery at *Donemutha*, apparently founded or refounded by Ecgfrith, which later attracted the attention of Eadbert and Æthelwold Moll. And there was the royal harbor of Jarrow Slake ... If *Arbeia* [a Roman fort identified by some as Urfa, site of Oswine's birth] was not the site of *Donemutha*, but was rather a residence of kings, the royal aspects of the region are even clearer. This is a cluster of royal sites which almost stands comparison with those in the Merovingian heartlands.[46]

Woods goes on to comment that historians are now reading Bede as more politically savvy than they thought in the past, and connects that to Jarrow as a former royal estate: 'Jarrow, I think, impinges more on Bede than we often realise'.[47] Royal uses of marsh and estuary are implicated in Bede's political coverage and silences. Wood earlier notes that Ecgfrith gave the land for Jarrow at a time of opposition to his attacks on Ireland (684) even while his half-brother Aldfrith was in exile in that land, and Bede 'attributes the failure of the Pictish campaign to divine displeasure over the king's earlier actions'.[48] Crossing some frontiers is costly. When Aldfrith returned and took the kingship at Ecgfrith's death, he initiated a friendlier policy towards Ireland and its missionaries in Britain – and inherited the bounty implied by a king's port and its trade at *Portus Ecgfridi.*

Alfred the Great (849–99) also has a close connection with fen and marsh, crucial to his story of survival against the Danes. In early January of 878, Vikings supposedly under truce came to Chippenham, a royal estate in Wiltshire, and took Wessex for themselves. Asser's *Life of King Alfred* tells us

> 53. At the same time King Alfred, with his small band of nobles and also with certain soldiers and thegns, was leading a restless life in great distress amid the woody and marshy places of Somerset. He had nothing to live on except what he could forage by frequent raids, either secretly or even openly, from the Vikings as well as from the Christians who had submitted to the Vikings' authority.[49]

Given earlier coverage of the rich ecologies in fenland, Alfred's 'distress' may indicate his unfamiliarity with fen environments and ecology, as it seems he should have been able to support himself without raids (though those may have been easier). We may hear an echo of his lapse into incompetence depicted in the famous tale of his burning the cakes of the swineherd's wife, although in multiple retellings connected with St Neot, Alfred understands the wife's rebuke as fulfilling Neot's comment that God punishes those whom he loves. Not used to such practical daily chores as foraging in the fen or minding the bread oven, he does nevertheless seem quickly to appreciate what the marshes offer. In the fens, Alfred proceeded to build a fortress at Athelney that March 'and from it with the thegns of Somerset he struck out relentlessly and tirelessly against the Vikings'.[50] Athelney means 'Athelings' (nobles') isle', as described in the *Life of Saint Neot*: 'it is surrounded on all sides by vast salt marshes and sustained by some level ground in the middle',[51] that is, the raised 'island' familiar in the eastern fenlands as well. Sometime later, he added another fortress and a church and monastery, described as

> surrounded by swampy, impassable and extensive marshland and groundwater on every side. It cannot be reached in any way except by punts or by a causeway which has been built by protracted labour between two fortresses. (A formidable fortress of elegant workmanship was set up by the command of the king at the

western end of the causeway.) In this monastery he gathered monks of various nationalities from every quarter, and assembled them there.[52]

In other words, the fen environment provides ideal cover while restricting access and increasing defensibility, whether for fortress or monastic foundation. Another set of terms suggests a persistent way of seeing fens as places to hide: *fenfreoðo* 'fen refuge'; *fenhleoðu* 'fen coverts'; *fenhop* 'fen hollow'. *Fengelād* especially may relate to the causeway mentioned here, a difficult path in an area prone to flooding. In place name contexts, Ann Cole's field work showed that a tendency to flooding was confirmed when she combined *gelād* places at rivers with observations in winters of dramatic flooding, at Cricklade, Evenlode, Lechlade and Abloads.[53]

Figurative frontiers

Hardship and heroism: the narrative impact of fens

Fens in Old English accounts are highly evocative symbolic frontiers as well: elegies, *Andreas* and *Beowulf*, for example, use fen landscapes to evoke particular cultural resonances in service of poetic effect and the construction of identity. While the shift from practical exploitation of the fens to how fens function in the imagination may seem a hard-right turn to some, as humans we map our learned experience and cultural structures onto the material world around us. Seeing an abandoned farmhouse in a field while on a walk is not the same experience as coming to it in the dark and knowing it is the only shelter for miles, or hearing its creaking timbers when there is no one else around. Choosing to walk around a graveyard rather than taking a shortcut through it might be a daily option on one's path, but the choice is made because of something besides efficiency, even if for some it is subconscious. Such cultural behaviour can make a physical space accessible both to practical exploitation and to the layers of memory and meaning a people invest in it. It is to this dual status, fenland as both quotidian borderland and liminal space loaded with cultural significance, that the discussion now turns. These poems and accounts show us ways that Anglo-Saxons processed their full experience of what fens could mean to them, psychological flesh on the bones of artefacts and settlement. While these accounts are both secular and religious, and the experiences of the educated religious elites would have been sometimes different from those, say, who kept stock in fenland, we should also remember that most often the elites of monasteries came from the same families who led secular society, and monks engaged in daily toil as did lay folk. Ely as a name promises that monks took to eeling just as other fen dwellers might. Surely those who told stories had mixed audiences, as the tale of Caedmon, the layman working at Whitby, shows us, or as sermons delivered to congregations suggest. Real differences exist between religious and secular, not least perhaps ideologically, but a shared communal understanding of the experience of the fens contributed to its depictions in cultural texts.

Thus the lovers of *Wulf and Eadwacer* may represent the tensions and personal hardships of tribal warfare or even contested rights, but the setting in the fens heightens the emotional impact. They are isolated from each other by hostile families, each on a separate island, but both anchored to those islands, embedded in the fens: *Fæst is þæt eglond fenne biworpen* 'Wulf is on an island, I on another./Fast is that island surrounded by fen'. *Beweorpan* usually means 'to cast/cast down or throw or plunge', though here it is generally rendered as 'surrounded'. John Donne's 'no man is an island' is here reversed: the environment reflects the isolation, each lover alone, islands unto themselves. The more usual meanings given for *beweorpan*, however, also suggest the fen works almost as a jailer, with the two on islands which are thrown or plunged into fens, where grasses and plants probably block any view and make locating someone difficult, increasing the despairing isolation voiced by the woman narrator. Whether she is hiding or has been put there, love and hostility are figured forth in the fen as a confining enclosure.

Even the gory cannibalism of the poem *Andreas*, in which the apostle Andrew rescues Matthew from the Mermedonians, has recently been placed in fens. Lindy Brady has argued that 'the poem aligns the cannibal nation with a more specific landscape within Anglo-Saxon England: that of the fens, a space which carried cultural baggage within the Anglo-Saxon corpus as a hiding place for a last population of Britons, a people associated with cannibalism in classical geographies'.[54] She notes that a long debate discussing whether a last remnant of Britons actually survived in the fens is less interesting than 'anxieties revealed by the Anglo-Saxon corpus that the fens might be harbouring such a population'.[55] Thus Mermedonia is described as a *mearc* and an *igland/ ealond*. One of the Old English words closest to meaning 'frontier' would be *mearc*, 'a bounded area or country, a monument erected to show limits or boundaries, an omen, indicator or characteristic, a sign, badge or brand on a person, a symbol or character other than a letter, etc.'[56] It also relates to the verb *mearcian*, to mark. Thus, when an Anglo-Saxon used the term, what s/he heard was the possibility of any of these meanings, but especially perhaps the close relationship between a region or boundary called a *mearc* and the act of marking or leaving a mark. The Old English *Andreas* is also unique in having Mermedonia be an *igland/ealand* (ll. 15, 28). Brady, as do most, interprets this as 'island' and links it to the Anglo-Saxon emphasis on Britain as an island (citing Nicholas Howe's work), though in *Beowulf* the same term is used to describe where the dragon ravages the coast: *ēalond ūtan* (l. 2334).[57] The very same phrase occurs in line 28 of *Andreas*, so perhaps the interpretation is less sure than we think. Certainly, a coastline reference does no damage to Brady's fen analogy.

Elsewhere I discuss St Guthlac's life in the fens more fully,[58] but for present purposes a few points are worth repeating, keeping in mind that these are shaped accounts, made to communicate chosen attitudes and ideological aims. He begins his life as a young war leader from one of the noblest houses in Mercia, fighting the British; his name translates as 'gift of war'. After a religious awakening, he retreats to the fens because of their isolation, taking two servants with him. There he acquires a reputation for holiness, but the illusion of isolation is dispersed as we read that his island in the fens has acquired accommodations for those who come to him, with thatch roofs (the raven who steals a glove is *uppe on anes huses þæce*)[59] as well as a landing place where visitors sound a signal, his *hȳðe*,[60] the same term discussed earlier. Guthlac also chooses a fen site previously occupied by Britons long gone, as evidenced by a burial mound (*hlaw mycel ofer eorðan geworht*)[61] and water reservoir or well (*mycel wæterseāð*),[62] over which he builds his house. The Old English homily on St Neot also mentions such a reservoir near that saint's hermitage, itself surrounded with other *myrige wæterseāðas*,[63] and George Younge posits that the detail is deliberately borrowed from the Guthlac *Life*, as it is not in other sources.[64] Later, in the time of Cœnred (704–09), king of the Mercians, the British are still fighting the English when Guthlac in his fen hears the voices of many cursed demons speaking *on bryttisc*, in British or a Celtic tongue. The political and religious are collapsed in this one detail, as his warrior past overlies his spiritual present, made possible by fens and their evocations. The burials and settlements of the Britons in fenland would have marked their past as both a precursor of the Germanic settlements and a history foreign to them. Haunted by fierce enemies who yield but leave their mark, the fens would provide both material evidence of Germanic settlements replacing those of Britons while preserving as well their memory and supernatural presence. But, more than that, for an elite warrior culture that made the lord's hall its psychological and cultural heart, when those same elites become religious figures, the absence of that hall is the ghost that haunts depictions of the fens. For literary parallels, we need think only of the Wanderer's homeless journey after his lord's death, haunted by the ghosts of lost companions, or the contrast evoked by the Seafarer between those who enjoy the riches of the land and his lonely sailing, loving the sea while at the same time seeing absence and transience in all around him. Rich as the fens are in resources, in these accounts poets play down that fact in favour of depicting the challenge and anxiety over being alone, beset by demons.

The fens and moors of *Beowulf* are perhaps the best known as a strange borderland, and the emphasis on Grendel and his mother inhabiting only such marginal areas, matching their own status as peripheral to humanity and the community of the hall, again depicts how suggestive the fen environment can be, especially if we bring to mind *Maxims II: Þyrs sceal on fenne gewunian/ana innan lande* 'The giant/monster must dwell in fens, alone in the land' (ll. 42b–43a).[65] Grendel is he who holds the moors, fen and stronghold: *se þe moras heold fen ond fæsten* (ll. 103–04).[66] He lies in wait as *sin-nihte heold/ mistige moras* 'perpetual night held the misty moors' (ll. 161b–162a), clearly a figurative description that nevertheless holds real horror, as Beowulf knows when he says Hrothgar need not worry about his burial if Grendel carries away his bloodied body to mark (*mearcað*) his *mōr-hopu* 'moor-hollow, mound or pool' (l. 450), a term echoed later when the dying Grendel wishes to flee to his *fen-hopu* (l. 764). When Grendel comes, he *cōm of more under mist-hleoþum* 'comes from the moor under misty hill hollows' (l. 710),[67] made more ominous by the poet's drum-beat repetition of how Grendel 'comes' three times within eighteen lines, but reversed in its effect when describing Beowulf's victory and Grendel's panicked flight under *fen-hleoðu* (l. 820). Grendel dies *in fen-freoðo*, his fen refuge. In her revenge, his mother snatches Hrothgar's closest advisor, Æschere, before returning *tō fenne* (l. 1295). Hrothgar then admits what he had not previously revealed: there were two creatures, not just one, *micle mearc-stapan mōras heldan* 'great march/border stalkers [who] held the moors' (l. 1348), where the walking of the moor boundaries forms the 'Mark' or country of these monsters. In the last mention of fens in the poem, Hrothgar describes the wolf coverts and windy headland of the monsters' region, reached by a perilous and wild fen path: *fen-gelād*, the term shown by Gelling and Cole's work to refer to a difficult water-crossing, here in the fens (see also Chapter 1 for discussion of water as physical and spiritual danger). Gelling references the work of Dennis Cronan on the related term *uncūð gelād* (l. 1410), which also occurs in *Exodus*.[68] He translates it as 'unknown water-passage' and Gelling adds,

The linking of *gelād* in place-names to particularly difficult river-crossings strengthens Cronan's perception of the sense of danger intended by the *Beowulf* poet. This is one of a number of instances in which landscape terms used in *Beowulf* can be better understood by a study of their use in place-names.[69]

Given the persistent linkage of Grendel and his mother to the fens and Brady's argument that the environment alone, regardless of mere geography, can be used to evoke cultural difference, we can wonder if some Anglo-Saxons might even have suspected Grendel on some level of being a Briton. The *mearc* of Cain takes on a different flavour in such a context.

A last example of how frontier fens in texts shape depictions of heroism and hardship shows a shift from earlier depictions of fens as threatening to fens as cultural shelter, doubtless influenced by Alfred's history and its place in creating the concept of Englishness. In this shift, it comes to dovetail with the late reclamation of coastal marshland and settlement densities that match those of dry land (see Chapter 4, 'The larger marshlands'). Hereward the Wake is one who even into the nineteenth century evoked a strong sense of identity for those in England. The earliest accounts are abbreviated notices in the Peterborough version of the *Anglo-Saxon Chronicle* for 1070–72. After the Norman Conquest, William begins to replace native churchmen and ransack monastic treasures, while at the same time, King Swein of Denmark arrives at the Humber, thinking to claim the throne. The English flock to him, and all come to the fens, to use as their stronghold. Hereward enters here (AD 1070), as Peterborough monastery discovers that he and his men plan to take the monastic treasures, ostensibly to keep them from the French abbot Turold even then on his way to the monastery. The 'outlaws' arrive at the monastery in ships and burn the monastery when the monks resist, afterwards taking substantial treasures from the church and returning to the fens of Ely. When William and Swein reconcile, the Danes take the treasures in ships which are dispersed by a storm to several countries or lost. Bishop Ælric excommunicates all those who have taken part. Given that the chronicle is written at the very monastery at the core of the events, an unbiased view is unlikely.

From this brief account, however, the genres of saga and romance augmented a character who, by using the fens as his base, came to represent Anglo-Saxon resistance and identity. The *Gesta Herewardi* was most likely written in Latin c.1109–30 by a man the *Liber Eliensis* calls Richard of Ely;[70] the *Liber Eliensis* itself borrows from and builds on the legend of Hereward as well. The *Gesta*'s introduction states that at first only a few damp manuscript remains were found in Old English, supposedly (and conveniently) written by Hereward's confessor Leofric, 'For it was the endeavour of this well-remembered priest to assemble all the doings of giants and warriors he could find in ancient fables as well as true reports, for the edification of his audience'.[71] It would seem already then that the environment of the fens as boundary frontiers had worked its magic, summoning 'giants and warriors' to what becomes not the wasted borderland of Grendel nor the secret and isolated retreat of holy men, but the very essence of England itself. Hereward's adventures are augmented in spectacular ways, except perhaps in the chapters claiming to report what his surviving mutilated comrades had to tell: 'These chapters (chs. XIV–XXXVI *passim*) are entirely different in tone from the preceding farago [*sic*]. Albeit the reminiscences of now elderly veterans, and no doubt recalled "with advantages," these tales of guerrilla skirmishes have the air of reality'.[72] This example of the merging of history, heroism and myth carries forward a nostalgic view of a unified past, but its catalyst is the fens, functioning as a frontier that links past and present. No wonder then that Charles Kingsley could turn to Hereward the Wake for proud nationalism in his 1866 novel. As David Roffe puts it, such resistance 'was perfectly fitted to the Victorians' image of themselves as a plucky little nation pitched against the odds in wild places'.[73] We have come full circle from where this chapter began, back to identity, but I will leave the last words to the man who celebrated Hereward's deeds in the *Gesta*, describing what it was like to learn of him from his own men about those heady days in Fenland:

I have frequently seen some of these men – tall in stature, well-built and exceptionally courageous ... men of distinguished appearance, although having lost the beauty of their limbs due to the trickery of enemies, being deprived of certain members through envy ... here is sufficient for you to understand how valorous their lord was, and how much greater his deeds were than those reported of him. For truly to know who Hereward was and to hear about his magnanimity and his exploits is conducive to magnanimous acts and generosity, especially in those wishing to undertake the warrior's life. So I urge you to pay attention, especially you who are concerned to hear of the exploits of brave men; listen carefully to this account of so great a man who, trusting in himself rather than rampart or garrison, alone with his men waged war against kings and kingdoms and fought against princes and tyrants, some of whom he conquered.[74]

That deft touch, *'some* of whom he conquered', pulls us back from legend to history. Admiration did not require perfection in this instance: Hereward defended the wealth of the fens from outsiders. Even if self-interest tainted pure patriotism, his sense of an England that needed to keep and defend its innermost and often sacred places speaks to how the frontier of the fens has become one with the boundaries of England itself as a frontier, a microcosm that stands for the greater whole. Indeed, it has in this case become its very heart, wild, rich and symbolic of Anglo-Saxon identity even as the Anglo-Normans recorded it in admiration, and as the multiple versions indicate, the popularity and fame of this story became part of daily life for those now conquered. The fens were still a boundary space, a frontier negotiating new interactions, but they also, in a real sense, shaped and formed a composite history that resisted Norman political and secular power, and that outlasted those influences in the end: the language of the English survived and replaced the French of the overlords. No English demons whispered to Norman saints in the frontier fens of England, but Hereward and his men strode through the imagination of a nineteenth-century English empire and its Anglo-Saxon past as it expanded its own new frontiers, for good or ill.

4

Marshlands and Other Wetlands

Stephen Rippon

> a most dismal fen of immense size ... now consisting of marshes, now of bogs, sometimes of black waters overhung by fog, sometimes studded with wooded islands, and traversed by the windings of tortuous streams.[1]

This famous quote from Felix's *Life of Saint Guthlac* presents one perception of wetlands in the early medieval period. Such early medieval documents are few in number and were written with a specific purpose in mind: while useful, they are not objective records of the past, and so this chapter considers how early medieval communities exploited the range of wetland environments that existed around England's coast and estuaries using a far wider range of evidence. It outlines how the drainage systems and canals of Roman Britain fell into disrepair, and how, as sea levels rose, coastal wetlands once again became saltmarsh environments. These landscapes were, however, rich in natural resources that were widely exploited, and, around the eighth century, the growing intensity of wetland use is reflected in the digging of drainage systems, changing the relationship between people and their environment. Around the tenth century, this process culminated in the reclamation of some, but not all, wetlands, a transformation of the landscape that would have profoundly affected the daily lives of the communities living there as new patterns of land use – and therefore annual cycles of living and working – were introduced. Those areas that remained as intertidal marshes were still economically important and were used for salt production and as grazing land.

Coastal wetlands: a mosaic of environments

Wetlands once formed an important and widespread type of environment covering around 11.5 per cent of the English landscape, with 210,000 hectares (ha) of lowland peatland and 740,000 ha of alluvial wetlands in coastal areas, mostly around the mouths of major coastal estuaries, and 550,000 ha of floodplains in river valleys.[2] Before human communities started to modify these coastal wetlands, they comprised a mosaic of natural environments, with unvegetated mudflats in the lower parts of the intertidal zone that would have been flooded by the sea twice a day, making this an unusual landscape for early medieval people to comprehend (Figure 4.1). Further inland there were extensive vegetated saltmarshes that occupied the higher parts of the intertidal zone: towards the coast, these would have been flooded quite frequently, although further inland the marshes may only have been inundated a few times each year during the very highest of spring tides (Figure 4.2). Beyond the limits of these tidal inundations lay a variety of freshwater wetlands, often covered by reed beds, sedge fens, alder-carr woodland and sphagnum-peat bogs.

During the Roman period, coastal wetlands were put to a variety of uses. Around most of Roman Britain, the marshes were unreclaimed

Fig. 4.1 *opposite* The unvegetated mudflats of the lower intertidal zone, grading into a vegetated saltmarsh in the foreground (looking north across the Taw Estuary from Bickington) (© Stephen Rippon).

Fig. 4.2 *above* High intertidal saltmarsh, its surface dissected by tidal creeks, in Bickington on the southern banks of the Taw Estuary, in Devon (© Stephen Rippon).

and used for grazing livestock and producing salt by heating sea water (using local peat for fuel), although around the Severn Estuary the construction of sea walls along the coast and beside tidal rivers, and the digging of extensive networks of drainage ditches, allowed for the intensification of agriculture on villa-based estates.[3] The rivers and estuaries that dissected the wetlands were important parts of the communication and supply network that supported the market-based Romano-British economy, and in Fenland these natural watercourses were supplemented by the building of artificial canals.[4] In the late and post-Roman period, however, the wetlands of southern England were extensively flooded. While this was no doubt associated in part with the collapse of the market-based economy and disappearance of non-agriculturally productive communities in towns, which resulted in a lower demand for food and so reduced pressure to farm more physically marginal areas, environmental factors may also have played their part as sea levels appear to have been rising. The result is that in coastal areas Romano-British landscapes are deeply buried under silty clays as these once agriculturally productive areas reverted to natural intertidal environments.[5] The cultural landscape had been wiped clean, and as early medieval communities once again started to exploit these marshland landscapes they encountered a wholly natural environment: the long process of transforming the mosaic of natural environments into cultural landscapes had to begin again.

Perceptions of the landscape

There is very little documentary evidence for how communities perceived their environment, and we must treat those sources with very great care (see Chapter 3 in this volume). Felix's eighth-century *Life of St Guthlac* portrays wetlands as hostile wildernesses, with Guthlac's dwelling in the Lincolnshire wetlands located within 'a most dismal fen of immense size … now consisting of marshes, now of bogs, sometimes of black waters overhung by fog, sometimes studded with wooded islands, and traversed by the windings of tortuous streams', and Guthlac and the monks at Crowland were said to have been troubled by 'the phantoms of demons'.[6] There are other documentary references that paint an equally dire view of how wetlands were viewed: in *Beowulf*, the demon Grendel lived in a fen, and the desolate nature of wetlands is also emphasized in the late tenth-century *Vita S. Neoti*.[7]

It is important to stress that the accounts given in these early medieval sources are, however, the perceptions of a very narrow section of society, notably early Christian communities. Felix refers to

Guthlac's wetland environment as a 'desert', and the significance of this concept of 'wilderness' is seen in the way that so many early monastic foundations were in physically isolated and environmentally challenging environments, notably on islands within wetland landscapes such as Fenland, the Somerset Levels, the Witham valley in Lincolnshire and the wetlands that fringe East Anglia.[8] This early association with wilderness areas increased in symbolic importance over time, which is reflected, for example, in the way that Glastonbury Abbey created and embellished its own history during the eleventh and twelfth centuries through the creation of a special jurisdiction – the 'Glastonbury Twelve Hides' – that embraced the peninsula of Glastonbury itself, the wetlands that surrounded it on three sides and a series of small but prominent islands that protruded through these wetlands.[9] Although some of the fertile dryland hinterland of Glastonbury was included within the Twelve Hides, it was clearly the islands and wetlands to the west that were perceived to be of primary importance to the monks. Accounts of Glastonbury's history, such as John of Glastonbury's mid-fourteenth-century *Cronica sive Antiquites Glastoniensis Ecclesie*, paint a similar picture: 'of all the places he [Patrick] might have chosen, he settled upon Glastonbury as the spot most apt for his triumphs over the devil, where he might be able to earn most fully the joys of a heavenly reward; for the place was then suited to heavenly vigils because of its remoteness from mankind, being almost inaccessible because of the marshes'.[10] In this early medieval period, Catherine Clarke has suggested that 'The topographical reality of Glastonbury's situation as a pleasant island amid the floods and marshes of the Levels provides a consistent focus for mythologisation of the abbey's spiritual identity and destiny', with 'the practicalities of land reclamation and cultivation … transformed into literary allegories of spiritual work and protection'.[11]

The territorial context of marshland utilization

Whilst documentary sources give us some idea of how ecclesiastical communities may have perceived wetlands, for the daily lives of rural communities we must rely upon archaeological evidence. While early Christian writers chose to stress the hostile nature of wetland landscapes for mythological reasons, these were actually resource-rich environments, although the exploitation of them would have been very different from that of their neighbours in dryland areas. The utilization of these wetland landscapes took place within different territorial contexts. Many coastal wetlands are relatively small in scale and lay within territories the greatest part of which lay on the adjacent drylands. An example is the landscape occupied by the community of

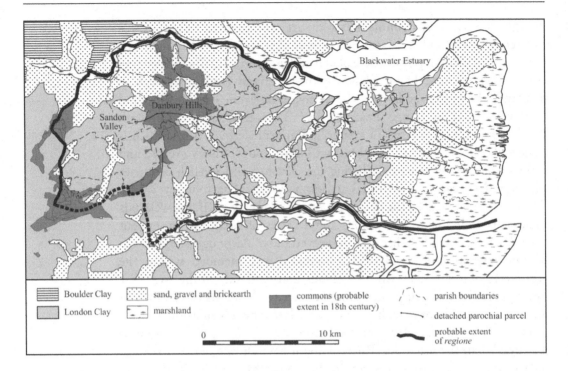

Boulder Clay   sand, gravel and brickearth   commons (probable extent in 18th century)   parish boundaries

London Clay   marshland   detached parochial parcel

0   10 km   probable extent of *regione*

Fig. 4.3 The *regione* of Dengie, in south-east Essex. Although the predominant surface geology is heavy London clay, diversity is provided by the lighter soils on drift deposits of sand/gravel/brickearth, and the rich grazing afforded by the coastal marshes that were once intercommoned (© Stephen Rippon).

Dengie, in Essex, which is recorded in a charter of *c.*706–*c.*709 that describes how King Swæfred of the East Saxons granted Ingwald, Bishop of London, *lxx cassatorum in regione qui dicitur Deningei* '70 hides in the district that is called Dengie' (in Essex).[12] A reconstruction of the possible extent of Dengie is shown in Figure 4.3, which is based upon a wide range of data such as the pattern of parochial detached parcels that reflect where communities once shared common resources.[13] This suggests that early medieval Dengie extended across the whole of the peninsula and later medieval Hundred of the same name, but also extended to the west of the Danbury Hills down into the Sandon Valley. The *regione* embraced a wide variety of landscape types, with fertile soils in the lowlands, wood pasture and heathland on the Danbury Hills and intertidal marshes around the coastal fringes, with the uplands and coastal marshes probably being common grazing. Over time, however, the early folk territory was broken up into a series of smaller estates, and this led to a need to define more closely where different communities had rights of grazing, which led to a distinctive pattern of parishes with detached parcels in what had been the extensive commons. That inland communities in Essex had rights of grazing in the coastal marsh can be inferred from the phrase 'pasture for sheep' that is commonly used in the Domesday folios; it has long been recognized that this pasture lay not within the main part of the parish,

but in detached parcels in distant coastal marshes (Figure 4.3).[14] This
pattern of landholding would have entailed the movement of livestock
over distances that cannot possibly have been travelled over the course
of a day, suggesting a transhumant cycle of moving animals to these
marshland grazings between periods when they were inundated. High
winter tides and the chances of storms make it likely that these marshes
were mostly grazed seasonally, meaning that for some within these
early medieval communities, their summers would have been spent in
temporary settlements on the marshes before returning to the inland
settlements in the winter.

The larger marshlands

Some parts of early medieval England – notably Fenland, the Somerset
Levels, Romney Marsh and the marshes around the Humber Estuary
– were sufficiently extensive to support communities whose entire
territory lay within the wetlands, and here there developed very
distinctive patterns of land use and daily life. By the eleventh century,
Domesday Book records a large number of settlements on these
wetlands, and the large populations and significant numbers of plough-
teams implies that they were permanent agricultural communities.
Although the densities of population and plough-teams for wetlands
such as Fenland are very low when mapped per square mile this
is because settlement was restricted to the coastal areas: the actual
numbers of plough-teams and people per vill was largely the same in
marshland settlements as on the adjacent dryland areas.[15] Excavation
and palaeoenvironmental analysis have confirmed that in Fenland
at least, reclamation dates to around the tenth century, and that on
the North Somerset Level it had occurred by the eleventh century.[16]
This reclamation represents the end of several centuries during
which the human utilization of these wetlands changed from simply
exploiting their rich natural resources, through modifying the natural
environment in order to make it suitable for limited agriculture, to
a full-scale transformation that finally changed the intertidal (salty/
brackish) environment into a reclaimed (freshwater) one. The clearest
evidence is from a series of excavations in Fenland. Sites dating to
the fifth to seventh centuries are characterized by the small-scale and
ephemeral nature of the occupation: the small, oval-shaped enclosures
at Third Drove in Gosberton and Leaves Lake Drove in Pinchbeck,
for example, were defined by relatively shallow gullies, and the scarcity
of domestic occupation has led these to be interpreted as haystack
mounds.[17] If, however, this was simply a small seasonal settlement
– perhaps little more than a shepherd's hut associated with pastoral

farming – then the material culture assemblage would be impoverished. That only a single post-hole was found within one of these enclosures might reflect the ephemeral and temporary nature of any house, and the loss of shallower features through later ploughing.[18]

Table 4.1
A comparison of the proportions of the bones of the main domesticated animals on eighth- to mid-ninth-century settlements on marshland sites, with the average across dryland areas.

	number of sites	total fragments	cattle	sheep/goat	pig
Dryland landscapes	15	4958	49%	38%	13%
Unreclaimed marshland	4	1552	41%	53%	6%

Around the eighth century, the character of settlement on Fenland changed, with a series of more substantial settlements emerging in new locations towards the coast.[19] These are characterized by a greater density of features, including substantial ditches that would have aided drainage, a greater amount and range of material culture, including pottery, and more evidence for agriculture, including arable cultivation. The animal bones and charred cereals from these marshland sites can be compared with those from dryland areas across southern England. A recent study has revealed that patterns of animal husbandry and cereal regimes vary considerably across different geologies,[20] and Table 4.1 provides an analysis of the animal bones of the main domesticates (cattle, sheep/goat[21] and pig) on sites dating to the eighth to mid-ninth centuries (which are often referred to as 'Middle Saxon'): unfortunately, there is insufficient data from fifth- to seventh- and late ninth- to mid-eleventh-century sites to make statistical analysis possible. Across dryland sites in southern England, sheep/goat account for 38 per cent of the cattle, sheep/goat and pig bones, while on marshland sites – all of which were unreclaimed intertidal marshes – sheep/goat were 53 per cent of the bones.[22] These proportions of bone fragments do not simply reflect the proportions of animals that were present – cattle bones, for example, are relatively large and so fragment into a larger number of fragments than sheep/goat and pig – and at Fishtoft, in Lincolnshire, for example, sheep/goat (with 53 per cent of the bone fragments) were actually around one and a half times as numerous as cattle.[23] That sheep were particularly common on saltmarshes is not surprising, as the salty conditions help to prevent foot rot and liver fluke, two of the major ailments that sheep suffer from on heavy freshwater soils (Figure 4.4).[24] There may also have been awareness of another benefit of grazing livestock on saltmarshes: classical and early medieval written sources describe giving salt or salted fodder to livestock to increase milk yields.[25]

Cereal grains preserved through charring can be used to reconstruct cereal regimes (Table 4.2). The only data for marshland sites once again comes from the eighth to mid-ninth centuries, a period for which there is unfortunately relatively little data for dryland sites,[26] although a marked contrast in cropping regimes is very clear. On dryland sites, wheat is dominant, but with significant amounts of barley, oats and rye: on marshland sites, in contrast, barley was overwhelmingly dominant. In discussing Fishtoft, in Lincolnshire, Gemma Martin notes previous studies that have suggested that the dominance of barley on marshland sites was due to salty soils, but rejects this on the basis that salt gets washed out of soil quite quickly, and that if land is tidally flooded it will be put down to pasture not arable. She concludes that 'this apparent dominance of barley in the local sites is therefore not necessarily a response to ecological factors or an accurate reflection of crop preference, but may be more to do with use of individual cereals'.[27] This may be an example

Fig. 4.4 Sheep grazing on an intertidal saltmarsh at Bickington, on the southern side of the Taw Estuary in Devon (© Stephen Rippon).

Table 4.2 A comparison of the proportions of the charred cereal grains on 'Middle Saxon' settlements on marshland sites, with the average across dryland areas.

	number of sites	number of grains	oats	barley	rye	wheat
Dryland landscapes	6	9236	16%	30%	9%	45%
Unreclaimed marshland	4	2714	1%	93%	0.1%	6%

of modern scholars shying away from acknowledging the potential role of the natural environment in shaping human behaviour, perhaps because they fear being labelled 'environmentally deterministic, even though it is very clear from later medieval documentary sources that patterns of agriculture varied enormously across different geologies'.[28] With regard to marshlands, it is true that salt washes out of soils quite quickly, but there is no need to use saltmarshes that are only occasionally flooded for pasture alone. Experimental crop growing on modern marshes has revealed that a number of cereals, especially barley, can be grown on a very high saltmarsh so long as they are not inundated during the seedling stage: the exception is wheat, which will not tolerate any salt.[29] In fact, the specialization in barley seen on marshland sites is part of a far wider pattern of crop husbandry seen in early medieval England that suggests that farmers were well aware of the soil preferences of particular crops: in the fifth to seventh centuries, for example, wheat was 63 per cent on Jurassic clays, 61 per cent on boulder clay, 39 per cent on river terraces, 7 per cent on heathland and 15 per cent in the south-west peninsula, while oats were 10 per cent on Jurassic clays, 10 per cent on boulder clay, 6 per cent on river terraces, 3 per cent on heathland but 20 per cent in the south-west peninsula.[30] Early medieval farmers were probably more in tune with their environment than we have given them credit for!

Whether these eighth- to ninth-century settlements were occupied in the summer months or all year round is essential to understanding the daily lives of the communities living there, but unfortunately the evidence is inconclusive. In *Anglo-Saxon Settlement*, by Andy Crowson and colleagues, there is an interesting reflective discussion. Before the analysis of all the evidence had been completed 'it had been wondered if occupation was specialised, perhaps some sort of seasonal "industrialised pastoralism" in the face of harsh winters', although it was finally concluded that 'There appears to be no good reason for thinking that occupation was seasonal, instead, it would appear that we are dealing with modest pioneer settlements in the fen, rather than large-scale directed settlement and a seasonal component of an upland economy'.[31] The reason for assuming that settlement was permanent is the presence of post-built timber houses and the nature of the animal bone assemblage: that the animals on these sites died as neonatal, under 6 months, between 6 and 12 months and older, is taken to suggest that livestock were present all year round, rather than having been brought to the area in just one season.[32] Other evidence, however, would support the idea that these were seasonal settlements. The animal bone report acknowledges that 'the identification of seasonal activities is tenuous' given the small sample sizes, and that the evidence 'does not exclude

seasonal activities'.[33] In the pits and ditches, layers of domestic refuse were interleaved with water-borne silt, suggesting periodic flooding, and the plants and animals living in the ditches show that tidal waters flowed through these ditches. A series of pits and gullies are interpreted as being associated with salt production which also suggests that these settlements were within the intertidal zone. If occupation had been all year round, this would have been an extremely hostile environment during winter storms and floods.

Whether or not these eighth- to ninth-century settlements were seasonal or occupied all year round, their creation is part of a marked intensification in how marshland landscapes were utilized. This must have been in response to wider socio-economic factors: this was the period of emerging stable kingship, the creation of defined landed-estates (initially granted to the Church and later to the secular elite) and increasing trade reflected in the creation of inland markets ('productive sites') and coastal emporia. Across southern England, there is evidence for agricultural intensification, reflected in the provision of infrastructure for collecting and processing agricultural surplus at estate centres such as Higham Ferrers in Northamptonshire. Some of these estate centres were equipped with watermills, for example, at Ebbsfleet in Kent, Old Windsor in Berkshire and Tamworth in Staffordshire,[34] showing how the control and management of water was increasingly seen as an important resource for early medieval communities. Communications were improved during

Fig. 4.5 Reconstruction by Peter Lorimer of the causeway and bridge across the Brue Valley, which linked Glastonbury to its estates on the Polden Hills (drawn from R. Brunning, *Somerset's Peatland Archaeology*, Fig. 196; © Somerset County Council).

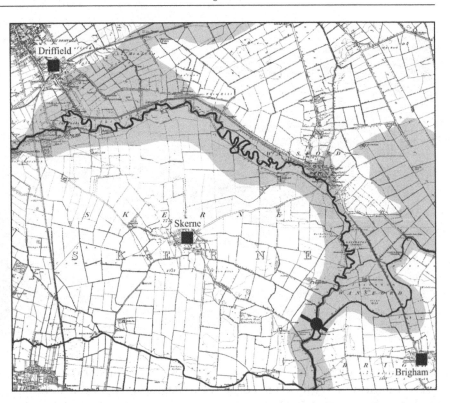

Fig. 4.6 The causeway and bridge in the Hull valley between Skerne and Brigham, south-west of the royal centre at Driffield (drawn by Stephen Rippon; OS First Edition Six Inch base map, 1891: © Crown Copyright and Landmark Information Group Limited (2013) all rights reserved).

the eighth century, and this included the construction of causeways, as at Mersea Island in Essex, across the Thames in Oxford, across the Brue Valley to Glastonbury in Somerset (Figure 4.5)[35] and in the Hull Valley at Skerne in Yorkshire (Figure 4.6).[36] By the tenth century, it appears that rivers were even being canalized.[37] The construction of such causeways and canals within these wetland environments will have expanded the world view of the nearby communities: landscapes that were once liminal to the daily lives of these early medieval communities, and for which there was no reason for people to travel through, will now have started to become part of their daily routine.

Another example of the investment of resources in intensifying how wetlands were exploited is the construction of large fish weirs in many intertidal areas (fishing and weirs are discussed at length in Chapter 6 of this volume, while some of the early documentary evidence is considered in Chapter 3). This would have meant that early medieval communities not only travelled through wetland landscapes, but spent a significant amount of time there. These fish weirs consisted of large V-shaped settings of upright timber posts, up to 60 metres long, the posts supporting hurdle fences that acted as a funnel channelling unwary fish towards a wicket basket at its apex. They are found as far

afield as the north Norfolk coast,[38] the estuaries of Suffolk and Essex (Figure 4.7),[39] the Thames[40] and the Severn Estuary.[41] The earliest of these fish weirs may date to the sixth and seventh centuries (e.g. Putney in the Thames and Holme Beach in Norfolk),[42] but most appear to start around the eighth century.[43] Many appear to be associated with monastic sites, which is not surprising as their construction, in such a difficult environment as an intertidal zone will have involved the utilization of considerable resources: the single fish weir complex at Collins Creek, in the Blackwater Estuary, Essex, probably involved the use of c.10,000 upright posts (Figure 4.7).[44] Unfortunately, the sites that are likely to have owned these fish weirs – such as the early monasteries at Bradwell-on-Sea and on Mersea Island – have yet to see extensive excavations with programmes of wet sieving that are necessary to produce fish bones, but there are a number of assemblages from lower-status rural communities and the species found here – notably eels and small flat fish such as plaice and flounder – are all predominantly inshore species.[45]

The construction of fish weirs represents a deliberate, conscious decision to harvest natural foodstuffs on a scale that had not previously been undertaken, and the early medieval period also saw the opportunistic exploitation of other resources, notably shellfish: on Fenland sites, for example, these were predominantly mussels along with a few oysters,

Fig. 4.7 The eighth-century fish weir on a shell and gravel bank at Collins Creek, in the Blackwater Estuary in Essex (Heppell, 'Saxon Fishtraps', Plate 2: © Essex County Council).

Fig. 4.8
Reconstruction
drawing by Nick
Nethercoat of an
eighth-century
fish weir in
the Blackwater
Estuary, Essex
(Hall and
Clarke, 'A Saxon
Intertidal Timber
Fish Weir',
Fig. 8: © Essex
County Council).

while at Flixborough, close to the Humber Estuary, oysters predominated.[46] Wild birds would also no doubt have been caught – as described in Ælfric's *Colloquy* – and the duck bones at Flixborough are probably wild mallards caught on the nearby wetlands; wild geese were also caught.[47] The evidence from Flixborough suggests that bottle-nosed dolphins may have been fished in the North Sea, while elsewhere the occasional naturally stranded dolphin/porpoise and whale will have been collected by coastal communities, providing some variety in their diet and bone for making artefacts.[48] Kelley Wickham-Crowley (Chapter 3) also explores some of plant resources available.

This increased exploitation of the rich natural resources that marshlands offered was not without its risks. Intertidal environments are potentially dangerous places, with tides advancing very quickly, and it would be easy for an unwary fisherman to become stranded on a sand bank as the tides race in (Figure 4.7). The positioning of fish weirs would have involved the development of a detailed understanding of tidal currents and the movements of fish. Damage to the wooded structures during winter storms would have required repairs in the spring (Figure 4.8), and the fishing communities must have lived close by in order to collect their catch before it became spoilt (dead fish rot quickly!). Wetland landscapes that were once peripheral to communities whose lives revolved around the daily, monthly and annual cycles of dryland agriculture now started to become focal to the existence of some communities. In addition to their acquiring the knowledge of where to position fish weirs, existing skills of hurdle making and basketry would have to have been adapted in order to construct them, and new skills developed into order to make nets with sufficient strength to withstand the ravages of tidal currents (early medieval netting needles and net-sinkers have been excavated at sites such as Flixborough in Lincolnshire and Skerne in Yorkshire).[49]

These coastal marshes will also have afforded the opportunity to produce salt. The earliest medieval site to be associated with salt production is at Fishtoft in the northern part of the Lincolnshire Fenland, dating to the eighth century, while there is possible evidence for salt production of the same date from Chopdike Drive in Gosberton to the south.[50] The method used to extract salt was the same on late prehistoric and Romano-British sites: heating water in large pans placed over fires or within ovens. By the tenth century, however, a new technique had been developed, as seen, for example, at Marshchapel, on the Lincolnshire Marshes, whereby intertidal sediment was collected, and the salt extracted by washing it with sea water that was then heated.[51] The extent of the industry by the eleventh century is in part reflected by the large number of salterns recorded in Domesday Book, although their absence from areas such as southern Essex (including Dengie) must surely be due to inconsistencies in what the Domesday survey compilers recorded: for example, no saltern is recorded at *Salcota* in Virley, on a creek that flows into the Blackwater Estuary to the north.[52] Domesday Book reveals that places typically had one to ten saltpans that would have provided some supplementary income for the communities that ran them, although there were places where producing salt was a major part of the economy: at Rye, in Sussex, for example, there were 100 salt pans valued at £8 15s. a year on a manor of 20 hides, 35 ploughlands and 99 villeins worth £50.[53] In contrast, at Charmouth, in Dorset, a three-hide and three-ploughland manor with three villeins and three slaves also had 16 salt workers, while at Ower, also in Dorset, a three-hide manor on which 'No plough is there' had 13 salt workers that paid 20s.[54]

While major causeways would have improved communications to and from major settlements – such as the Skerne causeway across the Hull Valley that lay to the east of the royal centre at Driffield (Figure 4.6), and the Street causeway across the Brue Valley that linked Glastonbury Abbey to its important estates on the nearby Polden Hills (Figure 4.5) – there would also have been a need to make crossing marshes easier for those communities engaged in fishing, grazing livestock and making salt. In the prehistoric period wetlands were traversed by timber and hurdle trackways that have been found in the Gwent Levels, Somerset Levels, Thameside marshes, Essex marshes and Humber Estuary.[55] There are, however, very few examples of early medieval trackways, although this scarcity almost certainly relates to taphonomic factors: wooden structures are preserved in wetlands because the permanent waterlogging prevents bacterial decay of organic material and so the deeply buried prehistoric structures – that lie below the water table – are well preserved. In the later deposits – that lie closer to the present-day ground surface – waterlogging is only seasonal, and so timber structures quickly decay away. Factors such as the cutting of peat for fuel and coastal erosion would also have led to the destruction of early medieval deposits within which trackways were probably once preserved. There are, however, a few examples such as the brushwood structure in the Crouch Estuary at Rettendon in Essex,[56] while posts and wattle structures such as those at Stratford in the Lea Valley and Stanford Wharf beside the Thames, also both in Essex, may be the remains of trackways that once crossed small saltmarsh creeks.[57]

Perceptions of a changing natural environment?

Whilst the intensification of wetland use was clearly in part a response to the general increase in agricultural productivity seen across southern England, it may also have occurred within the context of a changing natural environment. It is clear that there was a rise in sea levels in the early medieval period, although it is unclear whether local communities would have been aware of this. Under natural conditions, saltmarshes build up to the level of the highest Spring tides, and so we can reconstruct sea levels from dated saltmarsh surfaces. In the Somerset Levels, for example, the unreclaimed marsh surface in the late Roman period was c.0.7 metres below that of today,[58] although the time period over which this sediment deposition occurred is unclear. The coastal marshes were clearly reclaimed by the eleventh century, as there was extensive settlement recorded in Domesday Book. That Burnham[-on-Sea], for example, is recorded in Alfred's Will (873–888)[59] probably indicates that there was little or no tidal flooding by that date as place name *Burnhamm* means 'water meadow by the stream',[60] which is indicative of a freshwater landscape, not an intertidal marsh (it may have been the development of a natural bank of sand dunes that kept the tide at bay, rather than artificial sea walls). The lack of distinctive, late fourth-century pottery on Romano-British sites in the area suggests that tidal flooding may have resumed as early as the late fourth century, and so the maximum period of time over which this *c*.0.7 metres of alluvium was deposited is around 500 years (AD *c*.350–850). The deposition of this amount of alluvium over that period of time suggests that the sea level rose on average by about 0.14 metres per century over that time period, but what is not clear is whether this rise occurred gradually over this whole period, or more rapidly over a shorter period: if it was over the whole period, then the rise of sea level would have been imperceptible as it amounted to about 4 centimetres over the course of a generation (30 years). In Fenland, up to 0.7 metres of post-Roman alluvium was laid down in coastal areas: at Wygate Farm, in Spalding, deposition started after the fifth century, while at nearby Weston reclamation occurred around the tenth century,[61] giving a rate of sediment accumulation of perhaps 0.20–0.25 metres a century if it had occurred gradually over the entire period.

It is possible, however, that there was a more rapid rise in sea level over a shorter period of time: in the Thames Estuary, for example, sea level fell 1.5 metres between the late first and mid-third centuries (i.e. 0.6 m per century, or 20 cm a generation), which resulted in the need for successive rebuilding of London's quays.[62] This was probably environmental change at a pace that would have been perceptible to waterside communities, although the rate of the subsequent rise in sea level is, frustratingly, less clear: it had risen 1.5 metres by the twelfth or thirteenth centuries, but once again it is not clear whether this was over a short or a long period. In Romney Marsh, sea level appears to have fallen by as much as 2.5 metres over the course of the Roman period; although there are relatively few 'sea level index points' in the early medieval period, it appears to have been around 300 years before sea level started to rise again, whereafter there was a relatively rapid rise of 2.5 metres between around the eighth to tenth centuries (again, perhaps 0.6 m a century, or 20 cm a generation).[63] In flat landscapes such as wetlands, such rises is sea level could have made a very real difference to the natural environment within the lifetime of individuals, as once freshwater areas were periodically flooded by the tides, and we can only imagine what the early medieval mind would have made of it.

Conclusion

Wetlands were once a common sight in the English landscape that had been intensively exploited during the Roman period. Economic collapse and a rise in sea level meant that these physically marginal environments were used much less intensively at the start of the early medieval period.

The impression that is gained from the few documentary sources we have is that wetlands were seen as hostile environments, although this has more to do with mythologization by early Christian communities than reality. In practice, wetlands offer a wide range of natural resources that communities in the fifth to seventh centuries appear to have been exploited without any physical changes to the environment. The excavated settlements of the fifth to seventh centuries were small and ephemeral, and are probably indicative of seasonal grazing. Over time, however, communities were increasingly drawn to the marshes, and around the eighth century there was a marked intensification with the digging of drainage ditches, the cultivation of the highest intertidal marshes, particularly with barley, the production of salt by heating sea water and continued grazing, notably by sheep. Whether these settlements were seasonal is unclear, although it seems unlikely that activities such as salt production would have continued during the stormy winter months. Added to the seasonal cycle of activities such as arable cultivation, livestock grazing and probably salt production would have been repair of intertidal fish weirs to make them ready for the new fishing season, and then the twice daily trek to collect the latest catch (Figure 4.8). These early medieval communities would, therefore, have had a lifestyle very different from communities living in dryland areas, although, around the tenth century, many marshland landscapes were transformed through reclamation which would have finally kept the sea at bay. By the Domesday survey, the densities of settlement, population and plough-teams were little different from those on dryland areas, and the distinctiveness of these marshland communities would have started to diminish. Overall, wetlands would have been a challenging environment for communities to exploit, but one that rewarded their efforts with an abundance of resources.

5

Rivers, Wells and Springs in Anglo-Saxon England: Water in Sacred and Mystical Contexts

Della Hooke

... fram mænanlea on horsweg of horswege innan gatanstige þanon innon denebroc of denebroc innon tilnoþ ælong tilnoþes to halgan wyllan of þære wyllan in hreodcumb ...

... from the common wood to the horse way; from the horse way into the goat path; thence into valley brook, from valley brook into Tilnoth; along Tilnoth to the holy well; from the well to reed coomb ... (Bounds of Withington, Gloucestershire)[1]

Introduction

As an indispensable necessity for human life, water played a major role in most early religious beliefs. But water can also be regarded as 'other': 'it can refresh or it can kill ... it possesses life, yet is not itself alive ... Water further comes from below, from darkness, from the place where the dead (in cultures for which that is relevant) are buried, from the brooding presence beneath the feet'.[2] It could therefore be 'both a creator and destroyer of life'.[3] It was believed in many cultures across the world that bodies of water in the form of wells, lakes and pits might provide access to another world below that of man, a world inhabited by both spirits and the ancestors. On the edge of the everyday world, liminal areas on the fringe of human occupation, wetlands evidently held a special meaning, too, for many early British societies. For some, these were places to venerate divinity 'through the forces of nature, focusing upon the borderline territories between this world and the next – which were to become known in Christian spirituality as "thin places", where eternity and unity with the Spirit can best be glimpsed from this earthly dimension'.[4] The sacrifice of precious objects in wetlands and rivers was part of an extensive water cult found throughout northern Europe in prehistory. Votive offerings resulting from such beliefs are first manifest in Britain as early as the Mesolithic period. They reached a height in the Late Bronze and Iron Ages but continued even after the adoption of Christianity (see below).

Christianity also saw water as a powerful symbol: heathen shrines could be purified by sprinkling on 'holy' water; many springs and wells were to be linked to Christian saints and water was an essential part of Christian baptism – water was seen increasingly as a means of purification and blessing. Changing attitudes to water can be investigated through contemporary literary sources (see Chapter 1 in this volume), but the sacred association with water is also found in some place names and in charter evidence.

Water in pre-Christian belief in Britain

From very early times, access to water seems to have played a major role in the siting of some prehistoric monuments, many spanning the Neolithic and Bronze ages. On Salisbury Plain in southern England, occupation began in the Mesolithic when hunter-gatherers were attracted to the area by the plentiful supply of game – including the giant aurochs – and perhaps by another unique phenomenon. To the north-west of Amesbury, overlooking the River Avon at Blick Mead, close to a Mesolithic encampment, was a spring with unusual qualities. Flints dipped into its water were at first turned brown by the water's iron content, but after two to three hours of exposure the colour of the flint would change to a rich magenta – the result of certain rare algae in the water. In the Mesolithic period, no logical explanation for this would have been forthcoming, and it must have been seen as a magical transformation, perhaps leading to the early religious significance of the area.[5]

It was during the Neolithic period that a number of henge monuments were constructed in this area: one incorporating stone and timber circles at Durrington Walls (the former apparently later abandoned), associated with a large settlement site beside the Avon, with another smaller one at Woodhenge close by. Another, to become known as Stonehenge, just over 3 kilometres to the south-west, incorporated stone circles and other features, with a smaller henge called Bluestonehenge beside the river.

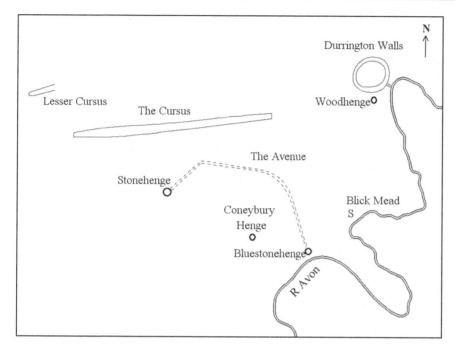

Fig. 5.1 The Stonehenge area, Salisbury Plain, Wiltshire (drawn by Della Hooke).

Both Stonehenge and Durrington Walls were linked to the river by avenues, giving the river itself, as a connecting link, also some religious significance (Figure 5.1). At the spring at Blick Mead, between the point at which the Stonehenge and Durrington Walls avenues reach the river, activity has also been attested from the sixth millennium BC, the spring acting as a place for depositing ritual items even in late Roman and early Anglo-Saxon times.[6]

The sources of rivers were often singled out for attention. Here the human world was impinging on the aqueous domain: places of liminality.[7] Further to the north in Wiltshire, the enigmatic monument known as Silbury Hill is an artificial mound begun as a relatively small mound around 2450 BC which was continually added to over a period of between 55 and 155 years. It stands above springs at the head of the West Kennet not far distant from Avebury henge, a tributary river which may have been perceived as the source of the Thames. Also in Wiltshire, the largest henge in the country, at Marden, stands at the head of the River Avon.[8]

There is also ample evidence for the significance of wetland sites – rivers, lakes or bogs – in Britain, as throughout northern Europe, as having been thought of as the rightful places for ritual offerings. Many of these date from the Neolithic but reached a peak in the late Bronze Age. They might be high-status articles such as armour and weaponry (mostly shields, swords, spears and arrows), coins, fertility and cult objects or valued animals such as horses, most prominent among the animal bones recovered. In the Somerset Levels, wooden figures had been deposited beside trackways around 2700 to 2400 BC, possibly ancestor figures guarding the route and preventing the passage of evil spirits or unwanted persons.[9] At Flag Fen on the western margins of the Fens near Peterborough in eastern England excavations have revealed a timber causeway running across the wetland, apparently constructed between 1365 and 967 BC, with a small island part way along the structure where religious ceremonies seem to have been carried out.[10] Many items denoting 'rank and prestige' were deposited in the surrounding water over a period of over 1,200 years, and, as elsewhere, many objects had been deliberately broken before deposition, perhaps to prepare them for conveyance into the spirit world.

Votive offerings cast into rivers remained a feature of Iron Age culture, represented by such finds as a decorative bronze shield dated to 400–c.250 BC recovered from the River Thames at Chertsey. One of the most impressive finds, however, was the collection of objects found in Llyn Cerrig Bach, a small lake in the north-west of the island of Anglesey in Wales, where over 150 objects of iron, bronze or copper alloy were found, including slave gang chains, swords, spearheads, a decorated bronze plaque and part of a trumpet and a shield, blacksmith's tools, fragments of two cauldrons and iron bars for trading (together with animal bone), forming one of the most important collections of La Tène style metalwork discovered in the British Isles. Many had been deliberately broken, not an unusual feature of votive offerings, as noted above, and it was first thought that the objects had been cast into the lake when the Romans were overthrowing local Iron Age tribal power. They are now believed to represent deposits made over a considerable period of time from about 300 BC to AD 100. As some seem to have originated in southern England, the lake may have had more than local significance, although they could also represent objects acquired by trade or warfare.[11] After the Roman Conquest, items continued to find their way into rivers such as the Thames, items that included metal figurines of animals, birds and gods, coins, the tools of everyday life and weapons, often mutilated as before. Even human skulls have been found in the river at Walbrook, perhaps a continuance of Celtic practice.[12] Occasionally, deposits have been found in Roman wells, but presumably at the end of the well's life as a source of clean water.

Human bodies have been found in bodies of water or peat bogs, thought by some to have been deliberately sacrificed. Lindow Man was deposited in Lindow Moss near Wilmslow in Cheshire, having experienced a violent death between 2 BC and AD 119, and mistletoe pollen, a plant thought by different European peoples including the Celts to have magical properties, was found within his stomach and may point to a ritual meal preceding his death. Over 100 bodies are now known from such a context, some 27 in lowland raised mires, dating from the early first to fourth centuries AD.[13]

In Roman Britain, as in ancient Greece and Rome, sacred springs continued to play an important role before the widespread adoption of Christianity in the fourth century AD, especially those thought to possess medicinal properties. The hot mineral water issuing from the Sacred Spring at Bath was beyond contemporary understanding and was believed to be the work of the ancient gods. A temple was constructed next to the spring and dedicated to the goddess Sulis Minerva, a deity with healing powers; a magnificent bath-house attracted pilgrims and visitors from all over the Empire.[14] Buxton in Derbyshire also had a thermal spring that encouraged the development of a Roman settlement known as Aquae Arnemetiae (or the spa of the goddess of the grove), and its baths were still in use in Tudor times but then attributed to St Anne, the well's Christian patroness. Springs and wells might thus be associated with divinities and especially with healing cults in Roman Britain. Springs might also be associated with 'wishing wells', but the requests were not always benign, as the dozens of tablets bearing curses found at Roman Bath reveal.[15] As Michelle Brown notes, water features could, along with other natural features such as rocks, trees, plants and creatures, be associated with animistic belief in the early stages of religious development:

> [These] were imbued with the attributes of deities and demons which needed to be appeased to ensure good fortune. Vestiges of such practices can be seen in the subsequent emphasis on sacred springs, wells and groves in ancient Celtic and Germanic religion and also in their continued use today as focal points for Christian and pagan alike.[16]

Rivers too might be named after Roman or Celtic goddesses: Tacitus names the River Severn as *Sabrina*, probably the name of the divinity of the river (see Chapter 2), and the *personae* of many other rivers were worshipped as named spirits. Such associations were not uncommon in ancient Gaul and throughout the Celtic world: in Ireland, almost all rivers have female names, some of them, according to medieval literary sources, the names of otherworld women.[17] In the case of the Severn, the regular surge of the bore may have been interpreted as a manifestation of the presence of the goddess (Figure 5.2). Other rivers named after

Fig. 5.2 The Severn bore (photograph by Della Hooke).

goddesses include the Dee, Clyde and Brent (see further Chapter 2). Rivers at their sources and confluences, particularly, were regarded as holy in Roman times: Condatis ('Watersmeet') was venerated in the Tyne Tees region of northern Britain, perhaps equated with Mars in his healing function. Anne Ross suggests that shrines may have been set up at the sources of some rivers.[18]

In relating beliefs to the natural landscape, it seems often to have been the juxtaposition of certain features which lent sacrality to a particular site: a notable tree growing close to a spring, perhaps with a particularly large stone or rock nearby, might attract attention as a sacred focus, especially in a period when landscape evolution was little understood. Although hard evidence can be difficult to find, both literature and folklore attest to the importance of wells and springs in Celtic belief pre-dating Christianity.[19] However, in exploring the history of 'holy wells', it is, as James Rattue warns, easy to be misled by a 'mystical consensus' fed by imaginative but unreal and irrational modern theories.[20]

The Anglo-Saxons, whose culture was gradually to dominate in England after the Roman withdrawal, were pagan upon their arrival. A belief in the sanctity of running water was widely prevalent among Germanic peoples: each brook, river and stream was supposedly haunted by a spirit who might be helpful or harmful. It might be propitiated by sacrificial offerings. Tacitus tells of a sacred lake in the homeland of certain Germanic tribes in which was an island with 'an inviolate grove'. Here was kept a chariot for the use of the goddess Nerthus, or Mother Earth. Following festivities, the chariot was washed in the lake and the slaves who had served there were drowned in its waters.[21] In Germanic lands there was also a belief that the gods resorted to the springs, and in AD 539 the Franks were sacrificing women and children to rivers.[22] Rudolph of Fulda's account of how the Saxons were defeated by Charlemagne in the 780s also notes how they 'exhibited the worship of leafy trees and springs' as well as the pillar 'Irminsul'.[23]

Anglo-Saxon and Norse paganism in England

Weapons, jewellery, horse equipment and tools continued to be cast into rivers in the Anglo-Saxon period, with over 100 Anglo-Saxon spearheads found within the River Thames, with those from the fifth and sixth centuries dominating, and others have been found in the rivers Cherwell, Kennet and Wey[24] (Figure 5.3). There was a resurgence of the practice of casting votive offerings in rivers in the later Anglo-Saxon period, perhaps following the influx of northern paganism after the Danish settlement. Animal skeletons and metalwork have been recovered from the River Hull, and in 1965 David Wilson noted 34 swords deposited in English rivers dating from between 850 and 1100, 24 from the Thames or its tributaries, especially within London.[25] A sword from the Thames at Chertsey (from the gravel of an old backwater of the river) must be added to this list. Others have come from the rivers Cam, Lea, Witham, Wensum, Nene, Frome, Great Ouse, Little Ouse and Kennet. In the Witham Valley in

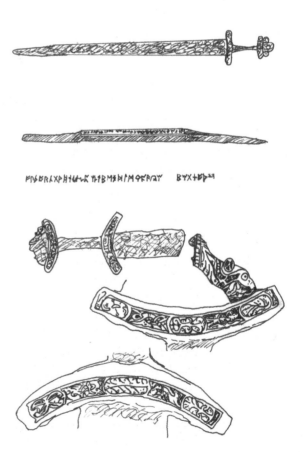

Fig. 5.3 Votive offerings found in rivers (drawn by Della Hooke).

Lincolnshire many of the metal objects (dating from prehistory to late Anglo-Saxon times and later) from the river were found close to causeways, often in wetland conditions, and included an eighth-century hanging bowl from Fiskerton, several late Anglo-Saxon swords from the ninth and tenth centuries and a range of other weaponry. Indeed, 'Some of the swords carry incantations inscribed into their blades which emphasise the superstitious (and presumably ritualistic) character of their depositions'.[26]

Other weapons deposited in water are also recorded in this period, including spearheads and scramasaxes from the River Thames, and a scramasax, sword and tools found in a hoard in the bank of a small stream in Lancaster, as well as weaponry from the rivers Lea and Witham. Horse equipment includes bronze stirrups from the Thames, Witham and (Wiltshire) Avon, plus a pair of stirrups decorated with inlaid brass wire from the bank of the River Cherwell near Magdalen Bridge, Oxford. Ornaments have come from the Nene, Thames and Witham. Many represent the highest craft levels of the time. It may be significant that most items have come from rivers draining into the North Sea (the exception being a sword from the Frome at Wareham in Dorset recorded in the 1920s) – regions within or close to those settled by Scandinavian incomers, although wetland depositions were by no means a Scandinavian introduction.[27] Some items are indeed unique, and several carry runic inscriptions. These include a ninth- to tenth-century iron scramasax from the Thames at Battersea, London (a unique object inlaid with copper, bronze and silver with runic letters and the masculine name *Beagnoth* inscribed on the blade), and a silver-gilt binding strip with an animal head and a runic inscription dating to the late eighth century found in the bank of the Thames near Westminster Bridge.[28] Ralph Merrifield raises the question of whether such objects might have been deposited in the rivers in the hope that they might rejoin their owner in Valhalla.[29]

With so many objects being found close to river crossings, Julie Lund raises the question whether these might relate to both the practical and the symbolic roles of the bridge in the landscape 'being a threshold and a passage between the living and dead'.[30] In Scandinavia, a watercourse often divided a settlement from its cemetery, and the same division between the living and the dead appears in Old Norse texts, while the word for 'bridge' might also appear in the decoration on many Viking Age rune stones. Even under Christianity the bridge maintained its role as a threshold for the dead, the soul believed to cross the bridge on its journey. (The interpretation of 'bridge' is discussed on pp. 158–59). There is also an indication of the continuance of votive deposits being cast into rivers in the Middle Ages, long after the acceptance of Christianity, in the case of pilgrim badges bearing images of a saint found at river crossings, perhaps to invoke a saint's protection for a safe journey.[31]

There is some indication of surviving pagan traditions in Old English literature. Although woods, wilderness and symbolic trees figure prominently,[32] watery places are also encountered. Fenlands were not only lonely and remote, part of the threatening wilderness, but might harbour monstrous beings.[33] In the Riddle on 'Creation', a free translation of Aldhelm's Latin riddle, *De Creatura*, the writer describes himself *ond ic fulre eom þonne þis fen swearte/þaet her yfle adelan stinceð*, translated by Paull F. Baum as 'And I am fouler than this black fen that evilly smells of filth' and by Robert K. Gordon as 'And I am fouler than this dark fen which here reeks of disease', and remarks how *eac ic under eorþan eal sceawige/wom wraðscrafu wraþra gæsta* 'I scan all things also under the earth, the dirty dens of evil spirits'/'I too see everything under the earth, the evil foul dens of malignant spirits'.[34] This attitude is also expressed in the Anglo-Saxon poem *Beowulf*. It particularly describes the monster Grendel, *mære mearcstapa,   se þe moras heold,/fen ond fæsten* 'a notorious prowler of the borderlands, who held the wastelands, swamps and fastness', his mother too dwelling *wæteregesan ... cealde streamas* 'in dreadful waters, cold currents'. It was in the lake in which they lived, *dygel lond ... flod under foldan* 'a secret land ... water under the earth', that Beowulf slew Grendel's dam, her blood melting the sword which he had used.[35] Even in pre-Conquest charters, a form of documentation often associated with the Christian Church, a sprinkling of minor place names recorded in charters also seems to refer to Grendel, implying that the work or the traditions which *Beowulf* was founded on may have been well known to the general populace. Grendel is associated, for instance, with a pit in Abbots Morton, Worcestershire (Figure 5.4), and with an unlocated mere in Old Swinford in the same county, and another at Ham, Wiltshire.[36]

Other associations between water sources and mythical figures also occur: Shobrooke in Devon is *sceoca broces ford* a 'demon's or goblin's brook' or 'haunted brook' (OE *sceocca* 'evil spirit, demon'),[37] and a *pucan wylle* at Bexhill in Sussex and at Weston near Bath in Avon may be 'goblin's spring' (OE *pūca* 'goblin' or alternatively '*Pūca's spring'*).[38] The place name Fritwell in Oxfordshire, *Fert(e)welle* 1086, may be 'the spring used for divination' (OE **freht* with *welle*, *wylla* 'augury');[39] a second is Freyewell at Moulsoe near Milton Keynes in Buckinghamshire, recorded before 1066; the name of Ladbroke in Warwickshire, *hlodbroc* in 998, *Lodbroc* in 1086, may also incorporate OE *hlot* 'lot' 'referring to a stream used for the purpose of divining the future or of drawing

Fig. 5.4
'Grendel's pit',
Abbots Morton,
Worcestershire
(photograph by
Della Hooke).

lots' while Holywell near Stamford in Lincolnshire recorded in 1190 may be from OE *hæl* 'omen'.[40] The attitude to wilderness found in the poem *Beowulf* re-emerges in more thoroughly Christian writings, as will be shown below.

A resurgence of pagan belief following the Viking conquests after the ninth century may have led to intensified pressure from the Church to suppress such beliefs. Old Norse literature from the Viking homelands contains many references to springs and wells, perhaps incorporating earlier beliefs, but these are recorded only in medieval literary sources (such as in Snorri Sturluson's *Poetic Edda*, which consists of traditional poems recorded in the thirteenth century).[41] The Norse Yggdrasill was a giant ash tree which extended from the underworld to the heavens, linking the cosmos, and beneath its roots was the well of Urðr or destiny, a realm denied and unknown to man.[42] Waters from the well kept the tree alive despite constant attacks from gnawing animals, and three maids, known as the Norns, sprinkled water daily from the spring over the ash to prevent its limbs from withering. In another of Sturluson's sagas, the *Ynglinga saga* (thirteenth century), Odin, the chief Norse god, is said to have travelled to Mímir's Well, near Jötunheimr, the land of the giants, disguised as Vegtam the Wanderer, where he drank from the Well of Wisdom, sacrificing an eye to do so.[43] He was thus able to see all the sorrows and troubles that would fall upon men and the gods and understand why the sorrows had to come to men. A somewhat earlier source tells of a spring next to the temple and tree of sacrifice at Gamla Uppsala in central Sweden: according to the eleventh-century writings of Adam of Bremen it was here that 'the pagans are accustomed to make their sacrifices, and into it to plunge a live man. And if he is not found, the people's wish will be granted'.[44] These sources therefore associate springs with destiny and divination (or, as Clive Tolley puts it, '*fate* and *fertility*').[45]

Some place names in Anglo-Saxon England also appear to recognize the association between water, crossing places and pre-Christian centres.[46] Weeford in Staffordshire (*Weforde* 1086) is 'heathen temple ford' (OE *wēoh* with *ford*) and Wyfordby in Leicestershire the same with Old Norse *by* 'village or farm'. Tyesmere in Worcestershire, a former lake close to the northern boundary of the Hwiccan kingdom, recorded in a ninth-century charter of *Coftune*, also names a mere after the god Tīw (a war god of the Germanic peoples) although no possible votive offerings have been located here.[47]

Christian belief

In the Christian world, the wastes and wildernesses of Britain were readily adopted as fearful places inhabited by devils, perhaps replacing the desert of Middle Eastern scriptures with the nearest European equivalents of wood and fenland (see additional discussion of fens and fen imagery in Chapters 3 and 4 of this volume). They were places which might test the faith of those true to God. Hermits would frequently seek out such remote places cut off by water, such as islands (like the Farne islands in the case of St Cuthbert) or places surrounded by extensive wetlands and marshes (like the eastern Fenlands of Crowland in the case of St Guthlac). For the ordinary people of early medieval England such wildernesses were places to be feared: they were remote from home and fields, sparsely populated and visited only by herdsmen and huntsmen, often on a seasonal basis. To the early medieval mind the division between the imagination and the real was not strongly defined, and these places, including extensive woodlands, could be fearsome: liminal places, where one might well expect to meet supernatural beings, and places where the veil between this and other worlds might be thin and easily broken.[48]

Thus, St Guthlac was drawn to places of 'wilderness' such as the fens of eastern England, as noted in Felix's *Life of St Guthlac*. Felix's *Life* was written in Latin in the eighth century, but Old English versions in eleventh-century sources follow the narrative outline quite closely:

> *Est in meditullaneis Brittanniae partibus inmensae magnitudinis aterrima palus, quae, a Grontae fluminis ripis incipiens, haud procul a castello quem dicunt nomine Gronte nunc stagnis, nunc flactris, interdum nigris fusi vaporis laticibus, necnon et crebris insularum nemorumque intervenientibus flexuosos rivigarum anfractibus, ab austro in aquilonem mare tenus longissimo tractu protenditur.*

There is in Britain a fen of immense size, which begins from the River Granta not far from the city of the same name, called Grantchester. There are immense swamps, sometimes dark stagnant water, sometimes foul rivulets running; and also many islands and reeds and tummocks and thickets. And it extends to the North Sea with numerous wide and lengthy meanderings.

Guthlac was told of a place which no man could endure

> *propter incognita heremi monstra et diversarum formarum terrores reprobaverant ... propter videlicet illic demorantium fantasias demonum*

because of various horrors and fears and because of the loneliness of the broad wilderness, a place where no one could live because of the dwelling-place there of accursed spirits.[49]

This is expressed in the Old English version as:

> *Wid is þes westen, wrǣcsetla fela,*
> *eardas onhǣle earmra gǣsta.*
> *Sindon wǣrlogan þe þa wic bugað.*

This wilderness is wide – [there are] many places of exile and secret dwelling places of wretched spirits. They are devils who dwell in this place.[50]

It was here that Guthlac chose to scorn the temptation of *contempto hoste, caelesti auxilio adiutus, inter umbrosa solitudinis nemora solus habitare coepit* 'the accursed spirits and was strengthened with heavenly support so that he began to live alone amidst the swampy thickets of the wilderness'.[51]

Sometimes the degree of 'dangerous watery wilderness' was indeed exaggerated in literary sources, including Saints' *Lives* (such as that of Guthlac, above). Gnomic poetry also tells that

> *Þyrs sceal on fenne gewunian*
> *ana innan lande.*

The giant shall dwell in the fen, alone in the land.[52]

Jennifer Neville has argued that Christianity may have fostered the idea that devils, along with elves, dwarves and other supernatural creatures, 'the previous inhabitants of the Anglo-Saxon landscape', continued to occupy the natural world, some 'fallen angels' also 'assigned residences in the sky, water and woods, like the demons who had taken up residence in Guthlac's fens'.[53]

However, the blessings of water were also recognized in Old English literature (see Chaper 1). In the Old English poem *The Phoenix*, the bird inhabited a wood within a 'noble land' where:

> *ac þær lagustreamas,*
> *wundrum wrætlice,   wyllan onspringað*

limpid streams, wondrous rare, spring freely forth.[54]

Here he tasted twelve times daily *of þam wilsuman   wyllgespryngum* 'of those pleasant springs of welling water'. It is here he returns after his death, again enjoying the *wylle-streama* 'welling streams'.[55]

There are references to 'still waters' as places of peace and healing in the Psalms, but the devastating effects of floods such as those described in the Bible also find a role in the Old English version of the life of St Andreas (St Andrew) taken initially from Greek texts. From his prison cell Andreas calls forth a flood which begins to pour forth at his command from the base of an old stone pillar. This threatens to drown his captors and their city until he calms the *geotende gegrind* 'rushing tumult', sending it down into an abyss that opens up, and asks God to spare the people, after which they recognize the power of *þe soð meotud* 'the true God'.[56]

On the European continent, ecclesiastical councils were attempting to ensure that heathen sites, some including springs, were taken over by Christianity. Around 452, the second Council of Arles declared that 'if in the territory of a bishop infidels light torches or venerate trees, fountains or stones, and he neglects to abolish this usage, he must know that he is guilty of sacrilege' and other later councils similarly denounced those 'who discharge vows among woods, or at sacred trees or springs'. Charlemagne (c.747–c.814) continued to condemn the worship of wells.[57] In England, Gildas, writing c.540, denounced the old pagan beliefs in which people 'heaped divine honours' upon 'the mountains and hills and rivers',[58] and in his letter to Mellitus in 601, Pope Gregory instructed missionaries to turn heathen temples into Christian places of worship. Even if actual archaeological evidence is thin, repeated Christian edicts, mostly uttered during the eleventh-century reformation of the Catholic Church, and perhaps partly occasioned by a resurgence of paganism following Danish settlement, frequently continue to attack the veneration of wells, trees and stones.[59]

> *Siquis ad arbores, vel ad fontes, vel ad lapides, sive ad cancellos ... votum voverit ... pœniteat*

> Punish those who dedicate votive offerings ... to trees, or to springs, or to stones, or to enclosures.[60]

> *Gif hwylc man his ælmessan gehate oðð e bringe to hwylcon wylle. oðð e to stane. oðð e to treowe. oðð e to ænigum oðrum gerceaftum. butan on Godes naman to Godes cyrican. fæste III. gear on hlafe 7 on wætere*

> If any man vows or brings to any spring or to a stone or to a tree or to any other element/thing/creature except in God's name to God's church, let him fast for 3 years on bread and water.[61]

These penitentials were one of the sources used in the so-called *Canons of Edgar* that are likely to date back to the early eleventh century and which were probably compiled by Wulfstan after he attained the see of Worcester in 1002.[62] In his writings, Wulfstan felt compelled to continue to forbid practices that included making offerings or practising divination as well as the 'worship of wells and trees'.[63] In his preamble to the laws of Edward and Guthrum, written in the early eleventh century, he reminded bishops of their duty to suppress heathenism diligently, and he drafted the law against idol-worship in 1020/21 which became part of Cnut's laws of c.1020–23, again banning the worship of:

> *idol weorðige, hæþne godas 7 sunnan oðð e monan, fyr oðð e flod, wæterwyllas oðð e stana oðð e æniges cynnes wudutreowa*

idols, heathen gods, and the sun or the moon, fire or water, springs
or stones or any kind of forest trees.[64]

Ælfric, a monk at the monastery of Cerne Abbas in Dorset and
later abbot of a new monastery founded at Eynsham (1000–c.1010), was
equally vehement about the need to stamp out heathen practices. In his
version of Augustine's homily 'On Auguries' he condemns the fact that

Sumne men synd swa ablende . þæt hi bringað heora lac
to eorðfæstum stane . and eac to treowum .
and to wylspringum . swa swa wiccan tæcað.

Some men are so blinded, that they bring their offerings to an
earth-fast stone, and also to trees, and to well-springs, just as
wizards teach.[65]

Many may have been seeking healing or good fortune, others signs
that would foretell the future,[66] but it is clear that such practices were
continuing to attract at least a sector of the population of eleventh-
century England despite the holding that the Church had over people's
everyday lives.

Since the fourth century, Gallic bishops 'had been resacralizing the
landscape, consecrating healing springs and associating trees with the
graves of saints'.[67] Wells were a source of pure water and could not be
neglected by the Church – water was essential for baptism, blessing and
other forms of Christian ritual such as the cleansing of the vessels used
in the Eucharist. Bede, in his *Historia ecclesiastica gentis Anglorum*, tells
how the bones of St Oswald upon their arrival at Bardney were washed,
and how the water, thereupon becoming holy, was poured away in a
corner of the cemetery:

Ex quo tempore factum est, ut ipsa terra, quae lauacrum unenerabile
suscepit, ad/abigendos ex obsessis corporibus daemones gratiae
salutaris haberet effectum.

Ever afterwards the soil which had received the holy water had
the power and saving grace of driving devils from the bodies of
people possessed.[68]

Thus, 'By the action of washing St Oswald's bones in the Witham
waters, the traditional power of these waters was henceforth attributed

to the saint, rather than to whatever water-spirit might have been resident previously'.[69] Such water might also have a healing effect: Bede recounts how an ailing woman, a thane's wife, was given holy water to drink (water blessed for the dedication of the church at Beverley), her wounds also washed with it, after which she rose cured, just as the mother-in-law of St Peter had been similarly cured of a fever.[70]

Many early churches and hermitages were established close to springs, and occasionally a church might actually be built over a spring, as in the case of St Kenelm's church at Romsley in Worcestershire or Kirkoswald in Cumbria. Wells in Somerset became an ecclesiastical centre when it became the focus of a new diocese in 909, and the fresh-water springs that gave rise to the place name still flow to the south-east of the cathedral (Figure 5.5). In the eighth century, when a grant of land on the River Wellow was made to St Andrew's minster *quod situm est juxta fontem magnum quem vocitant Wielea* (for *Wiella*) 'which is situated next to the great spring which is called *Wiella*', Wells was also known by its Latin form *Fontinetum* and as *(æt) Wyllan* '(at) the springs' (1061 x 1066).[71] In this case the minster seems to have been set over a Roman mausoleum, with several springs distributed around the site.[72] The cathedral at Winchester was also built on ancient wells, with one of the earliest in the Old Minster possibly dating from the seventh century and remaining in use until the church was demolished in the eleventh century. It was located in the north porticus flanking the main altar – a well which fed into a shallow sunken pool;[73] another was sunk in the late tenth century: the well in the eastern apse, almost doubled in length at this time, ensured that the community continued to have access to water for liturgical purposes and may have had an altar adjacent.[74] This tradition continued, and recent dating has identified a chapel at Camborne in Cornwall, for instance, that was built within an open enclosure around a holy well in the twelfth century.[75] In Scotland, Wales and Ireland many medieval churches were to be accompanied by a 'sacred spring'.[76] Not all such springs may have had any earlier link with sacrality, however – but the Church was perfectly happy to recognize certain 'wells' as 'holy' and might link these to a particular saint in order, perhaps, to legitimize such recognition.

John Blair has argued that some early Christian minsters may owe their locations in watery places almost encircled by water to another expression of liminality – 'enabling the minsters to be *in* the world but not quite *of* it'[77] (Eynsham, Oxford and Bampton are examples in Oxfordshire – see below). Rivers may, of course, also have provided the means for transporting the stone to build the minsters – that at Evesham in Worcestershire, founded in the eighth century, lay within a

meander of the River Avon – but other early minsters also lay along this river (at Fladbury, Pershore, Bredon, Stratford and probably Alcester) (Figure 5.6). David Stocker and Paul Everson go further and argue that the siting of a number of early churches and monasteries in the Witham Valley of Lincolnshire, such as Kirkstead and Bardney, may have been suggested by the previously existing water cults which involved places chosen to make votive offerings. Indeed, offerings including such meritorious objects as fine swords continued in the medieval period and in some places even increased in number: 'Clearly the practice had been Christianized in some way. The prehistoric ritual had been given a meaning that sat acceptably within the ideology of the new religion: a "conversion" had taken place'.[78] Moreover, the monasteries often assumed the responsibility for maintaining many of the earlier causeways that had provided access to the pools along the course of the river where votive offerings had been made since prehistoric times, signalling the triumph of Christianity.[79] It is notable how many early

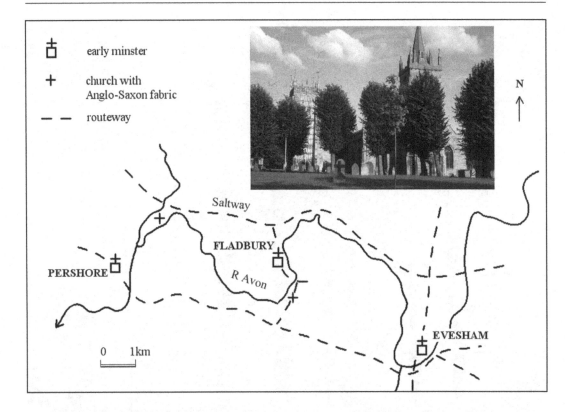

Fig. 5.6 Early Worcestershire minsters along the River Avon. Two post-Conquest churches and a Tudor bell tower (inset) are all that survive on the site of Evesham Abbey today (drawing and photograph by Della Hooke).

minsters were established at places with Old English *ēg* in the place name, signifying 'land surrounded by water'.[80]

Much Old English literature emanates from the Church, and references to ancient 'superstitions' are, not surprisingly, limited in number. In his homilies, Ælfric shows how, in the case of stones and trees, the oldest substratum of pre-Christian belief had been overlaid by Christian culture, but not directly in its pagan form absorbed into Christian practice.[81] However, the situation may have been different for holy water (see below). The *Charms* and the *Leechdoms* also appear to represent the Christianization of former pagan lore with survivals of paganism and magical practices being found in both (below). Grendon concludes that

> Heathen reminiscences and superstitious directions abound in the Old English charms ... Widely prevalent among Germanic peoples was a belief in the virtues and sanctity of running water. Each brook, river, and stream was supposedly haunted by a spirit, who might be helpful or harmful, and must be flattered by sacrificial offerings.[82]

It is recognized that much of the Old English medical literature contained in *Bald's Leechbook* is derived from Greek and Roman sources, re-written for the local needs of a Christian society.[83] Herbs, including bishopwort (also known as wood betony, *Stachys betonica* or *Stachys officinalis*), were, for instance, now to be shredded into holy water to be drunk in ale as a cure for 'one devil's sick'.[84]

One of the earliest of the leechdoms is known as the *Lacnunga* (*c*.1000), which may have been influenced by Celtic belief as well as Graeco-Roman material, and this also contains references to holy water. Thus as a 'bone salve' for 'a headache and for infirmity of all organs' the bark of several kinds of trees, including ash, ?myrtle, crab-apple and sallow together with the twigs of willow, were to be *wylle on haligwætere* 'boiled in holy water' to soften them and added to hazel, ivy-berries and certain herbs before being pounded, mixed with grease and old butter, reboiled and filtered several times and then mixed with additional ingredients before the resulting paste was stirred with a 'quick-beam' stick while psalms and prayers were sung over it; it was then applied to the head or wherever the sore might be.[85]

Blessing with holy water was not confined to healing human bodily ailments. In the *Lacnunga*, it is used in cures for diseases in horses, cattle and sheep. Water was also considered to be effective in various Old English healing charms: herbs and other ingredients were frequently sprinkled with holy water while Christian incantations were recited, with references to holy water almost certainly representing the Christianization of earlier charms.[86] *The Metrical Charms* preserved in Anglo-Saxon manuscripts include a charm, the '*Æcerbot*', 'For Unfruitful Land', written down in the early eleventh century: four turves from four sides of the land were taken at night before dawn and sprinkled from below with oil, honey, yeast and milk from cattle, plus a part of every kind of tree growing there except 'hard' trees, part of every known herb except burdock and *haligwæter* 'holy water' while prayers were said; the turves thereupon were taken to the church where masses were sung over them, returned to the field with other rituals being carried out and a poem recited; furthermore, a loaf of bread kneaded with milk and holy water was to be laid under the first furrow while another prayer was recited.[87] The instructions in *Metrical Charm 7* are to take various herbs *ofgeat mid ealaþ, do hæligwæter to*, 'steep in ale, add holy water', over which a charm is to be sung, to produce a medicine against *wæterælfadle* 'water-elf disease', perhaps chickenpox or measles.[88]

'Holy wells' in literature, documents and place names

'Holy wells' also reappear in Christian literature. In Bede's *Life of St Cuthbert*, written in two versions, in verse *c*.716 and in prose *c*.721, and drawing upon an earlier anonymous *Life*,[89] it is told how the seventh-century saint created a well on the island of Lindisfarne,

> *Quae uidelicet aqua mirum in modum primis contenta ripis, nec foras ebulliendo pauimentum inuadere, nec hauriendo nouit deficere, ita moderata gratia largitoris, ut nec necessitati accipientis superflueret, nec sustentandae necessitati copia deeset.*

> And this water was in a wonderful way kept within its first limits so that it never bubbled over and covered the floor, nor failed through the exhaustion of its supply; but the grace of the Giver so controlled it that it did not exceed the necessities of the receiver, nor was the supply for those necessities ever lacking.[90]

Bede compares such miracles with those performed by Benedict and Anthony, Benedict's a copious spring which flowed down the mountainside, but most powerful was the spring of St Alban which broke out at the place where he was to be martyred (see below).[91]

As the cult of saintly martyrdom began to grow, springs were also on occasion involved in the stories describing their deaths. In his *Historia ecclesiastica gentis Anglorum*, which he completed in 731,[92] Bede recounts in detail how St Alban was martyred near the Roman town of Verulamium at the hands of the heathen priests in the third or early fourth century AD. His cult had become established there soon afterwards and Offa of Mercia established a Benedictine monastery and an abbey *c*.793; probably sacked by the Danes in the ninth century, the abbey was rebuilt by the Normans. Bede recounts the story of how the saint selected the site of his martyrdom. Already the river which he had been led across had run dry to allow his passage. The site chosen was a small hill:

> *montem ... qui oportune laetus gratia decentissima quingentis fere passibus ab harena situs est, uariis herbarum floribus depictus, immo usquequaque uestitus; in quo nihil repente arduum, nihil praeceps, nihil abruptum, quem lateribus longe lateque deductum in modum aequoris Natura conplanat, dignum uidelicet eum pro insita sibi specie uenustatis iam olim reddens, qui beati martyris cruore dicaretur. In huius ergo uertice sanctus Albanus dari sibi*

a Deo aquam rogauit, statimque incluso meatu ante pedes eius fons perennis exortus est, ut omnes agnoscerent etiam torrentem martyri obsequium detulisse;

This hill lay about five hundred paces from the arena, and, as was fitting, it was fair, shining and beautiful, adorned, indeed clothed, on all sides with wild flowers of every kind; nowhere was it steep or precipitous or sheer but Nature had provided it with wide, long-sloping sides stretching smoothly down to the level of the plain. In fact its natural beauty had long fitted it as a place to be hallowed by the blood of a blessed martyr. When he reached the top of the hill, St. Alban asked God to give him water and at once a perpetual spring bubbled up, confined within its channel and at his very feet, so that all could see that even the stream rendered service to the martyr.

When the river had *ministerio persoluto, deuotione conpleta officii testimonium* 'fulfilled its duty and completed its pious service', it returned to its natural course.[93]

Another similar saint's *Life* is that of St Kenelm, a legend apparently composed in the middle of the eleventh century (probably between 1066 and 1075 but perhaps incorporating material already in circulation in oral tradition, as Kenelm was already venerated as a saint in the late tenth century); one version was probably written at Worcester in the third quarter of the eleventh century but with twelfth-century additions.[94] This contains a similar story of martyrdom and the appearance of a miraculous spring. It describes how the boy-king Kenelm (Cynehelm) was murdered in the wood of Clent in north Worcestershire by his foster-father Askebert at the instigation of his jealous sister, Quendrith. Much of the story involves a miraculous ash tree which grew from the staff planted by the child in the ground at the spot he chose for his murder, but, after the site of his burial had been revealed by a white cow and Kenelm's soul had appeared as a milk-white dove, it was a spring that was to gush forth on the spot:

Continuo uero fons erupit sub quadam petra, qua ablata totus cetus salutem bibit et processit. Fons autem hactenus in amnem decurrit.

And immediately a spring burst forth under a rock, which they lifted up, and the whole company drank healthfully before moving on. The spring runs into the river today.[95]

Fig. 5.7a
St Kenelm's Well,
Romsley, north
Worcestershire
(photograph by
Della Hooke).

Springs occur in other saints' *Lives* and similar literature. The association of the tree and the spring is one that regularly crops up in folk tradition. At Romsley, the site of Kenelm's murder below the Clent Hills, a church was built above the spring, but the latter was diverted when the building was restored in the nineteenth century; today the water flows a little to the east and feeds into a stone cistern and is still reputed to have healing powers (Figure 5.7a). According to the Middle English *Life of Kenelm* there was a second healing well and chapel on Salter's Hill to the east of his father's monastery at Winchcombe, to which Kenelm's body was conveyed; this probably lay beside an ancient saltway.[96] Such stories were not factual, although Kenelm (Cynehelm) was a Mercian ætheling who probably did predecease his father in 812.[97]

Such legends form part of a standard stock of early medieval/ medieval hagiographical literature: saints might be murdered, their staffs planted in the ground might grow into trees and, as here, springs might gush forth at the site of their martyrdom.

Holy wells in place names

Given the essential nature of accessibility to a clean water source, wells frequently gave rise to place names throughout the country. The name of Wells in Somerset, for instance, takes its name from the freshwater springs that still flow south-east of the cathedral, as has been noted

Fig. 5.7b The holy spring on the boundary of Withington, Gloucestershire (photograph by Della Hooke).

above. This minster site became the centre of a new bishopric founded in 909 when the old West Saxon diocese of Sherborne was subdivided.

There are several terms for springs found in Old English place names (see Chapter 2), including *ǣwelm*, *ǣwylle* 'a river-spring, the source of a river', which Margaret Gelling and Ann Cole suggest was one that was particularly prolific;[98] *spring*, *spryng*, usually with *ēa* 'stream' or *wella* 'well, spring, stream' as *ǣ-spring* or *wyll-spring*; *funta* 'spring'; and a rare term *celde*, but the term most commonly encountered is *wella*, *well(e)* (Anglian or Kentish form), *wiella*, *wielle*, *will(a)*, *wylle* (West Saxon) or *wælla*, *wælle* (Mercian). This could mean a well or a spring, or even refer to the headwaters of a stream issuing from a spring – *welle* and *wylle* are the forms usually met in charters. It is this term that is most frequently associated with the description 'holy'. Victor Watts also notes similar but different place name terms OE *wǣl*, *wēl* meaning 'a deep pool, a deep place in a river', a possible interpretation of the name Wellesbourne in Warwickshire.[99] A well is understood today to be a shaft artificially sunk into the earth to reach a water source, but in earlier times might instead describe a pool that was fed from a spring nearby.

Among the Old English terms, *funta* is a loan from late British (Primitive Welsh) **funtōn*, **font*, **funt*, itself from Latin *fontana* and surviving as Cornish *fenten*. Gelling has noted how the Latin loan-word **funta* 'spring, fountain', is found in a limited number of place names, chiefly in the southern England and often used for copious springs or wells close to a Roman road, perhaps with Roman masonry then visible, but no subsequent research has confirmed the latter.[100] However, Oliver Padel suggests that the Cornish term would also apply to a 'natural spring, not a dug well' (the latter *puth) 'though it can include a built superstructure, as at many of the holy wells'.[101] *Funta* names are particularly common in the southern chalklands of Dorset and Wiltshire, but the Roman or early medieval settlement sites were rarely located close to the actual springs.

References to holy wells are also frequent in place names, but such minor features rarely find their way into the documentary record before the medieval period, by which time 'holy' wells were proliferating. However, a number do appear as manor/estate names in Domesday Book. These include Halwill (*Halgewella* 1086), with a ruined chapel standing beside it, and Halwell in Brixton (*Hagawila* 1086), both in Devon; and Holy Well in the parish of Radipole, Dorset (*Halegewelle* 1086). Holy Well in Oxford (*Haliwele* 1086), now covered, was a spring lying to the north of St Cross church while at Holywell near St Ives, in Cambridgeshire (*Haliewelle* 1086), held by the Abbot of Ramsey in 1086, the well is tucked behind the church. A spring at Hinderwell, North Yorkshire (*Hildrewelle* 1086), may have been dedicated to St Hild of *Streoneshalh* whose monastery lies a few miles to the south-east (or merely be 'spring where elder grows': OE *hyldre* 'elder').[102] Of the holy wells that became parish names, the majority lie close to a church and many other holy wells also lie close to churches.[103] A 'holy' bourne, 'sacred stream' is also found: Holybourne in Hampshire (*Haliborne* 1086).

Not all holy wells were associated with church sites, however. Some of the earliest documented 'holy wells' occur as landmarks in pre-Conquest charter-bounds, all post-dating the mid-tenth century (one charter claiming to date from the mid-ninth century is known to be spurious). These early occurrences are found across the country, from Somerset to Northamptonshire and southwards to Hampshire, obviously coincident with charter coverage (such documents are largely absent from the north of the country and limited in the east). They often seem to refer to the headwater streams of brooks or to the headwater springs themselves. At Ruishton in Somerset the bounds of an estate owing dues to the Bishop of Winchester ran upstream along the *beadding broc*, a tributary of the River Tone which formed most of the eastern boundary of Ruishton, and beyond a bridge, to the brook's source at a *halgan wylle* (Figure 5.8a).[104] On the boundary of Withington in Gloucestershire, the south-eastern boundary of the estate follows the River Coln as far as another *halgan wyllan* (Figure 5.8b), taking in a small area beyond the

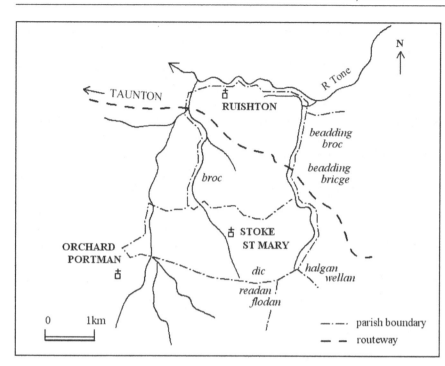

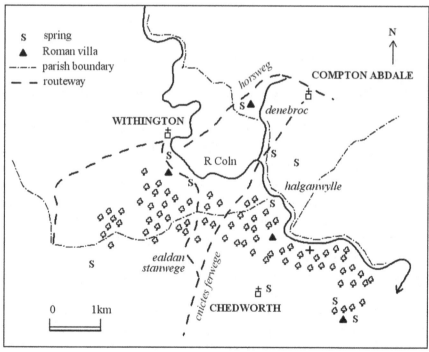

Fig. 5.8
a and b
Holy wells
on charter
boundaries:
Ruishton,
Somerset;
Withington,
Gloucestershire
(drawn by
Della Hooke).

river which lay not far distant from a Roman villa site in the adjacent parish of Chedworth; Roman finds have also been found in the vicinity of the spring (Figure 5.7b).[105] The villa site contained temples dedicated to various Roman gods, but also a spring-fed pool dedicated to the water-nymphs (a Nymphaeum) which supplied the villa with water. A Christian chi-rho symbol had been scratched on one of the rim-stones, probably in the fourth century AD, perhaps transforming it into a Christian baptistery.[106] This may indicate the reuse of a pagan shrine for the 'new' religion, offering a similar scenario for the nearby 'holy well'.

At Olney, Buckinghamshire, the bounds run up the 'holy brook' to the 'holy spring'; at Stoke near Ipswich in Suffolk the bounds note a *haligwylle* and on two occasions the springs are associated with fords, as at Stowe in Northamptonshire and at Sunbury in Surrey.[107] In these last two cases the ford may have crossed a brook where a road was running towards a 'holy' place, as the name Stowe would suggest. Another *halgan wyl* occurs on the boundary of Portisham, Dorset, and is recorded in 1024, here referring to a headwater stream near Rodden.[108] A number of charter springs, as in place names, are associated with saints: *cynburge wellan* at Chalgrove, Bedfordshire, may have been dedicated to St Cyniburg of Mercia, abbess of Castor; *eanswiþe wyllas* at Cold Ashton, Gloucestershire, to St Eanswith, abbess of Folkeston, and *ceollan wylle* at Barkham, Berkshire, to 'St' Ceolla, sister of St Helen of Helenstow, the founder of Abingdon Abbey. Post-Conquest references to such saintly associations become increasingly frequent.[109]

While water in the eyes of the Church and in reality remained a source of purification and blessing and was essential for life, its darker side did not disappear entirely. One river which was associated with a deliberate drowning was the Thames. One unusual documentary mention occurs in a twelfth-century record of an exchange of land in the tenth century between Æthelwold, bishop of Winchester, and a certain Wulfstan Uccea, sometime between 963 and 975. It describes how a widow and her son had been accused of driving an iron pin into Wulfstan's father Ælsi. When she was declared a witch, her estate was forfeited and the woman was drowned at London Bridge, her son becoming an outlaw.[110] There was also an execution site on an island in the Trent near Burton in Staffordshire. Two charter boundary clauses refer to this site: in 1008, King Æthelred granted an estate at Rolleston to Abbot Wulfgeat, the boundary of which ran *to ðan þorne þer ða þeofes licgan* 'to the thorn-tree where the thieves lie', a site referred to again in 1012 in a second grant to the abbot of the adjacent estate of Wetmoor in which the boundary clause begins *Ærst of trente þær þa ðeofes hangað on middan bere fordes holme* 'First from the Trent where the thieves hang in the middle of barley ford island', a place later known as Gallows Flat, perhaps the place where the abbey carried out justice.[111]

Holy wells and sacred rivers in later tradition
The role that 'holy wells' had played in ordinary people's lives ensured that they remained a strong tradition. 'Holy wells', whether ancient or not, were frequently associated with particular saints, thus Christianizing any possible 'pagan' element. At Penmon Priory on Anglesey a well that was probably one of the druidic shrines destroyed by Paulinus in the first century AD was enclosed by a dry-stone beehive cell in the early Christian period and became associated with St Seiriol, the sixth-century founder of Penmon church and the monastery on nearby Puffin Island (Ynis Seiriol or Priestsholm).[112] In Wales, Frances Jones notes no fewer than 437 'holy' wells which bear the names of saints, together with another 65 indicative of Christian practice, while of those bearing saints' names some 119 are also regarded as healing wells.[113]

Wells associated with saints reappear in medieval hagiographic literature: *The Life of St Nectan*, for example, in its present form was probably composed at the end of the twelfth century and tells again of a fifth-century holy man who lived alone in the solitude of the woods in a remote valley of northern Devon near 'a town called Stokes' (Stoke in Hartland, known as *Nectanestoke* in 1189). He was beheaded by two robbers trying to steal his cows but then miraculously carried his own head to the 'fountain' near his hut, laying it down on a certain stone that remained bloodied thereafter. The remainder of his body was subsequently placed by the repentant thief alongside. St Nectan's Well lies at Hartland, and his church was to be built close by, becoming the site for many miracles.[114] In Cornwall and Devon, many 'holy wells' claim to have a pre-Christian ancestry. Robert Hope records as many as over 50 'holy wells' in these two counties – far more than he records elsewhere.[115] Scraps of material are still regularly placed around such wells by those seeking cures to this day.

Some stories associating springs and wells with particular saints may have an earlier basis in fact. St Frideswide, patron saint of Oxford city and the university, is said to have hidden in a wood near Bampton to escape the clutches of the lecherous Algar (Æthelbald), a Mercian king – a common hagiographical theme in female saints' lives. Here she sought refuge, but the water in which she had washed her hands miraculously cured a girl of blindness. With so many pilgrims being attracted to the site she was forced to flee again to another secluded site at Thornbury near Binsey where she established an oratory. A well near the church of St Margaret at Binsey which is said to have been 'made to flow by the prayers of St Frideswide' was later reputed to possess healing powers. According to the twelfth-century accounts of Frideswide's *Life*, she was the daughter of a sub-king Didan who ruled over what was to become west Oxfordshire, and it was he who founded the monasteries at Eynsham, Bampton and Oxford, all on gravel islands within the various channels of the braided River Thames (that at Oxford on the site of the present Christ Church Cathedral), all therefore at crossing points of the river. It is at Oxford that Frideswide became an abbess. Archaeology has now produced evidence of an earthwork enclosure at Thornbury, similar to other enclosures of possibly Iron Age or sub-Roman date, but possibly reused as the hedged enclosure of a religious site, and of eighth-century burials at the Oxford site. Again, there are links between a 'holy well' and a medieval saint's *Life*.[116]

In medieval times, holy wells proliferated, and many were also to become associated with the name of a particular saint, something which gave them legitimacy, as previously noted. Some were to be associated, as 'Lady Wells', with the Virgin Mary, or her mother Anne, popular in the fifteenth century. Others were associated with St Helen, whose cult was widespread in medieval England but most popular in the East Midlands of England and Yorkshire; her wells, however, lie mainly in the Pennine spine of northern England: some 43 wells in total, perhaps 'survivals from rather more pastoral societies'.[117] Her day, 3 May, may have been particularly appropriate for 'the time of year when popular tradition held that the "powers" of water were at their fullest' and when the measure of the flow or dryness might portend good or evil fortune, the adoption of such a saint the 'simple and appropriate choice of patron in the course of Christianisation'.[118] Many were thought to have healing powers: the holy well at Holwell near Sherborne, Dorset, for instance (recorded by the fifteenth century), is next to St Laurence's church and was used for baptisms and as a domestic water supply, but its waters were also reputed to cure sore eyes.[119] Many holy wells also remained associated with trees, perhaps seen as offering protection to the sacred spring or well.[120]

The tales of swords cast into lakes purport to be early traditions, but usually come from later literary sources: King Arthur is said to have retrieved his sword from 'the Lady of the Lake', and old sagas from Iceland also sometimes have a hero *lose* a sword in a lake or the sea only to have it magically recovered again later. Rivers, too, continued to play a role in folklore. Some were believed to demand a regular human sacrifice: the River Spey in Scotland was said to require one life a year whereas the 'bloodthirsty Dee, required three', as did the Welsh River Dee, in the latter case to ensure success in battle; some Scottish lochs similarly demanded a sacrifice.[121] Southern English rivers in this category included the 'cruel' Dart, the Tavy and the East Okement in Devon and the Parrett in Somerset; others further north included the Trent in Derbyshire, the Ure in North Yorkshire, the Ribble in Lancashire and the Wye in Herefordshire.[122] Some were thought to be inhabited by spirits who dragged people (especially children) into the water to drown them.[123] However, few such stories can be traced back earlier than the nineteenth century. Even the dressing of wells in springtime cannot be reliably traced back into medieval times, although it is claimed that the wells at Tissington in Derbyshire were first dressed with flowers in 1349 as a way of giving thanks for the purity of the water drawn during the period of the Black Death. However, such associations in legend and folklore with healing, sacrality or even death obviously draw upon long-established traditions.

Conclusion

The sacred association of water must be set within a broad time-frame. It appears to have been present in Britain from at least Mesolithic times. The Anglo-Saxon period is important because this is when pagan traditions were being overtaken by Christianity, a process that can be investigated in contemporary literary and documentary sources. Whatever the role of water in pre-Christian belief, as an essential for life it could not be ignored, and it therefore readily gained recognition as a means of purification, blessing and healing within the Church.

6

Food from the Water: Fishing

Rebecca Reynolds

Nis min sele swige, ne ic sylfa hlud
*ymb * * * unc dryhten scop*
siþ ætsomne. Ic eom swifter þonne he,
þragum strengra, he þreotigra.
Hwilum ic me reste; he sceal yrnan forð.
Ic him in wunige a þenden ic lifge;
gif wit unc gedælað, me bið dead witod.[1]

Not silent is my hall, nor I myself am loud
... for us two the Lord ordained
Our ways together. I am swifter than he
And at times stronger; [he] is more enduring.
Often I rest; he must run on.
With him is my home all my life long.
If we two are parted my death is destined.

Exeter Riddle 85 (Fish and River)[2]

The importance of fishing in the later medieval period is well attested and understood. Both freshwater and marine fish were consumed, either fresh or preserved.[3] Freshwater fish ponds were also prominent features of display on religious and secular elite settlements.[4] However, the level of fishing during the Anglo-Saxon period is more complex to decipher. While the remains of fish are generally common on urban settlements of the middle and late Anglo-Saxon period, it was once thought that marine fish were not a common foodstuff until the later part of the late Anglo-Saxon period.[5] This picture is slowly beginning to change as further excavations reveal the presence of fish remains and material remains associated with fishing, as well as evidence from landscape studies. Combining all these different sources of evidence allows us to draw a picture of what constitutes a fishing identity: who were the people fishing and consuming fish? What were they fishing? Where were they fishing and consuming fish? How were they fishing? When were they fishing and consuming fish? Why were they fishing and consuming them? The exploitation of fish in Anglo-Saxon England changes, and it is this change that is important to explore.

Fishing in early Anglo-Saxon England

One of the most obvious pieces of evidence for the consumption of fish is the retrieval of fish bones from settlements. The presence of fish bones on archaeological sites is, however, fraught with problems. Their small size makes them vulnerable to destruction, and if extensive sieving is not conducted during excavation then the bones of larger species such as cod will be recovered in preference to those of smaller but equally important species such as eel and herring. Fish remains have been recovered from a great many sites across the Anglo-Saxon periods; however, it is extremely difficult to compare them, as many sites have not been sieved, and this thus has had a great impact on the presence or absence, abundance and diversity of species recovered.

Fish remains can be recovered from a variety of different features, although the feature in question may have an impact on the likelihood of recovering any fish remains. In the early Anglo-Saxon period, the features excavated were primarily occupation layers from dwellings or post-holes, and these tend to be poor in fish remains. Nevertheless, fish remains were recovered from several sites, but never in any great amounts. West Stow, Suffolk, revealed one of the biggest fish assemblages dominated by freshwater fish, such as pike, tench and a few other cyprinids, the largest family of freshwater fish.[6] Marine species were found on some sites, though rarely in great numbers. Six bones were found at Bonners Lane, Leicester.[7] Three bones and one were found at Clerkenwell and Hammersmith, respectively, both sites being situated close to the River Thames.[8] A different situation is exhibited by the early phase of the occupation at Redcastle Furze, Thetford, where 24 bones of herring, 17 bones of eel, and potential single bone finds of pike and perch were recovered.[9] The excavations at Lyminge, Kent, have revealed a long and rich sequence of occupation. A large post-built hall and other elite trappings have been found.[10] Analysis of the faunal remains are still ongoing, but the remains of herring and other marine fish have been found.[11] At Bloodmoor Hill, Suffolk, marine species such as smelt, halibut and herring dominated, though no species exhibited 'number of identified specimens' (NISP) in numbers greater than 12. In addition, six fish hooks were revealed from that site.[12]

Fishing material culture has only been found on one other early Anglo-Saxon site: Ramsgate, Kent.[13] One fish hook and two fired perforated ceramic discs were found here. The ceramic discs are the only ones of their kind. One of them has a barnacle on the inside, which strengthens its interpretation as a fishing implement, possibly a line or net weight.

Fish weirs or traps dating from this period have also been found. These are primarily from around the River Thames and its tributaries. Some of these early weirs bridge the late Roman/early Anglo-Saxon period such as the remains of the weir from Shepperton Lane.[14] Other early weirs on the Thames are found at Putney, Barn Elms, Nine Elms and Hammersmith.[15] While fish have been found on some early Anglo-Saxon sites and there is evidence that they were being caught with the use of large structures such as weirs, the fish-bone evidence suggests that their consumption was not very widespread. A number of early Anglo-Saxon cemeteries have revealed skeletons that have been sampled for carbon and nitrogen stable isotope signatures. The results reveal that marine protein did not play a particularly significant role in the diet of these individuals as most seem to have had a largely terrestrial diet. The small variations that are noticeable are most likely due to environmental factors.[16]

Other isotopic surveys of Anglo-Saxon diet have noted that a change occurs in the early part of the middle Anglo-Saxon period, suggesting that elites in certain areas, particularly the east of England, begin to show evidence for the consumption of marine protein.[17] There are still many problems surrounding isotope analysis such as contamination and understanding more precisely what animals the proteins have come from. Other recent work on early Anglo-Saxon burials has shown that it is possible to discern between the protein signatures of freshwater, migratory and marine fish.[18] This study showed that some of the skeletons that displayed elite trappings from inland cemeteries were getting their protein from estuarine or marine fish, but the amount consumed was likely to be very small. Overall, the isotopic signature for marine fish consumption for Anglo-Saxon England as a whole is not very encouraging. This conclusion is hampered by the fact that the majority of cemeteries sampled were of early Anglo-Saxon date, and it is only during the middle and late periods that marine fish are found more frequently.

There exists some pictorial evidence in the form of shield *appliqués* and occasionally belt buckles with fish in the design. Along with other *appliqués* depicting animals such as eagles, they have been interpreted as emblems of protection.[19] Due to the environment fish live in and the dangers associated with fishing them, it is possible that they were associated with great men. Watery environments in the early Anglo-Saxon period seem to have been places of mystery and were to be feared due to the creatures dwelling there (see also Chapter 1 of this volume).[20] This may help explain the small number of bones found on sites dating to the early Anglo-Saxon period. Their appearance on sites such as Bloodmoor Hill and the earlier phases at Lyminge, which also show signs of developing social complexity, may suggest that marine and freshwater fishing were activities that required the conquering of wild environments. These acts required courage and perhaps were used by these developing elites to differentiate themselves from others. A similar situation has been noticed with wild mammal exploitation, in particular, with deer.[21]

One very curious deposit of fish remains from the later part of the early Anglo-Saxon period has been discovered during the excavations at King's Garden Hostel, Cambridgeshire. The grave of a woman was accompanied by the bones of three complete eels placed in a hanging bowl at her head.[22] As this is the only find of fish bones that seems to have been deliberately placed, it is very difficult to understand the reason behind such deposition. The symbolic meaning of an object or foodstuff can acquire a different meaning when placed in a funerary context, so remains of food and drink may not just have been provisions for the afterlife.[23] They could have represented a gift of food for the dead, in which case they were to be consumed by the deceased in the next world, or they were meant to be consumed by someone else in the afterlife. Similarly, this deposit may have been a reflection of the woman's status: perhaps she gathered fish from a weir on a regular basis or was a member of a group who helped build and then subsequently owned a fish weir. By the middle Anglo-Saxon period the possible taboo surrounding water environments seems to disappear. Elites may still have led the way, but fish now appear on a greater number and variety of sites.

Fishing in mid-Anglo-Saxon England

A distinct change in the use and perception of the environment, especially water, occurred during the middle of the Anglo-Saxon period. This change is not only evident in the increased levels of fish found on archaeological sites, but also in the location of these settlements. An increased number of settlements appeared in the Fens,[24] small rural settlements as well as early ecclesiastical sites, perhaps drawn here by this strange 'wilderness' that could be tamed by Christianity[25] (see Chapter 3 of this volume).

The new acceptance of watery environments seems to have changed the perception of fish as a comestible, though the isotopic evidence is still very slight. A recent survey by Bradley Hull and Tamsin O'Connell has indicated that a change is noticeable during the mid-Anglo-Saxon period,[26] a change also reflected in the zooarchaeological remains of fish found; in this period the number of sites with fish increases significantly, as do the amounts found on them. Several excavations from mid-Anglo-Saxon London and *Hamwic* (Southampton), for example, have recovered numerous fish remains. The species found on these settlements could easily have been caught locally; eel and other cyprinids could be found in the river, and herring, whiting, flatfish and small cod would have been available around London and *Hamwic*.

Remains of marine fish have been found on a small handful of coastal rural settlements. At *Sandtun*, West Hythe, Kent, numerous continental artefacts were also found alongside the high number of marine fish remains.[27] At Fishtoft, Lincolnshire, large numbers of fish, specifically flatfish, were found alongside evidence of salt making.[28] It is possible that the fish were consumed at these sites or transported inland. There is a possibility that Lyminge had ties with the settlement at *Sandtun*, though this is not entirely certain.[29]

The mid-Anglo-Saxon period sees the development of social differentiation visible through settlements: along with the *emporia* (early urban settlements) along rivers and estuaries appear religious and secular elite settlements. While a number of these have been excavated, only a small number have been subject to extensive sieving. Research at Flixborough, Lincolnshire, has recovered the largest assemblage comprised of freshwater and estuarine fish (such as cyprinids, eel, pike and flatfish). The remains of bottle-nose dolphins were also present in the assemblage. The mid-Anglo-Saxon phases at Lyminge have so far revealed a marine assemblage dominated by cod with over 600 fragments and a total assemblage of over 4,000 fragments.[30] Another elite settlement, Sedgeford, Norfolk, also has an assemblage rich in fish, though not as much as Flixborough and Lyminge. This lower amount is probably due to the fact that over its 17 years of continuous excavation, the sieving strategy has unfortunately not been very consistent. Nevertheless, herring, cyprinids, flatfish and some cod have been identified at this site.[31] Textual evidence contemporary with such finds confirms the variety of fish consumed in the period; a passage from Bede mentions the fame that Britain enjoyed in this middle period for its abundance, including 'its rivers, which abound in fish, particularly salmon and eels, and for copious springs. Seals as well as dolphins are frequently captured and even whales; besides these there are various kinds of shellfish' (particularly mussels and whelks).[32]

The finds of fishing material culture do not abound in the mid-Anglo-Saxon period. Flixborough revealed the largest assemblage of fish hooks and lead weights, though some of these date to the late Anglo-Saxon period or come from unstratified contexts.[33] An intriguing object consisting of an axially perforated sheep/goat metacarpal has been found at Southampton and Ipswich. Ian Riddler believes that such objects may have been used as net sinkers.[34] If this is indeed how they were used, then they would have been attached to the ends of nets in order to drag a section of the net to the bottom. The large numbers of herring found during excavations here alongside these items that may have been used to catch them seems to be more than just a coincidence.

During the mid-Anglo-Saxon period there is a surge in the building of weirs. Numerous weirs have been found on the River Thames, the Blackwater Estuary in Essex, Holbrook Bay and Barber's Point in Suffolk and Holme Beach in Norfolk.[35] Many more weirs have been found at Colwick, Nottinghamshire; West Cotton, Northamptonshire; the Wootton-Quarr coast of the Isle of Wight and the River Severn.[36] Many of these were built in the later part of the mid-Anglo-Saxon period or the early half of the late Anglo-Saxon period. In fact, most of the weirs built show continuous repair and upkeep, suggesting in some cases that they were in use over many decades, if not centuries.

All of the weirs in England are timber built, with the exception of one found at Wareham, Dorset.[37] These seem to be V-shaped in structure, with the apex of the V being where the fish were caught. They are all post-built, and sometimes consist of double rows of posts. This construction would have allowed for wattle fences to be placed between these rows of posts. Otherwise, wattle fencing may have been attached to these individual posts. Wattle fragments have been found at Collins Creek in the Blackwater.[38] The method of trapping the fish in the apex is likely to have been accomplished by placing a conical basket at the opening. At Shepperton Lane, some stone weights were found in proximity to the weir and have been interpreted as being used to fix the basket in place.[39] Fragments of basket have also been found at Collins Creek.[40]

Certain features identified as weirs resemble a fence crossing the body of water. It is likely that these would have served to trap fish. Over time these would have become overgrown with algae, effectively becoming self-baiting.[41] It is also possible for these to have been baited with small hooks to catch fish. The extensive size of these weirs has led to many suggesting that these weirs were constructed by elites. This argument is supported by the fact that the timber used in the construction of these weirs has come from managed woodland, and textual evidence links several of these weirs to monasteries or bishops.[42] However, it is

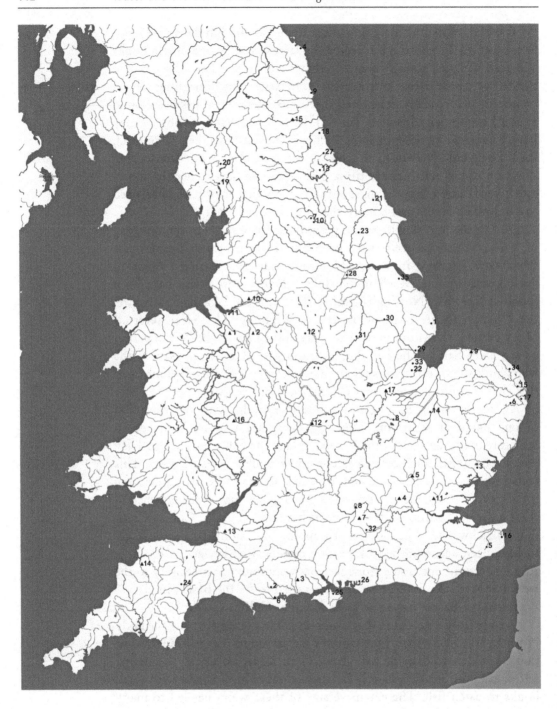

Fish place names

Weir place names

[+]Place-names recorded after 1086 (Domesday Book). All others are either first recorded in 1086 or before.

*May refer to cattle/sheep stall rather than fishing.

Table 6.1
Fish- and weir-related place names from Figure 6.1

Fig. 6.1 *opposite* Locations of English fish-related (circle) and weir-related (triangle) place names. Each place-name and its county are listed in Table 6.1.

also possible that these weirs were built by communities in order to supplement their diet.[43]

The upkeep of these weirs would have taken considerable time and effort. Weirs are angled to catch fish on the ebbing tide, and so, twice a day, as the tide retreats, the fish caught in them have to be collected before they spoil. Such work would have been necessary whatever the weather or time of day, and would have acted as a strict control on time. Depending on the height of the waters, it is possible for women and children to have been able to gather the fish from the weir. The gathering of marine foodstuffs has been seen to be the work of women in many traditional societies.[44] Not only would weirs have controlled the daily lives of those living nearby, they would also have been important markers in people's memories in travelling and orienting themselves.[45] Their immense size would have been very noticeable, especially at low tide. This fact may explain why certain place names are related to weirs.

A very basic preliminary survey of fish-related place names indicates that a number of major place names contain elements designating weirs and fish (Table 6.1 and Figure 6.1). Place names related to eel are common, and coupled with the fact that eel are one of the most common finds on archaeological sites, suggest that river fishing for eel with weirs and eel baskets was a common activity. Many fish-related place names are located on rivers as opposed to being directly on the coast. There is unfortunately not much correlation between the location of place names, weirs and the finds of fish bones. There are a few exceptions: Edgware in London is not such a great distance from the Thames, nor is the complex of weirs at Holme Beach from Warham. Many of these place names may have been settlements, though the exact nature of these locations requires further exploration. Harold Fox has suggested that many early coastal fishing settlements would have been seasonal, and therefore probably not very significant.[46] These may thus be linked to other settlements further inland where the fishermen may have resided the rest of the year. It is also possible that certain fishing settlements and weirs were associated with elite settlements, and charters discussing boundaries of these settlements may shed further light on these relationships. Place names related to watermills can be related to estate centres, and several sources suggest that mills and weirs are related.[47] Most of the place names discussed so far do not appear in written form before Domesday Book (see, too, Della Hooke, Chapter 2). However, it is likely that some of these were in use for many years before, such as Ely, the district of eels, whose name first appears in 731 and which perfectly demonstrates encroachment into the wet environments that is witnessed in the mid-Anglo-Saxon period.

Late Anglo-Saxon period

By the late Anglo-Saxon period, fish remains are found on almost all sites, though their actual numbers vary greatly depending on whether the site was sieved or not. What is most evident is that fish remains are now found on inland sites such as the urban centres of Oxford, Hereford and York.[48] Some of these have only revealed a few bones of herring, while others, such as most of the excavations within Norwich, have revealed important amounts of herring and other marine fish. Herring have also been found on inland rural sites such as Wraysbury, Berkshire.[49]

Unfortunately, many of the elite settlements of this period have not been subject to sieving, which makes it very difficult to get a full picture of how all sections of society perceived fish. Nevertheless, the odd cod bone has been recovered at sites such as Goltho, Lincolnshire.[50] When sites have been sieved, such as Flixborough in its mid-Anglo-Saxon phases, the later finds continue to be dominated by freshwater and estuarine fish as well as bottle-nose dolphins. The assemblage from Bishopstone, East Sussex, was entirely dominated by marine fish, with the exception of eel. In addition, estimates of size from the bones recovered indicate that some of the cod caught were over a metre long. Castle Mall, Norwich, has also revealed an assemblage that contained herring along with other freshwater and marine fish.[51]

With the exception of Westminster Abbey, no other ecclesiastical settlement of this late period has been subject to any sieving. The assemblage was made up of almost 3,000 herring fragments and over 1,000 plaice/flounder and sprat fragments each. Other marine species were also present.[52] This assemblage forms one of the biggest recovered from the Anglo-Saxon period.

Alongside the increased levels of fish remains in the late period, we also find an increase in the numbers of fish hooks and weights, either of lead, clay or stone. There do seem to be some regional and chronological differences: the large numbers of fish hooks from Flixborough are from the ninth to tenth centuries, along with the fish hooks from Fishergate and Coppergate, York, from the eighth, ninth and tenth centuries.[53] As we move into the eleventh and twelfth centuries, the number of occurrences of fish hooks increases, with several being recovered from the various excavations in Norwich, London and further finds from York.[54] Three fish hooks were recovered from Bishopstone, East Sussex.[55] The south-east of England seems to demonstrate a progression of fishing with fish hooks, among other items. This progression continues on into the medieval period as demonstrated by the fish hook finds from

Sandtun, New Romney and Dover.[56] New Romney and Dover were both later part of the confederation of Cinque Ports.[57]

The largest fish hooks are generally post-Conquest in date. A small hook, however, does not preclude the fishing of large fish, within reason. The larger concentrations of fish hooks have come from late Anglo-Saxon York, Norwich, Thetford and London.[58] In York these would have been used purely for freshwater fishing, whereas at both Norwich and London they may have been used for estuarine and freshwater fishing. At Bishopstone it is likely that the hooks found would have been used for marine fishing,[59] supported by the fact that the fish bone assemblage consisted primarily of marine fish and included some very large cod.

Gorges, grooved objects pointed at both ends and often made of wood or bone, are a rarer find, but, according to Riddler, this may be due to their being confused with pin beaters,[60] a very common artefact associated with the textile industry which is found on many sites. Both items are very similar in appearance and perhaps may have had dual functions, though the interpretation of these finds is of course dependent on the location of the sites on which they are found.[61] Given that objects can go through different uses throughout their lifetime, it may be worthwhile to reconsider the interpretation of artefacts in light of the developing understanding of fishing in Anglo-Saxon England. Hook and line fishing would have required the use of weights to pull them down and hold them in place. Weights made of both stone and lead have been recovered from numerous sites. Lead weights have been found at Coppergate, Fishergate and Flixborough,[62] and stone weights have also been found at Fishergate.[63]

Textual sources discussing fish or fishing are rare before the late Anglo-Saxon period, and even in this period they are scant. Ælfric's *Colloquy* recalls a discourse had with a fictional fisherman. The fisherman explains that with the use of his boat along with lines or nets he catches a very wide variety of fish. In rivers and estuaries the freshwater fish include *Anguillas et lucios, menas et capitones, tructas et murenas, et qualescumque in amne natant. Saliu.* 'Eels and pike, minnows and turbot, trout and lamprey and whatever swims in the water. Small fish'. When he ventures out to sea, his catch includes *Alleces et isicios, delfinos et sturias, ostreas et cancros, musculas, torniculi, neptigalli, platesia et platissa et polipodes et similia* 'Herrings and salmon, porpoises and sturgeon, oysters and crabs, mussels, winkles, cockles, plaice and flounders and lobsters, and many similar things'.[64] When questioned further he points out that he does not fish out at sea due to the dangers, such as being eaten by a large fish! Ælfric's fisherman may not want to fish in the sea, but the zooarchaeological record suggests that some did, perhaps even many, as Ælfric's fisherman says that he cannot catch enough fish for the demand at market. There are several documents from the late Anglo-Saxon period that demonstrate that elites sought to control aquatic resources through ownership of fisheries.[65] From these documents it appears that there were many different types of weirs, such as 'pusting were' or *cytweras*.[66] A tenth-century charter from the estate at Tidenham, Gloucestershire, mentions the ownership of numerous *cytweras* 'basket-weirs' on the rivers Severn and Wye, along with a smaller number of *hæcweras* 'hackle weirs' on the Wye, and states that 'every alternate fish belongs to the lord of the manor and every rare fish which is of value – sturgeon or porpoise, herring or sea fish'.[67] Other textual sources indicate that the remains of cetaceans belonged to the king, though most of these refer to the finds of beached cetaceans.[68] Hirokazu Tsurushima argues that herring were fished at the request of elites, probably using several boats.[69]

The presence of large fish on elite settlements may exemplify the elite role in fishing clearly. The cod remains recovered from Bishopstone suggest that several of the fragments came from individuals sometimes over a metre in length (above). The mid-Anglo-Saxon fish remains from Lyminge have also revealed an assemblage of large cod remains, and the later phases are likely to have even more. While urban settlements were now also consuming marine fish, the elites continued to differentiate themselves by consuming bigger fish which required more skill, manpower and courage to land them.

Implications

The great increase in the numbers of fish found on late Anglo-Saxon sites coupled with the increased numbers of fish hooks and other fishing material culture support the theory that a 'fish event horizon' occurred during the late Anglo-Saxon period. However, when we look more closely at the earlier periods alongside other forms of evidence like weirs and place names it becomes clear that the picture is very complex. This complexity is made more obvious when one looks at the zooarchaeological evidence. Due to the small size and fragility of some of the species of fish likely to be recovered, it becomes very difficult to compare different sites over different periods. At the same time, it is important to know where fish have been recovered, regardless of how small in quantity the fish are. Such a comparative approach has been used for this study, and should be borne in mind. Other limiting factors, as discussed, are the lack of finds on sites that have not been sieved.

As it stands, the evidence seems to suggest that marine fishing may, to an extent, have been an elite activity. The lack of fish consumption during the early Anglo-Saxon period is probably due to a taboo surrounding aquatic environments. However, this begins gradually to change by the late seventh and early eighth centuries, coinciding with the development of a more complex social hierarchy evident in some settlements, such as Bloodmoor Hill and Lyminge. During the mid-Anglo-Saxon period fish appear on a variety of sites but the small number of elite settlements that have been sieved reveal larger assemblages with a greater variety of species that can include large fish or cetaceans. The catching of large fish would have required venturing out into more open waters, which comes with its own dangers and thus could have been appealing to elites in a similar way as hunting deer. The bottle-nose dolphins found at Flixborough were probably herded up the estuary and then killed with spears. The act of killing with such weapons held strong metaphors associated with warfare.[70]

It is very difficult to establish who specifically is fishing. Ælfric's fisherman fishes for himself in order to sell at the market; it is very likely that some of the sporadic finds of fish bones from small settlements dating to the early and middle Anglo-Saxon periods represent fish caught by their inhabitants for their own consumption. The pictorial evidence may suggest that it was men who wandered into these mystical environments and caught fish. Whether it was only men who consumed fish is harder to determine. Who was fishing and consuming fish on elite and religious settlements is even more difficult to ascertain. These settlements could be very large and be comprised of many different inhabitants: men, women, children and a variety of people of different status. It is possible that the larger fish such as cod and bottle-nose dolphin were consumed by the elite inhabitants, perhaps reserved for certain celebrations.

The isotope samples generally come from both men and women. The individual reports do not mention any visible differences between the values from men and women. Simon Mays and Nancy Beavan were the only ones to notice a small elevation in $\partial_{15}N$ levels in men over 30 years of age from riverine areas, but the reasons for this are numerous, and it is not possible to say if this difference is due to a higher proportion of riverine or marine protein.[71] As mentioned above, most of these samples also come from the early Anglo-Saxon period, which is the time when the evidence for fishing is most scant. To be able to establish more precisely whether women as well as men were consuming fish in the later period, more research into isotopes must first be undertaken.

The reasons for consuming fish are likely to be varied and complex. We have already discussed the possibility that elites consumed large fish as a way of differentiating themselves. Many textual sources from the later medieval period describe fishing to be a noble pursuit suitable for kings and other aristocrats.[72] The methods described for catching fish in these sources are identical to those supposed to have been used during the Anglo-Saxon periods, which we can glean from the archaeological record and some textual sources.[73] Those in rural areas and urban centres may have eaten fish occasionally to diversify their diet and because they were locally available.

Religious beliefs and the impact of the Rule of St Benedict have often been believed to be the reason for the increased levels of fish found in later Anglo-Saxon England.[74] This rule forbade the consumption of flesh from quadrupeds on saints' days and Fridays; fish and birds provided perfect substitutes. The Rule of St Benedict would have been known to ecclesiasts such as Wilfrid and Benedict Biscop, and it is likely that they introduced some aspects of it into their own monasteries.[75] The oldest known copy of the Rule in England dates to the seventh or eighth century.[76] Many studies have tried to identify the zooarchaeological markers of a monastic diet.[77] However, it is difficult to evaluate the extent to which this rule was adhered to and its impact on secular members of society. Richard Gem explains that the practising of the Rule was reinforced by religious reforms of the late ninth and early tenth centuries.[78] Before this, monasteries practised a *regula mixta*, where no single rule was predominant and was either the choice of the abbot or of the founders and local rulers who wished further to exert their influence.[79]

As a result of the Benedictine Rule, assemblages rich in fish remains have often been thought to be indicative of a monastic diet. For the Anglo-Saxon period, it is difficult to test this theory, as few monastic sites have been extensively sieved. For instance, the faunal assemblages from the double monasteries of Wearmouth and Jarrow were not sieved, neither were the early phases at Eynsham Abbey and so revealed no fish remains and only one well deposit at Lewes Priory was sieved, revealing an assemblage of marine fish.[80] Westminster Abbey revealed the largest assemblage with over 9,000 fragments. The settlement at Flixborough seems to have changed character during the ninth century, and this site has been described as exhibiting a monastic character. James Barrett applied correspondence analysis to the fish assemblage recovered from Flixborough and noted the difficulty associated with the small dataset available for the Anglo-Saxon period.[81] As a result, the analysis incorporated data from later medieval monastic sites as well. The results indicated that flatfish seem to be a trait of monastic houses. However, the number of identified flatfish does not vary greatly over the different phases at Flixborough.

Incidentally, flatfish have also been found on numerous other site types of the Anglo-Saxon period: at Fishtoft, flatfish were one of the most abundant species recovered, leading to the suggestion that a fishery focusing on flatfish was located there.[82] Other sites that have revealed significant numbers of flatfish are *Sandtun,* Sedgeford and Bishopstone. Analysis of the assemblage from the first season of excavation from Lyminge, Kent, dated to the late seventh and eighth centuries, and material believed to be pre-seventh century in date also revealed flatfish. A mid-Anglo-Saxon monastery is believed to exist at Lyminge,[83] but at present it is hard to assign a distinct monastic signature to the assemblage.[84] Other studies have shown that herring and cod, most likely preserved through drying for the former and salting or brining for the latter, were also an important element of monastic diets.[85] Fishponds were common features on estates and monasteries in the later medieval period,[86] and it is possible that monasteries further inland would have relied more on their ponds, while those closer to the sea would have benefited from a better access to marine fish, both fresh and preserved.

Kristopher Poole has suggested that both Sedgeford and Bishopstone display attributes that have often been associated with monasteries.[87] At Sedgeford a large number of bones from immature chickens were found, which is similar to what was found at Eynsham and St Alban's Abbey, along with a strong degree of evidence for dairying. Like Sedgeford, Bishopstone also revealed high numbers of domestic fowl, but these settlements lack the other attributes associated with monasteries. Christopher Loveluck has highlighted the similarities in the material culture between secular elite and monastic sites.[88] Therefore, not one zooarchaeological marker can be used to determine the status of a settlement; all faunal evidence must be examined alongside material remains.

The principles of humoral balance may also have had an influence on increased levels of fish consumption within certain sections of society. A healthy body was dependent on a careful balance of one's humours (blood, phlegm, black bile and yellow bile), which was intrinsically linked to the four elements of earth, fire, water and air as well as the seasons. Men were believed to be hotter and drier, whereas women were cold and moist. Diet was believed to be able to impact the humours. The temperament of men, for instance, was thought to be able to be quelled by the consumption of fish. The origins of these principles lie in the writings of Hippocrates and Galen,[89] and there is no doubt that they were known to some Anglo-Saxon ecclesiasts;[90] what is less clear is how much their knowledge of humoral balance extended into diet.[91] As with trying to establish the degree of adherence to the Rule of St Benedict, zooarchaeological assemblages do not easily lend themselves to answering these questions. It is very probable that in some situations certain belief systems did affect people's attitudes and desire to consume fish.

Conclusion

The interdisciplinary approach used in this study demonstrates that fishing and the consumption of fish in Anglo-Saxon England may have been more prevalent than previously thought.[92] The evidence for consumption of fish during the early Anglo-Saxon period is still not very strong, but what we do begin to see is that some settlements, mainly those that show the beginnings of social differentiation, have fish remains along with the means to catch them. By the mid-Anglo-Saxon period, fish appear on many more sites, and there are also a large number of fish weirs built at this time whose use seems to continue into the late Anglo-Saxon period and beyond. In the late Anglo-Saxon period, fish are found on almost all sites, and, had more sites been sieved, the quantities are likely to have been even greater. Marine species such as herring are found further inland, indicating the existence of demand and a supply network. Fish hooks are also found on numerous urban settlements of this time, indicating the inhabitants went out to catch fish, possibly even out to sea.[93]

While a taboo may or may not have existed during the early Anglo-Saxon period, it seems as if the elites may have helped to change this view. However, they continued to differentiate themselves as fish became more popular and did so by catching and consuming large fish such as cod and bottle-nose dolphin. Cetaceans and fish were probably seen as similar creatures due to their identical habitats, and therefore any large sea creature may have been a worthy prize. Human control also extended to the smaller fish species through involvement in the building of weirs, as well as in ownership of the numerous fisheries that dotted coastal and inland waters by the time of Domesday Book.

The reasons for the exploitation of the waters must have been numerous. Some would have caught small freshwater fish to add variety to their diet, but for others it is likely that a deeper meaning may have played a part. The impact of the Benedictine Rule may have had a role, as perhaps did humoral theory. The relationships among small coastal settlements where fish remains have been found, those settlements with fish elements in their place names and elite centres, still require further investigation. Only through further analysis of sieved assemblages can more light be shed on these questions. The change in landscape perception that resulted in increased fish consumption resulted in a trend that would last well into the late medieval period and beyond.

7

Inland Waterways and Coastal Transport: Landing Places, Canals and Bridges

Mark Gardiner

Ego ascendo nauem cum mercibus meis, et nauigo ultra marinas partes, et uendo meas res et emo res pretiosas, que in hac terra non nascuntur.[1]

I board my ship with my cargo and sail to overseas lands, and sell my goods and buy precious things which are not made in this country. (Ælfric's *Colloquy*)

To appreciate the experience of the Anglo-Saxons one needs to think oneself into another world in which water was a major, perhaps *the* major, means of communication, where its characteristics were vital to trade and to agriculture.[2]

In the passage above, David Pelteret expressed a suspicion which some historians of the early Middle Ages have long harboured: in a period when little effort was expended on maintaining roads, water transport offered a faster, more reliable and perhaps even a more commonly used means of moving around. Yet, before we accept the idea that this was '*the* major means of communication', we need to bear in mind that water transport was not without its own difficulties. There was an equal lack of investment in keeping rivers clear of obstruction and providing for mariners the basic infrastructure for passage at sea, including lights or other sea-marks. The reality may have been that the problems for boatmen and shipmasters were equal to or even greater than those experienced by horsemen and carters. This chapter seeks to evaluate the evidence for and importance of water transport in Anglo-Saxon England, considering not only the practicalities of moving around on the rivers and sea, but also the facilities on land associated with watery environments, including landing places, bridges and causeways. Ships and boats are not discussed at any length since the evidence for these has been recently and very adequately summarized.[3]

The core problem is to determine whether boats and ships were widely used for the daily movement of people and goods. References in the *Anglo-Saxon Chronicle* to boats or the preparation of fleets give little impression of the frequency of everyday usage: they were connected with events that were worthy of particular note. Equally, we cannot draw conclusions from the number of finds of ancient boats. These were rarely abandoned to rot in creeks or besides rivers, though the tenth-century Graveney boat is a notable exception.[4] Losses on the high seas may also have been relatively infrequent. Most boats were broken up after they ceased to be serviceable and incorporated into burials, waterfronts and embankments, or perhaps were simply used for firewood.[5] Logboats were treated rather differently as they were not so easy to dismember. They too were occasionally employed for burials, as at Snape, but more generally logboats were abandoned in the middle reaches of rivers or in fens where they had been used.[6] In spite of the number of boat fragments and logboats now found, and the growing number of dates available for them, the remains must still represent a fraction of those built.[7] A more effective way of identifying the use of ships and boats is to examine the impact made by water transport. We can see evidence for the use of water transport in the distribution of goods, the construction of landing places and the management of waterways.

Archaeologists have long used pottery as a convenient indicator of trade and long-distance transport. Pottery was traded as a commodity in itself, but also as a container for other goods. In both situations, it provides a tool for understanding the movement of mundane items. The distribution patterns of pottery types can be interpreted to show the operation of waterborne transport and to identify those waterways which were passable. Ipswich Ware was produced in that port from about 720 until 850. It was widely distributed overland throughout East Anglia and has been found on many local farmsteads of the period. Close to its production centre it was sold as a domestic vessel for cooking as well as for storing goods, though it may also have arrived as a container for traded items. However, beyond Norfolk and Suffolk, the pattern is rather different (Figure 7.1). Most of the Ipswich Ware vessels found at a distance from the place of manufacture were large jars used as containers for traded goods. Its find-spots

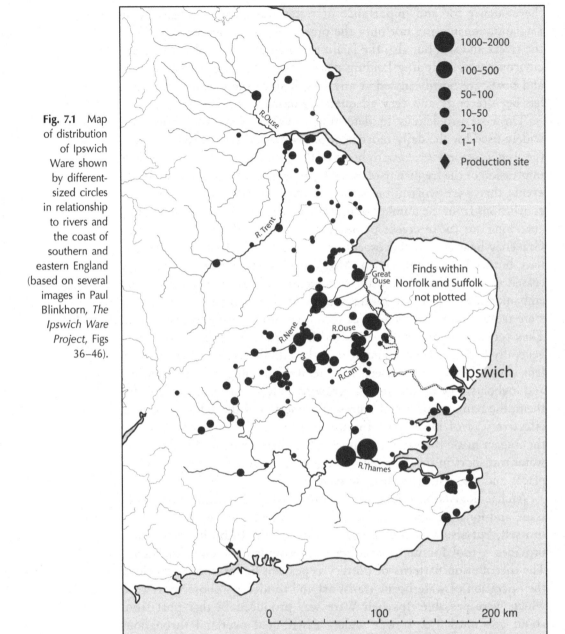

Fig. 7.1 Map of distribution of Ipswich Ware shown by different-sized circles in relationship to rivers and the coast of southern and eastern England (based on several images in Paul Blinkhorn, *The Ipswich Ware Project*, Figs 36–46).

are significant: it generally occurs at major trading centres, lordly settlements, ecclesiastical centres and some rural sites which seem to be involved in specialized agricultural production. At such places Ipswich Ware may be found alongside imported continental pottery and Mayen lava millstones originating in the Eifel region of Germany, suggesting it was one commodity amongst others being moved by water. Certainly, it is apparent from the distribution of Ipswich Ware that its movement was often by sea and river. To the south of Ipswich, the distribution is predominantly coastal, and extends up the Thames to Barking Abbey, London, and beyond. Kent shows a similar pattern of coastal and riverine sites with the addition of a small number of finds in or around Canterbury. The proximity of find-spots to rivers is equally significant, with finds in the East Midlands concentrated around the upper Thames, Trent, Nene, Great Ouse and Cam. Only in Lincolnshire is the distribution less firmly governed by the proximity of waterways, and, there, movement along Roman roads may also have been important.[8]

The distribution of another pottery type, Torksey Ware, provides a similar insight for the later Anglo-Saxon period. This was produced from the late ninth to mid-eleventh centuries at a site near the junction between the River Trent and Foss Dyke. It is not surprising that the pottery seems to have moved up and down the Trent, but it was also carried along the Roman canal, Foss Dyke, which seems to have remained passable into the medieval period, as far as Lincoln, which was a major market for the ware. From there it travelled on down the Witham towards the Wash. It was distributed along the south bank of the Humber and up the Ouse to York. Again, it seems apparent that land transport was important over shorter distances in moving the pottery from the source to consumers in Lincolnshire.[9] But, at the end of the Anglo-Saxon period, water transport seems to become less important in the movement of pottery as the number of local production centres increased. An earlier suggestion that the shelly wares found in London were produced in Oxford and shipped down the Thames has had to be revised; it is now clear that there were a number of kilns in the Home Counties, and possibly in London itself, producing a similar product.[10]

The complexity of using archaeological finds to trace patterns in the movement of goods is also evident from the distribution of Mayen lava quernstone (see Chapter 9 of this volume for related discussion). This stone was exported to England from Germany in partially finished 'blanks' which were then completed by craftsmen in urban centres. Unfinished querns have been found on Middle Saxon sites in Ipswich and on a late tenth-century site in London. The movement beyond these centres is more complex, as studies of two areas have demonstrated. The limited number of finds in Kent shows a strongly coastal distribution, but the pattern in Yorkshire does not appear to be dependent on water for the transport of millstones. Mayen querns are found, for example, at Cottom on the Yorkshire Wolds well away from major rivers. It is hardly surprising that Cottom otherwise has little material traded over a long distance.[11]

These examples suggest that while goods might be carried by water in the Anglo-Saxon period, overland transport was also used. The distance from waterways did not prevent the distribution of such fragile items as pottery or such bulky items as millstones. As in the later medieval period, millstones were probably moved as far as convenient by water and then put on a cart to complete the journey to the mill.[12] Inland rivers and coastal transport were just one of the means used in the early Middle Ages, but there is no evidence that people or goods had to rely exclusively upon water transport, unless travelling overseas.

The conditions of rivers

A critical factor in interpreting water transport is to determine how far rivers in the Anglo-Saxon period resemble those we now find in lowland England. Would the rivers have been as deep or deeper than current watercourses and have had a similar speed of flow? Studies of the archaeology and geomorphology of floodplains have shown the complexity of these questions. Local factors had a considerable influence on the conditions of specific lengths of river and the timing of changes. For example, the very detailed examination of the Trent at Hemington and Colwick has shown that the bridge just above the confluence with the Derwent was constructed over channels of unstable shallow sand and gravel, but this was not typical of the middle courses of most lowland rivers.[13] They were generally of two types: a stable, single-channel form and anastomosing rivers. The latter term is used for watercourses with an unstable pattern of numerous branching channels. While rivers with anastomosing forms persisted well after the Anglo-Saxon period, particularly in the lower reaches, there was a tendency for increasing sedimentation, which has been recorded in numerous river valleys in the later first millennium AD, to lead to the development of single, deeper river channels.[14]

The effects of these changes on river transport have barely been considered. The branched channels found on both the middle and lower courses of anastomosing rivers would have presented considerable problems for navigation. The dispersed nature of the water flow would have made individual channels shallow, and it would have required experienced navigators to pick their way through the network of watercourses. However, the development of a stable bed and aggrading bank form with a single channel river course would have favoured the passage of boats. On some rivers this happened with the increased supplies of sediment introduced by intensive Iron Age and Roman farming, but the decline in cereal cultivation after AD 400 reduced alluviation. It was not until towards the end of the first millennium that expanded agriculture again led to an increase in valley sedimentation and the trend towards single channel rivers resumed.[15]

English rivers, therefore, varied in their suitability for navigation in the Anglo-Saxon period. While some would have been similar to the present with a single, well-defined channel set between natural levees and very suitable for the passage of boats, others would have had stretches of shallows and divided channels. Fallen trees and obstructions from driftwood may also have presented problems. The suggestion by Ann Cole that the inhabitants of settlements with the name *ēa-tūn*, the 'river settlement' (Eaton, Eton and so on) might have been specifically charged with the duty of keeping certain stretches of river open seems overly conjectural.[16] It is not clear who would have compelled this activity, nor how it could have been managed. Not until the later tenth century do we begin to see work to improve inland waterways.

Canals

The growing appreciation that canals were constructed in late Anglo-Saxon England has necessitated a reappraisal of the use of inland waterways. The construction of canals suggests that there was a demand for improvements from boatmen already travelling along rivers. The best-documented example is the artificial channel constructed above Thrupp, Oxfordshire, on the River Thames. The twelfth-century chronicle of Abingdon Abbey records that in the time of Abbot Orderic (1052–66) the citizens of Oxford petitioned for a channel to be constructed to the south of the Thames because the river at that point was particularly shallow and caused problems for the passage of boats. In return for this, it was agreed that a toll of one hundred herrings should be paid by each passing vessel.[17] The course of this canal, which measures 1.8 kilometres, has been identified by John Blair and still survives as a stream. Whether the canal was constructed by the monks or the townspeople is not clear, but its purpose was: it was intended to make passage up and down the Thames easier. The payment of herring must surely imply that this was one of the cargoes being brought upstream for sale in Oxford.[18] Similar improvements also took place on the River Itchen, where a new cutting was made early in the eleventh century from close to the tidal limit to allow boats to pass as far as Bishopstoke. The canal enabled goods to move upstream in the direction of Winchester, though it is improbable that it was possible to go by water all the way to the city.[19]

These two canals were constructed to ease the movement of goods to commercial centres; two others were constructed to enable goods to be moved to monasteries. The artificial channel known as Cnut's Dyke extends for 16 kilometres to the south-east of Peterborough. It has been suggested that the canal was constructed in connection with the foundation of Ramsey Abbey in the later tenth century.[20] However, the Tudor historian William Camden has another explanation for its building. He reports a tale that the servants of King Cnut were passing over Whittlesey Mere in the Fens when a storm arose and imperilled their lives. In order to ensure such a thing should not happen again, Cnut is said to have laid out a canal which consequently was called Cnut's Delf or *Swerdesdelf*.[21] While the details of the account may be fanciful, the connection with Cnut and his ealdorman Siward is curious and may have some historical veracity. In that case, the canal would date from the 1020s or 1030s and might be connected with a later building phase at the abbey. The other monastic canal was also constructed in a marshland location. A channel 1.6 kilometres long was dug from the River Brue in the Somerset Levels along the north edge of Wearyall Hill to end near St Benedict's Church in Glastonbury. The foundation of that church appears to be mentioned in an account of the translation of the remains of St Benignus by boat in 1091. The church was constructed at the place at which the body was rested when it arrived from the boat and was originally dedicated to that saint.[22] The account suggests that the canal was already in use by the end of the eleventh century, and this is confirmed by radiocarbon dates from oak stakes from the edge of the watercourse.[23]

These four canals by no means exhaust the channels which have been attributed to the late Anglo-Saxon period, but other examples are less certain. The late tenth- and eleventh-century dates for these canals seem to reflect the start of a period of waterway improvement which continued into the twelfth century and beyond. This is in contrast to the very limited evidence for earlier canal-building and suggests that construction was a response to an increasing level of commercialization and the need to move goods.[24]

Bridges and causeways

In the early Middle Ages, the term 'bridge' (OE *brycg* and its Latin equivalent, *pons*) referred not only to a bridge in the modern sense, but also to a causeway across wetlands. Such a causeway may have led, not to a dry crossing over a river, but to a ford or ferry, and yet would have been described in sources as a 'bridge'. This creates a problem which has scarcely been acknowledged by historians: we simply do not know how many bridges in the modern sense there were in early medieval England, and how often these were simply causeways and fords.[25] The duty of bridge work recorded from at least the eighth century may have been an obligation to maintain causeways rather than construct a span over a river.[26] The construction of even a timber structure over a watercourse is likely to have been beyond the capabilities of most peasants, but building a causeway was a simpler operation and a reasonable demand on labour.

There is a good argument that there were very few real bridges before the tenth century (see Chapter 9 of this volume).[27] The Thames between Southwark and London, admittedly a major engineering challenge, does not seem to have been spanned by London Bridge before the beginning of the eleventh century. The Severn at Gloucester may have been crossed only by a causeway in the late eleventh century.[28] The situation at Oxford, where there has been extensive excavation, is more complex. A causeway was established in the ninth century to provide access from the south, and a timber bridge was constructed over at least one of the river channels. A ford was constructed in the tenth century. Whether this supplemented the earlier bridge or replaced it is uncertain. It is not until the late eleventh century that a causeway with stone flood arches and a stone bridge was built.[29] Further down the Thames, the crossing at Wallingford made by the army of William the Conqueror in 1066 is described by William of Poitiers as 'by ford and bridge', which seems contradictory unless we understand the 'bridge' to be a causeway.[30] The one detailed record we have for work on a bridge, an account of the labour services for repairing the crossing at Rochester, also suggests that Anglo-Saxon structures over rivers may have been uncommon. The account, which is attributed to the eleventh century, records the duties of various vills to provide three horizontal beams between the bridge piers and the planking to go on top and form the roadway. No arrangements are noted for the maintenance of the piers themselves, which seem almost certainly to have been those constructed in the Roman period and which continued to be used until the late fourteenth century.[31] The minimal work undertaken in the eleventh century on this bridge tends to reinforce the impression that the construction of structures over water was a relatively uncommon Anglo-Saxon practice.

There seem to have been few dry crossings over English rivers before the tenth century, and perhaps not many before the mid-eleventh. It is a conclusion which has implications for water transport, because bridges could create significant obstructions for river traffic. The bridge abutments hemmed in the river, and the water was channelled through relatively narrow openings between the piers. The height of the span of the bridge might constrain the vessels which could pass beneath it, so that sailing vessels could be restricted to the lengths of river downstream from the lowest bridge unless the mast could be lowered and the ship rowed through. For example, the bridge at Bramber, West Sussex, impeded ships from passing up the River Adur in 1103, which they had done before the Conquest.[32] However, if there were few bridges in the Anglo-Saxon period, it would have been easier for vessels to pass upstream without the need to transfer goods from seagoing ships to river boats.

Landing places and waterfronts

The study of early medieval ports in the past has been very closely linked with the examination of the trading centres or *emporia*, the quasi-urban centres dating from the late seventh to mid-ninth century.[33] In more recent years, it has become clear that there was a greater variety of trading sites and a greater diversity of landing places than had been supposed. Bawsey, Burnham and West Walton in Norfolk have been identified as commercial centres on the evidence of the quantities of coins and other metalwork found there, and limited excavations at the latter produced one sherd of North French Blackware and one of Tating Ware,[34] but not at possible landing places. It may have been the presence of a place of trade rather than the conditions on the coast which determined the location of landing sites, as many places were suitable for beaching boats.[35] Concentrations of coins and imported pottery may provide the best indicator of early landing places, but some are also mentioned in written sources. For example, Aldhelm's poem, *Carmen rhythmicum*, written around the start of the eighth century, seems to make allusion to a port at Lyme, Dorset.[36] By the eleventh century, when there is a much greater abundance of written sources and commercial trade was flourishing, it is possible to identify a significant number of landing places along the coast of south-east England.[37]

Many potential landing sites required little preparation for the arrival of ships. Early medieval vessels were intended to be beached rather than berthed against a quayside, so a gently shelving sand or shingle foreshore was ideal.[38] Shores with some protection from wind and waves were preferable to more exposed lengths of coast. Landing places on muddy foreshores required some work to ensure that ships did not get stuck. Branches had been placed beneath the tenth-century Graveney Boat, which had been run up into a creek.[39] Given the rudimentary character of such sites, it is not surprising that few Anglo-Saxon ports have been identified in excavations, though from the eleventh century onwards there is evidence for increasing investment in harbours. The earliest waterfront at New Fresh Wharf in London dating to around AD 1000 was formed by a spread of stone rubble up to one metre thick lying on the shore, with some branches to prevent the hulls of boats rubbing against the hard-standing. Boats could be beached on the rubble parallel to the shore and loaded and unloaded at low tide. In addition, a timber jetty was constructed beyond the end of the rubble to allow goods to be transferred to and from boats moored at the edge of the Thames.[40] A similar hard-standing formed of flint gravel was found at Lewes, Sussex, extending parallel to the River Ouse below the causeway across the river valley (Figure 7.2).[41] A further example was found on the River Kennet at Reading Abbey, where the banks were surfaced with stone.[42] More substantial works were proposed for an intended harbour to be established near Sandwich, Kent, a place which in the middle of the eleventh century was described as *omnium Anglorum portuum famosissimus* 'the most well-known of all the ports of the English'.[43] Around 1025 to 1040, Abbot Ælfstan planned to build a 'wharf' to protect a landing place at Stonor on the opposite side of the Wantsum Channel 'against the raging tide'.[44] The term 'wharf' seems to have been used, not to indicate a quay, but to describe a breakwater protecting the landing site, suggesting a growing appreciation of the worth of investment in harbour infrastructure.[45]

There was a gradual shift during the tenth and eleventh centuries from unestablished landing places to sites marked by some form of structure. Before the mid-tenth century, the term *hȳð* 'hythe' is rarely recorded in place names or in charter bounds, but it occurs with increasing frequency thereafter, though this must be set within the general context of the growth in documentary records from that time. A 'hythe' simply means a landing place, but its use in place names suggests it was not applied to any site at which boats landed, but to specific locations, probably with a wharf or other facilities. A grant of ten hides at Yaxley and Farcet made in 956 mentions a notable number of landing places amongst the bounds – *dichȳthe, norðhȳthe, suðhȳthe* and *færresheafde hȳthe* – which must reflect the importance that water transport had in the Fens.[46] Hythes are also mentioned at Stoke by Ipswich and at *Rameslie* (probably to be identified with Rye, Sussex), the latter described in an earlier charter as a *portus* 'port', again suggesting perhaps more than just a place at which ships might be pulled up.[47] The distribution of early *hȳð* names is quite distinctive, with concentrations not only in the Fens, but also along the Thames and the lower part of the River Trent. This may suggest areas where riverine landing places were particularly important.[48]

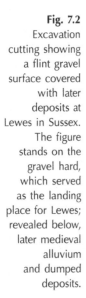

Fig. 7.2
Excavation cutting showing a flint gravel surface covered with later deposits at Lewes in Sussex. The figure stands on the gravel hard, which served as the landing place for Lewes; revealed below, later medieval alluvium and dumped deposits.

There were similar minor landing places around the English coast. These served, amongst others, the crews of fishing vessels which followed the migrating shoals of herring moving down the East Coast between August and November each year.[49] Most of the evidence for the herring fleets is later, but there is sufficient indication in Domesday Book to show that the fishery already formed an important part of the economy of many coastal communities. For example, according to Domesday Book, the 'king's peace' was proclaimed in Dover while the crews were away between 29 September and 30 November. The start date implies that the Dover ships travelled up as far as the coast of southern Lincolnshire or Norfolk, the point reached by the herring shoals by the end of September. Certainly, ships from Hastings were sailing as far north as Saltfleet in Lincolnshire, where they put ashore and were charged tolls.[50] A considerable number of vills along the Norfolk, Suffolk, Kent and Sussex coast also paid renders of herring in the late eleventh century, which implies that fishing vessels were based not only in the larger ports, but in many coastal settlements.[51] Many must have been simply hauled up on to beaches or moored in creeks, and they may not have ventured as far in pursuit of their catch as the Dover and Hastings ships.

Such minor sites should be clearly distinguished from the major coastal and estuarine ports which were visited by foreign merchants and which operated under special rules. Arrangements were made at such ports to tax goods brought from abroad and to allow the king to purchase them at preferential rates. In London a distinction was made in the ninth century between those goods offered for sale in the area of the port, that is south of Thames Street and subject to the right of royal pre-emption, and those sold in the city to the north.[52] Foreign merchants in the thirteenth century and possibly as early as the eleventh century were permitted to stay for no more than forty days.[53] They had to lodge with Londoners who took responsibility for their behaviour, an arrangement known as 'hosting', which seems to have had its origins in the seventh century. In return for this duty, the English hosts had the right to buy a proportion of the merchants' goods before they were offered for general sale.[54] Similar rules may well have applied in other ports, but the evidence is largely later in date. Such strict regulations emphasize that foreign trade had a particular financial and even diplomatic importance.[55]

Sea travel and belief

In many cultures, there was a sharp divide between the terrestrial and maritime worlds, both in systems of behaviour and belief. The attitudes of seafarers are sometimes dismissed as superstitious, but can more constructively be regarded as a representing a shifted cultural perspective.[56] Sailors occupied a perilous environment which was peripheral to the experience of most of their contemporaries, and they sought to make sense of it in terms of a series of beliefs. If we can draw conclusions from the cautious comments of the fisherman in Ælfric's *Colloquy*, it is that there was an awareness of the very considerable risks of venturing out to sea.[57]

While it is almost impossible to recover any of the folk beliefs of Anglo-Saxon seafarers, we can make a start in understanding their religious perspective by looking at their relationship with churches. Coastal churches served both as sea-marks by which sailors could locate themselves and as places of worship when they came to land. In Scandinavia, the use of religious monuments as sea-marks has been noted: Late Iron Age burial cairns may have served this purpose, and stone crosses certainly did after Christianization.[58] In Anglo-Saxon England, sea-marks acted various purposes. Gillian Hutchinson has argued that the church at Bosham, Sussex, served as a sea-mark to guide ships to the landing place. It lies directly at the head of the navigable channel in Bosham Creek, a port used in the eleventh century.[59] Further along the coast, the eleventh-century church of St Mary-in-the-Castle was built on the hill overlooking Dover, immediately next to the Roman lighthouse. The church had a first-floor gallery at the west end which apparently provided a link to a now-blocked door in the lighthouse.[60] The construction of the church effectively Christianized an existing sea-mark. Another coastal church which served as a sea-mark was the seventh-century building at Reculver. The ruins of the church and its added Norman towers were purchased in 1809 by Trinity Board to ensure it might continue to act as a mark for ships in the Thames estuary, but its function in the Anglo-Saxon period was rather different. It then stood in the ruins of a Roman fort on the west side of the entrance to the Wantsum Channel and marked the beginning of the route from the Thames estuary to the English Channel, avoiding North Foreland.[61] Churches such as these also served for sailors staying on land, and if there was no church at a landing site frequented by them, seafarers often constructed a chapel. Such a chapel was built on the shore at Great Yarmouth in the early twelfth century to serve the fishermen who came there, according to an early fourteenth-century record. There was also a chapel for sailors at Ringmore, Devon, on the Teign estuary, dedicated appropriately to the patron saint of seafarers, St Nicholas. It dates to the twelfth century or before.[62]

Conclusion

The evidence does not exist to support the confident assertion cited at the opening of this chapter that water transport was *the* major means of communication in Anglo-Saxon England. However, it has been possible to begin to define the circumstances in which river and sea transport played an important role. There is good evidence for the use of water transport on major rivers, such as the Thames and Trent, and also on the larger marshes, such as the Fens and the Somerset Levels, where 'hythe' place names were common and canals were constructed. These waterways were used for the transport of goods, both for long-distance trade and perhaps also for the daily movement of people, some livestock and produce.[63] Coastal communities, too, may have made wider use of water transport since they had access to boats for fishing and perhaps for trade. The later tenth and the eleventh centuries have emerged in the discussion as a crucial period in the development of water transport. The first post-Roman canals were constructed, the number of 'hythe' place names increased and a growing number of sea ports were recorded from this period onwards. The deepening commercialization of England created a greater need for transport, which was met in part by moving goods by water.

The construction of a boat, even a logboat, represented a considerable investment of time and was not therefore something that people did unless there was an evident need.[64] The knowledge of how to handle a boat may have been no more common than at present, and travelling by water was always risky in a society where swimming was not a common skill.[65] There is, however, one strand of evidence which might suggest that knowledge of boats was rather more widespread. From the early eleventh century, the large ecclesiastical estates had their lands divided into areas known as shipsokes, each of which had to supply a ship, a crew and the equipment for them. This meant that of necessity some of the vessels came from inland areas of the country, such as the bishop of Worcester's soke of Oswaldslow.[66] It also raises the question where the ships were normally kept – was the Oswaldslow ship normally moored on the upper Severn? How did the crew acquire training, without which they would have been more a hindrance than a benefit? The places providing seamen for a ship of St Paul's in London were situated mostly near to the coast or the Thames, and it is conceivable that they might have sent those who had worked as sailors. An alternative interpretation is that those vills might have merely paid such money as was necessary to support experienced sailors to serve in St Paul's ship.[67] Yet shipsoke cannot have been just a fiscal matter. Eadric the steersman (or captain) of the bishop of Worcester's vessel was also a tenant of the bishop, suggesting that the link between the shipsoke and the ship also involved personnel.[68] The operation of shipsoke seems to imply that an experience of boats was more extensive than we have assumed.

It is perhaps inevitable that the subject of water transport remains somewhat obscure. Although the sea is used as a common metaphor in Old English literature, it remains a symbolic space rather than one described in a realistic manner. It is hard even to draw any very solid conclusions about contemporary attitudes to the sea.[69] The material remains are equally difficult to pin down, and not until the end of the period can we begin to identify specific traces connected with water transport. We face the risk that we mistake the absence of evidence for the absence of the thing itself, however, and what trace should we expect from a passing boat? At the same time, the lack of remains should be given some credence. We cannot really imagine that water transport was as important as has been claimed while so little provision was made for it. Transport on inland rivers and on the seas played a small, but growing role in Anglo-Saxon England, one of considerable economic importance.

8

Watermills and Waterwheels

Martin Watts

Seo heofen belicð on hire bosme ealne middaneard, 7 heo æfre tyrnð onbuton us swyftre ðonne ænig mylenhweowul, eal swa deop under þyssere eorðan swa heo is bufon. Eall heo is sinewealt 7 ansund 7 mid steorrum amett.

The heaven encompasses in its bosom the whole earth, and it turns constantly around us more swiftly than any mill-wheel, going as far below the earth as it does above. It is completely circular and entire, and adorned with stars.[1]

Introduction

The Anglo-Saxon achievement in the development of water-power to drive millstones for grinding grain is underlined by references to over 6,000 mills in England at the time of the Domesday survey of 1086, the majority of which must have been established by or during the late Anglo-Saxon period. Following an overview of previous research on Anglo-Saxon mills and the lack of evidence for a Roman legacy, I will review the documentary and archaeological evidence for watermills in the Anglo-Saxon period. I will also discuss the provision and control of a manageable water supply, using fresh or salt water, waterwheels and the mill buildings themselves and finally consider the relationship between watermills and those who built and ran them.

The research background

In their comprehensive history of grain milling written at the end of the nineteenth century, Richard Bennett and John Elton found no evidence to support the theory that the Romans introduced the watermill into

England, suggesting that it reached Britain 'in due course' and 'was extensively adopted throughout the kingdom by the Saxons: displacing its early forerunner, the Norse mill, except in the more distant and secluded parts of the country'.[2] Within a decade of this statement, the archaeologist F. Gerald Simpson excavated a Roman building at Haltwhistle Burn Head, just south of Hadrian's Wall in Northumberland, which he interpreted as a watermill dating from the third century AD.[3] A small number of Roman watermill sites have subsequently been identified in Britain, all of which had vertical waterwheels.[4] Further evidence of the widespread distribution of Roman watermills is suggested by finds of milling stones that are considered too large to have been querns, small diameter millstones turned by hand.[5] These sites and finds span the period between the second and fifth centuries AD. There is currently a lack of firm evidence for continuity in the use of water-power in Britain in the post-Roman period, although the possibility of a 'continuance of tradition' in water milling has been mooted at Ickham, Kent.[6] Richard Holt has suggested that the economic, political and social upheaval that occurred in Britain after the Roman withdrawal was greater than in mainland Europe, which may have made survival of watermills less likely, but if there was no continuity of use of the watermill from the Roman period, then it was fairly quickly re-established.[7] In Ireland, early medieval law tracts dealing with the construction, ownership and water rights of mills, as well as archaeological finds, indicate that watermills were established features of the landscape there by the early seventh century.[8] In England, the earliest archaeological evidence for Anglo-Saxon watermills dates from the late seventh century, and the first documentary references are found in eighth-century charters. By the time of the Domesday survey in 1086, there were over 6,000 mills established on English manors, on average one to every 40 households.[9] The use of water-power and the mechanization of grain milling may perhaps be regarded as useful indicators of increasing stability and settlement.

Concerning Anglo-Saxon mills, little collective research has been published, partly due to the paucity of evidence; the first physical remains of a mill were not discovered until the 1950s. H.P.R. Finberg briefly summarized some of the evidence from England and mainland Europe in 1972, referring to watermills as 'one important feature of the agrarian landscape'.[10] There is also a short section on milling in David Wilson's *Archaeology of Anglo-Saxon England* published in 1976.[11] Following up on his excavation at Tamworth in 1971, Philip Rahtz collaborated with Donald Bullough to provide the first comprehensive overview of the evidence for Anglo-Saxon mills in a joint article published in 1977.[12]

Rahtz also summarized his thoughts on milling in the early and later medieval periods in a volume on medieval industry.[13] David Hill's map, published in 1981, brought together evidence from charters, place names and archaeological excavations to show a total of 52 sites.[14] Richard Holt briefly discussed the documentary and archaeological evidence in 1988,[15] and, more recently, Ann Hagen produced a useful overview of milling, based on information compiled from a variety of sources, as part of a study of Anglo-Saxon food.[16] By far the largest and most informative corpus of material on early medieval mills, however, comes from Ireland, where the remains have been found of over 150 mills dating back to the early seventh century, which used both horizontal and vertical waterwheels, sometimes on the same site. The work of Colin Rynne and others provides an important yardstick against which the English evidence needs to be assessed.[17]

A note on terminology

The terms 'vertical' and 'horizontal' are used to describe the two principal types of waterwheel used in the Anglo-Saxon period (Figure 8.1). 'Mill', or 'watermill', describes the building and its working parts, including the millstones for grinding grain. The terms 'Vitruvian', for a vertical-wheeled mill with a single pair of millstones driven through a pair of gears, and 'Norse', for a mill with a horizontal waterwheel, which have frequently been used in the recent past, are deliberately avoided, as neither can now be considered accurate or appropriate.[18]

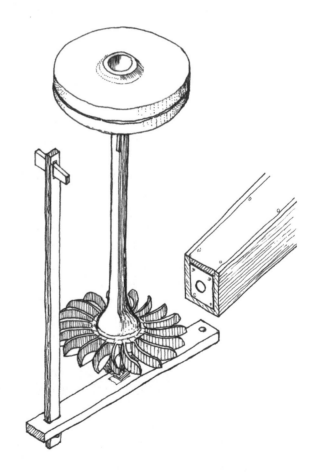

Fig. 8.1a Reconstruction drawing of a horizontal waterwheel driving a pair of millstones (drawn by Martin Watts).

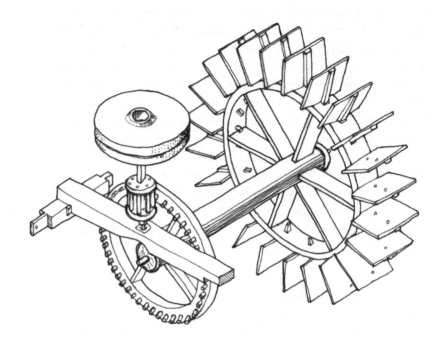

Fig. 8.1b
Reconstruction drawing of a vertical undershot waterwheel driving a pair of millstones (drawn by Martin Watts).

Documentary evidence

Recent research by the writer has identified over 90 pre-Conquest references to mill locations in charters and other documentary sources, either directly or by implication through place and river or stream names. The earliest definitive reference to a mill in England, cited by Bennett and Elton and referred to by many subsequent writers, is from the year AD 762.[19] This is in a charter by which Æthelbert II, king of Kent, confirmed an arrangement whereby the monastery of St Peter and St Paul, Canterbury, exchanged half a mill at Chart for swine pasture in the Weald of Kent.[20] Susan Kelly has suggested the mill was located at Ripton, about four miles from the Anglo-Saxon royal estate centre at Wye.[21] In the eleventh century, Domesday Book records that St Augustine's held a manor there with a quarter of a mill, the only mill fraction held by them at that time. It is perhaps significant that this early reference should refer to half a mill, an aspect of mill ownership considered further below.

Two earlier eighth-century charters suggest the presence of mills, but one is of doubtful authenticity and the other is lost. The first refers to a *mylen weg* at Notgrove, Gloucestershire, reputedly dated 737 to 740; the same mill appears to be referred to as *þaere ealden mylne* in a 963 charter of Harford.[22] The second is a reference in a lost charter of 740 to 756 to *Muleburnam*, possibly identified as Whitwell on the Isle of Wight, part of a large land endowment by Cuthred, king of the West Saxons, to the Church of Winchester.[23]

The number of documentary references to mills increases during the ninth and tenth centuries. Over 30 charters refer to water-related features connected with mills. Examples are *Melebroc*, 'Millbrook', near Southampton (AD 956; 1045); *mylenburnan*, 'mill-burn/bourne', at Bradford Abbas, Dorset (933), one of several West Country instances of that name; *mylendic*, 'mill-dyke', at Hardenhuish, Wiltshire (854), and *myle streame* at Uffington, Berkshire (c.931).[24] The terms 'brook', 'burn/bourne' and 'stream' may refer to natural features that were made use of, perhaps with minor adaptation, to drive waterwheels, while mill-dyke seems more likely to refer to an artificial channel or leat. These terms are discussed in more detail by Della Hooke in Chapter 2.

There were mill fords near Staunton on Arrow, Herefordshire, and Sherburn in Elmet in Yorkshire in the mid-ninth century, and an intriguing *hweoulforda*, 'wheel ford', at Abbots Wootton, Dorset, in 1044.[25] The reference to *mylen fleotes*, 'mill fleet', at Reculver on the Kent coast in 949[26] is considered significant in terms of salt water being used to drive waterwheels, as evidenced by the early eighth-century tide mill excavated at Northfleet in north Kent, which is discussed below. Mill pools are referred to in Gloucestershire in two ninth-century charters, the first in the bounds of Withington and the second in those of a property at Stoke Bishop which was surrendered by the monastic community at Berkeley in exchange for exemption from supplying food-rents to the king. The site of a triangular pond is still recognizable in the modern suburbs of Bristol on the River Trym, upstream from Millpill Bridge.[27] The presence of a weir, to raise the water level and provide a take-off point for an artificial channel – a leat or ditch – along which water was conveyed to a mill site, is instanced at least six times from the early tenth century onwards.[28] Finally, a *myle wylle*, 'mill spring', occurs at Bishops Cleeve, Gloucestershire, in a boundary clause added to a late eighth-century grant.[29]

These water-related features form the most dominant group in the charter evidence, the remainder being comprised of locative and personal names, as well as the simple term *myln*, which occurs in both charters and place names from about the mid-tenth century. An example is Mells, Somerset, *Milne* in 942, the mill there perhaps belonging to the monastic settlement at Frome.[30] The association of mills with other settlement elements is apparent in the eighth-century name of *Mylentun*, near Kemsing, Kent, and *Mulecote*, Milcote in Warwickshire, which appears in a spurious charter of 710 and cannot be confirmed as a place name before the third quarter of the tenth century.[31] The term *mylensteall* occurs in four charters, one from the ninth and three from the tenth century; if interpreted as the site for a mill rather than an extant mill, then, as Della Hooke has suggested, these charters may indicate the provision of suitable sites for building mills.[32] The *mylenstede*, 'mill stead' referred to at Padworth, Berkshire, in 956, also indicates the site of a mill, but whether a mill was already standing there is unclear.[33]

Archaeological evidence

Until the excavation of the foundation timbers of two phases of a horizontal-wheeled watermill at Tamworth, Staffordshire, in 1971, the only physical evidence for an Anglo-Saxon watermill that had ever been identified was the enigmatic structure interpreted as a 'large and sophisticated mill, with three vertical water-wheels' found at Kingsbury, Old Windsor, Berkshire, in 1955.[34] The number of sites identified by archaeological excavation has, however, increased significantly in recent decades to nine, and paddles from horizontal waterwheels, described below, have been found at two further sites, although neither has been precisely dated. Watercourses or water control features that are considered to be of Anglo-Saxon origin have also been excavated or identified at a number of locations.[35]

The site of a probable royal residence at Kingsbury, which was occupied three or four centuries before the Norman Conquest, was partially excavated in the 1950s by Brian Hope-Taylor, under the auspices of the then Ministry of Works. An initial interpretation of the timber structure found at the base of a large artificial channel which took water from the River Thames, was that it was a bridge. The channel, referred to as a 'great ditch or leat' was over 1 kilometre in length and at the mill site about 5.3 metres wide, its flat bed being about 1.8 metres below the modern ground surface. The mill evidence is based largely on horizontal oak cill beams set across the base of the channel, three of which survived *in situ*, with some remains of and mortises for vertical posts. Hope-Taylor considered this to be an 'outstanding structure', which he interpreted as a 'large and sophisticated mill, with three vertical water-wheels ... working in parallel'.[36] Preliminary dating put the structure as ninth-century, and evidence from the remains of other buildings nearby suggested it had been destroyed by fire in the late ninth or early tenth century. Subsequent dendrochronological analysis indicated that the base timbers had been felled in the late seventh century. Deposits overlying these timbers suggest that the mill was out of use by the early to mid-ninth century. A narrow channel cut into the filling of the

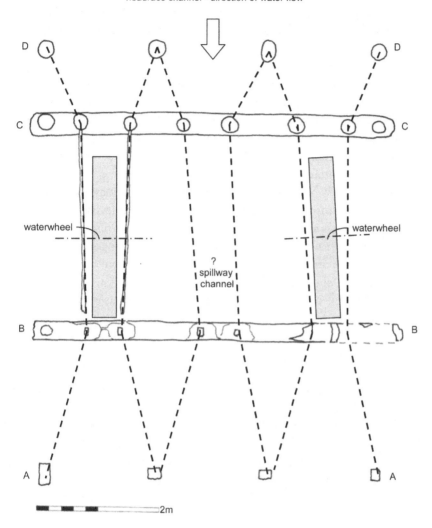

Fig. 8.2 Diagrammatic plan showing possible layout of two vertical waterwheels with a central spillway at Kingsbury, Old Windsor, Berkshire, based on the positions of the four cross timbers (A–D) excavated by Brian Hope-Taylor in 1955.

earlier leat was interpreted as having been made 'to feed the horizontal water-wheel of a mill of the so-called "Norse" type'.[37]

Recent analysis by Brian Durham and the writer based on the site plans and sections drawn during the excavation suggests, however, that there were probably only two vertical waterwheels in parallel, each serving a mill building on opposite sides of the watercourse (Figures 8.2 and 8.6).[38] The positions of the wheels, within timber-framed structures with headraces funnelled into them and tail-water channels splaying out below them, reflect early medieval undershot waterwheel technology known from other sites.[39] The wheels would have worked off a relatively low head, but with a plentiful water supply, considering the size of the watercourse. Water would have been let onto the wheels by raising sluice gates on the upstream side. The third, central channel is unlikely to have housed a waterwheel, as there would be no method of taking power from its horizontal shaft if it was placed between the two outer wheels. It is more likely that this channel acted as a spillway, with a sluice at its upstream end for controlling the water level and flow. No evidence of other water control features was found within the area excavated. The smaller, later ditch, cut into the west side of the silted-up channel, which was itself filled in the eleventh century, does not appear to have been a leat, and there is no evidence to suggest that it served a horizontal waterwheel. Similarly, there is no evidence of the size or extent of the mill buildings. While the scale of the installation may have appeared unusual in the 1950s, there were then no comparable finds to gauge it against. The mills at Old Windsor may have formed an impressive group in the eighth century, but their scale does not appear to be exceptional.

When a site in Bolebridge Street, Tamworth, on the edge of the defences at the south-east corner of the Saxon *burh*, was excavated by Philip Rahtz in 1971, the base timbers of two phases of horizontal-wheeled watermill were found.[40] Originally dated by radiocarbon to the eighth century, the mill was thought to have been connected with Offa's royal palace; timbers from the mill and millpond were subsequently dated by dendrochronology to the mid-ninth century, however. Two phases of construction were identified, the later, mid-ninth-century mill overlying the earlier, with the possibility that some of the timbers from the first mill were reused. Close above the mill site, a contemporary timber structure was identified as the end of the mill pond or pool. The interpretation of the second phase Tamworth mill, for which the evidence was clearer and better preserved than the first, was a single horizontal waterwheel fed by an inclined timber trough, which had not survived.

A second trough position implied by a cut-out in the rear cill beam was interpreted as a spillway (Figure 8.3, right). By comparison with contemporary examples of horizontal-wheeled mills found in Ireland, however, there can be little doubt that the Tamworth mill had two wheels, each fed by its own trough, and the large number of millstone fragments (over 200 pieces from a possible 26 millstones) appears to confirm this. Two other significant finds were a single paddle, its shape confirming that it was from a horizontal wheel, and a steel bearing worn on both sides which would have been the basal or foot bearing of the waterwheel and shaft assembly. This is the only example in steel that has been found, such bearings usually being of stone.[41] There have been several reconstructions of the Tamworth mill, both on paper and in model form, which vary considerably in their interpretation. Reconstructions of the

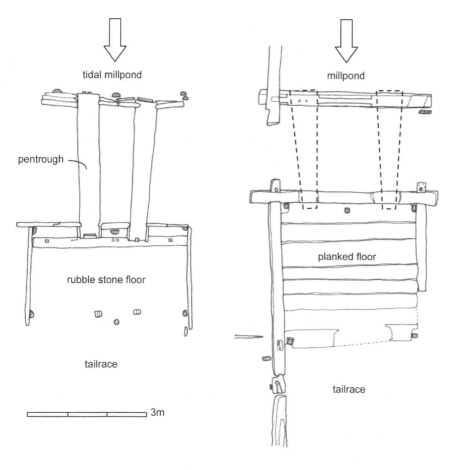

tidal millpond

millpond

pentrough

rubble stone floor

planked floor

tailrace

tailrace

3m

Fig. 8.3 Comparative plans of Ebbsfleet and Tamworth horizontal-wheeled mills. The undercrofts of the horizontal-wheeled mills at Ebbsfleet, Northfleet, Kent, late seventh century (left), show the two pentroughs found in position, and the second phase mill at Tamworth, Staffordshire, mid-ninth century (right). The probable positions of the two pentroughs at Tamworth are indicated by the broken lines (Northfleet plan courtesy of Oxford Archaeology; Tamworth after Rahtz and Meeson, *An Anglo-Saxon Watermill at Tamworth*, Fig. 31).

waterwheel generally show it as having 12 paddles, but, again, based on finds from early medieval Ireland, it is likely that there were more than this, the Irish examples usually having upwards of 19.[42] The mill appears to have been destroyed by fire in the late ninth or early tenth century. Its location just outside the boundary of the *burh* and away from the earlier royal centre make its exact relationship to that site uncertain.

At both Old Windsor and Tamworth, the initial identification of the finds was not clear cut, and Brian Hope-Taylor and Philip Rahtz are to be applauded for realizing that they had found the remains of Anglo-Saxon watermills. The importance of Tamworth as the first horizontal-wheeled mill to be identified in England should not be underestimated. However, the feasible reinterpretations of Old Windsor as having had only two vertical waterwheels and Tamworth as a double horizontal-wheeled mill suggest that some of the interpretations that have been put forward for more recent excavations need to be critically re-examined in the light of present knowledge.

Two long-term projects on deserted settlement sites, at Wharram Percy, North Yorkshire, and West Cotton, Raunds, Northamptonshire, have produced evidence of watermills from the later Anglo-Saxon period.[43] The dam site to the south of the main settlement areas at Wharram Percy was investigated in 1982, but the evidence for a watermill was hardly conclusive, other than a large quantity of quern fragments which suggested that some milling activity had taken place there. Crop-processing waste dumps had been incorporated into the earliest dam in the ninth or early tenth centuries. An analysis of the configuration of the pond suggested that regulation of water pressure onto a waterwheel was perhaps more important than the creation of a large reservoir,[44] which further suggested that the mill, of which little evidence survived, probably had a horizontal waterwheel fed by an inclined timber trough.[45]

At West Cotton, three phases of watermills were identified in what was described as 'a complex stratigraphic sequence'.[46] The watermill system appeared to be part of the original establishment of the settlement in the mid-tenth century, but the structural elements of the mills, which were on slightly different alignments, were poorly preserved. Although there was evidence of eighth- or ninth-century use of an adjacent river channel, it was suggested that the first mill dated from the second half of the tenth century and was abandoned and its leat backfilled by the end of that century. The second mill was broadly ascribed to the first half of the eleventh century, both sites being dated from pottery evidence. The third mill was also dated to the eleventh century, from pottery finds and three radiocarbon dates, two of which 'both centred on the eleventh century'. It was suggested that the latter mill may have been the low-value mill recorded in Domesday Book.[47] All three mills were fed by flat-bottomed leats. The shape of the phase one waterwheel emplacement was seen to have a close parallel with an eighth-century timber structure excavated at Morett, County Laois, with a timber headrace funnelling water into a narrow timber channel which would have housed an undershot wheel, with the tailrace widening out from its downstream end (Figure 8.4).[48] The fragmentary remains of the wheel emplacement of the second mill had been disturbed by the construction of the final mill, the latter being interpreted as having had a horizontal wheel, using Tamworth as a model. However, the hydraulic system is not notably different from the earlier phases, and the plan, with a stout vertical timber on either side of the watercourse, bears a close affinity to that of a vertical-wheeled Roman watermill excavated at Fullerton in Hampshire.[49]

Two further discoveries which were identified as the remains of mills dating from the Anglo-Saxon period were made in the 1980s, at Barking,

Essex, and Worgret, near Wareham, Dorset.[50] At Barking, an excavation on part of the early Saxon abbey complex found part of a leat which had been used over many years, with several phases of woodwork dating from the early eighth to the early ninth centuries. Several piles and cleft oak planks defined the sides of a leat which appears to have funnelled inwards to feed a vertical waterwheel, similar to that inferred at Old Windsor and West Cotton. The excavation area stopped just short of the mill site.[51] At Worgret, a timber frame, rectangular in plan with its lower end open, was excavated on the route of a pipeline. At first thought to be of Roman origin, the timbers were subsequently dated by dendrochronology to the late seventh century.[52] In 2000, a frame closely comparable to that at Worgret was found in advance of gravel extraction at Wellington, near Hereford.[53] In both cases, the lack of associated features has made interpretation difficult. It was initially suggested that both structures housed vertical waterwheels, but comparison of the arrangement of the timbers with securely identified horizontal-wheeled mill structures excavated in Ireland provides an acceptably close parallel (Figure 8.5).

A timber structure on the north bank of the River Tyne near Corbridge in Northumberland, formerly thought to be the remains of a bridge or a wharf,

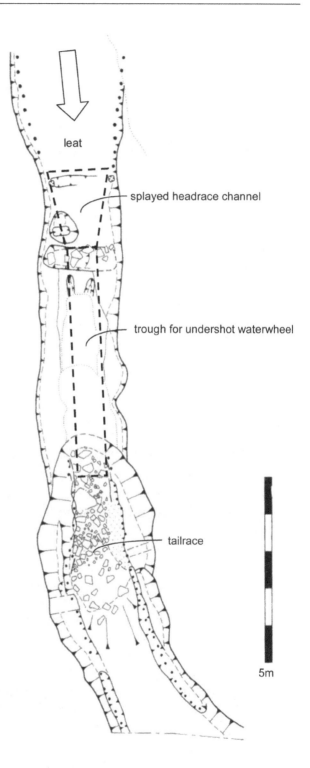

leat

splayed headrace channel

trough for undershot waterwheel

tailrace

5m

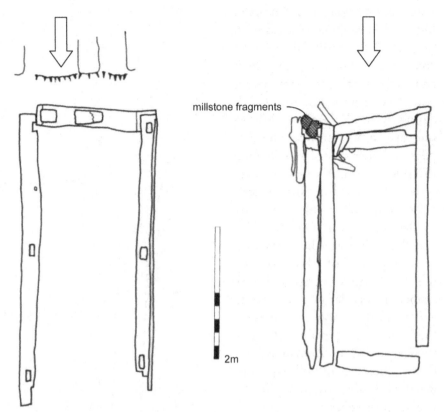

Fig. 8.5 Comparative plans of the ground frames of two late seventh- to early eighth-century, single horizontal-wheeled mills at Worgret, Dorset (left), and Wellington, Herefordshire (right). The arrows indicate the direction of the water flow (Worgret after Maynard 'Excavations on a Pipeline near the River Frome', Fig. 4; Wellington courtesy of Worcester Archaeology).

was re-assessed in the mid-1990s and is now considered to be the foundations of a late Saxon watermill.[54] The reconstruction of this mill on paper again used Tamworth as its model, although its identification as a horizontal-wheeled mill, as with the later phase mill at West Cotton, is open to debate. Its location and topography, as well as the layout of the foundations timbers, can more readily be interpreted as suitable for a vertical-wheeled mill. Although sited on the bank of a large river, the foundations may not have been on the main channel in the Anglo-Saxon period, but further away, fed by a leat system from a smaller tributary, the Cor Burn, the possible course of the leat being implied by a row of timber stakes upstream of the site.

The most recent significant archaeological find was made at Northfleet, in the Ebbsfleet valley in Kent, where the excavation of a large area with evidence of Roman and Anglo-Saxon occupation was undertaken on the route of the Channel Tunnel rail link in 2002. Two inclined oak pentroughs – enclosed timber troughs – both of which would have fed horizontal waterwheels, were found, together with the timber structure of the undercroft of the mill, which was dated by

dendrochronology to AD 692 (Figures 8.3 (left) and 8.7).[55] As well as
the pentroughs and other water control features, the remains of two
paddles from a horizontal wheel were also found. The mill was built
on the edge of a tidal estuary, on a small sandbank consolidated with
timber stakes and wattle screens, and worked by salt water which was
impounded in a pond at high tide and released through the pentroughs
when the tide had ebbed below the level of the horizontal waterwheels.
It is thought that the Northfleet mill flourished during the reign of
Wihtred (*c.*691–725), the last strong king of Kent, and was deliberately
dismantled after about 30 years or so. A short distance from the mill
site, close to where the tidal sluice gates appear to have been positioned,
a curved timber with regularly spaced mortises through it was found.
This appears to be part of a vertical waterwheel and, although not dated,
its dimensions and curvature closely resemble a similar artefact found
at the late seventh- or early eighth-century Merovingian watermill site
excavated at Dasing in Bavaria in 1993.[56]

Water supply and control

It has been suggested that mills do not require leats when sited on
larger streams or rivers, and one reason they are not built across main
channels is that they would form obstacles to access up and down the
stream.[57] Nevertheless, the creation of a controllable water supply and

Fig. 8.7
opposite
Excavation of
the late seventh-
century, double
horizontal-
wheeled tide
mill at Ebbsfleet,
Northfleet,
Kent, by
Oxford Wessex
Archaeology
in 2002. The
millpond area is
to the bottom
right, with
two inclined
pentroughs
which fed the
horizontal
wheels in the
undercroft,
centre left
(courtesy
of Oxford
Archaeology).

the construction of weirs, leats, ponds and sluices is essential to regulate both the flow and the head of water at any mill site. The need to create an artificial channel to lead water from a weir to a waterwheel, or the provision of a pond, in effect a reservoir to provide a working water supply, depends, to a certain extent, on topography and the gradient of the stream. The documentary evidence as well as that from the excavated sites indicates that all of the principal features – weirs, dams, leats and ponds – were known in or by late Anglo-Saxon times. It is also likely that some of these features which survive at extant mill sites were established during this period, even if no documentary or archaeological evidence is available to confirm this.

The late sixth-century description by Gregory of Tours of a weir created to raise the level of the water to serve a new mill at the monastery of Loches, on the Indre river in France, is the first to detail such a construction, 'by driving down a double row of poles and interlacing them, in the usual way, with wickers, commingled also by an admixture of straw and stones'.[58] Such weirs, or simpler structures made by piling stones across the flow of a stream, served to raise the water level upstream and direct the flow into an artificial channel off one end, or sometimes both ends. Building weirs for the purpose of supplying mills or for fishing could be contentious, potentially restricting access for water-borne craft. The distinction between weirs built for fishing and those built for mills is not always clear, and many probably served both needs. The duties of the reeve, set out in the tenth- or eleventh-century *Gerefa*, link them together: *Me mæig in Maio Jun Julio on sumera fealgian ... fiscwer and mylne macian* 'In May and June and July, in summer ... one may construct a fish-weir and a mill'.[59] The early summer months would also be when water levels were likely to be at their lowest.

The size of the 'great ditch or leat' at Old Windsor appears to be more than would be required for a mill, even a double one, so it may also have had a defensive function and could have been used for water transport, the importance of which for carrying building stone to high-status sites has been emphasized.[60] The engineering of such watercourses was certainly within the capabilities of the later Anglo-Saxons.[61] The Chronicle of Abingdon Abbey describes how, in about 960, Abbot Æthelwold diverted part of the Thames into a leat over 1 kilometre long to supply a new mill and cut a tailrace to rejoin the main river somewhere near St Helen's church. From this description, there seems little doubt that Æthelwold's mill stood on the same site as the present Abbey Mill.[62] Æthelwold was also responsible for reorganizing the monastic mills and their watercourses at Winchester later in the ninth century.[63]

As mentioned earlier, salt water was used as well as fresh water

supplies from rivers and streams. The horizontal waterwheels of the seventh-century mill at Northfleet were turned by water from a tidal pond, and two of the earliest Irish mill sites at Nendrum, County Down, and Little Island, Cork, both dated to the early seventh century, were also tide mills.[64]

Waterwheels

In making an analogy between the rotation of the heavens and that of a mill wheel, Ælfric, cited at the beginning of this chapter, introduces an ambiguity that is a particular dilemma with regard to the interpretation of Anglo-Saxon waterwheels. Was the waterwheel in Ælfric's mind rotating vertically or horizontally? Donald Bullough saw this metaphor as clearly relating to the rise and fall of a vertical wheel, but the heavens could also be thought of as turning around the earth like a horizontal waterwheel.[65] In either case, water droplets spinning off the paddles or floats of a turning waterwheel and catching the light could be likened to stars.

The archaeological evidence indicates that both vertical and horizontal waterwheels were used during the Anglo-Saxon period. The use of horizontal wheels has been seen by some as a symptom of technical

regression, as was implied in the interpretation of Old Windsor, but such is not the case. As Holt points out, the Irish used them by choice, sometimes alongside vertical-wheel installations, and recent research suggests that the output of millstones is closely comparable, whether they are driven by a horizontal or a vertical undershot waterwheel.[66] The physical evidence for horizontal waterwheels in England is limited, however, to a possible six paddles and one fragment from four sites. Only those from Tamworth and Northfleet are securely associated with mills, and if the dating evidence for these sites is followed, those from Northfleet are likely to date from the late seventh or early eighth century and that from Tamworth may be mid-ninth century. A possible paddle from Oxford found in a shallow gulley downstream of the Castle Mill site and upstream of Trill Mill may date from the tenth century. It is not clearly associated with either site, although it is perhaps more likely to have been washed downstream than up.[67] Its form is flat, in contrast to the Northfleet and Tamworth finds, which are scoop-shaped, and its identification is therefore open to question. Both flat and scoop-shaped paddles from early medieval horizontal waterwheels have been found in Ireland, the latter cut and shaped from a single block of oak, as at Tamworth. The two Northfleet paddles are different in that they are made of two pieces, a flat board being pegged to the underside of the scoop.[68] Two elongated, scoop-shaped paddles, along with a fragment now lost, were recovered during road works near Egypt Mills, Nailsworth, Gloucestershire, in 1967. These are not precisely provenanced and are undated, but are considered to be pre-1300, based on a lack of any evidence for horizontal-wheeled mills in southern England after that date.[69] They are similar in shape and dimensions to each other and probably came from the same waterwheel which, unlike those at Northfleet and Tamworth, would have rotated in an anti-clockwise direction.[70] Their form, however, differs from other known early medieval examples.

The isolated find at Northfleet of a curved section of oak with a series of regularly spaced mortises through it, mentioned above, is probably part of a vertical waterwheel, but no other components have as yet been identified from the Anglo-Saxon period.[71]

Mill buildings

Ælfric Bata's *Grammar* of *c.*1000 describes monastic buildings, including the granary and the mill, as being some of wood and some of stone,[72] but the available evidence suggests that Anglo-Saxon mills were generally timber-framed, with some form of cladding, perhaps boards or wattles, between the posts. While the dimensions of the undercrofts, where the horizontal wheels were housed, are available from Tamworth and Northfleet (Figure 8.3), there is no evidence for the size of the upper houses, where the millstones were located and the milling took place. Similarly, no clear evidence of mill buildings, or their extent, was found in association with the vertical waterwheel emplacements at Old Windsor, West Cotton and Corbridge. At both Old Windsor and Tamworth, the mills appear to have been destroyed by fire, and it is thought that the Northfleet mill was deliberately dismantled after a relatively short working life of perhaps 30 years or so.[73] The available evidence suggests that timber-built mills, sited in what must be seen as relatively aggressive environments, were fairly short-lived structures, perhaps working for no more than 20 to 30 years before major rebuilding was required (Figure 8.7).

Functions

The evidence from the majority of watermill sites that have been excavated is that they were used for grinding cereal grains. At Tamworth, this is confirmed by the large number of millstone fragments. Millstones were also found at West Cotton, and at Wellington where one corner of the

Fig. 8.8
opposite
Horizontal-wheeled mill in Norway, one of five at Skor. This contemporary photograph shows a small timber-built mill perched on rough stone piers, its waterwheel fed from an open timber trough. The construction and the location on the bank of the river underline the vulnerability of such mills and how little might survive in the archaeological record (photograph by Martin Watts).

base frame was underpinned by a large piece of millstone.[74] At other sites the evidence is less clear. At Wharram Percy, careful analysis of the large number of milling stone fragments recovered from the dam site identified them as being from querns rather than from power-driven millstones.[75] A fragment of a stone described as a quern, from its small size, was also found at Worgret, and some small fragments of lava stone were recorded on the site drawings as querns at Old Windsor.[76] At Wellington, slag, probably from smithing, was associated with the buried mill structure, while the pit containing the Worgret timbers had been backfilled with 3.5 tonnes of iron slag.[77] The interesting question as to whether either of these sites provides evidence of water-power being used for iron working in the Anglo-Saxon period remains unanswered.

It is worth noting that while the presence of milling tools and mills is implied by the amount of bread referred to in various documents,[78] there is almost no information about the process of milling or the technology of water-power in contemporary sources. The craft of the miller can be seen to come between that of the ploughman and the baker, both of whom have roles in Ælfric's *Colloquy*. The ploughman, he says, 'feeds us all', and the importance of bread is stressed: the baker states that 'without my craft every table would seem empty; and without bread all food would seem distasteful', but regarding the miller the dialogue is mute.[79]

Ownership, millers and millwrights

There is no mention of mills or provision for the use of water-power in Anglo-Saxon laws, unlike those of early medieval Ireland and medieval Wales,[80] only indirect references which imply the use of milling techniques on more than a domestic scale. That querns were used by female grinding slaves in early seventh-century Kent is implicit in a law of Æthelberht, which places the value of a grinding slave between that of a king's handmaiden and one of the third class,[81] indicating that some status was afforded to those who processed grain. In an early eighth-century law of Ine, food renders from an estate of ten hides included 300 loaves, 12 ambers of Welsh ale and 30 ambers of clear ale.[82] The meal and flour from which the bread was baked and the malt for the ale must have been ground, and the quantities appear to be in excess of what might comfortably be produced using querns. The reintroduction of watermill technology appears, on current evidence, to have taken place in the middle Anglo-Saxon period, the first mills perhaps being built in the south-east and eastern counties. It has been suggested that the construction of a watermill may be seen as evidence of a high-status or royal site and also as an indicator of a settled society: 'A mill within an estate was a valuable fixed economic asset, arguably a secular equivalent to the fixed religious asset of the Church'.[83] The documentary evidence suggests that many mills existed on royal and ecclesiastical estates, often forming part of gifts of land. Ælfric, writing at the end of the tenth century, could comment ruefully that 'some men let out churches for hire, just like common mills'.[84]

An Irish law tract dating from *c.*700 indicates that a lord or prosperous commoner would have had his own mill, and less affluent landowners would have jointly owned or shared a mill.[85] Milling time was fairly divided between the owner of the land on which the mill was situated, the owner of the land from which water was drawn, the owner of the land in which the mill pond was situated and, if applicable, the operator and constructor of the mill. Such an arrangement, which must have been difficult to manage in practice, as well as divisions of property through inheritance, may have existed in late Anglo-Saxon England and may perhaps account for the shares or fractions of mills that are a feature of most counties recorded in Domesday Book.

There is also some evidence that mills were built, owned and worked communally. At St Dennis in Cornwall, an early eleventh-century document refers to a communally owned mill, and it has been suggested that such an arrangement might account for the extremely low number of mills recorded in Cornwall in Domesday Book.[86] It is also possible that the earliest mill at Wharram Percy was communal, its eventual demise resulting from changes in manorial administration after the Norman Conquest.[87] The value of mills as manorial assets forms a significant part of the Domesday record, although how these values were assessed and when the soke rights by which some tenants were compelled to have their grain ground at the lord's mill with payment in kind were established, requires further research.

The earliest mention of a miller occurs in the tenth-century will of Æthelgifu, who bequeathed one Wine *mylnere*, miller, along with land at Langford, Bedfordshire, to Ælfnoth. The bequest indicates that Wine was not a free man, but attached to the estate and, presumably, a mill.[88] A *mylewerde*, mill ward or keeper, is referred to among other workmen in the *Gerefa*.[89] Only six millers and two mill-keepers are referred to as such in Domesday Book, suggesting that the majority of the mills recorded in 1086 were worked by manorial servants or tenants of middling status. The rise of specialist millers appears to have taken place in the later medieval period, perhaps with the increasing value of mills as sources of income for manorial landlords.[90] Of the millwrights who designed and built the mills nothing is documented, although, as

Wilson pointed out, 'the large number of mills in Anglo-Saxon England might suggest their presence'.[91]

Were all late Anglo-Saxon mills and those recorded in Domesday Book watermills? This is not a question that can be readily answered and is beyond the scope of this chapter. However, while there is no evidence for windmills in England until the late twelfth century,[92] three references to mill oxen in Huntingdonshire in late tenth-century documents and the possible identification of an animal-powered mill at the Anglo-Saxon royal palace at Cheddar, Somerset, does suggest that not all Anglo-Saxon mills were water-powered.[93] Domesday Book provides clear evidence for the widespread distribution of mills in late Anglo-Saxon England. Earlier documentary sources, as outlined above, may be considered meagre, but they point to a legacy of water-power use that has had a lasting effect on the landscape. A combination of archaeological investigation and historical study can also enable us to look at the technology of watermills and to place them in a developing framework of agricultural and social activity.

9

Water, *Wics* and *Burhs*

Hal Dalwood[†]

quorum metropolis Lundonia ciuitas est, super ripam praefati fluminis posita, et ipsa multorum emporium populorum terra marique uenientium[1]

Its chief city is London, which is on the banks of that river [the Thames] and is an emporium for many nations who come to it by land and sea.

Introduction

There was no doubt in the mind of Bede that London was both a city (*civitas*) and a trading place (*emporium*) in the early eighth century, a river port that was the destination for long-distance trade 'by land and sea'. Towns, trade, navigable rivers and seaways were closely associated across western and northern Europe in the early medieval period. The aim of this chapter is to investigate those connections and explore the wider role of water in the urban environment and in the everyday lives of Anglo-Saxon town dwellers.

There is an extensive literature on many aspects of Anglo-Saxon towns, but despite many decades of research, basic questions remain about urban origins and urban economies. Martin Biddle defined a research framework for Anglo-Saxon towns in 1976[2] which remains relevant today.[3] The documentary evidence is fundamental but limited in quantity, so it is through detailed surveys of individual towns and archaeological excavations that knowledge has advanced. One focus of this chapter is the location of many Anglo-Saxon towns on navigable rivers. The reasons for such sitings included military strategy and new administrative arrangements, but through the Anglo-Saxon period it was access to navigable rivers and the sea that was important for economic development. Rivers and seaways formed the principal trade routes of the early medieval period, and it was the successful exploitation of these routes that was key to the economic prosperity of towns at this period.

The study of towns in Anglo-Saxon Britain must take into consideration the extensive urban landscape of Roman Britain.[4] Many Roman towns had been established on navigable rivers, at fordable or bridgeable locations, and the larger towns had stone walls. At the outset of the Anglo-Saxon period the Roman towns lay abandoned, in many cases after a long period of decline. Urban life had ended in any meaningful sense, but there was an impressive legacy of urban ruins.[5]

Middle Saxon high-status settlements and *wics*

Urban settlements were absent from early Anglo-Saxon England, but in the seventh century, high-status, proto-urban settlements appeared, based around royal palaces and minsters. These were important places during the development and consolidation of Anglo-Saxon kingdoms during the seventh century. These settlements were occupied by the elite as well as by their families, servants and household attendants, but their permanent populations were small and dependent on renders of tribute.[6] Some high-status settlements developed within the circuits of Roman walled towns, such as Winchester (in the kingdom of Wessex), London (in Mercia) and Canterbury (in Kent), and clearly these former Roman towns were regarded as having a high status by both Royalty and the Church. Other high-status settlements were on new sites. The archaeological and historical evidence have been much debated.[7]

There were a few Middle Saxon trading settlements, where archaeological excavation has identified distinctive urban communities, including merchants, craftsmen and food producers. These new trading sites are known as *wics* or *emporia* (both meaning 'trading place'). Comparable sites are found on the opposite side of the English Channel, such as *Quentovic* in Normandy and Dorestad in the Netherlands. Four Anglo-Saxon *wics* are fairly well known: *Lundenwic* (in the modern Strand area, west of the Roman city of London), *Hamwic* (Southampton, Hampshire), *Eoforwic* (south of the walls of Roman York) and *Gippeswic* (Ipswich, Suffolk).[8] Some *wics* were close to high-status settlements where important churches and royal administrative centres were located. The *wics* at London and York were outside but close to the Roman walled towns within which stood important churches and probably royal palaces. *Hamwic* was sited at the mouth of the River Itchen and lay 18 kilometres downriver from Winchester, the royal and ecclesiastical centre of the kingdom of Wessex.[9] A more complicated pattern existed in Kent, with a *wic* at Fordwich on the River Stour, close to the royal and ecclesiastical centre at Canterbury, and with two other *wic*s in the kingdom of Kent, at Sandwich and at Dover.[10] In all these places it was access to the sea that was crucial, as the *wic*s were focused on overseas trade and controlled imports and exports under royal officials. The *wic*s were not the only places involved in trade. A network of smaller trading places (known as 'productive sites') has begun to emerge through the recovery of coins and metalwork; the *wic*s were part of a complex economic network inside the Anglo-Saxon kingdoms.[11]

The re-emergence of trading towns in the late seventh century was a phenomenon that occurred across western Europe.[12] The seagoing craft used for crossing the North Sea are well known from excavated wrecks: shallow clinker-built boats propelled by oars and sail that could navigate shallow rivers and could easily be beached.[13] Consequently, the *wic*s did not require elaborate harbours or quays, as seagoing boats could be drawn up on sloping river banks to be offloaded and to take on new cargo. All the early coastal *wic*s were located on the south and east coasts, and the archaeological evidence shows that trade was with France and the Rhineland as well as along the coast between the *wic*s themselves. The inhabitants of these new trading towns were an urban population of merchants and craftsmen, including textile workers, smiths, jewellers, potters, tanners and bone and antler workers. Excavation of workshop sites in *wic*s has allowed detailed understanding of technologies of production and the range of goods manufactured, such as the closely related crafts of working with bone, antler and horn.[14]

The emergence of recognizable trading places marks an important stage in the development of towns in Anglo-Saxon England: these were urban settlements that looked outward across the sea. However, this vibrant stage was relatively short-lived, and the *wic*s were in decline from the late eighth century. One factor in this decline was certainly disruption caused by Viking raids and the vulnerability of the *wic*s to attack, but there was a more general decline in trade at this period. The details of the transition from *wic*s to later towns are unclear, but it is clear that the factors that determined the location of the *wic*s remained important in subsequent centuries.[15]

Later Anglo-Saxon towns

There was a revival in towns from the late ninth century onwards, and urban communities became important settlements in the Anglo-Saxon landscape, although only a small proportion of the population lived in them.[16] The major impetus was the foundation of the new settlements called *burh*s in Wessex and Mercia in the late ninth and early tenth century, by Alfred and his successors. The *burh*s included some sites that were simply military forts and, more importantly, other sites that were both defensible places and intentional, planned towns from their foundations. The sites chosen for *burh*s included Roman walled towns, as well as many new sites.[17] The process of *burh* foundation was complex, but there is evidence that the economic role of *burh*s was recognized from the beginning.[18] Fortified Roman towns that had been used as royal and ecclesiastical centres from the seventh century onwards took on new urban characteristics when they were established as *burh*s. They developed a range of commercial functions, and populations grew. In southern England, the Roman walled towns of London, Winchester, Canterbury, Chichester, Exeter, Lincoln, Chester, Gloucester and Rochester developed a fully urban character during the later Anglo-Saxon period.[19] New *burh* foundations included Shaftesbury, Malmesbury, Wallingford and Oxford in Wessex; Hereford, Gloucester and Worcester in western Mercia; and Bedford, Stamford and Nottingham in areas that had been under Scandinavian rule. The excavated evidence from the *burh*s is fairly extensive, and includes Chester, London, Lincoln, Oxford, Stafford, Wallingford, Winchester and Worcester.[20]

The foundation of *burh*s was a royal policy with the primary aim of organizing effective defence, but it has long been argued, based on their planning and locations, that the *burh*s were intended to be towns with permanent populations from the outset, rather than simply defensible sites that could be used in times of war.[21] The settlements were well organized within their defences, with metalled streets and a regular pattern of narrow properties lining the street frontages, often with buildings oriented with the gable end facing the street, for which the best evidence comes from Anglo-Scandinavian York.[22] Late Saxon *burh*s had populations of merchants, craftsmen and food producers. Many of the *burh*s in the Midlands and East Anglia were pottery-manufacturing centres (including Ipswich, Thetford, Stamford, Stafford, Nottingham, Norwich, Torksey, Northampton and Lincoln).[23] A wide range of other industries has been identified, including smithing, metal-working, wood turning, leather- and bone-working, glass making and cloth weaving.[24] By the eleventh century, the *burh*s had developed into complex urban settlements, tied into networks of regional and international trade, and had become a vital part of the economy of Anglo-Saxon England. Many of the *burh*s were located on navigable rivers, accessible to the seagoing, shallow-drafted ships of the Anglo-Saxon period. The urban communities of the *burh*s took on the roles of merchants, traders and sailors that had been seen in the *wic*s.

Towns and rivers in defensive strategy

There was a high level of warfare in early medieval England, but the walled Roman towns were not reoccupied as settlement sites before the ninth century, a pattern that is found across western Europe and which has been attributed to the nature of warfare at this period, but which is not entirely explicable.[25] The Middle Saxon *wic*s in England were undefended, although most *wic*s were close to defensible sites, such as the *wic*s at London and York, which lay outside the Roman walled towns, although there was a defensive ditch at *Lundenwic* at a late period in its occupation.[26]

The appearance of defended towns and other fortified sites across western Europe in the late ninth century has long been seen as a response to the new military threat of Viking raids and attacks.[27] In England, this period saw the rapid establishment of the *burh*s in Wessex and in Mercia as a coherent defensive strategy, and was advanced as territory was re-conquered from the Danelaw. The location of many *burh*s at river crossings is attributed to this defensive strategy, in order to deter the passage of Viking warships up rivers, and to prevent Viking armies crossing rivers by fords or bridges.[28] The defence of the Anglo-Saxon kingdoms depended on the military support of those who held land, and, from the late eighth century onwards, charters refer to the 'three common burdens' on all landholders, including religious houses: the provision of men to fight in the army, the construction and maintenance of fortifications and the upkeep of bridges.[29] The military strategy behind the foundation of *burh*s seems to have been effective from the late ninth century onwards.[30] The major *burh*s of Wessex, Mercia and the newly conquered 'boroughs' of the Danelaw became the administrative centres of shires and were responsible for local administration, taxation and defence.[31] The defensive strategy of an established army working in tandem with the garrisons of *burh*s included the control of navigable rivers.[32] Whilst the threat of longships striking up rivers remained, the townspeople of the *burh*s were part of the defensive strategy of England.

Towns and river crossings

River crossings were required at early medieval towns located on rivers. People, animals and goods would usually cross rivers by fords and ferries, and more rarely by bridges. During the Roman period, the development of towns and a road network included the construction of substantial bridges. The major Roman bridges took the form of stone piers with a timber superstructure, which required regular upkeep and substantial repair when damaged by flooding. The clearest evidence for Roman bridges remaining in use in the Anglo-Saxon period is at Rochester, and the Roman bridges at Chester, London, Huntingdon, Nottingham and Cambridge were probably all capable of being used during the period. Substantial timber bridges were also constructed in the Anglo-Saxon period.[33] However, in general there were few major bridges in use before the tenth century, when the growth in local and regional trade stimulated the construction of new bridges to replace fords.[34]

Natural fording places (due to irregularities in river-beds) were the focus of long-standing overland routes, and such intersections of land and river routes were a factor in the location and development of towns such as Oxford, Wallingford and Bedford, as fords were critical locations on the transport network (see Chapter 7 of this volume for related discussion). At Oxford, there is archaeological evidence for the construction of crossing points over the Thames, which may be typical of the development of river crossings at towns. There were a number of small islands in the wide floodplain of the River Thames, and to cross some of the channels a timber trestle bridge associated with the minster church of St Frideswide was built in the mid-Anglo-Saxon period. As the *burh* developed in the early tenth century, a cobbled ford was constructed. The timber bridge, crossing at least part if not all of the Thames, was maintained up to end of the eleventh century, when a stone bridge was built.[35] Fords were suitable for pack animals and men on horseback, and some could be crossed on foot when the river was low, but travellers used ferries as well. Ferry boats required a small community of ferrymen, associated with the boatmen involved in long-distance river trade.

Towns, trade and the wider world

Connections between Britain and the continent depended on seagoing vessels for millennia, and archaeological evidence demonstrates that well-established seaways linked the continent, Britain, Ireland and the northern islands long before 4000 BC.[36] In Roman Britain, substantial quaysides were constructed for handling large ships, as at London,[37] and navigable rivers were an integrated part of the transport network. River navigation was important throughout England from the Anglo-Saxon period up to the thirteenth century, although it declined in importance from the fourteenth century.[38] The relative importance of river trade in the Anglo-Saxon period is a matter of debate, but there is a wide range of evidence which attests to its importance (see Chapter 7 of this volume).

The boats used in the Anglo-Saxon period were the product of a long tradition of clinker-built shipbuilding, the origins of which have been traced back to the Iron Age. Ships with shallow drafts were capable of crossing the North Sea and of travelling long distances up rivers. A few boats have been excavated in England, including the warship buried at Sutton Hoo, but the majority of travel was by smaller vessels such as the Graveney boat (dating to about AD 900) which was 14 metres long and capable of carrying six to seven tons of cargo.[39] A well-established cross-channel trade network operated in the sixth to seventh centuries, and can be traced through the discovery of Frankish metalwork in Kent and English metalwork in France; and it is also possible that slaves were an important element of trade from England.[40] Small cargoes of high-value goods could be landed on beaches and river-mouths and did not require permanent trading stations. However, the development of trade on a more substantial scale required permanent ports. There was a need for merchants to organize the trade, shipbuilders and other specialist craftspeople and sailors and boatmen to crew the ships. The *wics* provided a place for the people to live upon whom the maritime and riverine trade depended. The *wics* were also convenient points of embarkation for long-distance journeys with purposes other than trade, such as the regular visits of English churchmen to Rome and beyond.[41] It is apparent that the church establishment was itself involved in overseas trade, as the bishops of London, Minster-in-Thanet, Rochester and Worcester were all exempted from royal tolls on their ships at *Lundenwic*.[42] Pottery manufactured at Ipswich (Ipswich Ware) was widely traded in the Middle Saxon period, and has been found in quantity at London, York and Canterbury; its widespread distribution in the form of jars and pitchers probably indicates that the pottery was used as containers for foodstuffs in regional trade from Ipswich.[43] The distribution of Ipswich Ware has been interpreted as evidence for the importance of coastal and river trade (see Chapter 7 of this volume). Place name evidence provides further support for Anglo-Saxon river trade, identifying many small landing places on rivers where shallow-drafted boats could be beached.[44] Such landing places were undoubtedly involved in short-distance travel, but it is likely that they represent elements of regional trade networks that developed in association with the growth of the *wics*.

The *wics* developed from the late seventh century in a period which saw a rise in the volume of trade across the Channel. In the early eighth century, silver coins (*sceattas*) were introduced, in smaller weights than the existing high-value gold coins, a change that has been attributed to the growth of trade and the greater need for coins in commerce. The mints were located in the *wics*, such as *Hamwic* and Ipswich.[45] The actual nature of trade can only be glimpsed from the limited evidence, but imports included wine (required by the Church) and exports included slaves, textiles, wool, metal ingots (such as lead) and hides.[46] Imported pottery from France, the Low Countries and the Rhineland has been found at *Lundenwic* in the mid-eighth to ninth centuries.[47] One major import was wine (although not directly visible in the archaeological evidence). This was supplied from the great wine markets at St Denis (drawing on the vineyards along the Seine) and Dorestad (exporting wine from the Rhine and the Main).[48] It has been suggested that wool was exported from *Lundenwic* and shipped down the Thames from monastic estates, together with salt produced at Droitwich in Worcestershire.[49]

Bulky trade goods could be handled more easily at *wics*, where goods could be stored in warehouses ready for onward transportation. It is clear that the *wics* were carefully controlled by royal authority: in the eighth century, *Lundenwic* was controlled by the kings of Mercia, and all ships coming to the port paid a toll to royal officials stationed there.[50] The principal export that passed through the *wics* may have been wool.[51]

The people who lived in the *wics* are beginning to be revealed by archaeological excavations. Grave goods are evidence that wealthy foreigners were buried in the cemeteries at Ipswich, *Hamwic* and *Lundenwic*. These are likely to have been merchants and their families involved in the overseas trade with Francia and Frisia.[52] The *wics* were undoubtedly where high-status goods were landed. All the *wics* have produced fragments of glass vessels, including palm cups and funnel beakers, some of which were probably produced on the Rhine or in south-west France. It seems likely that the vessels were destined for aristocratic and ecclesiastical sites and were broken in transit, although some parts were recycled and used to manufacture glass beads in the *wics*.[53] A range of imported pottery from northern France has been excavated from *Hamwic*, which seems to have been mostly utilized in the trading settlement itself. Although some imported pottery was used to transport goods such as honey, the majority was used in domestic households, and this has been interpreted as evidence for resident foreign merchants and other immigrants in *Hamwic* with strong connections across the Channel.[54] When the settlement focus shifted from *Hamwic* to Southampton, the new site continued as a port trading with northern France, and continued to have a population of foreign merchants and other immigrants using imported pottery.[55] The extensive evidence from

Hamwic and late Anglo-Saxon Southampton indicates that some trading places had a distinctive material culture, even in relation to contemporary sites in Wessex, and this has been interpreted as indicating a foreign element in the population of the port. Early medieval trading towns were not only involved in the day-to-day business of maritime trade, but had horizons that reached beyond England to France and further afield.

High-status goods remained an important feature of early medieval trade after the development of new towns in the later ninth century. In Ælfric's *Colloquy* the role of the merchant as the foundation of wealth is expounded: the merchant travelled and brought back valuable goods including 'purple cloth and silks, unusual clothes and spices, wine and oil, ivory and bronze, copper and tin, sulphur and glass'.[56] The Anglo-Saxon merchants might travel to France or the Rhineland, but goods such as silk had been transported over long-distance trade routes from Constantinople and western Asia, along new routes opened up by Viking traders.[57] Silk was a luxury good, but silk decorative strips for headgear have been recovered from Lincoln, so it seems to have been accessible to some of the inhabitants.[58] A Norwegian called Ohthere visited Alfred's court and described the value of products from the Arctic, including whalebone, walrus ivory and furs.[59] The tolls on goods imported to London from Germany included quantities of pepper (transported on long-distance trade routes from India), vinegar and cloth, whereas the exports included wool, glassware and fat.[60] Overseas trade was carefully regulated: the tolls that were collected at London by royal officials were laid down and varied depending on the size of the ship and the value of the goods offloaded (such as wine, cloth, timber and fish).[61]

The long-established river trade routes on the Severn and the Thames expanded in the later Anglo-Saxon period with the development of trade along rivers in eastern England flowing into the North Sea.[62] Many towns emerged as nodal points in trade networks where overland routes met navigable rivers, and the archaeological evidence shows that rivers were important for inter-regional trade, as indicated by pottery. However, the road network was an important part of the trade network as well, as is shown by the development of towns at a distance from navigable rivers.[63] River trade was particularly important in eastern England, due to the important trade links with Scandinavia, the Netherlands and France.[64] The bishops of Worcester had a quay and commercial property at London, and the evidence suggests they were also directly involved in river trade from Worcester,[65] as in earlier centuries. It seems likely that the motivation for a distant bishopric to be involved in trade in London was to secure access to imported specialist goods required by the Church (such as wine and silk), but undoubtedly other more commercial interests became important over time.

Bulky and heavy goods included grain, wool, cloth and minerals (such as salt from Droitwich in Worcestershire) which were transported by river from the interior to the coasts.[66] Pottery production became an important industry in towns, and evidence for kilns has been found at Exeter, Gloucester, Stafford, Lincoln, Newark, Ipswich, Thetford and Torksey (and probably York and Derby). The increase in the consumption of sea fish (probably air-dried 'stockfish') in towns in the late tenth century, probably imported from Scandinavia and the Baltic, is a further example of the growth of overseas trade in bulky goods of relatively low value.[67] Other bulky or heavy goods have been traced along their trade routes. Lava quernstones were widely traded from the Eifel region near Mayen in north-west Germany. These were imported to Anglo-Saxon England in large numbers from the ninth century, and were the principal cargo of the tenth-century Graveney Boat mentioned above.[68] The trade was long-lasting, initially in finished quernstones from manufacturing centres at Hedeby and Dorestadt, but in the late tenth century unfinished quernstones were imported to London and completed in workshops and distributed to rural settlements throughout the hinterland.[69] In a well-known letter from Charlemagne to King Offa of Mercia in 796 there is mention of an exchange of prestige goods, comprising lengths of English cloth and 'black stones' from the continent.[70] Although the reference to 'black stones' has usually been interpreted as a reference to quernstones, it has been suggested that these were in fact stone columns (such as porphyry) from demolished Roman buildings offered to Offa for use in a new building in England.[71] However Charlemagne's letter is interpreted, there is no doubt that the transportation of building stone for churches was widespread in the later Anglo-Saxon period, both by sea and by river.[72]

A complex web of people and places sustained the expanded trade system of the late Anglo-Saxon period. Urban merchants would have been involved in purchasing the cargos, organizing the finishing of goods ready for sale, warehousing and onward sale and distribution. The transportation of bulky goods (such as bales of wool or barrels of wine or dried fish) required warehouses for secure storage before local sale or transport to the hinterland. In turn, the operation of the import and export trade required the hire of casual labourers for moving goods around.

Archaeological excavations have revealed the facilities for loading and offloading boats, and shown how these developed as trade increased.

At the *wics*, river banks were used for beaching both river craft and seagoing ships, but improvements were made. At *Lundenwic* there was a wide brushwood and rubble embankment beside the Thames, which was used to tie up ships for unloading as well as the conduct of trade.[73] In the late ninth century, the riverside below the Roman walls of London was developed for commercial trade, following the switch in settlement focus to within the Roman walls. In 898/899, the king granted the Bishop of Worcester and the Archbishop of Canterbury the right to moor ships at their land at *Ætheredeshyd* (later Queenshithe).[74] Excavation at this location, on the river bank in front of the Roman walls, has shown that boats were beached on the river bank and tied to mooring posts, while parts of the foreshore were used for trade, as at *Lundenwic*.[75] In the eleventh century, more substantial embankments with timber revetments were constructed at a number of locations along the Thames, indicating an increase in the volume of trade and the number of boats calling at London.[76] A similar development occurred at Lincoln, where settlement developed within the walled Roman city from the late ninth century (initially under Viking control). Immediately outside the walls, the bank of the River Witham was stabilized and a rubble jetty constructed, followed by reclamation and the construction of a quay by the mid-eleventh century.[77] Undoubtedly, such developments were common.

Larger types of seagoing sailing vessels with deep and broad hulls reflected the growth in the volume of trade. This is typified by excavated boats from Denmark and north Germany, including 'Skudelev 1', capable of carrying 25 tons of cargo, and 'Hedeby 3', 25 metres long and capable of carrying 60 tons. Such vessels could cross the North Sea or even the Atlantic, but they were easier to offload when docked at quays rather than when beached on a river bank.[78] International trade grew and expanded through the ninth and tenth centuries, and Bristol, Gloucester and Chester developed as ports trading with Ireland and northern Britain.[79] Imports were probably livestock and grain as well as furs – the last, including marten furs, were particularly valued.[80] Anglo-Saxon towns involved in long-distance trade were also ports where passage could be obtained for foreign travel. Long-distance travel to Rome on pilgrimage or on ecclesiastical business was common.[81]

The use of water in crafts and industries

A range of urban industries have been recorded in both the *wics* and the *burhs* of the late ninth century and later, as at Winchester, although the widest range of archaeological evidence is from Anglo-Scandinavian

York. Production was mostly on a household scale: in London, there is evidence for smithing, weaving, wool preparation, wood turning, bone working, dyeing and glass making.[82]

Flowing water was required for processes involved in the textile industries, including washing wool and fulling (finishing woollen cloth). The processing of flax into linen required retting (soaking the flax plants in running water). The hides from slaughtered animals were processed into leather in tanneries, which also required large quantities of water, as well as urine, wood ash, lime and dog dung.[83] The treatment of animal hides to produce leather may have been a specifically urban industry in the early medieval period, as it was in later centuries in England, because of efficiencies in processing large numbers of hides and their availability from urban butchers. Vegetable tanning of leather required fairly substantial and fixed processing plants (especially timber-lined tanning pits) and a constant water supply, and leather production and leather working in towns seems to have increased substantially in the tenth century.[84] There is archaeological evidence for a tannery from eleventh-century Winchester at the Lower Brook Street site.[85] The process was odoriferous, but, just as in later medieval English towns, it was access to water that was the important factor: in *Lundenwic*, tanning was undertaken in the middle of the settlement. In Oxford, flax retting (another process that produced unpleasant smells and waste) was carried out in timber-lined gullies and in natural river channels next to the town.[86] Ale brewing also required large quantities of water. Ale was widely drunk, and it seems likely that brewing was undertaken on a commercial scale in towns. It was commonplace for later medieval urban trades and crafts to be grouped together, often reflected in street names, but, so far, the evidence indicates that was not necessarily the case in Anglo-Saxon towns such as London.[87]

As urban populations grew, disputes inevitably arose over the use of water supplies, between people who needed clean water (such as the brewers of ale) and craftsmen whose work led to the production of large volumes of contaminated water (such as tanners), and this is well documented in the later medieval period. There were some watermills in Anglo-Saxon towns, such as that excavated at Tamworth,[88] but it was common for households to own rotary querns and to grind their own corn by hand. In the later medieval period, mills were very common in towns (see Chapter 8 of this volume).

The majority of urban industries in Anglo-Saxon towns were concerned with supplying the needs of townspeople. The various types of evidence for regional and international trade have already been considered, but we can also infer the existence of a group of townspeople directly involved in the business of maritime and river trade: boatmen, shipbuilders, ropemakers, coopers and labourers. Evidence for these crafts is limited before the late medieval period.[89] Shipbuilding was a particularly important and skilled industry, and fragments of Anglo-Saxon ships excavated in London have been interpreted as evidence of a local ship-building industry.[90]

Fish in the urban food supply

Fish were a regular part of the Anglo-Saxon diet by the middle of the period, an aspect of consumption perhaps related to the many non-meat-eating days in the Christian calendar, and fish were an important source of food for growing urban populations. The evidence for fishing and fish consumption is varied (see Chapter 6 of this volume for related discussion). The many references to small and large fisheries in charters (interpreted as constructions such as fish weirs) indicate the economic importance of fish throughout the early medieval period.[91] The charter evidence shows that the right to take fish from rivers was carefully controlled, for instance on the River Severn,[92] so this valuable resource was not a free supply of food for the local population (for fisheries more generally, see Chapter 2 of this volume). Archaeological excavations have shown that freshwater fish (such as the carp family and pike) and migratory fish (European eel, salmon, trout, smelt and flatfish) were consumed by the inhabitants of the *wics*, together with some marine fish. However, in the late tenth century, a change in fish consumption occurred and marine fish (herring and cod-like species) became dominant in towns such as York.[93] This change can be interpreted as the result of a substantial increase in demand from growing urban populations. The source of the marine fish is uncertain, but it may have been Norway or the Baltic in the form of 'stockfish' (air-dried fish). The change in fish consumption seems also to be concurrent with the development of larger cargo ships in the late tenth century, which made the transportation of low-value and high bulk goods both cheaper and easier. However, migratory fish (such as salmon and eel) remained important in urban diets.[94]

Where towns stood on major rivers, local fish were probably sold by the fishermen directly at the riverside, as in the later medieval period. By contrast, the trade in stockfish must have been organized by merchants who could store the goods and supply the fishmongers. Fishermen were probably common in towns due to the scale of the demand, although the fish they caught and sold were probably less varied than described by the fisherman in Ælfric's *Colloquy*.[95]

Water supply and drainage in towns

Archaeological excavation in early medieval towns shows that water supply and drainage were common concerns. In Middle Saxon *Lundenwic*, the houses were accompanied by timber-lined wells in the backyards, and the gravelled street was lined with timber drains to remove surface water.[96] At *Hamwic* there were timber-lined wells 3.5 metres to 4 metres deep, mostly located in backyards, but some were next to street frontages and may have been communal.[97] The wells found in *wics* were undoubtedly used to meet domestic needs, but many of the crafts and industries recorded at the *wics* required a good supply of water, and this probably accounts for the number and size of the wells.

Wells were also fairly common in late Anglo-Saxon *burhs*. Other sources of water would have included rainwater, which could have been collected in water-butts. There were natural springs in some towns: at Lincoln these provided a plentiful source of water in the middle of the town, although wells were also dug.[98] In Winchester, natural watercourses flowed through the walled area, and by the late tenth century these had been carefully channelled; these watercourses were sufficient to drive mills inside the walls as well as providing water for domestic and industrial purposes.[99] Palaeoenvironmental evidence from York indicates that river water was used for domestic supply and was not heavily contaminated, whilst the evidence for wells is limited.[100]

Waste water and human effluent were regularly disposed of close to houses, into pits or other open features. Excavation in many Anglo-Saxon towns shows that pits were ubiquitous in back yards, and detailed analysis of fills from York shows that the primary purpose of such pits was as cess pits, which led to rather noxious conditions with pit fills infested with flies and a generally unhealthy environment.[101] The proximity of cess pits to wells in back plots led to dangerous but undetectable pathogens entering the water supply, a situation that prevailed in towns until the dangers were understood in the nineteenth century. Textile processing produced large quantities of foul waste water, and it has been suggested that ditches and gullies in York were dug to carry away large volumes of waste water from textile processing in domestic plots. Rivers were an efficient means of disposing of unpleasant waste materials, which led to the contamination of the river water – a practice that was often the cause for complaints in towns in the later medieval period. At Oxford, the shallow channels of the Thames were used to dump butchery waste in the tenth century,[102] and it must have been a common practice to use rivers to carry away waste. The conclusion must be that the general environment of Anglo-Saxon towns was rather noxious and unhealthy.

Ritual

The evidence for the significance of water in Anglo-Saxon towns has focused on practical necessities, including defence, trade and everyday life. However, some evidence indicates that water played a larger role in the world view of Anglo-Saxon townsmen, reflecting the sacred significance of water in many contexts (see Chapter 5 of this volume for related discussion). During excavations in London, close to the Roman walls, two Anglo-Saxon burials were recorded: one was in a grave in the river bank, and the other had been lain on the foreshore and covered with moss and bark.[103] Why these individuals were not buried in a cemetery cannot be ascertained, but the physical location on the river bank was surely significant for the society that buried them there. The River Thames at London has produced a wide range of Viking-type weapons, which may have been lost during one of the Viking attacks on London. It has also been suggested that some were votive offerings to the river,[104] comparable to similar finds across England (see Chapter 5 of this volume), an interpretation which sets Anglo-Saxon townspeople in a complex relationship with their environment.

Conclusions

This chapter has focused on the relationship between water and Anglo-Saxon towns. Rivers and seaways were particularly important in the emergence of towns in the Anglo-Saxon kingdoms. The flow of trade through *wics* and *burhs* brought foreign merchants who settled there. As the economies of towns developed, regional and international trade became particularly important for the wealth of England, and so the livelihoods of many members of the urban communities were tied to riverine and seagoing trade.

Of course, access to a water supply is important for any community, and the growth of Anglo-Saxon urban populations led to increasing demand, particularly for the needs of the cloth and leather industries. The archaeological evidence highlights aspects of the disposal of contaminated water and other effluent which indicates something of the nature of the environment in which Anglo-Saxon townspeople lived their lives.

Notes

Special thanks to Tiffany Conley for her assistance in editing the notes for this volume and her assistance with the compilation of the index.

Introduction

1   Della Hooke, *The Anglo-Saxon Landscape: The Kingdom of the Hwicce* (Manchester: Manchester University Press, 1985), pp. 3–23, Figs 1 and 2.

2   The boundaries of drainage provinces referred to here are based upon the drainage systems depicted by Brian K. Roberts and Stuart Wrathmell, *Region and Place: A Study of English Rural Settlement* (London: English Heritage, 2002), p. 34, Fig. 2.2. Tom Williamson considers this as a division of his 'North Sea Province' which he takes to include a further drainage system around the Wash: Tom Willamson, *Environment, Society and Landscape in Early Medieval England: Time and Topography* (Woodbridge: Boydell, 2013), p. 58.

3   Barbara Yorke, 'The Jutes of Hampshire and Wight and the Origins of Wessex', in Stephen Bassett (ed.), *The Origins of Anglo-Saxon Kingdoms* (London: Leicester University Press, 1989), pp. 84–96.

4   Aneurin Owen (ed.), *Ancient Laws and Institutions of Wales*, vol. 1 (London: 1841), p. 77.

5   Della Hooke, *Anglo-Saxon Territorial Organization: The Western Margins of Mercia* (Birmingham: Department of Geography, University of Birmingham, 1986).

6   Della Hooke, 'Saxon Conquest and Settlement', in Roger Kain and William Ravenhill (eds), *An Historical Atlas of South-Western England* (Exeter: University of Exeter Press, 1999), p. 95.

7   Treaty of Alfred and Guthrum, 1: Frederick L. Attenborough (trans. and ed.), *The Laws of the Earliest English Kings* (Cambridge: Cambridge University Press, 1922), pp. 98–99.

8   Nicholas Higham, *The Origins of Cheshire* (Manchester: Manchester University Press, 1993), pp. 85, 89, Fig. 3.6; Della Hooke, 'Names and Settlement in the Warwickshire Arden', in Della Hooke and David Postles (eds), *Names, Time and Place: Essays in Memory of Richard McKinley* (Oxford: Leopard's Head Press, 2003), pp. 67–99, esp. pp. 69–71 and Fig. 2.1. The early kingdom of Kent is discussed by Mark Gardiner, 'The Colonisation of the Weald of South-east England', *Medieval Settlement Group Annual Report* 12 (1997), pp. 6–8, and by Nicholas Brooks, 'The Creation and Early Structure of the Kingdom of Kent', in Bassett, *The Origins of Anglo-Saxon Kingdoms*, pp. 55–74. Pagan and place names in Sussex are discussed by Martin G. Welch, *Early Anglo-Saxon Sussex*, British Archaeological Reports, British Series 112 (Oxford: British Archaeological Reports, 1983).

9   Hooke, *Anglo-Saxon Territorial Organization*, pp. 21–23; Bruce Coplestone-Crow, *Herefordshire Place-Names*, British Archaeological Reports, British Series 214 (Oxford: British Archaeological Reports, 1989), pp. 6–9.

10   Hooke, *The Anglo-Saxon Landscape*, pp. 85–86.

11   *The Anglo-Saxon Chronicle*, e.g. 800, MS C: Katherine O'Brian O'Keefe (ed.), *The Anglo-Saxon Chronicle: A Collaborative Edition*, vol. 5 (Cambridge: D.S. Brewer, 2001), p. 51; Susan Irvine (ed.), *The Anglo-Saxon Chronicle: A Collaborative Edition*, vol. 7 (Cambridge: D.S. Brewer, 2004), p. 43.

12   Victor Watts (ed.), *The Cambridge Dictionary of English Place-Names* (Cambridge: Cambridge University Press, 2004) (*CDEPN*), p. 425, citing Margaret Gelling.

13   See also Della Hooke, *The Landscape of Anglo-Saxon England* (London: Leicester University Press, 1998), pp. 177–79.

14   Mark G. Macklin, Anna F. Jones and John Lewin, 'River Response to Rapid Holocene Environmental Change: Evidence and Explanation in British Catchments', *Quaternary Science Reviews* 29 (2010), pp. 1555–76, esp. p. 1571.

15   Hooke, *Landscape of Anglo-Saxon England*, pp. 170–76. However, the fens were not abandoned to the same degree as once thought, with recent interpretation of archaeological and other evidence showing continuous occupation scattered across fenland throughout the early medieval period. See Susan Oosthuizen, 'Culture and Identity in the Early Medieval Fenland Landscape', *Landscape History* 37.1 (2016), pp. 5–21.

16   Hooke, *Landscape of Anglo-Saxon England*, pp. 176–77.

17   Ian D. Rotherham, *The Lost Fens: England's Greatest Ecological Disaster* (Stroud: The History Press, 2013), pp. 22–24, 39–47.

18   Hooke, *Landscape of Anglo-Saxon England*, pp. 182–84 and Fig. 61a.

19   *The Anglo-Saxon Chronicle*, trans. and ed. Michael Swanton (London: Dent, 1996), p. 145: translation of the Peterborough MS (E), Oxford, Bodleian Library MS Laud 636.

20   David Hill, *An Atlas of Anglo-Saxon England* (Oxford: Basil Blackwell, 1981), p. 10.

21   *CDEPN*, p. 253.

22   Albert L.F. Rivet and Colin Smith, *The Place-Names of Roman Britain* (London: Batsford, 1979), pp. 212–13.

23   Williamson, *Environment, Society and Landscape*.

24   Richard Jones and Della Hooke, 'Methodological Approaches to Medieval Rural Settlements and Landscapes', in Neil Christie and Paul Stamper (eds), *Medieval Rural Settlement: Britain and Ireland, AD 800–1600* (Oxford: Oxbow, 2012), pp. 186–205.

Chapter 1: Anglo-Saxon Poetry

1   *Solomon and Saturn*, ll. 225–29, in Elliott Van Kirk Dobbie (ed.), *The Anglo-Saxon Minor Poems*, Anglo-Saxon Poetic Records 6 (New York: Columbia University Press, 1942), p. 39. All translations from Old English are mine, unless otherwise noted.

2   *Bede's Ecclesiastical History of the English People*, ed. and trans. Bertram Colgrave, with an introduction by Judith McClure and Roger Collins (Oxford: Oxford University Press, 1994), i.1, p. 9.

3   David M. Wilson, *The Anglo-Saxons* (Harmondsworth: Penguin, 1975), p. 91.

4   Wilson, *The Anglo-Saxons*, p. 77. See also Chapter 8 of this volume for evidence about the numbers, kinds and functions of water-wheels within Anglo-Saxon society.

5   Della Hooke, *The Landscape of Anglo-Saxon England* (London and New York: Leicester University Press), p. 92. See also Chapter 5 of this volume for Della Hooke's discussion of water as a symbolic boundary.

6   Jennifer Neville's book, *Representations of the Natural World in Old English Poetry* (Cambridge: Cambridge University Press, 1999) provides a comprehensive and valuable analysis of this subject.

7   See, for instance, Katrin Thier's article, 'Steep Vessel, High Horn-Ship: Water Transport', in Maren Clegg Hyer and Gale R. Owen-Crocker (eds), *The Material Culture of Daily Living in the Anglo-Saxon World* (Exeter: University of Exeter Press, 2011), pp. 48–72.

8   Neville, *Representations of the Natural World*, p. 22.

9   Hugh Magennis, *Anglo-Saxon Appetites: Food and Drink and their Consumption in Old English and Related Literature* (Dublin: Four

Courts, 1999) observes that in the traditional world of Old English poetry, drinking is a social activity that involves not water, but alcohol (p. 64).

10   George Philip Krapp and Elliott Van Kirk Dobbie (eds), *The Exeter Book, Anglo-Saxon Poetic Records* 3 (New York: Columbia University Press, 1936), pp. 227–29.

11   Krapp and Dobbie, *The Exeter Book*, p. 160.

12   The term 'sapiential literature', or 'wisdom literature', is difficult to define exactly, but Thomas D. Hill quotes Aristotle's definition of maxim as a reasonable starting place: '"a statement, not however concerning particulars ... but with the objects of human actions, and with what should be chosen or avoided with reference to them" ... To this we may add statements concerning the natural order, some of which seem to have immediate moral implications and others seem to be direct natural observation' ('Wise Words: Old English Sapiential Poetry', in David F. Johnson and Elaine M. Treharne (eds), *Readings in Medieval Texts: Interpreting Old and Middle English Literature* (Oxford: Oxford University Press, 2005), p. 167).

13   *The Anglo-Saxon Minor Poems*, p. 39.

14   'The Rune Poem', *Anglo-Saxon Minor Poems*, p. 29 of 28–30.

15   *The Vercelli Book*, in George Philip Krapp (ed.), *Anglo-Saxon Poetic Records* 2 (New York: Columbia University Press, 1932), p. 8.

16   'In the Open Air', in Martin O.H. Carver, Alexandra Sanmark and Sarah Semple (eds), *Signals of Belief in Early England* (Oxford: Oxbow, 2010), p. 30.

17   The exact definition of *mere* is troublesome; for a discussion of its semantic and cultural range, see Roberta Frank, '"Mere" and "Sund": Two Sea-Changes in *Beowulf*', in Phyllis Rugg Brown, Georgia Ronan Crampton, Stanley B. Greenfield and Fred C. Robinson (eds), *Modes of Interpretation in Old English Literature* (Toronto: University of Toronto Press, 1986), pp. 153–72.

Chapter 2: Charters, Laws and Place Names

1   Peter H. Sawyer, *Anglo-Saxon Charters: An Annotated List and Bibliography* (London:

18   *The Exeter Book*, p. 158.

19   See Psalm 106: 23–30 and Matthew 14: 22–33.

20   *The Exeter Book*, pp. 134–37.

21   *Battle of Maldon, The Anglo-Saxon Minor Poems*, pp. 7–16.

22   *Battle of Maldon, The Anglo-Saxon Minor Poems*, pp. 15–16.

23   For comparison's sake, other examples of kennings for ocean include *fifelwæg* 'sea-monster's way' (*Elene* 237b), *fisces eþel* 'fish's kingdom' (*Judgement Day I*, 39b), *ganotes bæþ* 'gannet's bath' (*Rune Poem* 79a), *hwælweg* 'whale's way' (*Seafarer*), *mæwes eþel* 'seagull's kingdom' (*Husband's Message* 26b), *seglrad* 'sail's road' (*Beowulf* 1429) and *seolhbæþ* 'seal's bath' (*The Exeter Book*, Riddle 10).

24   *Exeter Book*, pp. 180–210, 229–43. Although Craig Williamson has renumbered the riddles for his study and edition, *The Old English Riddles of the* Exeter Book (Chapel Hill: University of North Carolina Press, 1977), here I follow the standard numbers of Krapp and Dobbie's *Anglo-Saxon Poetic Records* edition.

25   *Old English Riddles of the* Exeter Book, pp. 127–33.

26   Donald K. Fry, 'Exeter Book Riddle Solutions', *Old English Newsletter* 15.1 (1981), pp. 22–33 provides a catalogue of all riddle solutions through 1980; Williamson, *The Old English Riddles of the* Exeter Book, pp. 127–33 offers a comprehensive overview of the solution process.

27   *The Exeter Book*, p. 2.

28   *The Anglo-Saxon Minor Poems*, pp. 111–12.

29   Magennis, *Anglo-Saxon Appetites*, p. 135.

30   Magennis, *Anglo-Saxon Appetites*, p. 137.

31   Magennis, *Anglo-Saxon Appetites*, p. 137.

32   Williamson, *The Old English Riddles of the* Exeter Book, pp. 369–74 explains in detail the process of its solution.

33   *The Exeter Book*, pp. 15–27.

34   *The Exeter Book*, pp. 143–47.

Royal Historical Society, 1968), S 770; Exeter, Dean and Chapter 2521v (saec. xi²), reproduced in Della Hooke, *Pre-Conquest Charter-Bounds of Devon and Cornwall* (Woodbridge: Boydell, 1994), pp. 41–42.

2   S 7; also S 1648; S 10; S 13; S 15 and many other charters: Della Hooke, 'The Early Charters of Kent' (unpublished manuscript). S 178, for example, notes rights in 'fishing, fowling, waters and marshes' at *Seleberhting lond* in the district of Faversham, Kent, in AD 815.

3   S 489; S 168.

4   S 89 (Ismere); S 52 (Ripple 20); S 24 and S 512 (Thanet in the mouth of the River Limen).

5   'Capitulare Aquigranense' (801–13) c.19, in Alfredus Boretius (ed.), *Capitularia regum Francorum*, vol. 1, Monumenta Germaniae Historica (Hanover: Hahn, 1883).

6   Felix Liebermann, *Die Gesetze der Angelsachsen* (Leipzig, 1903), Gerefa 9: 1.454; Paul D.A. Harvey, 'Rectitudines Singularum Personarum and Gerefa', *English Historical Review* 108 (1993), pp. 1–22.

7   S 926; S 1562: Cyril R. Hart, *The Early Charters of Eastern England* (Leicester: Leicester University Press, 1966), no. 30, p. 33; Della Hooke, 'Uses of Waterways in Anglo-Saxon England', in John Blair (ed.), *Waterways and Canal-Building in Medieval England* (Oxford: Oxford University Press, 2007), pp. 37–54, esp. pp. 45–54.

8   S 391; Agnes J. Robertson (ed.), *Anglo-Saxon Charters*, 2nd edn (Cambridge: Cambridge University Press, 1956) (*ASC*), no. 23, pp. 46–47, 302.

9   S 54; Della Hooke, *Worcestershire Anglo-Saxon Charter-Bounds* (Woodbridge: Boydell, 1990), pp. 36–40.

10   S 849; Hooke, 'Uses of Waterways in Anglo-Saxon England', p. 46.

11   For rights *in þæm pusting were/in ðaem pusting uuerae*, see Kent charters S 123 and S 125. *Pusting* was perhaps intended for **pöting*, a word derived from *pöte* 'burbot' (inf. Richard Coates). In the nineteenth century, a *putts* weir consisted of baskets known as *putts* set between pairs of stakes, 'puttchers' but then correlated with *cytweras*: Hooke, 'Uses of Waterways in Anglo-Saxon England', p. 49, citing Frederic Seebohm, *The English Village Community*, 4th edn (London: Longmans, Green, 1905), pp. 150–53. S 227 (Meare); S 1555; S 1426 (Tidenham).

12   S 433 (Topsham): Hooke, *Pre-Conquest Charter-Bounds of Devon and Cornwall*, pp. 122–26.

13   Richard Hamer, *A Choice of Anglo-Saxon Verse* (London: Faber and Faber, 1970), p. 33.

14   *Ælfric's Colloquy*, ed. and trans. George N. Garmonsway, rev. edn (Exeter: University of Exeter Press, 1991), pp. 26–29.

15   S 1463; Domesday Book, fol. 205.

16   Victor Watts (ed.), *The Cambridge Dictionary of English Place-Names* (Cambridge: Cambridge University Press, 2004) (*CDEPN*), p. 109.

17   *CDEPN*, p. 194.

18   *Bede's Ecclesiastical History of the English People*, ed. and trans. Bertram Colgrave and Roger A.B. Mynors, rev. edn. (Oxford: Clarendon Press, 1969), iv.19, pp. 396–97.

19   S 186; S 821; S 767.

20   S 1142; Florence E. Harmer, *Anglo-Saxon Writs* (Manchester: Manchester University Press, 1952), no. 98, pp. 362–63.

21   Hooke, 'Uses of Waterways in Anglo-Saxon England', pp. 42–44.

22   S 1449; *ASC*, no. XLIX, pp. 102–05.

23   S 1489; *ASC*, no. XXVI, pp. 70–73.

24   S 98.

25   S 959; *ASC*, no. LXXXII, pp. 158–59.

26   S 1555.

27   S 1612; S 29; S 959; *ASC*, no. LXXXII, pp. 158–59.

28   Della Hooke, *The Anglo-Saxon Landscape: The Kingdom of the Hwicce* (Manchester: Manchester University Press, 1985), p. 59, Fig. 13.

29   S 1591a; S 80; Hooke, *Worcestershire Anglo-Saxon Charter-Bounds* (Woodbridge: Boydell, 1990), pp. 377–82, 46–57.

30   S 1303; Hooke, *Worcestershire Anglo-Saxon Charter-Bounds*, pp. 256–61.

31   S 450; S 951; S 1005; S 1019; S 1027; Hooke, *Pre-Conquest Charter-Bounds of Devon and Cornwall*, pp. 22–27; 55–59, 62–69.

32   S 878; Della Hooke, *The Landscape of Anglo-Saxon Staffordshire: The Charter Evidence* (Keele: Department of Adult Education, University of Keele, 1983), pp. 88–91.

33   S 770; Hooke, *Pre-Conquest Charter-Bounds of Devon and Cornwall*, pp. 41–43.

34   The author is indebted to Professor

Richard Coates for his many valuable observations in this section.

35 Tacitus, *Cornelii Taciti Annalium*, 12.31, in Charles D. Fisher (ed.), *Tacitus, Cornelii Taciti Annalium* (Oxford: Clarendon Press, 1906), pp. 320–21; *CDEPN*, p. 537; Geoffrey of Monmouth, *The History of the Kings of Britain*, trans. Lewis Thorpe (London: Guild Publishing, 1982), ii. 1–5, pp. 75–77; Anne Ross, *Pagan Celtic Britain: Studies in Iconography and Tradition* (London: Routledge and Kegan Paul, 1967), p. 21.

36 *CDEPN*, pp. 537–38.

37 Ross, *Pagan Celtic Britain*, pp. 21–22.

38 Discussed in *CDEPN*, p. 627.

39 Eilert Ekwall, *English River-Names* (Oxford: Clarendon Press, 1928) (*ERN*), pp. liv–lv.

40 Space does not allow full reference to word derivations, but minor river names are found in *ERN*, many updating the county volumes of the English Place-Name Society, while major river names are discussed in *CDEPN*.

41 *CDEPN*, p. 82, citing David D. Dixon, *Upper Coquetdale, Northumberland: Its History, Folk-Lore and Scenery* (Newcastle upon Tyne: R. Redpath, 1903), p. 79.

42 *ERN*, pp. lvi–xii.

43 Kenneth Jackson, *Language and History in Early Britain* (Edinburgh: Edinburgh University Press, 1953); map reproduced in Margaret Gelling, *Signposts to the Past: Place-Names and the History of England* (London: J.M. Dent and Sons, 1978), p. 89, Fig. 3.

44 David Parsons, 'Shropshire River-Names', lecture presented in 'A Tribute to Margaret Gelling', Society for Name Studies in Britain and Ireland Autumn Conference, Shrewsbury, 25 October 2014.

45 Ann Cole, *The Place-Name Evidence for a Routeway Network in Early Medieval England*, British Archaeological Reports, British Series 589 (Oxford: British Archaeological Reports, 2013).

46 Cole, *The Place-Name Evidence*, p. xc.

47 Margaret Gelling and Ann Cole, *The Landscape of Place-Names*, new edn (Donington: Shaun Tyas, 2014), pp. xiii–xvi, 1–35.

48 Joseph Bosworth, *An Anglo-Saxon Dictionary Based on the Manuscript Collections of the Late Joseph Bosworth*, ed. T. Northcote Toller (Oxford: Clarendon Press, 1898); Alistair Campbell, *An Anglo-Saxon Dictionary, Supplement* (Oxford: Oxford University Press, 1921); *ERN*.

49 Albert H. Smith, *English Place-Name Elements, Parts I–II*, English Place-Name Society, 25 and 26 (Cambridge: Cambridge University Press, 1956) (*EPNE I, EPNE II*).

50 Jane Roberts and Christian Kay with Lynne Grundy, *A Thesaurus of Old English in Two Volumes*, vol. 1 (London: Centre for late Antique and Medieval Studies, King's College, London, 1995).

51 Including Gelling, *Signposts to the Past*.

52 Barrie Cox, 'The Place-Names of the Earliest English Records', *Journal of the English Place-Name Society* 8 (1975–76), pp. 12–66.

53 Margaret Gelling, *Place-Names in the Landscape* (London: Dent, 1984); Gelling and Cole, *The Landscape of Place-Names*.

54 *CDEPN*.

55 Dictionary of Old English Project, Centre for Medieval Studies, University of Toronto: Pontifical Institute of Medieval Studies (ongoing).

56 Ann Cole, '*Burna* and *Brōc*: Problems Involved in Retrieving the Old English Usage of these Place-Name Elements', *English Place-Name Society Journal* 23 (1991), pp. 26–48. Richard Coates draws attention to the German term *bruch*.

57 Gelling and Cole, *The Landscape of Place-Names*, p. 21.

58 *EPNE II*, pp. 121–22.

59 *EPNE II*, p. 172.

60 S 786; Hooke, *Worcestershire Anglo-Saxon Charter-Bounds*, pp. 177–90.

61 S 469; *CDEPN*, p. 188.

62 Hooke, *Worcestershire Anglo-Saxon Charter-Bounds*; Hooke, *Pre-Conquest Charter-Bounds of Devon and Cornwall*.

63 S 218.

64 *EPNE II*, pp. 74, 75.

65 *CDEPN*, p. 233.

66 Hooke, *Pre-Conquest Charter-Bounds of Devon and Cornwall*, pp. 132, 159.

67 R. Coates, 'Reflections on Some

Major Lincolnshire Place-Names Part Two: Ness Wapentake to Yarborough, *Journal of the English Place-Name Society* 41 (2009), pp. 57–102, esp. pp. 81–83.

68   Ann Cole, 'The Place-Name Evidence for Water Transport in Early Medieval England', in John Blair (ed.), *Waterways and Canal-Building in Medieval England* (Oxford: Oxford University Press, 2007), pp. 77–78; John Blair, 'Transport and Canal-Building on the Upper Thames, 1000–1300', in Blair, *Waterways and Canal-Building*, pp. 270–71, 278.

69   *ERN*, p. 192.

70   Richard Coates, 'The Two Goxhills', *Journal of the English Place-Name Society* 27 (1995), pp. 5–13.

71   Gelling and Cole, *The Landscape of Place-Names*, p. 1.

72   *EPNE I*, p. 7.

73   *ASC*, pp. 176–77.

74   S 116; *CDEPN*, p. 265.

75   A.G.C. Turner, 'Notes on Some Somerset Place-Names', *Proceedings of the Somerset Archaeological and Natural History Society* 95 (1950), pp. 112–24.

76   Hooke, *Pre-Conquest Charter-Bounds of Devon and Cornwall*, p. 174.

77   Turner, 'Notes on Some Somerset Place-Names', p. 24.

78   Jane Roberts and Christian Kay, *A Thesaurus of Old English*, vol. 1 (London: King's College London Centre for Late Antique and Medieval Studies, 1995), p. 12.

79   A.G.C. Turner, 'Some Old English Passages Relating to the Episcopal Manor of Taunton', *Proceedings of the Somerset Archaeological and Natural History Society* 98 (1953), pp. 119, 123, but see below.

80   Smith, PNE II, p. 178.

81   Helen Maynard, 'The Use of the Place-Name Elements *Mōr* and *Mersc* in the Avon Valley', *Transactions of the Birmingham and Warwickshire Archaeological Society* 86 (1974), pp. 80–84.

82   C. Morris (ed.), *The Illustrated Journeys of Celia Fiennes 1685–c.1712* (Stroud: Alan Sutton Publishing, 1995), p. 82.

83   Gelling and Cole, *The Landscape of Place-Names*, pp. 62–63.

84   Some observations on changing Gloucestershire river names are made by Stephen Yeates, 'River-Names, Celtic and Old English: Their Dual Medieval and Post-medieval Personalities', *Journal of the English Place-Name Society* 38, pp. 63–81.

85   *ERN*, pp. xl–xli.

86   A. Mawer and F.M. Stenton with F.T.S. Houghton, *The Place-Names of Worcestershire*, English Place-Name Society 4 (Cambridge: Cambridge University Press, 1927), p. 10.

87   *CDEPN*, p. 170.

88   S 786; Hooke, *Worcestershire Anglo-Saxon Charter-Bounds*, pp. 208–19.

89   *CDEPN*, p. 582.

90   A.H. Smith, *The Place-Names of Gloucestershire, Part I*, English Place-Name Society 38 (Cambridge: Cambridge University Press, 1964), p. 11; Richard Coates, '*Stour* and *Blyth* as English River-Names', *English Language and Linguistics* 10.1 (2006), pp. 23–29.

91   *ERN*, pp. 272–73.

92   *ERN*, pp. 373–74.

93   *ERN*, pp. 320–22.

94   S 1348; Hooke, *Worcestershire Anglo-Saxon Charter-Bounds*, pp. 200–32; S 550.

95   S 206; Hooke, *Worcestershire Anglo-Saxon Charter-Bounds*, pp. 100–01. In this charter of AD 855, a grant of privileges to the bishop of Worcester and his community at Worcester, the estate was freed from the duty of pasturing the king's swine.

96   *ERN*, pp. 15–16.

97   *CDEPN*, p. 365.

98   Della Hooke, *Trees in Anglo-Saxon England: Literature, Lore and Landscape* (Woodbridge: Boydell, 2010).

99   Stefan Buczacki, *Fauna Britannica* (London: Hamlyn, 2002), p. 214.

100   *ERN*, pp. 237–38.

101   See George Monbiot, *Feral: Rewilding the Land, Sea and Human Life* (London: Penguin, 2013), pp. 118–19.

102   Hooke, *Worcestershire Anglo-Saxon Charter-Bounds*, mapped pp. 255, 270, 378–79, 265, 227.

103   Della Hooke, *The Anglo-Saxon Landscape: The Kingdom of the Hwicce*, p. 164.

104   The river names discussed here are mostly those included in *CDEPN*.

105   *CDEPN*, p. 95.

106   *CDEPN*, p. 390.

107   Hooke, *Pre-Conquest Charter-Bounds of Devon and Cornwall*, pp. 193–95.

108   Bruce Coplestone-Crow, *Herefordshire Place-Names*, British Archaeological Reports, British Series 214 (Oxford: British Archaeological Reports, 1989), pp. 11, 166–67.

109   *CDEPN*, p. 175.

110   *CDEPN*, p. 621.

111   *CDEPN*, p. 122.

112   *CDEPN*, p. 357.

113   *CDEPN*, p. 157.

114   *ERN*, p. 135.

115   But see R. Coates, *Transactions of the Philological Society* 103.3 (2005), pp. 303–22, where it is suggested that the meaning of *Granta* is a completely open question.

116   Hooke, *Worcestershire Anglo-Saxon Charter-Bounds*, pp. 235–39.

117   *CDEPN*, p. 252.

118   *CDEPN*, p. 364.

119   *ERN*, p. 138.

120   *CDEPN*, p. 405.

121   *CDEPN*, p. 410.

122   *CDEPN*, p. 325.

123   Margaret Gelling, *The Place-Names of Shropshire, Part 5*, English Place-Name Society 82 (Nottingham: English Place-Name Society, 2006), p. 153.

124   Revd C.B. Crofts, 'St. Buryan: An Attempt to Restore and Identify the Charter Placenames', *Devon and Cornwall Notes and Queries* 24 (1950–51), pp. 6–8.

125   S 165; Hooke, *Pre-Conquest Charter-Bounds of Devon and Cornwall*, pp. 165–68.

126   Della Hooke, in preparation.

127   Carole Hough, 'Commonplace Place-Names', *Nomina* 30 (2007), pp. 101–20, esp. pp. 105, 107.

128   R. Coates, 'Beverley: A Beaver's Lodge Place', *Journal of the English Place-Name Society* 34 (2002), pp. 17–22.

129   S 361; B 607.

Chapter 3: Fens and Frontiers

1   *The Peterborough Chronicle of Hugh Candidus*, ed. W.T. Mellows (Oxford: Oxford University Press, 1949), p. 2.

2   Kelley M. Wickham-Crowley, 'Living on the *Ecg*: The Mutable Boundaries of Land and Water in Anglo-Saxon Contexts', in Clare A. Lees and Gillian R. Overing (eds), *A Place to Believe In: Locating Medieval Landscapes* (University Park: Pennsylvania State University Press, 2006), p. 85.

3   Susan Oosthuizen, 'Culture and Identity in the Early Medieval Fenland Landscape', *Landscape History: Journal of the Society for Landscape Studies* 37.1 (2016), p. 8: citing Sam Lucy and Andrew Reynolds (eds), *Burial in Early Medieval England and Wales* (London: Society for Medieval Archaeology, 2002). My thanks to Della Hooke for providing a pre-publication copy of this article.

4   Oosthuizen, 'Culture and Identity', p. 10.

5   Oosthuizen details evidence for Brittonic and Late Spoken Latin in the early medieval fenland, as well as discussing Anglo-Saxon

royal genealogies with British Celtic elements ('Culture and Identity', pp. 8, 16–17).

6   See 'Major Wetland Areas of England', in John Coles and David Hall (eds), *Changing Landscapes: The Ancient Fenland*, Wetland Archaeology Research Project (WARP) (Cambridge: Cambridgeshire County Council, 1998), p. 2, Fig. 1.1.

7   Margaret Gelling and Ann Cole, *The Landscape of Place-Names* (Stamford: Shaun Tyas, 2000), p. xv.

8   Gelling and Cole, *The Landscape of Place-Names*, p. xiii.

9   Gelling and Cole, *The Landscape of Place-Names*, p. xv.

10   Gelling and Cole, *The Landscape of Place-Names*, p. xv.

11   Gelling and Cole, *The Landscape of Place-Names*, p. xvi.

12   Gelling and Cole, *The Landscape of Place-Names*, p. xvii.

13   For further discussion of place-name elements in Brittonic or Late Spoken Latin, as well as Old English elements preserving 'minor clan'

names and the term '-*wealh*', Briton or foreign speaker, see Oosthuizen, 'Culture and Identity', pp. 14–19.

14 See Chapter 4 of this volume for the somewhat scanty evidence for settlement ('The Larger Marshlands').

15 Gelling and Cole, *The Landscape of Place-Names*, pp. 44–45.

16 Gelling and Cole, *The Landscape of Place-Names*, p. 58.

17 Gelling and Cole, *The Landscape of Place-Names*, p. 44.

18 Gelling and Cole, *The Landscape of Place-Names*, p. 45.

19 *Bede's Ecclesiastical History of the English People*, ed. and trans. Bertram Colgrave and Roger A.B. Mynors, rev. edn. (Oxford: Clarendon Press, 1969), iii.20, pp. 276–77.

20 Colgrave and Mynors, *Bede's Ecclesiastical History*, iv.6, pp. 354–55.

21 Colgrave and Mynors, *Bede's Ecclesiastical History*, iv.19, pp. 390–93.

22 Kenneth Penn, 'Introduction', in Andy Crowson, Tom Lane, Kenneth Penn and Dale Trimble, *Anglo-Saxon Settlement on the Siltland of Eastern England*, Lincolnshire Archaeology and Heritage Reports Series 7 (Sleaford: Heritage Trust of Lincolnshire, 2005), p. 3.

23 David Roffe, 'The Historical Context', in Crowson et al., *Anglo-Saxon Settlement*, p. 265.

24 Roffe, 'Historical Context', p. 265.

25 Roffe, 'Historical Context', p. 276, for example.

26 Roffe, 'Historical Context', pp. 266, 268.

27 See the work of Alan Everitt on Kent and the Weald, for example, in its shared woodlands, shielings and droveways: *Landscape and Community in England* (London: Hambledon Press, 1985), esp. chaps 3 and 4. Della Hooke also discusses the subdivision of Fenland grazings in *The Landscape of Anglo-Saxon England* (London: Leicester University Press, 1998), pp. 172–73 and Susan Oosthuizen also discusses regional polities and intercommoning in 'Culture and Identity', pp. 10–14.

28 Roffe, 'Historical Context', pp. 273–4.

29 Penn, 'Introduction', in Crowson et al., *Anglo-Saxon Settlement*, p. 4.

30 Val Fryer and Kenneth Penn, 'Crafts and Production', in Crowson et al., *Anglo-Saxon Settlement*, p. 210.

31 Polydora Baker, 'Animal Bone', in Crowson et al., *Anglo-Saxon Settlement*, p. 217.

32 C.P. Biggam, 'The True Staff of Life: The Multiple Roles of Plants', in Maren Clegg Hyer and Gale R. Owen-Crocker (eds), *The Material Culture of Daily Living in the Anglo-Saxon World* (Exeter: University of Exeter Press, 2011), p. 34.

33 Peter Bierbaumer and Hans Sauer, with Helmut W. Klug and Ulrike Krischke (eds), *Dictionary of Old English Plant Names*, q.v. '*fen-minte*' (2007–09) <http://oldenglish-plant-names.org> [accessed 19 May 2015].

34 *Dictionary of Old English Plant Names*, q.v. '*mersc-mealwe*', '*mersc-mear-gealla*', *mersc-hōfe*'.

35 Paul Blinkhorn, 'Pottery', in Crowson et al., *Anglo-Saxon Settlement*, p. 211.

36 Blinkhorn, 'Pottery', p. 212.

37 See Mark Gardiner, Chapter 7, for further discussion of hythes; see Stephen Rippon (Chapter 4) and Della Hooke (Chapters 2 and 5) for further discussion of water and waterway terms.

38 Ann Cole, 'The Place-Name Evidence for Water Transport in Early Medieval England', in John Blair (ed.), *Waterways and Canal-Building in Medieval England* (Oxford: Oxford University Press, 2007), p. 66.

39 *The Electronic Sawyer: Online Catalogue of Anglo-Saxon Charters*, revised and expanded version of Peter Sawyer's *Anglo-Saxon Charters: An Annotated List and Bibliography*, Center for Computing in the Humanities at King's College London, 2015 <www.esawyer.org.uk/charter/595.html#> [accessed 3 June 2015].

40 Cole, 'Water Transport', p. 74.

41 Cole, 'Water Transport', p. 74.

42 Gelling and Cole, *The Landscape of Place-Names*, p. 86.

43 Cole, 'Water Transport', p. 68.

44 Jo Caruth, 'Recent Work on the Anglo-Saxon Cemeteries of RAF Lakenheath', *Saxon: The Newsletter of the Sutton Hoo Society* 32 (2000), pp. 1–2 <http://suttonhoo.org/wp-content/uploads/2016/02/Saxon32.pdf> [accessed 21 February 2017].

45   Ian Wood, *The Origins of Jarrow: The Monastery, the Slake and Ecgfrith's Minster*, Bede's World Studies 1 (Jarrow: Bede's World, 2008), pp. 8–9, Fig. 1.

46   Wood, *Origins of Jarrow*, p. 31.

47   Wood, *Origins of Jarrow*, p. 33.

48   Wood, *Origins of Jarrow*, p. 7.

49   Asser, 'Life of King Alfred', in Simon Keynes and Michael Lapidge (eds), *Alfred the Great: Asser's Life of King Alfred and Other Contemporary Sources* (Harmondsworth: Penguin, 1983), ch. 53, p. 83.

50   Asser, 'Life of King Alfred', ch. 55, p. 84.

51   Quoted in 'Alfred and the Cakes' in Keynes and Lapidge, *Alfred the Great*, p. 197.

52   Asser, 'Life of King Alfred', ch. 92, p. 103.

53   Gelling and Cole, *The Landscape of Place-Names*, p. 81.

54   Lindy Brady, 'Echoes of Britons on a Fenland Frontier in the Old English *Andreas*', *Review of English Studies* 61.252 (2010), p. 669.

55   Brady, 'Echoes', pp. 676–77.

56   Joseph Bosworth and T. Northcote Toller, *An Anglo-Saxon Dictionary* (Online), compiled by Sean Christ and Ondřej Tichý, Faculty of Arts, Charles University, Prague, q.v. *mearc* <http://bosworth.ff.cuni.cz/055183> and <http://bosworth.ff.cuni.cz/022482> [accessed 23 May 2015].

57   *Beowulf: A Dual-Language Edition*, ed. Howell D. Chickering, rev. edn (New York: Anchor, 2006).

58   Wickham-Crowley, 'Living on the *Ecg*', pp. 85–110.

59   Paul Gonser, *Das angelsächsische Prosa-Leben des hl. Guthlac*, Anglistische Forschungen Heft 27 (Heidelberg: Carl Winter, 1909; repr. Amsterdam: Swets & Zeitlinger, 1966), ch. 11, l. 17, p. 144.

60   Gonser, *Guthlac*, ch. 11, l. 23, p. 145.

61   Gonser, *Guthlac*, ch. 4, ll. 6–7, p. 117.

62   Gonser, *Guthlac*, ch. 4, ll. 11–12, p. 118.

63   Rubie D.N. Warner (ed.), 'Of Seinte Neote', *Early English Homilies from the Twelfth Century Ms. Vesp. D. XIV* (London: Kegan Paul, Trench, Trübner and Co. for the Early English Text Society, 1917; repr. New York: Kraus, 1971), ll. 10 and 30, p. 130.

64   George Ruder Younge, '"Those Were Good Days": Representations of the Anglo-Saxon Past in the Old English Homily on Saint Neot', *Review of English Studies*, New Series 63.260 (2012), p. 356.

65   Old English Poetry, 'Maxims II', The Complete Corpus of Anglo-Saxon Poetry, <http://www.sacredtexts.com/neu/ascp/a15.htm> [accessed 18 May 2015].

66   All line references with translation can be found in *Beowulf*, ed. Chickering (2006).

67   Margaret Gelling, 'The Landscape of *Beowulf*', *Anglo-Saxon England* 31 (2002), p. 8.

68   Dennis Cronan, 'Old English *gelad*: "A Passage across Water"', *Neophilologus* 71 (1987), pp. 316–19, cited in Gelling and Cole, *The Landscape of Place-Names*, p. 83.

69   Gelling and Cole, *The Landscape of Place-Names*, p. 83.

70   *Liber Eliensis: A History of the Isle of Ely from the Seventh Century to the Twelfth*, trans. Janet Fairweather (Woodbridge: Boydell, 2005), II.107, p. 222: 'They are to be found, however, more fully recounted ... by Richard of blessed memory, a venerable man and a most learned brother of ours'.

71   *Hereward the Wake*, trans. Michael Swanton, in Stephen Knight and Thomas Ohlgren (eds), *Robin Hood and Other Outlaw Tales*, TEAMS Middle English Texts Series (Kalamazoo: Medieval Institute Publications, 1997) <http://d.lib.rochester.edu/teams/text/hereward-the-wake> [accessed 22 May 2015].

72   *Hereward the Wake*, 'Introduction', in Knight and Ohlgren, *Robin Hood and Other Outlaw Tales*.

73   Roffe, 'Context', in Crowson et al., *Anglo-Saxon Settlement*, pp. 264–65.

74   *Hereward the Wake*, 'Preface', in Knight and Ohlgren, *Robin Hood and Other Outlaw Tales*.

My gratitude to research assistant Robert Lee Wolfe III for early help on sources.

Chapter 4: Marshlands and Other Wetlands

1   Bertram Colgrave, *Felix's Life of Saint Guthlac* (Cambridge: Cambridge University Press, 1956), pp. 86–87.

2   Robert Van de Noort, William Fletcher, Gavin Thomas, Ian Carstairs and David Patrick, 'Monuments at Risk in England's Wetlands', University of Exeter for English Heritage, 2002 <http://hdl.handle.net/10036/29596> [accessed 28 July 2014], pp. 4–5.

3   Stephen Rippon, *The Transformation of Coastal Wetlands* (Oxford: Oxford University Press, 2000); Tom Lane and Elaine L. Morris (eds), *A Millennium of Saltmaking: Prehistoric and Romano-British Salt Production in the Fenland*, Lincolnshire Archaeology and Heritage Reports Series 4 (Sleaford: Heritage Trust of Lincolnshire, 2001); Stephen Rippon, *Landscape, Community and Colonisation: The North Somerset Levels during the 1st to 2nd Millennia AD*, Council for British Archaeology Research Report 152 (York: Council for British Archaeology, 2006); Edward Biddulph, Stuart Foreman, Elizabeth Stafford, Dan Stansbie and Rebecca Nicholson, *London Gateway: Iron Age and Roman Saltmaking in the Thames Estuary. Excavation at Stanford Wharf Nature Reserve, Essex*, Oxford Archaeology Monograph 18 (Oxford: Oxford Archaeology, 2012).

4   Rippon, *Transformation of Coastal Wetlands*, pp. 69–71; Heather Wallis, *Roman Routeways across the Fens: Excavations at Morton, Tilney St Lawrence, Nordelph and Downham West*, East Anglian Archaeology Occasional Paper 10 (Gressenhall: East Anglian Archaeology, 2002); Brian B. Simmons and Paul Cope-Faulkner, *The Car Dyke: Past Work, Current State and Future Possibilities*, Lincolnshire Archaeology and Heritage Reports Series 8 (Sleaford: Heritage Trust of Lincolnshire, 2004).

5   Rippon, *Landscape, Community and Colonisation*, pp. 80–81.

6   Colgrave, *Felix's Life of Saint Guthlac*, pp. 86–87; John Hines, *Voices in the Past: English Literature and Archaeology* (Woodbridge: Boydell and Brewer, 2004), pp. 62–70. See also Chapter 5 of this volume.

7   Mark Gardiner, 'The Wider Context', in Luke Barber and Greg Priestley-Bell (eds), *Medieval Adaptation, Settlement and Economy of a Coastal Wetland: The Evidence from around Lydd, Romney Marsh, Kent* (Oxford: Oxbow, 2008), pp. 297–304. Chapters 1, 3, 5 and 6 discuss other literary evidence for how water and wetlands were perceived in this period.

8   For Fenland, see Gardiner, 'The Wider Context', pp. 299–300. For Congresbury, in Somerset, see Rippon, *Landscape, Community and Colonisation*, p. 134 and Figs 6.4 and 12.2. For Muchelney, see Michael Aston, 'An Archipelago in Central Somerset: The Origins of Muchelney Abbey', *Proceedings of the Somerset Archaeological and Natural History Society* 150 (2007), pp. 63–72. For Glastonbury, see Stephen Rippon, '"Making the Most of a Bad Situation"? Glastonbury Abbey, Meare and the Medieval Exploitation of Wetland Resources in the Somerset Levels', *Medieval Archaeology* 48 (2004), pp. 91–130. For the Witham Valley in Lincolnshire, see David Stocker and Paul Everson, 'The Straight and Narrow Way: Fenland Causeways and the Conversion of the Landscape in the Witham Valley, Lincolnshire', in Martin Carver (ed.), *The Cross Goes North: Processes of Conversion in Northern Europe AD300–1300* (York: York Medieval Press, 2003), pp. 271–88. For East Anglia, see Richard Hoggett, *The Archaeology of the East Anglian Conversion* (Woodbridge: Boydell, 2010), pp. 71–77.

9   Rippon, 'Making the Most of a Bad Situation'.

10   James P. Carley, *The Chronicle of Glastonbury Abbey: An Edition, Translation and Study of John of Glastonbury's* Cronica sive Antiquites Glastoniensis Ecclesie (Woodbridge: Boydell, 2001), p. 101.

11   Catherine A.M. Clarke, *Literary Landscapes and the Idea of England: 700–1400* (Cambridge: D.S. Brewer, 2006), p. 68; and see C. Clarke, 'The Allegory of Landscape: Land Reclamation and Defence at Glastonbury Abbey', in Mary Carr, Kenneth P. Clarke and Marco Nievergelt (eds), *On Allegory: Some Medieval Aspects and Approaches from Chaucer to Shakespeare* (Newcastle upon Tyne: Cambridge Scholars, 2008), pp. 87–103.

12   Peter H. Sawyer, *Anglo-Saxon Charters: An Annotated List and Bibliography* (London: Royal Historical Society, 1968), S 1787; Cyril Hart, *The Early Charters of Essex*, Department of English Local History Occasional Paper 1st Series 10, rev. edn (Leicester: Leicester University Press, 1971), no. 7.

13   The methodology for reconstructing early folk territories such as these is described in Stephen Rippon, *Beyond the Medieval Village* (Oxford: Oxford University Press, 2008) and Stephen Rippon, *Making Sense of an Historic Landscape* (Oxford: Oxford University Press, 2012).

14   Horace C. Round, 'The Domesday Survey', in *The Victoria History of the Counties of England: A History of the County of Essex*, vol. 1 (Westminster: Constable, 1903), pp. 368–74; Henry Clifford Darby, *The Domesday Geography of Eastern England* (Cambridge: Cambridge University Press, 1971), pp. 241–44; Rippon, *Transformation of Coastal Wetlands*, pp. 201–07.

15   See, for example, Darby, *The Domesday Geography of Eastern England*, pp. 47–54. The significance of wetlands as frontier regions is discussed in Chapter 3 and Stephen Rippon, 'Focus or Frontier? The Significance of Estuaries in the Landscape of Southern Britain', *Landscapes* 8(i) (2007), pp. 23–38.

16   Andy Crowson, Tom Lane, Ken Penn and Dale Trimble, *Anglo-Saxon Settlement on the Siltland of Eastern England*, Lincolnshire Archaeology and Heritage Reports Series 7 (Sleaford: Lincolnshire Archaeology, 2006), pp. 171–90 and pp. 190–205; Rippon, *Landscape, Community and Colonisation*.

17   Crowson et al., *Anglo-Saxon Settlement*, pp. 19–35 and 35–48.

18   It is also worth noting that most of the interior of the southern enclosure at Third Drove was destroyed by a later ditch. See Crowson et al., *Anglo-Saxon Settlement*, Figs 6 and 8.

19   Rose Hall Farm in Walpole St Andrew, Hay Green in Terrington and Ingleborough in West Walton: Crowson et al., *Anglo-Saxon Settlement*, pp. 126–89; Clampgate Road in Fishtoft: Paul Cope-Faulkner, *Clampgate Road, Fishtoft: Archaeology of a Middle Saxon Island Settlement in the Lincolnshire Fens*, Lincolnshire Archaeology and Heritage Reports Series 10 (Sleaford: Lincolnshire Archaeology, 2012).

20   Stephen Rippon, Adam Wainwright and Chris Smart, 'Farming Regions in Medieval England: The Archaeobotanical and Zooarchaeological Evidence', *Medieval Archaeology* 58 (2014), pp. 205–66.

21   The vast majority of the bones of goats and sheep cannot be identified to species, and so they can only be identified as 'sheep or goat'.

22   For dryland sites, see Rippon et al., 'Farming Regions'; the marshland sites are Ingleborough in West Walton, Norfolk; Rose Hall Farm in Walpole St Andrew, Norfolk; Hay Green in Terrington St Clement, Norfolk (Crowson et al., *Anglo-Saxon Settlement*) and Clampgate Road, Fishtoft, Lincolnshire (Cope-Faulkner, *Clampgate Road*).

23   Cope-Faulkner, *Clampgate Road*, p. 96.

24   C. French, 'Molluscan Analysis', in R.P.J. Jackson and Tim W. Potter (eds), *Excavations at Stonea, Cambridgeshire: 1980–85* (London: British Museum, 1996), pp. 639–54; Keith Dobney, Deborah Jaques, James Barrett and Cluney Johnstone, *Farmers, Monks and Aristocrats: The Environmental Archaeology of Anglo-Saxon Flixborough* (Oxford: Oxbow, 2007), p. 193; Sue Stallibrass, 'Animal Bones', in Jackson and Potter, *Excavations at Stonea*, pp. 587–612.

25   Dobney et al., *Farmers, Monks and Aristocrats*, p. 143.

26   The sample size was so small that the data was not published in Rippon et al., 'Farming Regions'. The six sites are Church View, in Lower Slaughter, Gloucestershire (David Kenyon and Martin Watts, 'An Anglo-Saxon Enclosure at Copsehill Road, Lower Slaughter: Excavations in 1999', *Transactions of the Bristol and Gloucestershire Archaeological Society* 124 (2006), pp. 73–109); Hillside Meadow, in Fordham, Cambridgeshire (Richard Cuttler, Helen Martin-Bacon, Kirsty Nichol, Catharine Patrick, Rob Perrin, Stephanie Rátkai, Martin Smith and Josh Williams, *Five Sites in Cambridgeshire: Excavations at Woodhurst, Fordham, Soham, Buckden and St Neots, 1998–2002*, British Archaeology Report

British Series 528 (Oxford: British Archaeology, 2011)); West Fen Road (Consortium site), in Ely, Cambridgeshire (Andrew Mudd and Michael Webster, *Iron Age and Middle Saxon Settlements at West Fen Road, Ely, Cambridgeshire: The Consortium Site*, British Archaeology Report British Series 538 (Oxford: British Archaeology, 2011)); Bestwall Quarry, in Wareham, Dorset (W. Carruthers, 'Bestwall Quarry, Wareham: The Charred Plant Remains from Iron Age, Romano-British and Later Contexts', unpublished report, 2006); Church Field, in Shapwick, Somerset (Christopher Gerrard and Michael Aston, *The Shapwick Project, Somerset: A Rural Landscape Explored*, Society of Medieval Archaeology Monograph 25 (Leeds: Society of Medieval Archaeology, 2007)); Yarnton, in Oxfordshire (Gill Hey, *Yarnton: Saxon and Medieval Settlement and Landscape*, Thames Valley Landscapes Monograph 20 (Oxford: Oxford Archaeology, 2004)).

27   Gemma Martin, 'Botanical Remains', in Cope-Faulkner, *Fishtoft*, pp. 109–14.

28   For example, Joan Thirsk, 'The Farming Regions of England', in Joan Thirsk (ed.), *The Agrarian History of England and Wales*, vol. 4, *1500–1640* (Cambridge: Cambridge University Press, 1967), pp. 1–112; J. Thirsk, *Agricultural Regions and Agrarian History in England, 1500–1750* (Basingstoke: Macmillan Education, 1987); Bruce M.S. Campbell, *English Seigniorial Agriculture 1250–1450* (Cambridge: Cambridge University Press, 2000).

29   Willem van Zeist, 'Palaeobotanical Studies of Settlement Sites in the Coastal Area of the Netherlands', *Palaeohistoria* 16 (1974), pp. 223–371; W. van Zeist, T.C. Van Hoorn, S. Bottema and H. Woldring, 'An Agricultural Experiment in the Unprotected Saltmarsh', *Palaeohistoria* 18 (1976), pp. 111–53; S. Bottema, T.C. Van Hoorn, H. Woldring and W.H.E. Gremmen, 'An Agricultural Experiment in the Unprotected Marsh Part II', *Palaeohistoria* 22 (1980), pp. 127–40; Karl-Ernst Behre and S. Jacomet, 'The Ecological Interpretation of Archaeobotanical Data', in Willem Van Zeist, Krystyna Wasylikowa and Karl-Ernst Behre (eds), *Progress in Old World Palaeoethnobotany* (Rotterdam: A.A. Balkema,

1991), pp. 81–108; J.D. Rhoades, A. Kandiah and A.M. Mashali, *The Use of Saline Water for Crop Production*, Food and Agriculture Organization Irrigation and Drainage Paper 48, Rome: Food and Agriculture Organization of the United Nations, 1992) <www.fao.org/docrep/T0667E/T0667E00.htm> [accessed 29 May 2015].

30   Rippon et al., 'Farming Regions', Table 12.

31   Crowson et al., *Anglo-Saxon Settlement*, pp. 217–26, 293.

32   Crowson et al., *Anglo-Saxon Settlement*, p. 125.

33   Crowson et al., *Anglo-Saxon Settlement*, pp. 218, 228.

34   Stephen Rippon, 'Landscape Change in the "Long Eighth Century"', in Nicholas Higham and Martin J. Ryan (eds), *The Landscape Archaeology of Anglo-Saxon England* (Woodbridge: Boydell, 2010), pp. 39–64.

35   Philip Crummy, Jennifer Hillam and Carl Crossan, 'Mersea Island: The Anglo-Saxon Causeway', *Essex Archaeology and History* 14 (1982), pp. 77–86; B. Durham, 'Archaeological Investigations at St Aldates, Oxford', *Oxoniensia* 42 (1977), pp. 83–203; Richard Brunning, *Somerset's Peatland Archaeology: Managing and Investigating a Fragile Resource* (Oxford: Oxbow, 2014), pp. 212–37.

36   John Dent, Chris Loveluck and Will Fletcher, 'The Early Medieval Site at Skerne', in Robert Van de Noort and Stephen Ellis (eds), *Wetland Heritage of the Hull Valley: An Archaeological Survey* (Hull: University of Hull Press, 2000), pp. 217–42.

37   Stephen Rippon, 'Making the Most of a Bad Situation', pp. 91–130.

38   David Robertson and John Ames, 'Early Medieval Inter-Tidal Fishweirs at Holme Beach, Norfolk', *Medieval Archaeology* 54 (2010), pp. 329–46.

39   L. Everitt, 'Targeted Inter-Tidal Survey', Suffolk County Council Archaeological Services Report 2007/192 <https://content.historicengland.org.uk/images-books/publications/suffolk-rczas-targeted-inter-tidal-survey-report/2007192targetedinter-tidalsurveyreport.pdf/> [accessed 20 February 2017]; Ellen M. Heppell, 'Saxon Fishtraps in the Blackwater Estuary, Essex: Monitoring Survey at Collin's

Creek, Pewet Island and The Nass 2003–2007', *Transactions of the Essex Society for Archaeology and History* 2 (2011), pp. 76–97.

40   Robert Cowie and Lyn Blackmore, *Early and Middle Saxon Rural Settlement in the London Region*, Museum of London Archaeological Service Monograph 41 (London: Museum of London Archaeological Service, 2008), pp. 115–24; N. Cohen, 'Early Anglo-Saxon Fishtraps on the River Thames', in Stuart Brookes, Sue Harrington and Andrew Reynolds (eds), *Studies in Early Anglo-Saxon Art and Archaeology: Papers in Honour of Martin G. Welch*, British Archaeological Reports Series 257 (Oxford: British Archaeology, 2011), pp. 231–38.

41   Steve Godbold and Rick Turner, 'Medieval Fishtraps in the Severn Estuary', *Medieval Archaeology* 38 (1994), pp. 19–54; Richard Brunning, 'A Millennium of Fishing Structures in Stert Flats, Bridgwater Bay', *Archaeology in the Severn Estuary* 18 (2007), pp. 67–83; Adrian M. Chadwick and Toby Catchpole, 'Casting the Net Wide: Mapping and Dating Fish Traps through the Severn Estuary Rapid Coastal Zone Assessment Survey', *Archaeology in the Severn Estuary* 21 (2010), pp. 47–80; T. Catchpole, R. Brunning and A. Chadwick, 'Casting the Net Wider: Further Dating and Discussion of Fish Traps Recorded by the Severn Estuary Rapid Coastal Zone Assessment Survey', *Archaeology in the Severn Estuary* 22 (2013), pp. 71–91.

42   Robertson and Ames, 'Early Medieval Inter-Tidal Fishweirs'; Cowie and Blackmore, *Early and Middle Saxon Rural Settlement in the London Region*, p. 117.

43   Peter Murphy, 'The Landscape and Economy of the Anglo-Saxon Coast: New Archaeological Evidence', in Higham and Ryan, *Landscape Archaeology*, pp. 211–22.

44   Stephen Rippon, 'Essex *c*.700–1066', in Owen Bedwin (ed.), *The Archaeology of Essex* (Chelmsford: Essex County Council, 1997), pp. 117–28; R.L. Hall and C.P. Clarke, 'A Saxon Intertidal Timber Fish Weir at Collins Creek in the Blackwater Estuary', *Essex Archaeology and History* 31 (2000), pp. 125–46.

45   Crowson et al., *Anglo-Saxon Settlement*, pp. 90, 120, 140, 167, 188; Cope-Faulkner, *Clampgate Road*, pp. 98–102; Dobney et al.,

Farmers, Monks and Aristocrats, pp. 52–53. Fishing in the early medieval landscape is also discussed in Chapter 6.

46   Crowson et al., *Anglo-Saxon Settlement*, pp. 120, 130, 133, 167, 170, 231; Cope-Faulkner, *Clampgate Road*, pp. 97–98; K. Dobney et al., *Farmers, Monks and Aristocrats*, pp. 211–12.

47   *Ælfric's Colloquy*, ed. and trans. George N. Garmonsway, 2nd edn (London: Methuen, 1947); Dobney et al., *Farmers, Monks and Aristocrats*, pp. 179, 193; D.H. Evans and C. Loveluck, *Life and Economy at Early Medieval Flixborough, c.AD600–1000: The Artefact Evidence* (Oxford: Oxbow, 2009), pp. 249–52.

48   Mark Gardiner, 'The Exploitation of Sea-Mammals in Medieval England: Bones and Their Social Context', *Archaeological Journal* 154 (1997), pp. 184–95; Mark Gardiner, John Stewart and Greg Priestley-Bell, 'Anglo-Saxon Whale Exploitation: Some Evidence from Dengemarsh, Lydd, Kent', *Medieval Archaeology* 42 (1998), pp. 96–101; Flixborough: Dobney et al., pp. 204–07. See also Chapter 6.

49   Evans and Loveluck, *Life and Economy at Early Medieval Flixborough*, pp. 236, 249–52; Dent et al., 'The Early Medieval Site at Skerne', p. 233. See also Chapter 6.

50   Cope-Faulkner, *Clampgate Road*; Crowson et al., *Anglo-Saxon Settlement*, pp. 76–77, 96.

51   Helen Fenwick, Henry Chapman, Will Fletcher, Gavin Thomas and Malcolm Lillie, 'Archaeological Survey of the Lincolnshire Marsh', in Stephen Ellis, Helen Fenwick, Malcolm Lillie and Robert Van de Noort, *Wetland Heritage of the Lincolnshire Marsh: An Archaeological Survey* (Kingston upon Hull: Humber Wetlands Project, 2001), pp. 99–202.

52   H.C. Darby, *Domesday England* (Cambridge: Cambridge University Press, 1977), pp. 263–65.

53   Their location is likely to have been spread across Walland Marsh (the western part of what is today known as Romney Marsh): S.H. King, 'Sussex', in H.C. Darby and Eila M.J. Campbell (eds), *The Domesday Geography of South East England* (Cambridge: Cambridge University Press, 1962), pp. 407–82.

54   Ann Williams and G.H. Martin, *Domesday Book: A Complete Translation* (London: Penguin, 2002), pp. 207, 213.

55   Martin Bell, Astrid Caseldine and Heike Neumann, *Prehistoric Intertidal Archaeology in the Welsh Severn Estuary*, Council for British Archaeology Research Report 120 (York: Council for British Archaeology, 2000); Bryony Coles and John Coles, *Sweet Track to Glastonbury: The Somerset Levels in Prehistory* (London: Thames and Hudson, 1986); Elizabeth Stafford, *Landscape and Prehistory of the East London Wetlands*, Oxford Archaeology Monograph 17 (Oxford: Oxford Archaeology, 2012); Tony J. Wilkinson and Peter L. Murphy, *The Archaeology of the Essex Coast*, vol. 1, *The Hullbridge Survey*, East Anglian Archaeology 71 (Chelmsford: East Anglian Archaeology, 1995); Robert Van de Noort, *The Humber Wetlands: The Archaeology of a Dynamic Landscape* (Macclesfield: Windgather, 2004).

56   Wilkinson and Murphy, *The Archaeology of the Essex Coast*, pp. 198–200.

57   Andrew B. Powell, *By River, Fields and Factories: The Making of the Lower Lea Valley. Archaeological and Cultural Heritage Investigations on the Site of the London 2012 Olympic and Paralympic Games*, Wessex Archaeology Report 29 (Salisbury: Wessex Archaeology, 2012), pp. 81–82; Biddulph et al., *London Gateway*, p. 177.

58   Stephen Rippon, 'Roman Settlement and Salt Production on the Somerset Coast: The Work of Sam Nash: A Somerset Archaeologist

and Historian 1913–1985', *Proceedings of the Somerset Archaeological and Natural History Society* 139 (1995), pp. 99–117; Stephen Rippon, 'The Romano-British Exploitation of Coastal Wetlands: Survey and Excavation on the North Somerset Levels, 1993–97', *Britannia* 31 (2000), pp. 69–200; Rippon, *Landscape, Community and Colonisation*.

59   Herbert P.R. Finberg, *The Early Charters of Wessex* (Leicester: Leicester University Press, 1964), no. 25, pp. 32 and 122.

60   Victor Watts (ed.), *The Cambridge Dictionary of English Place-Names* (Cambridge: Cambridge University Press, 2004), p. 102.

61   M. Wood, 'Archaeological Investigation along the Weston Bypass, Weston, Lincolnshire (WPB01)', Archaeological Project Services report 145/06 <http://archaeologydataservice.ac.uk/archiveDS/archiveDownload?t=arch-1045-1/dissemination/pdf/4115_Archaeological InvestigationsalongtheWestonBypass_Weston.pdf> [accessed 4 August 2014].

62   Rippon, *Transformation of Coastal Wetlands*, p. 29.

63   Martyn Waller and Anthony Long, 'The Holocene Coastal Deposits of Sussex: A Re-Evaluation', in Erik Thoen, Guus J. Borger, Adriaan M.J. de Kraker, Tim Soens, Dries Tys, Lies Vervaet and J.T. Weerts (eds), *Landscapes or Seascapes? The History of the Coastal Environment in the North Sea Area Reconsidered*, CORN (Comparative Rural History of the North Sea Area) Publication 13 (Turnhout: Brepols, 2013), pp. 31–59, Fig. 3.2.

Chapter 5: Sacred and Mystical Contexts

1   Peter H. Sawyer, *Anglo-Saxon Charters: An Annotated List and Bibliography* (London: Royal Historical Society, 1968), S 1556 (British Museum, MS Cotton Nero E I, pt. 2, fol. 181: bounds of Withington (eleventh century)).

2   James Rattue, *The Living Stream: Holy Wells in Historical Context* (Woodbridge: Boydell, 1995), p. 10.

3   Miranda J. Green, *Celtic Myths* (London: British Museum Press, 1993), p. 51.

4   Michelle P. Brown, *Pagans and Priests: The Coming of Christianity to Britain and Ireland* (Oxford: Lion Hudson, 2006), p. 28.

5   David Jacques and Tom Phillips, 'Mesolithic Settlement near Stonehenge: Excavations at Alcot Mead, Vespasian's Camp, Amesbury', *Wiltshire Archaeological and Natural History Magazine* 107 (2014), pp. 7–27, esp. p. 23.

6   David Jacques, Tom Phillips and Tom Lyons, 'Vespasian's Camp, Cradle of Stonehenge?', *Current Archaeology* 271 (2012), pp. 28–33.

7   Ken Dowden, *European Paganism: The Realities of Cult from Antiquity to the Middle Ages* (London and New York: Routledge, 2000), p. 29.

8   Jim Leary and Matthew Symonds,

'The Many Faces of Silbury Hill', *Current Archaeology* 293 (2014), pp. 12–18; Jim Leary, David Field and Gill Campbell (eds), *Silbury Hill: The Largest Prehistoric Mound in Europe* (Swindon: English Heritage, 2013).

9   Bryony Coles, 'Wood Species for Wooden Figures: A Glimpse of a Pattern', in Alex Gibson and Derek Simpson (eds), *Prehistoric Ritual and Religion* (Sutton: Stroud, 1998), pp. 163–73.

10   Francis Pryor, *Flag Fen: Life and Death of a Prehistoric Landscape* (London: Tempus, 2005).

11   National Museum of Wales, 'Artefacts from Llyn Cerrig Bach' <www.museumwales. ac.uk/2363> [accessed 11 March 2014].

12   Ralph Merrifield, *The Archaeology of Ritual and Magic* (London: Guild Publishing, 1987), p. 27; Geoff Marsh and Barbara West, 'Skullduggery in Roman London', *Transactions of the London and Middlesex Archaeological Society* 32 (1981), pp. 86–102.

13   Rick C. Turner, 'Recent Research into British Bog Bodies', in Rick C. Turner and Robert G. Scaife (eds), *Bog Bodies: New Discoveries and New Perspectives* (London: British Museum, 1995), pp. 108–22.

14   Michael Havinden, *The Somerset Landscape* (London: Hodder and Stoughton, 1981), p. 67.

15   Roger S.O. Tomlin, 'The Curse Tablets', in Barry Cunliffe (ed.), *The Temple of Sulis Minerva at Bath*, vol. 2, *The Finds from the Sacred Spring*, Oxford University Committee for Archaeology Monograph 16 (Oxford: Oxford University Committee for Archaeology, 1988), ch. 4, pp. 59–277.

16   Brown, *Pagans and Priests*, pp. 15–16.

17   Anne Ross, *Pagan Celtic Britain: Studies in Iconography and Tradition* (London: Routledge and Kegan Paul, 1967), pp. 21, 232.

18   Ross, *Pagan Celtic Britain*, p. 232.

19   Green, *Celtic Myths*, p. 51.

20   Rattue, *The Living Stream*, pp. 1–3.

21   Tacitus, *Germania* 40, *Tacitus, Dialogus, Agricola, Germania*, trans. and ed. William Peterson (London: William Heinemann, 1914), pp. 320–21.

22   Francis Jones, *The Holy Wells of Wales* (Cardiff: University of Wales Press, 1992), p. 13, citing James Hastings (ed.), *Encyclopaedia of Religion and Ethics*, vol. 9, *Mundas-Phrygians*, pp. 241, 253 (Edinburgh: T&T Clark, 1917).

23   Dowden, *European Paganism*, pp. 118–19.

24   Michael Swanton, *A Corpus of Pagan Anglo-Saxon Spear-Types*, British Archaeological Reports, British Series 7 (Oxford: British Archaeological Reports, 1974), pp. 31–89; Nathalie Cohen, 'Boundaries and Settlement: The Role of the River Thames', *Anglo-Saxon Studies in Archaeology and History* 12 (2003), pp. 9–21, esp. p. 11; Merrifield, *The Archaeology of Ritual and Magic*, pp. 107–08.

25   David M. Wilson, 'Some Neglected Late Anglo-Saxon Swords', *Medieval Archaeology* 9 (1965), pp. 32–54; see also <www.vikingage.org> [accessed 28 July 2014].

26   David Stocker and Paul Everson, 'The Straight and Narrow Way: Fenland Causeways and the Conversion of the Landscape in the Witham Valley, Lincolnshire', in Martin Carver (ed.), *The Cross Goes North: Processes of Conversion in Northern Europe, AD 300–1300* (Woodbridge: York Medieval, 2003), pp. 271–88, esp. pp. 280–81.

27   Julie Lund, 'At the Water's Edge', in Martin Carver, Alex Sanmark and Sarah Semple (eds), *Signals of Belief in Early England: Anglo-Saxon Paganism Revisited* (Oxford: Oxbow, 2010), pp. 49–66, esp. pp. 53–54.

28   David M. Wilson, *Catalogue of Antiquity of the Later Saxon Period*, vol. 1, *Anglo-Saxon Ornamental Metalwork, 700–1100, in the British Museum* (London: British Museum, 1964), pp. 144–46; Gale R. Owen-Crocker, *Rites and Religions of the Anglo-Saxons* (Newton Abbot: David & Charles, 1981), p. 72; Lund, 'At the Water's Edge', p. 54.

29   Merrifield, *The Archaeology of Ritual and Magic*, p. 108.

30   Lund, 'At the Water's Edge', p. 54.

31   J. Lund, 'Våben i vand: om deponeringer i vikingetiden', *Kuml: Årbog for Jysk Arkæologisk Selskab* (2005), pp. 197–220; Lund, 'At the Water's Edge', pp. 53–54, 108–09.

32   Della Hooke, *Trees in Anglo-Saxon England: Literature, Lore and Landscape* (Woodbridge: Boydell, 2010).

33   Jennifer Neville, *Representations of the Natural World in Old English Poetry*

(Cambridge: Cambridge University Press, 1999), pp. 70–71.

34   Riddle: Baum 11, Krapp and Dobbie 40, ll. 31–33, 40–41: *The Exeter Book*, in George Philip Krapp and Elliott Van Kirk Dobbie (eds), *Anglo-Saxon Poetic Records* 3 (New York: Columbia University Press, 1936), p. 201; trans. Robert K. Gordon, *Anglo-Saxon Poetry* (London: Dent, 1954), p. 302; Paull F. Baum, *Anglo-Saxon Riddles of the Exeter Book* (Durham, NC: Duke University Press, 1963), pp. 12–13.

35   *Beowulf*, ll. 103–04, 1260–61, 1357, 1361: trans. and ed. Michael Swanton (Manchester: Manchester University, 1978), pp. 38–39, 94–95, 98–99, 111.

36   S 78; S 579; Della Hooke, *Worcestershire Anglo-Saxon Charter-Bounds* (Woodbridge: Boydell, 1990), pp. 43–46, 162–67; S 416.

37   S 387; Victor Watts (ed.), *The Cambridge Dictionary of English Place-Names* (Cambridge: Cambridge University Press, 2004) (*CDEPN*), p. 546.

38   S108; S 508.

39   Carole Hough, 'The Place-Name Fritwell', *English Place-Name Society Journal* 29 (1997), pp. 65–69; *CDEPN*, p. 242.

40   *CDEPN*, pp. 242, 356; Graham Jones, *Saints in the Landscape* (Stroud: Tempus, 2007), pp. 126–27.

41   *The Poetic Edda*, trans. Carolyne Larrington (Oxford: Oxford University Press, 1996).

42   Paul C. Bauschatz, *The Well and the Tree* (Amherst: University of Massachusetts Press, 1982), pp. 3–29, 125; also discussed in Hooke, *Trees in Anglo-Saxon England*, pp. 15–16.

43   *Ynglinga Saga*, ed. Edward M. Bridle (Armidale, NSW: Midgard Books, 1998).

44   Adam of Bremen IV, Scholium 138 [134], trans. Francis J. Tschan, *Adam of Bremen: History of the Archbishops of Hamburg-Bremen*, Records of Civilization (New York: Columbia University Press, 1959), p. 207; Bauschatz, *The Well and the Tree*, pp. 82, 60.

45   Clive Tolley, *Shamanism in Norse Myth and Magic* (Helsinki: Suomalainen Tiedeakatemia, 2009), vol. 1, p. 328.

46   Lund, 'At the Water's Edge', p. 55.

47   Della Hooke, *The Anglo-Saxon Landscape: The Kingdom of the Hwicce* (Manchester: Manchester University Press, 1985), p. 40; *Worcestershire Anglo-Saxon Charter-Bounds*, p. 135; S 1272.

48   Della Hooke, 'Wilderness and Waste – "The Weird and Wonderful": Views of the Midland Region', in Paul S. Barnwell and Marilyn Palmer (eds), *Post-Medieval Landscapes* (Macclesfield: Windgather Press, 2007), pp. 137–50.

49   *Felix's Life of Saint Guthlac*, ed. Bertram Colgrave (Cambridge: Cambridge University Press, 1956), XXIV, XXV, pp. 86, 88; 'The Life of Saint Guthlac', trans. Michael Swanton, in *Anglo-Saxon Prose* (London: Dent, 1975), pp. 39–62. The passages quoted here are on p. 44.

50   *St Guthlac*, in Krapp and Dobbie, *The Exeter Book*, p. 58, ll. 296–98; trans. Neville, *Representations of the Natural World*, p. 127, n. 165.

51   *Felix's Life of Saint Guthlac*, ed. Colgrave, XXV, p. 88; 'The Life of Saint Guthlac', Swanton, *Anglo-Saxon Prose*, p. 44. Also discussed by Kelley M. Wickham-Crowley, 'Living on the *Ecg*: The Mutable Boundaries of Land and Water in Anglo-Saxon Contexts', in Clare A. Lees and Gillian R. Overing (eds), *A Place to Believe In: Locating Medieval Landscapes* (University Park: Pennsylvania State University Press, 2006), pp. 85–110.

52   *Maxims II*, in Elliott Van Kirk Dobbie (ed.), *The Anglo-Saxon Minor Poems*, *Anglo-Saxon Poetic Records* 6 (New York: Columbia University Press, 1942), p. 56, ll. 42–43; trans. Neville, *Representations of the Natural World*, pp. 71–72 n. 67.

53   Neville, *Representations of the Natural World*, pp. 104–05.

54   *The Phoenix*, in Krapp and Dobbie, *The Exeter Book*, p. 95, ll. 62–63; Israel Gollancz (trans. and ed.), *The Exeter Book: An Anthology of Anglo-Saxon Poetry* (London: Early English Text Society, 1895), Part I, pp. 204–05.

55   *The Phoenix*, in Krapp and Dobbie, *The Exeter Book*, ll. 109, 362; trans. Gollancz, *The Exeter Book: An Anthology of Anglo-Saxon Poetry*, Part I, pp. 206–07, 222–23.

56   *Andreas*, ll. 1590, 1602, in George Philip Krapp (ed.), *The Vercelli Book*, *Anglo-Saxon*

Poetic Records 2 (New York: Columbia
University Press, 1932), pp. 3–51, esp. p. 48;
trans. Gordon, *Anglo-Saxon Poetry*, pp. 206–08.

57 Rattue, *The Living Stream*, p. 78, citing
Janet Bord and Colin Bord, *Sacred Waters:
Holy Wells and Water Lore in Britain and
Ireland* (New York: Granada Publishing, 1985;
repr. London: Paladin, 1986), p. 31 and Jocelyn
N. Hillgarth (ed.), *Christianity and Paganism,
350–750: The Conversion of Western Europe*
(Philadelphia: University of Pennsylvania Press,
1986), p. 103; Hooke, *Trees in Anglo-Saxon
England*, p. 22; F. Jones, *The Holy Wells of
Wales*, p. 22.

58 *Gildas: The Ruin of Britain and Other
Works*, trans. and ed. Michael Winterbottom
(Chichester: Phillimore, 1978), 4.3, p. 17.

59 John Blair, *The Church in Anglo-Saxon
Society* (Oxford: Oxford University Press, 2005),
p. 481; Dorothy Bethurum (ed.), *The Homilies of
Wulfstan* (Oxford: Clarendon Press, 1957), p. 319
nn. 165–68.

60 Peonitentiale Pseudo-Theodore XXVII,
in Benjamin Thorpe (ed.), *Ancient Laws and
Institutes of England*, Monumenta Ecclesiastica
(London: G.E. Eyre and A. Spottiswoode, 1840),
p. 293.

61 Poenitentiale Pseodo-Egberti ii.22:
Thorpe, *Ancient Laws*, p. 371.

62 Roger Fowler (ed.), *Wulfstan's Canons of
Edgar*, Early English Text Society, Old Series
266 (London: Early English Text Society, 1972),
pp. xvi–xxix.

63 Hooke, *Trees in Anglo-Saxon England*,
pp. 31–32.

64 Agnes J. Robertson (trans. and ed.), *The
Laws of the Kings of England from Edmund to
Henry I* (Cambridge: Cambridge University
Press, 1925), II Cnut, c. 5.1, pp. 176–77.

65 Ælfric, 'On Auguries', ll. 129–36, in
Walter E. Skeat (ed.), *Ælfric's Lives of the Saints*,
vol. 1, Early English Text Society, Old Series
76 (London: Early English Text Society, 1881),
pp. 372–74; trans. Blair, *The Church in Anglo-
Saxon Society*, p. 482.

66 Richard Morris, *Churches in the
Landscape* (London: Dent and Sons, 1989),
pp. 84–85; G. Jones, *Saints in the Landscape*,
pp. 15–17.

67 Blair, *The Church in Anglo-Saxon
Society*, p. 226.

68 *Historia ecclesiastica gentis Anglorum
(HE): Bede's Ecclesiastical History of the
English People*, ed. and trans. Bertram Colgrave
and Roger A.B. Mynors, rev. edn. (Oxford:
Clarendon Press, 1969), iii.11, pp. 246–47.

69 Stocker and Everson, 'The Straight and
Narrow Way', p. 282.

70 Colgrave and Mynors, *Bede's
Ecclesiastical History*, v.4, pp. 463–64.

71 S 262; Walter de Gray Birch, *Cartularium
Saxonicum*, 3 vols (1885–99; repr. Cambridge:
Cambridge University Press, 2012), B 200; S 250;
B 142; S 115; *CDEPN*, p. 661.

72 Warwick Rodwell, 'From Mausoleum
to Minster: The Early Development of Wells
Cathedral', in Susan M. Pearce (ed.), *The Early
Church in Western Britain and Ireland: Studies
Presented to C.A. Ralegh Radford*, British
Archaeological Reports, British Series 102
(Oxford: British Archaeological Reports, 1982),
p. 52.

73 Birthe Kjølbye-Biddle, 'Anglo-Saxon
Baptisteries of the 7th and 8th Centuries:
Winchester and Repton', *Acta XIII Congressus
Internationalis Archaeologiae Christianae*, Studi
di antichità cristiana 54 (Vatican City: Pontificio
Istituto di Archeologia Cristiana, 1998), pp. 759–
60; Helen Gittos, *Liturgy, Architecture, and
Sacred Places in Anglo-Saxon England* (Oxford:
Oxford University Press, 2013), p. 202.

74 Rattue, *The Living Stream*, p. 58; Gittos,
Liturgy, Architecture, and Sacred Places, p. 91
and Fig. 29, pp. 172, 185.

75 Blair, *The Church in Anglo-Saxon
Society*, pp. 375–78.

76 Rattue, *The Living Stream*; F. Jones, *The
Holy Wells of Wales*.

77 Blair, *The Church in Anglo-Saxon
Society*, p. 194, citing Helen Gittos, 'Sacred
Space in Anglo-Saxon England: Liturgy,
Architecture and Place' (unpublished DPhil.
thesis, University of Oxford, 2002), pp. 39–42.

78 Stocker and Everson, 'The Straight and
Narrow Way', pp. 277–79, 281.

79 Stocker and Everson, 'The Straight and
Narrow Way', p. 284.

80 Della Hooke, in preparation.

81 E.g. *Ælfric's Homilies*, 1.31, 'Kalandas Septembris. Passio Sancti Bartholomei Apostoli', l. 312, in Peter Clemoes (ed.), *Ælfric's Catholic Homilies. The First Series, Text*, Early English Text Society, Supplementary Series 17 (Oxford: Oxford University Press, 1997), p. 450. There is some indication that the planting of yews in churchyards as a symbol of resurrection may draw upon ancient roots: Hooke, *Trees in Anglo-Saxon England*, pp. 207–11. For a recent discussion of the absorption of pagan beliefs into Christianity, see Michael Bintley, *Trees in the Religions of Early Medieval England* (Woodbridge: Boydell, 2015).

82 Felix Grendon, *Anglo-Saxon Charms* (Norwood, PA: Norwood Editions, 1976), p. 16.

83 Charles H. Talbot, 'Some Notes on Anglo-Saxon Medicine', *Medical History* 9 (1965), pp. 156–69.

84 *Leechbook III*, lxvii, in Thomas O. Cockayne (ed.), *Leechdoms, Wortcunning and Starcraft of Early England*, Rolls Series (London: Longman, Green, Longman, Roberts, and Green, 1865), vol. 2, pp. 354–57, fol. 126b. Bishopwort is still thought to cure or alleviate several ailments, which interestingly include delirium, nervous headaches and other nervous complaints – both perhaps once thought of as being caused by devilish influence.

85 *Lacnunga XXXIa*, in John H.G. Grattan and Charles Singer (eds), *Anglo-Saxon Magic and Medicine*, Publications of the Wellcome Historical Medical Museum, New Series 3 (London: Oxford University Press, 1952), pp. 110–13.

86 Grendon, *Anglo-Saxon Charms*, pp. 16–17.

87 *The Metrical Charms* 1, 'For Unfruitful Land', in Elliott Van Kirk Dobbie (ed.), *The Anglo-Saxon Minor Poems*, Anglo-Saxon Poetic Records 6 (New York: Columbia University Press, 1942), pp. 116–18, ll. 9, 72–80.

88 *The Metrical Charms* 7, in Dobbie, *The Anglo-Saxon Minor Poems*, pp. 124–25; Malcolm L. Cameron, *Anglo-Saxon Medicine*, Cambridge Studies in Anglo-Saxon England 7 (Cambridge: Cambridge University Press, 1993), p. 154.

89 *Bedae Vita Sancti Cuthberti*, trans. and ed. B. Colgrave, *Two Lives of Saint Cuthbert* (Cambridge: Cambridge University Press, 1940), pp. 1–16; Ann Williams, Alfred P. Smyth and David P. Kirby (eds), *A Biographical Dictionary of Dark Age Britain: England, Scotland and Wales c.500–c.1050* (London: Seaby, 1991), p. 2.

90 *Bedae Vita Sancti Cuthberti*, ed. Colgrave, ch. XVIII, pp. 218–19.

91 *Bedae Vita Sancti Cuthberti*, ed. Colgrave, ch. XIX, pp. 220–23; Gittos, *Liturgy*, pp. 32–34.

92 Colgrave and Mynors, *Bede's Ecclesiastical History*, p. xvii.

93 *HE*, I, vii, pp. 32–33.

94 David W. Rollason, 'The Cults of Murdered Royal Saints in Anglo-Saxon England', *Anglo-Saxon England* 11 (1983), p. 8; *Vita et Miracula Sancto Kenelmi*, trans. and ed. Rosalind Love, *Three Eleventh-Century Anglo-Latin Saints' Lives* (Oxford: Clarendon Press, 1996), pp. xci, cxii–cxiii.

95 Love, *Three Eleventh-Century Anglo-Latin Saints' Lives*, pp. 70–71.

96 Love, *Three Eleventh-Century Anglo-Latin Saints' Lives*, p. 70 n. 2.

97 Williams, Smyth and Kirby, *A Biographical Dictionary*, p. 98.

98 Margaret Gelling and Ann Cole, *The Landscape of Place-Names* (Stamford: Shaun Tyas, 2000), p. 1.

99 *CDEPN*, p. 660.

100 Margaret Gelling, 'Latin Loan-Words in Old English Place-Names', *Anglo-Saxon England* 6 (1977), pp. 1–13; Margaret Gelling, *Signposts to the Past: Place-names and the History of England* (London: Dent and Son, 1978), p. 86; Ann Cole, 'Topography, Hydrology and Place-Names in the Chalklands of Southern England: **funta, æwiell* and *æwielm*', *Nomina* 9 (1985), pp. 3–19, but see Gelling and Cole, *The Landscape of Place-Names*, p. 18.

101 Oliver J. Padel, *Cornish Place-Name Elements*, English Place-Name Society 56/57 (Cambridge: Cambridge University Press, 1985), p. 97.

102 For individual names, see the various volumes of the English Place-Name Society, and, for major names, *CDEPN*.

103 Blair, *The Church in Anglo-Saxon Society*, pp. 377–78.

104   S 352, allegedly 979 for 879 but of doubtful authenticity; S 310, allegedly 854 but again a spurious document: George B. Grundy, *The Saxon Charters and Field Names of Somerset* (Taunton: Somerset Archaeological and Natural History Society, 1935), pp. 22–28.

105   S 1556; Royal Commission on Historical Monuments (England), *Ancient and Historical Monuments in the County of Gloucester*, vol. 1, *Iron Age and Romano-British Monuments in the Gloucestershire Cotswolds* (London: HMSO, 1976), p. 25.

106   Roger J.A. Wilson, *A Guide to the Roman Remains in Britain* (London: Constable, 2002), p. 197.

107   S 834; S 781; S 615; S 702.

108   S 961; George B. Grundy, 'Dorset Charters', *Proceedings of the Dorset Natural History and Archaeological Society* 59 (1937), p. 118. Later a 'holy well' was located at the Norman Saint Catherine Chapel, at Abbotsbury, frequented by maidens wishing for a husband: Robert C. Hope, *Legendary Lore of the Holy Wells of England, including Rivers, Lakes, Fountains and Springs* (London: Elliot Stock, 1983), p. 67.

109   S 396; S 414, but a spurious charter, S 559; G. Jones, *Saints in the Landscape*, pp. 125–27.

110   S 1377; Birch, B 1131; Agnes J. Robertson, *Anglo-Saxon Charters*, 2nd edn (Cambridge: Cambridge University Press, 1956), no. 37, p. 68; Swanton, *Anglo-Saxon Prose*, pp. 28–29.

111   S 920; S 930; Della Hooke, *The Landscape of Anglo-Saxon Staffordshire: The Charter Evidence* (Keele: Department of Adult Education, University of Keele, 1983), pp. 93–101.

112   Brown, *Pagans and Priests*, p. 46.

113   Jones, *The Holy Wells of Wales*, pp. 6–7, 10–11.

114   Revd Gilbert H. Doble, *The Saints of Cornwall*, Part 5 (Truro: Dean and Chapter, 1964), pp. 59–79; Hope, 'Summary of Wells', *Legendary Lore*. See also Sam Turner, *Making a Christian Landscape: The Countryside in Early Medieval Cornwall, Devon and Wessex* (Exeter: University of Exeter Press, 2006), pp. 132–33.

115   Hope, 'Summary of Wells', *Legendary Lore*.

116   Christopher Catling, 'Saints and Miracles: The Holy Well at Binsey', *Current Archaeology* 297 (2014), pp. 16–23; Lydia Carr, Russell Dewhurst and Martin Henig (eds), *Binsey: Oxford's Holy Place: Its Saint, Village, and People* (Oxford: Archaeopress, 2014); J. Blair, 'Saint Frideswide Reconsidered', *Oxoniensia* 52 (1987), pp. 71–127; 'St Frideswide's Monastery: Problems and Possiblities', *Oxoniensia* 53 (1988), pp. 221–58; for the longer and shorter Lives of St Frideswide, see <http://d.lib.rochester.edu/teams/text/reames-middle-english-legends-of-women-saints-legend-of-frideswide-introduction> [accessed 21 February 2017].

117   Jones, *Saints in the Landscape*, p. 126 and Fig. 4.

118   Jones, *Saints in the Landscape*, p. 127.

119   Bord and Bord, *Sacred Waters*, p. 189.

120   Hooke, *Trees in Anglo-Saxon England*, p. 105.

121   Bord and Bord, *Sacred Waters*, p. 150.

122   Bord and Bord, *Sacred Waters*, pp. 150–52; Roy Palmer, *Herefordshire Folklore* (Almeley: Logaston Press, 2002), p. 16.

123   Jacqueline Simpson and Steve Roud (eds), *A Dictionary of English Folklore* (Oxford: Oxford University Press, 2000), pp. 297, 381.

Chapter 6: Fishing

1   Riddle 85, *The Exeter Book*: George Philip Krapp and Elliott Van Kirk Dobbie (eds), *The Exeter Book, Anglo-Saxon Poetic Records* 3 (New York: Columbia University Press, 1936), p. 238.

2   Exeter Riddle 85: Paul F. Baum, *Anglo-Saxon Riddles of the Exeter Book* (Durham, NC: Duke University Press, 1963), no. 62, pp. 49–50.

3   Alison Locker, *The Role of Stored Fish in England 900–1750 AD: The Evidence from Historical and Archaeological Data* (Sofia: Publishing Group Limited, 2001); David Orton, James Morris, Alison Locker and James H. Barrett, 'Fish for the City: Meta-Analysis of Archaeological Cod Remains and the Growth of London's Northern Trade',

Antiquity 88 (2014), pp. 516–30; Dale Serjeanston and Chris M. Woolgar, 'Fish Consumption in Medieval England', in Chris M. Woolgar, Dale Serjeanston and Tony Waldron (eds), *Food in Medieval England: Diet and Nutrition* (Oxford: Oxford University Press, 2006), pp. 102–30.

4   Michael Aston (ed.), *Medieval Fish, Fisheries and Fishponds in England* (Oxford: British Archaeological Reports, 1988).

5   James H. Barrett, Alison M. Locker and Callum Roberts, '"Dark Age Economics" Revisited: The English Fish Bone Evidence AD 600–1600', *Antiquity* 78 (2004), pp. 618–36; Naomi J. Sykes, *The Norman Conquest: A Zooarchaeological Perspective* (Oxford: British Archaeological Reports, 2007).

6   Pamela Crabtree, personal communication.

7   Ian L. Baxter, 'Animal, Bird, Reptile and Amphibian Bones', in Neil Finn (ed.), *The Origins of a Leicester Suburb: Roman, Anglo-Saxon, Medieval and Post-Medieval Occupation on Bonners Lane* (Oxford: British Archaeological Reports, 2004), pp. 132–48.

8   Robert Cowie and Lynn Blackmore, *Early and Middle Saxon Rural Settlement in the London Region*, Museum of London Archaeological Services Monograph 14 (London: Museum of London Archaeological Services, 2008).

9   Rebecca A. Nicholson, 'Fish Remains', in Phil Andrews (ed.), *Excavations at Redcastle Furze, Thetford, 1988–89*, East Anglian Archaeology Report 72 (Norwich: East Anglian Archaeology, 1995), pp. 128–31.

10   Gabor Thomas, 'Life Before the Minster: The Social Dynamics of Monastic Foundation at Anglo-Saxon Lyminge, Kent', *Antiquaries Journal* 93 (2013), pp. 109–45.

11   Rebecca Reynolds, 'Lyminge 2010 Analysis of Fish Remains from Environmental Samples', unpublished report, University of Nottingham, 2013.

12   Sam Lucy, Alison Dickens and Jess Tipper, *The Anglo-Saxon Settlement and Cemetery at Bloodmoor Hill, Carlton Colville, Suffolk*, East Anglian Archaeology 131 (Dereham: East Anglian Archaeology, 2010), p. 316.

13   Ian Riddler, 'Anglo-Saxon Ceramic Weights from Ramsgate Harbour Approach Road', in Paul Bennett (ed.), *Canterbury's Archaeology 1998–1999* (Canterbury: Canterbury Archaeology, 2000), pp. 64–65.

14   D.G. Bird, 'Possible Late Roman or Early Saxon Fish Weirs at Ferry Lane, Shepperton', *Surrey Archaeological Collections* 86 (1999), pp. 105–23.

15   Cowie and Blackmore, *Early and Middle Saxon Rural Settlement in the London Region*.

16   For further information on the study of isotopes, see Gundüla H. Müldner, 'Investigating Medieval Diet and Society by Stable Isotope Analysis of Human Bone', in Roberta Gilchrist and Andrew Reynolds (eds), *Reflections: 50 Years of Medieval Archaeology* (Leeds: Maney, 2009), pp. 327–46.

17   Bradley D. Hull and Tamsin C. O'Connell, 'Diet: Recent Evidence from Analytical Chemical Techniques', in Helena Hamerow, David A. Hinton and Sally Crawford (eds), *The Oxford Handbook of Anglo-Saxon Archaeology* (Oxford: Oxford University Press, 2010), pp. 667–87.

18   Simon Mays and Nancy Beavan, 'An Investigation of Diet in Early Anglo-Saxon England Using Carbon and Nitrogen Stable Isotope Analysis of Human Bone Collagen', *Journal of Archaeological Science* 39 (2012), pp. 867–74.

19   Tania M. Dickinson, 'Symbols of Protection: The Significance of Animal-ornamented Shields in Early Anglo-Saxon England', *Medieval Archaeology* 49 (2005), pp. 109–63.

20   Julie Lund, 'At the Water's Edge', in Martin Carver, Alex Sanmark and Sarah Semple (eds), *Signals of Belief in Early England: Anglo-Saxon Paganism Revisited* (Oxford: Oxbow, 2010), pp. 49–66; Sara Semple, 'In the Open Air', in Carver, Sanmark and Semple, *Signals of Belief in Early England*, pp. 21–48.

21   Naomi Sykes, 'Deer, Land, Knives and Halls: Social Change in Early Medieval England', *Antiquaries Journal* 90 (2010), pp. 175–93.

22   Natasha Dodwell, Sam Lucy and Jess Tipper, 'Anglo-Saxons on the Cambridge Backs: The Criminology Site and King's Garden Hostel

Cemetery', *Proceedings of the Cambridge Antiquarian Society* 43 (2004), pp. 95–124.

23   Guy Halsall, 'Burial, Ritual and Merovingian Society', in Joyce Hill and Mary Swan (eds), *The Community, the Family and the Saint: Patterns of Power in Early Medieval Europe* (Turnhout: Brepols, 1998), pp. 325–38.

24   Andy Crowson, Tom Lane, Kenneth Penn and Dale Trimble, *Anglo-Saxon Settlement on the Siltland of Eastern England*, Lincolnshire Archaeology and Heritage Report Series 7 (Exeter: Lincolnshire Archaeology and Heritage, 2005); Peter Murphy, 'The Landscape and Economy of the Anglo-Saxon Coast: New Archaeological Evidence', in Nicholas J. Higham and Martin J. Ryan (eds), *The Landscape Archaeology of Anglo-Saxon England* (Woodbridge: Boydell, 2010), pp. 211–21.

25   Alex Pluskowski, *Wolves and the Wilderness in the Middle Ages* (Woodbridge: Boydell, 2006).

26   Hull and O'Connell, 'Diet', p. 682.

27   Mark Gardiner, R. Cross, N. MacPhearson-Grant and Ian Riddler, 'Continental Trade and Non-Urban Ports in Middle Anglo-Saxon England: Excavations at Sandtun, West Hythe, Kent', *Archaeological Journal* 158 (2001), pp. 161–290.

28   Paul Cope-Faulkner, *Clampgate Road, Fishtoft: Archaeology of a Middle Saxon Island Settlement in the Lincolnshire Fens*, Lincolnshire Archaeology and Heritage Reports Series 10 (Sleaford: Lincolnshire Archaeology and Heritage, 2012).

29   Susan Kelly, 'Lyminge Minster and its Early Charters', in Simon Keynes and Alfred P. Smyth (eds), *Anglo-Saxons: Studies Presented to Cyril Hart* (Dublin: Four Courts, 2006), pp. 98–113.

30   Rebecca Reynolds, 'Food for the Soul: The Social and Economic Context of Fishing and Fish Consumption in Anglo-Saxon England, AD 400–1100' (unpublished doctoral thesis, University of Nottingham, 2015).

31   Reynolds, 'Food for the Soul'.

32   *Bede's Ecclesiastical History of the English People*, ed. and trans. Bertram Colgrave and Roger A.B. Mynors, rev. edn. (Oxford: Clarendon Press, 1969), i.1, pp. 14–15.

33   Patrick Ottaway, 'Iron Fish Hooks', in David H. Evans and Christopher Loveluck (eds), *Life and Economy at Early Medieval Flixborough c.AD 600–1000: The Artefactual Evidence* (Oxford: Oxbow, 2009), p. 252; Lisa M. Wastling, 'Evidence for Fishing and Netting Birds', in Evans and Loveluck, *Life and Economy at Early Medieval Flixborough*, pp. 249–52.

34   Ian Riddler, 'Early Medieval Fishing Implements of Bone and Antler', in Marnix Pieters, Frans Verhaeghe and Glenn Gevaert (eds), *Fishing, Trade and Piracy: Fishermen and Fishermen's Settlements in and around the North Sea Area in the Middle Ages and Later*, Archeologie in Vlaanderen 6 (Brussels: Archeologie in Vlaanderen, 2003), pp. 171–80.

35   Cowie and Blackmore, *Early and Middle Saxon Rural Settlement in the London Region*; David Strachan, 'Inter-tidal Stationary Fishing Structures in Essex: Some C14 Dates', *Essex Archaeology and History* 29 (1998), pp. 274–82; L. Everett, *Targeted Inter-Tidal Survey* (Ipswich: Suffolk County Council Archaeological Service, 2007); David Robertson and John Ames, 'Early Medieval Inter-tidal Fishweirs at Holme Beach, Norfolk', *Medieval Archaeology* 54 (2010), pp. 329–46.

36   P.M. Losco-Bradley and Christopher R. Salisbury, 'A Saxon and a Norman Fish Weir at Colwick, Nottinghamshire', in Aston, *Medieval Fish, Fisheries and Fishponds*, pp. 239–82; Christopher Salisbury, 'Flood Plain Archaeology: The Excavation of Hemington Fields', *Current Archaeology* 145 (1995), pp. 34–37; Andrew Chapman, *West Cotton, Raunds: A Study of Medieval Settlement Dynamics AD 450–1450: Excavation of a Deserted Medieval Hamlet in Northamptonshire, 1985–1989* (Oxford: Oxbow, 2010); David J. Tomalin, Rebecca D. Loader and Roger G. Scaife (eds), *Coastal Archaeology in a Dynamic Environment: A Solent Case Study* (Oxford: Archaeopress, 2012); S. Godbold and R.C. Turner, 'Medieval Fishtraps in the Severn Estuary', *Medieval Archaeology* 38 (1994), pp. 19–54.

37   J.G.D. Clarke, 'The Development of Fishing in Prehistoric Europe', *Antiquaries Journal* 28 (1948), pp. 45–85.

38   R.L. Hall and C.P. Clark, 'A Saxon Inter-tidal Timber Fish Weir at Collins Creek in the Blackwater Estuary', *Essex Archaeology and History* 31 (2000), pp. 125–46.

39   Bird, 'Possible Late Roman or Early Saxon Fish Weirs', p. 199.

40   Hall and Clark, 'Saxon Inter-tidal Timber Fish Weir', p. 125.

41   Thomas McErlean and Aidan O'Sullivan, 'Foreshore Tidal Fishtraps', in Thomas McErlean, Rosemary McConkey and Wes Forsythe (eds), *Strangford Lough: An Archaeological Survey of its Maritime Cultural Landscape* (Belfast: Blackstaff, 2002), pp. 144–80.

42   Strachan, 'Inter-tidal Stationary Fishing Structures', p. 280; Nathalie Cohen, 'Early Anglo-Saxon Fish Traps Along the River Thames', in Stuart Brookes, Sue Harrington and Andrew Reynolds (eds), *Studies in Early Anglo-Saxon Art and Archaeology: Papers in Honour of Martin G. Welch* (Oxford: British Archaeological Reports, 2011), pp. 131–38.

43   Cowie and Blackmore, *Early and Middle Saxon Rural Settlement in the London Region*; Aidan O'Sullivan, 'Place, Memory and Identity Among Estuarine Fishing Communities: Interpreting the Archaeology of Early Medieval Fish Weirs', *World Archaeology* 35 (2004), pp. 449–68.

44   Sharyn Jones, *Food and Gender in Fiji: Ethnoarchaeological Explorations* (Lanham, MD: Lexington Books, 2009); Thomas Malm, 'Women of the Coral Gardens: The Significance of Marine Gathering in Tonga', *SPC Traditional Marine Resource Management and Knowledge Information Bulletin* 25 (2009), pp. 2–15.

45   O'Sullivan, 'Place, Memory and Identity', pp. 449–68.

46   Harold Fox, *The Evolution of the Fishing Village: Landscape and Society along the South Devon Coast, 1086–1550* (Oxford: Leonard's Head, 2001).

47   Della Hooke, 'Uses of Waterways in Anglo-Saxon England', in John Blair (ed.), *Waterways and Canal-Building in Medieval England* (Oxford: Oxford University Press, 2007), pp. 37–54.

48   Sheila Hamilton-Dyer, 'Fish Bones', in Alan Thomas and Andy Boucher (eds), *Hereford City Excavations*, vol. 4, *1976–1990* (Logaston: Hereford City and County Archaeological Trust, 2002), pp. 117–19; Claire Ingrem, 'The Bird, Fish and Small Mammals', in Z. Kamash, D.R.P. Wilkinson, B.M. Ford and J. Hiller (eds), 'Late Saxon and Medieval Occupation: Evidence from Excavations at Lincoln College Oxford 1997–2000', *Oxoniensia* 67 (2002), pp. 199–286; Terry P. O'Connor, *Bones from Anglo-Scandinavian Levels at 16–22 Coppergate*, The Archaeology of York 15.3 (York: York Archaeological Trust, 1989); Terry P. O'Connor, *Bones from 46–54 Fishergate* (London: Council for British Archaeology, 1991); Alison Locker, 'Fish Bones', in Brian S. Ayers (ed.), *Excavations at Fishergate, Norwich, 1985* (Norwich: Norwich Museums Service, 1994), pp. 42–44; Alison Locker, 'The Fish Remains', in Brian S. Ayers (ed.), *Excavations at St. Martin-at-Palace Plain, Norwich, 1981* (Norwich: Norwich Museums Service, 1987), pp. 114–17; Rebecca Nicholson, 'Fish Bones', in Andy Shelley (ed.), *Dragon Hall, King Street, Norwich: Excavation and Survey of a Late Medieval Merchant's Trading Complex* (Norwich: Norfolk and Norwich Heritage Trust, 2005), pp. 167–70; Rebecca Nicholson, 'Avian and Fish Bone', in Phillip A. Emery (ed.), *Norwich Greyfriars: Pre-Conquest Town and Medieval Friary* (Dereham: East Anglian Archaeology, 2007), pp. 217–22; Andrew K.G. Jones and Sally Scott, 'The Fish Bones', in M. Atkin, A. Carter and D.H. Evans (eds), *Excavations in Norwich, 1971–1978, Part II* (Norwich: East Anglian Archaeology, 1985), pp. 223–28; Andrew K.G. Jones, 'Fish Remains', in Brian Ayers and P.A. Murphy (eds), *Waterfront Excavation at Whitefriars Street Car Park, Norwich, 1979* (Dereham: East Anglian Archaeology, 1983), pp. 32–34.

49   Jennifer Coy, 'Animal Bones', in G.G. Astill and S.J. Lobb (eds), 'Excavations of Prehistoric, Roman and Saxon Deposits at Wraysbury, Berkshire', *Archaeological Journal* 146 (1989), pp. 68–134.

50   R. Jones and I. Reuben, 'Animal Bones with Some Notes on the Effects of Differential Sampling', in Guy Beresford (ed.), *Goltho: The Development of an Early Medieval Manor c.850–1150* (London: English Heritage, 1987), pp. 197–26.

51   Umberto Albarella, Mark Beech, Julie Curl, Alison Locker, Marta Moreno-Garcia and Jacqui Mulville, *Norwich Castle: Excavations and Historical Survey 1987–98, Part III: A Zooarchaeological Study* (Dereham: East Anglian Archaeology, 2010).

52   Alison Locker, 'The Fish Bones', in P. Mills (ed.), 'Excavations at the Dorter Undercroft, Westminster Abbey', *Transactions of the London and Middlesex Archaeological Society* 46 (1997), pp. 69–124.

53   Patrick Ottaway, *Anglo-Scandinavian Ironwork from 16–22 Coppergate, London* (York: York Archaeological Trust and Council for British Archaeology, 1992); Nicola S.H. Rogers, *Anglian and Other Finds from 46–54 Fishergate, London* (York: York Archaeological Trust and Council for British Archaeology, 1993).

54   V. Williams, 'Iron Objects', in Ayers, *Excavations at St. Martin-at-Palace Plain*, pp. 67–71; V. Williams, 'Iron Objects', in Ayers, *Excavations at Fishergate, Norwich, 1985*, p. 14; V. Williams, 'Non-Ferrous Metal Objects', in Ayers, *Excavations at Fishergate, Norwich, 1985*, p. 14; F. Pritchard, 'The Small Finds', in Alan Vince (ed.), *Aspects of Saxo-Norman London 2: Finds and Environmental Evidence*, London and Middlesex Archaeological Society Special Paper 12 (London: London and Middlesex Archaeological Society, 1991), pp. 120–78; Rogers, *Anglian and Other Finds*; Alan Vince, *Saxon London: An Archaeological Investigation* (London: Seaby, 1990).

55   Gabor Thomas (ed.), *The Later Anglo-Saxon Settlement at Bishopstone: A Downland Manor in the Making* (York: Council for British Archaeology, 2010).

56   Mark Gardiner, R. Cross, N. MacPhearson-Grant and Ian Riddler, 'Continental Trade and Non-Urban Ports in Middle Anglo-Saxon England: Excavations at Sandtun, West Hythe, Kent', *Archaeological

Journal* 158 (2001), pp. 161–290; Gillian Draper and Frank Meddens, *The Sea and the Marsh: The Medieval Cinque Port of New Romney Revealed through Archaeological Excavations and Historical Research* (London: Pre-Construct Archaeology, 2009); Keith Parfitt, Barry Corke and John Cotter (eds), *Townwall Street, Dover: Excavations 1996, Canterbury* (Canterbury: Canterbury Archaeological Trust, 2006).

57   Draper and Meddens, *The Sea and the Marsh*; Parfitt et al., *Townwall Street*.

58   Rogers, *Anglian and Other Finds*; Ottaway, *Anglo-Scandinavian Ironwork*; S. Atkin, E. Crowfoot, P.J. Drury, B. Ellis, I.H. Goodall, S. Jennings, S. Margeson and D. Smith, '"Excavations on Alms Lane": The Artefacts', in Atkin, Carter and Evans, *Excavations in Norwich, 1971–1978, Part II*, pp. 179–219; V. Williams, 'Iron Objects' (*St Martin-at-Palace Plain*); V. Williams, 'Iron Objects' (*Fishergate*); V. Williams, 'Non-Ferrous Metal Objects'; Ian H. Goodall and Patrick Ottaway, 'Iron Objects', in C. Dallas (ed.), *Excavations in Thetford by B.K. Davidson between 1964 and 1970* (Dereham: East Anglian Archaeology, 1993), pp. 96–115; Pritchard, 'The Small Finds'.

59   Gabor Thomas and Luke Barber, 'Fishing Weights', in Thomas, *The Later Anglo-Saxon Settlement at Bishopstone*, p. 133.

60   Riddler, 'Fishing Implements', p. 172.

61   Riddler, 'Fishing Implements', p. 172.

62   A.J. Mainman and Nicola S.H. Rogers, *Craft, Industry and Everyday Life: Finds from Anglo-Scandinavian York* (York: Council for British Archaeology, 2000); Rogers, *Anglian and Other Finds*; Williams, 'Non-Ferrous Metal Objects'; Wastling, 'Evidence for Fishing and Netting Birds'.

63   Rogers, *Anglian and Other Finds*.

64   *Ælfric's Colloquy*, ed. and trans. George N. Garmonsway (Exeter: University of Exeter Press, 1978), pp. 27–29.

65   Richard C. Hoffmann, *Fishers' Craft and Lettered Art: Tracts on Fishing from the End of the Middle Ages* (Toronto: University of Toronto Press, 1997); Hooke, *Anglo-Saxon Waterways*; Hirokazu Tsurushima, 'The Eleventh Century in England through Fish-eyes: Salmon, Herring,

Oysters, and 1066', in Christopher P. Lewis (ed.), *Anglo-Norman Studies 29: Proceedings of the Battle Conference* (Woodbridge: Boydell, 2007), pp. 193–213.

66   Hooke, *Anglo-Saxon Waterways*, p. 47. See also Chapter 2 of this volume.

67   Agnes Jane Robertson, *Anglo-Saxon Charters* (Cambridge: Cambridge University Press, 1956), no. 109, pp. 204–07; Peter H. Sawyer, *Anglo-Saxon Charters: An Annotated List and Bibliography* (London: Royal Historical Society, 1968), no. 1555.

68   Mark Gardiner, 'The Exploitation of Sea-Mammals in Medieval England: Bones and their Social Context', *Archaeological Journal* 154 (1997), pp. 173–95.

69   Tsurushima, 'Eleventh Century in England through Fish-eyes'.

70   Naomi Sykes, *Beastly Questions: Animal Answers to Archaeological Issues* (London: Bloomsbury, 2014).

71   Mays and Beavan, 'Investigation of Diet'.

72   Richard C. Hoffmann, 'Fishing for Sport in Medieval Europe: New Evidence', *Speculum* 60 (1985), pp. 877–902.

73   Hooke, *Anglo-Saxon Waterways*.

74   Barrett et al., 'Dark Age Economics'.

75   Sarah Foot, *Monastic Life in Anglo-Saxon England*, c.600–900 (Cambridge: Cambridge University Press, 2006), p. 54.

76   David Farmer, 'St. Augustine's Life and Legacy', in Richard Gem (ed.), *St. Augustine's Abbey Canterbury* (London: B.T. Batsford/ English Heritage, 1997), pp. 15–32; Benedict of Nursia, *The Rule of St. Benedict*, trans. and ed. Cardinal Gasquet (New York: Cooper Square Publishers, 1966).

77   Keith Dobney and Deborah Jaques, 'Avian Signatures for Identity and Status in Anglo-Saxon England', *Acta Zoologica Cracoviensia* 45 (2002), pp. 7–21; Anton Ervynck, 'Following the Rule? Fish and Meat Consumption in Monastic Communities in Flanders (Belgium)', in Guy de Boe and Frans Verhaege (eds), *Environment and Subsistence in Medieval Europe: Papers of the 'Medieval Europe Brugge 1997' Conference* (Zellik: Instituut voor het Archeologisch Patrimonium, 1997), pp. 67–81.

78   Richard Gem, 'Introduction', in Gem, *St Augustine's Abbey Canterbury*, p. 12.

79   John Blair, *The Church in Anglo-Saxon Society* (Oxford: Oxford University Press, 2005); Foot, *Monastic Life*; Henry M.R.E. Mayr-Harting, *The Venerable Bede, the Rule of St. Benedict and Social Class*, Jarrow Lecture 1976 (Newcastle upon Tyne: J. and P. Bealls, 1976).

80   Patricia Stevens, 'The Animal Bones', in Malcolm Lyne (ed.), *Lewes Priory: Excavations by Richard Lewis 1969–1982* (Lewes: Lewes Priory Trust, 1997).

81   Keith Dobney, Deborah Jacques, James Barrett and Cluny Johnstone, *Farmers, Monks and Aristocrats: The Environmental Archaeology at Flixborough* (Oxford: Oxbow, 2007), pp. 231–33.

82   Cope-Faulkner, *Clampgate Road, Fishtoft*.

83   Gabor Thomas, 'Bringing A Lost Anglo-Saxon Monastery to Life: Excavations at Lyminge 2008–2009', *Medieval Archaeology* 54 (2010), pp. 409–14.

84   Rebecca Reynolds, 'Surf 'n' Turf: The Components and Influences of a Middle Anglo-Saxon Diet from Lyminge, Kent' (unpublished MSc. dissertation, University of Nottingham, 2009).

85   Locker, *Role of Stored Fish*.

86   Aston, *Medieval Fish, Fisheries and Fishponds in England*.

87   Kristopher Poole, 'The Nature of Anglo-Saxon Society' (unpublished doctoral thesis, University of Nottingham, 2010).

88   Christopher Loveluck, 'Problems of the Definition and Conceptualisation of Early Medieval Elites, AD 450–900: The Dynamics of the Archaeological Evidence', in F. Bougard, H.W. Goetz and R. Le Jan (eds), *Théorie et pratiques des élites au Haut Moyen Âge: conception, perception et réalisation sociale* (Brepols: Turnhout, 2011), pp. 22–67.

89   Noga Arikha, *Passions and Tempers: A History of the Humours* (New York: Harper Collins, 2007); Vivian Nutton, *Ancient Medicine* (London and New York: Routledge, 2004).

90   Peter S. Baker and Michael Lapidge (eds), *Byrhtferth's Enchiridion* (Oxford: Oxford University Press, 1995); Malcolm L. Cameron, *Anglo-Saxon Medicine* (Cambridge: Cambridge

University Press, 1993); Roy M. Liuzza (ed.), *Anglo-Saxon Prognostics: An Edition and Translation of Texts from London, British Library, MS Cotton Tiberius* (Cambridge: D.S. Brewer, 2011).

91   László Sándor Chardonnens, *Anglo-Saxon Prognostics: 900–1100: Study and Texts* (Leiden: Brill, 2007), p. 33.

Chapter 7: Landing Places, Canals and Bridges

1   *Ælfric's Colloquy*, ed. G.N. Garmonsway (London: Methuen, 1947), p. 33, ll. 153–55.

2   David A.E. Pelteret, 'The Role of Rivers and Coastlines in Shaping Early English History', *Haskins Society Journal* 21 (2009), p. 21.

3   Katrin Thier, 'Steep Vessel, High Horn-Ship: Water Transport', in Maren Clegg Hyer and Gale R. Owen-Crocker (eds), *The Material Culture of Daily Living in the Anglo-Saxon World* (Exeter: University of Exeter Press, 2011), pp. 48–72.

4   Valerie Fenwick, *The Graveney Boat: A Tenth-Century Find from Kent* (Oxford: British Archaeological Reports, 1978).

5   For examples, see Stuart Brookes, 'Boat-Rivets in Graves in pre-Viking Kent: Assessing Anglo-Saxon Boat-Burial Tradition', *Medieval Archaeology* 51 (2007), pp. 1–18; Anne Dodd (ed.), *Oxford before the University: The Late Saxon and Norman Archaeology of the Thames Crossing, the Defences and the Town* (Oxford: Oxford Archaeology, 2003), p. 33; Gustav Milne, *Timber Building Techniques in London c.900–1400* (London: London and Middlesex Archaeological Society, 1992), p. 80; Julian Ayre and Robin Wroe-Brown, 'The Post-Roman Foreshore and the Origins of the Late Anglo-Saxon Waterfront and Dock of Æthelred's Hithe: Excavations at Bull Wharf, City of London', *Archaeological Journal* 172 (2015), p. 165.

6   William Filmer-Sankey and Tim Pestell, *Snape Anglo-Saxon Cemetery: Excavations and Surveys 1824–1992* (Ipswich: East Anglian Archaeology, 2001), pp. 199–203; Sean McGrail, *Logboats of England and Wales with Comparative Material from European and Other Countries* (Oxford: British Archaeological Reports, 1978), pp. 330–31.

92   Barrett et al., 'Dark Age Economics'; Sykes, *The Norman Conquest*.

93   Katrin Thier, 'Steep Vessel, High-Horn Ship: Water Transport', in Maren Clegg Hyer and Gale R. Owen-Crocker (eds), *The Material Culture of Daily Living in the Anglo-Saxon World* (Exeter: University of Exeter, 2011), 49–72.

7   Sean McGrail and Roy Switsur, 'Medieval Logboats', *Medieval Archaeology* 23 (1979), pp. 229–31; more recent finds are mentioned in 'Hamble River Logboat: Report on Recent Investigation by HWTMA', Hampshire and Wight Trust for Maritime Archaeology, 2010, p. 7 n. 1 <www.maritimearchaeologytrust.org/uploads/publications/Hamble_Logboat_ShortReport_sept2010.pdf> [accessed 15 April 2015].

8   Paul Blinkhorn, *The Ipswich Ware Project: Ceramics, Trade and Society in Middle Saxon England* (London: Medieval Pottery Research Group, 2012).

9   Jane Young and Alan Vince, *A Corpus of Anglo-Saxon and Medieval Pottery from Lincoln* (Oxford: Oxbow Books, 2005), pp. 88–90; Alan Vince, 'Pottery Production and Use in Northern England in the Fifth to Twelfth Centuries', in Jan Klápště and Petr Sommer (eds), *Arts and Crafts in the Medieval Rural Environment* (Turnhout: Brepols, 2007), pp. 260–62; Leigh Andrea Symonds, *Landscape and Social Practice: The Production and Consumption of Pottery in 10th Century Lincolnshire* (Oxford: British Archaeological Reports, 2003), pp. 161, 168.

10   Lyn Blackmore and Jacqueline Pearce, *A Dated Type Series of London Medieval Pottery, Part 5: Shelly-Sandy Ware and the Greyware Industries* (London: Museum of London Archaeology, 2010), pp. 24, 82.

11   Jonathan Parkhouse, 'Putting Lava on the Map', in Gale R. Owen-Crocker and Susan D. Thompson (eds), *Towns and Topography: Essays in Memory of David H. Hill* (Oxford: Oxbow Books, 2014), pp. 20–21; John Naylor, *An Archaeology of Trade in Middle Saxon England* (Oxford: Archaeopress, 2004), pp. 73–74, 114; Julian Richards, 'Anglian and

Anglo-Scandinavian Cottam: Linking Digital Publication and Archive', *Internet Archaeology* 10 <http://intarch.ac.uk/journal/issue10/richards/discuss.html> [accessed 15 April 2015].

12   David Farmer, 'Millstones for Medieval Manors', *Agricultural History Review* 40 (1992), p. 102.

13   M.P. Taylor, M.G. Macklin and K. Hudson-Edwards, 'River Sedimentation and Fluvial Response to Holocene Environmental Change in the Yorkshire Ouse Basin, Northern England', *The Holocene* 10 (2000), p. 210; A.G. Brown, L. Cooper, C.R. Salisbury and D.N. Smith, 'Late Holocene Channel Changes of the Middle Trent: Channel Response to a Thousand-Year Flood Record', *Geomorphology* 39 (2001), pp. 69–82; Susan Ripper and Lynden P. Copper, *The Hemington Bridges: The Excavation of Three Medieval Bridges* (Leicester: University of Leicester Archaeological Services, 2009).

14   John Lewin, 'Medieval Environmental Impacts and Feedbacks: The Lowland Floodplains of England and Wales', *Geoarchaeology: An International Journal* 25 (2010), pp. 298–301; A.G. Brown and M.K. Keough, 'Holocene Floodplain Metamorphosis in the Midlands, United Kingdom', *Geomorphology* 4 (1992), pp. 433–45. Della Hooke in Chapter 2 above suggests that the character of rivers might be investigated using the evidence of place names.

15   J. Lewin, M.G. Macklin and E. Johnstone, 'Interpreting Alluvial Archives: Sedimentological Factors in the British Holocene Fluvial Record', *Quaternary Science Reviews* 24 (2005), Fig. 11.4; Antony G. Brown, 'Colluvial and Alluvial Response to Land Use Change in Midland England: An Integrated Geoarchaeological Approach', *Geomorphology* 108 (2009), p. 104.

16   Ann Cole, 'The Place-Name Evidence for Water Transport in Early Medieval England', in John Blair (ed.), *Waterways and Canal-Building in Medieval England* (Oxford: Oxford University Press, 2007), pp. 78–82.

17   *Chronicon Monasterii de Abingdon* 1, ed. Joseph Stevenson, Rolls Series 2 (London: Longman, 1858), pp. 480–81.

18   John Blair, 'Transport and Canal-Building on the Upper Thames', in Blair, *Waterways and Canal-Building*, pp. 258–59, Fig. 61.

19   Christopher K. Currie, 'Early Water Management on the Lower River Itchen in Hampshire', in Blair, *Waterways and Canal-Building*, pp. 244–53.

20   David Hall, *The Fenland Project, Number 6: The South-western Cambridgeshire Fenlands* (Cambridge: East Anglian Archaeology, 1992), p. 42.

21   James Bond, 'Canal Construction in the Early Middle Ages: An Introductory Review', in Blair, *Waterways and Canal-Building*, p. 181; William Camden, *Britannia*, Huntingdon, §8 (1607 edition).

22   *William of Malmesbury: Saints' Lives. Lives of Ss Wulfstan, Dunstan, Patrick, Benignus and Indract*, ed. Michael Winterbottom and R.M. Thomson (Oxford: Oxford University Press, 2002), pp. 360–65.

23   Charles and Nancy Hollinrake, 'Glastonbury's Anglo-Saxon Canal and Dunstan's Dyke', in Blair, *Waterways and Canal-Building*, pp. 235–38.

24   Richard H. Britnell, *The Commercialisation of English Society, 1000–1500* (Manchester: Manchester University Press, 1996), pp. 5–52.

25   The problem is identified, but the consequences are not pursued, in David Harrison, *The Bridges of Medieval England: Transport and Society 400–1800* (Oxford: Clarendon Press, 2004), pp. 25–26. For an alternative view of bridges, see Chapter 9.

26   Alan Cooper, *Bridges, Law and Power in Medieval England, 700–1400* (Woodbridge: Boydell, 2006), pp. 24–38 offers a rather different interpretation of the problem of 'bridge-work but no bridges'.

27   Cooper, *Bridges, Law and Power*, pp. 8–15; Harrison, *Bridges of Medieval England*, pp. 35–43 seems to prefer an early chronology for constructing bridges in the current sense.

28   Bruce Watson, Trevor Bingham and Tony Dyson, *London Bridge: 2000 Years of a River Crossing* (London: Museum of London Archaeological Service, 2001), pp. 52–60; John

Rhodes, 'The Severn Flood-Plain at Gloucester in the Medieval and Early Modern Periods', *Transactions of the Bristol and Gloucestershire Archaeological Society* 124 (2006), p. 31.

29   Dodd, *Oxford before the University*, pp. 14–16, 33, 53–54.

30   *The Gesta Gvillelmi of Williams of Poitiers*, trans. and ed. Ralph H.C. Davies and Marjorie Chibnall (Oxford: Clarendon Press, 1998), pp. 146–47, *uado simul atque ponte*.

31   Nicholas P. Brooks, 'Rochester Bridge, AD 43–1381', in Nigel Yates and James M. Gibson (eds), *Traffic and Politics: The Construction and Management of Rochester Bridge, AD 43–1993* (Woodbridge: Boydell, 1994), pp. 16–25. An edition of the text for the bridgeworks at Rochester is given in Yates and Gibson, *Traffic and Politics*, pp. 362–69.

32   *Cartae Antiquae* 2, ed. James Conway Davies, Pipe Roll Society New Series 33 (London: Pipe Roll Society, 1960), p. 150.

33   Chris Loveluck and Dries Tys, 'Coastal Societies, Exchange and Identity along the Channel and Southern North Sea Shores of Europe, AD 600–1000', *Journal of Maritime Archaeology* 1 (2006), p. 143; John Naylor, 'Access to International Trade in Middle Saxon England: A Case of Urban Over-Emphasis?', in Marinella Pasquinucci and Timm Weski (eds), *Close Encounters: Sea- and Riverborne Trade, Ports and Hinterlands, Ship Construction and Navigation in Antiquity, the Middle Ages and in Modern Time* (Oxford: Archaeopress, 2004), pp. 139–48.

34   Andrew Rogerson, 'Six Middle Anglo-Saxon Sites in West Norfolk', in Tim Pestell and Katharina Ulmschneider (eds), *Markets in Early Medieval Europe: Trading and Productive Sites, 650–850* (Macclesfield: Windgather, 2003), pp. 112–15, 118–19; Andy Crowson, Tom Lane, Kenneth Penn and Dale Trimble, *Anglo-Saxon Settlement of the Siltland of Eastern England* (Sleaford: Heritage Trust of Lincoln, 2005), p. 179; Loveluck and Tys, 'Coastal Societies', p. 151.

35   Mark Gardiner, 'Hythes, Small Ports and Other Landing Places in Later Medieval England', in Blair, *Waterways and Canal-Building*, pp. 85–109.

36   Katherine Barker, '*Usque Domnoniam*: The Setting of Aldhelm's *Carmen Rhythmicum*, Literature, Language and the Liminal', in Katherine Barker and Nicholas Brooks (eds), *Aldhelm and Sherborne: Essays to Celebrate the Founding of the Bishopric* (Oxford: Oxbow, 2010), pp. 34–36, 77–79.

37   Mark Gardiner, 'Shipping and Trade between England and the Continent during the Eleventh Century', *Anglo-Norman Studies* 22 (2000), p. 86.

38   Edwin Gifford and Joyce Gifford, 'The Art of Anglo-Saxon Shipbuilding', in Jane Hawkes and Susan Mills (eds), *Northumbria's Golden Age* (Stroud: Sutton, 1999), p. 83.

39   Fenwick, *The Graveney Boat*, p. 183.

40   Ken Steedman, Tony Dyson and John Schofield, *Aspects of Saxo-Norman London: III: The Bridgehead and Billingsgate to 1200* (London: London and Middlesex Archaeological Society, 1992), pp. 99–104. For similar structures, see Gustav Milne and Damian Goodburn, 'The Early Medieval Port of London AD 700–1200', *Antiquity* 64 (1990), p. 630 and Ayre and Wroe-Brown, 'The Post-Roman Foreshore', p. 164.

41   Mark Gardiner, Miles Russell and David Gregory, 'Excavations at Lewes Friary, 1985–86 and 1988–89', *Sussex Archaeological Collections* 134 (1996), pp. 75–78.

42   John W. Hawkes and P.J. Fasham, *Excavations on Reading Waterfront Sites, 1979–1988* (Salisbury: Wessex Archaeology, 1997).

43   *Encomium Emmae Reginae*, ed. Alistair Campbell (London: Royal Historical Society, 1949), pp. 20–21.

44   Peter H. Sawyer, *Anglo-Saxon Charters: An Annotated List and Bibliography* (London: Royal Historical Society, 1968) [hereafter cited simply as 'Sawyer' with the charter number], S 1467; *Charters of Christ Church Canterbury, Part 2*, ed. Nicholas P. Brooks and Susan E. Kelly (Oxford: The British Academy, 2013), 164.

45   A.G. Dyson, 'The Terms "Quay" and "Wharf" and the Early Medieval London Waterfront', in Gustav Milne and Brian Hobley (eds), *Waterfront Archaeology in Britain and Northern Europe* (London: Council for British Archaeology, 1981), pp. 37–38.

46   Sawyer 595; the bounds are discussed in Cyril R. Hart, *The Early Charters of Eastern England* (Leicester: Leicester University Press, 1966), pp. 164–65.

47   Sawyer 781, 911; Charles H. Haskins, 'A Charter of Canute for Fécamp', *English Historical Review* 33 (1918), pp. 342–44.

48   Margaret Gelling and Ann Cole, *The Landscape of Place Names* (Donnington: Shaun Tyas, 2000), pp. 83–84.

49   Maryanne Kowaleski, 'The Seasonality of Fishing in Medieval Britain', in Scott G. Bruce (ed.), *Ecologies and Economies in Medieval and Early Modern Europe: Studies in Environmental History for Richard C. Hoffmann* (Leiden: Brill, 2010), pp. 120–22.

50   Domesday Book, published as *Libri Censualis, Vocati Domesday-Book*, ed. H. Ellis (London; Record Commissions, 1816), I, 1a; 375b.

51   James Campbell, 'Domesday Herrings', in Christopher Harper-Bill, Carole Rawcliffe and Richard G. Wilson (eds), *East Anglia's History: Studies in Honour of Norman Scarfe* (Woodbridge: Boydell, 2002), pp. 7–8.

52   Neil Middleton, 'Early Medieval Port Customs, Tolls and Controls on Foreign Trade', *Early Medieval Europe* 13 (2005), pp. 335–36 based on his interpretation of Sawyer 46, 1628.

53   Mary Bateson, 'A London Municipal Collection of the Reign of John', *English Historical Review* 17 (1902), pp. 725; for dating, see Middleton, 'Early Medieval Port Customs', p. 334 n. 100.

54   Middleton, 'Early Medieval Port Customs', pp. 337–38, citing Felix Liebermann, *Die Gesetze der Angelsachsen* (Halle: Niemeyer, 1903), vol. 1, pp. 9–11.

55   Middleton, 'Early Medieval Port Customs', pp. 350–51; Susan Kelly, 'Trading Privileges from Eighth-Century England', *Early Medieval Europe* 1 (1992), pp. 3–28.

56   Christer Westerdahl, 'Sea versus Land: An Arctic and Subarctic "Cosmology"?', in Christer Westerdahl (ed.), *A Circumpolar Reappraisal: The Legacy of Gutorm Gessing (1906–1979)* (Oxford: Archaeopress, 2010), pp. 301–05.

57   The Anglo-Saxon caution about the sea is discussed further in Chapter 1.

58   Christer Westerdahl, 'Ancient Sea Marks: A Social History from a North European Perspective', *Deutsches Schiffahrtarchiv* 33 (2010), pp. 76, 83, 118–24.

59   Gillian Hutchinson, *Medieval Ships and Shipping* (London: Leicester University Press, 1994), pp. 171–72; Philip Macdougall, 'Bosham: A Key Anglo-Saxon Harbour', *Sussex Archaeological Collections* 147 (2009), pp. 51–60.

60   Kevin Booth, 'The Roman *Pharos* at Dover Castle', *English Heritage Historical Review* 2 (2007), p. 21.

61   H.M. Taylor and Joan Taylor, *Anglo-Saxon Architecture*, vol. 2 (Cambridge: Cambridge University Press, 1965), p. 504.

62   Harold Fox, *The Evolution of the Fishing Village: Landscape and Society along the South Devon Coast, 1086–1550* (Oxford: Leopard's Head Press, 2001), pp. 137–38.

63   For the use of water transport on marshlands, see Gardiner, 'Hythes, Small Ports and Other Landing Places', pp. 93–95, 108.

64   Damian Goodburn and Mark Redknap, 'Replicas and Wrecks from the Thames Area', *London Archaeologist* 6 (1988), pp. 7–22.

65   On the later rise of swimming, see C. Love, 'An Overview of the Development of Swimming in England, *c.*1750–1918', *International Journal of the History of Sport* 24 (2007), pp. 568–85; see also on the knowledge of swimming, Daniel Anlezark, 'All at Sea: Beowulf's Marvellous Swimming', in Daniel Anlezark (ed.), *Myths, Legends, and Heroes: Essays on Old Norse and Old English Literature in Honour of John McKinnell* (Toronto: University of Toronto Press, 2011), pp. 225–41.

66   On shipsoke, see Nicholas Hooper, 'Some Observations on the Navy in Late Anglo-Saxon England', in Matthew Strickland (ed.), *Anglo-Norman Warfare* (Woodbridge: Boydell, 1992), pp. 22–26; James Campbell, Eric John and Patrick Wormald, *The Anglo-Saxons* (London: Phaidon, 1982), pp. 172–73.

67   Agnes J. Robertson, *Anglo-Saxon Charters* (Cambridge: Cambridge University Press, 1956), pp. 144–45, 389–92; Susan E. Kelly, *Charters of St Paul's, London* (Oxford: Oxford University Press, 2004), pp. 97–100, 192–201;

M.K. Lawson, 'The Collection of Danegeld and Heregeld in the Reigns of Aetheldred II and Cnut', *English Historical Review* 99 (1984), p. 726. However, Cyril Hart, *The Danelaw* (London: Hambledon, 1992), pp. 208–10, envisages that the vills did supply individuals to man the St. Paul's ship.

Chapter 8: Watermills and Waterwheels

1   *Ælfric, De temporibus anni*, trans. and ed. Martin Blake (Woodbridge: Boydell, 2009), pp. 76–77.

2   Richard Bennett and John Elton, *History of Corn Milling*, vol. 2 (Liverpool: Simpkin Marshall, 1899).

3   F. Gerald Simpson, *Watermills and Military Works on Hadrian's Wall* (Kendal: Titus Wilson, 1976), pp. 26–50.

4   Summarized in Martin Watts, *The Archaeology of Mills and Milling* (Stroud: Tempus, 2002), pp. 50–57; see also Robert Spain, *The Power and Performance of Roman Water-Mills* (Oxford: British Archaeological Reports, 2008); for a recent view of Roman power-driven millstones, see David Peacock, *The Stone of Life: The Archaeology of Querns, Mills and Flour Production in Europe up to c.AD500* (Southampton: Highfield, 2013), pp. 98–119.

5   A preliminary figure of about 180, based on research by David King presented to the Quern Study Group in 1998, updated by the writer.

6   Paul Bennett, Ian Riddler and Christopher Sparey-Green, *The Roman Watermills and Settlement at Ickham, Kent* (Canterbury: Archaeological Trust, 2010), p. 345.

7   Richard Holt, *The Mills of Medieval England* (Oxford: Blackwell, 1988), p. 3.

8   Watts, *Archaeology of Mills*, pp. 65–67.

9   Usefully summarized in Henry Clifford Darby, *Domesday England* (Cambridge: Cambridge University Press, 1977), pp. 270–75.

10   Herbert P.R. Finberg, 'Mills', in Herbert P.R. Finberg (ed.), *The Agrarian History of England and Wales*, vol. 1.2 (London: Cambridge University Press, 1972), pp. 498–99.

11   David M. Wilson (ed.), *The Archaeology of Anglo-Saxon England* (London: Methuen, 1976), pp. 275–76.

68   Hooper, 'Some Observations on the Navy', pp. 23–24.

69   Antonina Harbus, 'The Maritime Imagination and Paradoxical Mind in Old English Poetry', *Anglo-Saxon England* 39 (2011), pp. 21–42. See also Chapter 1 for the uses of water in Anglo-Saxon literature.

12   Philip Rahtz and Donald Bullough, 'The Parts of an Anglo-Saxon Mill', *Anglo-Saxon England* 6 (1977), pp. 15–37.

13   In David Wyatt Crossley (ed.), *Medieval Industry*, Council for British Archaeology Research Report 40 (London: Council for British Archaeology, 1981), pp. 1–15.

14   David Hill, *An Atlas of Anglo-Saxon England* (Oxford: Blackwell, 1981), p. 114.

15   Holt, *Mills of Medieval England*, pp. 3–7.

16   Ann Hagen, *A Handbook of Anglo-Saxon Food: Processing and Consumption* (Pinner: Anglo-Saxon Books, 1993), pp. 3–6.

17   For a summary, see Colin Rynne, 'Waterpower in Medieval Ireland', in Paolo Squatriti (ed.), *Working with Water in Medieval Europe* (Leiden: Brill, 2000), pp. 1–50; for a detailed report on a recent excavation, see Neil Jackman, Catríona Moore and Colin Rynne, *The Mill at Kilbegly* (Dublin: National Roads Authority, 2013). See also Niall Brady, 'Mills in Medieval Ireland: Looking Beyond Design', in Stephen A. Walton (ed.), *Wind & Water in the Middle Ages* (Tempe, AZ: ACMRS, 2006), pp. 39–68. I am grateful to Colin Rynne for providing me with many useful references and for valued discussion on early medieval mills.

18   For further discussion, see Watts, *Archaeology of Mills*, pp. 48–50, 78.

19   Bennett and Elton, *Corn Milling*, p. 86; S 25: this and other charter references are from Peter H. Sawyer, *Anglo-Saxon Charters: An Annotated List and Bibliography* (London: Royal Historical Society, 1968).

20   Susan E. Kelly (ed), *Charters of St Augustine's Abbey, Canterbury and Minster-in-Thanet* (Oxford: Oxford University Press, 1995), pp. 44–47.

21   Kelly, *Charters*, p. 47.

22   S 99; Della Hooke, *The Anglo-Saxon*

Landscape (Manchester: Manchester University Press, 2009), p. 128; S 1304.

23 Herbert P.R. Finberg, *The Early Charters of Wessex* (Leicester: Leicester University Press, 1964), pp. 27–28.

24 S 636; S 1008/9; S 422; S 308; S 1208.

25 S 677; S 712; S 1004.

26 S 546.

27 S 218; S 1556; James Bond, *Monastic Landscapes* (Stroud: Tempus, 2004), p. 313.

28 S 620; S 955; S 1560; S 495; S 1001; S 586.

29 S 141; Hooke, *Anglo-Saxon Landscape*, p. 243.

30 S 481; Michael Costen, *Anglo-Saxon Somerset* (Oxford: Oxbow, 2011), p. 136.

31 S 186; S 81; for Milcote see Hooke, *Anglo-Saxon Landscape*, p. 128.

32 Della Hooke, 'Uses of Waterways in Anglo-Saxon England', in John Blair (ed.), *Waterways and Canal-Building in Medieval England* (Oxford: Oxford University Press, 2007), p. 43.

33 S 1275; S 418; S 1310; S 1337; S 620.

34 Reported in David M. Wilson and John G. Hurst, 'Medieval Britain in 1957', *Medieval Archaeology* 2 (1958), pp. 183–85. The site archive is now deposited with the Royal Commission on the Ancient and Historical Monuments of Scotland, Canmore. Some of the drawings and photographs are available online <www.scran.ac.uk/> [accessed 29 April 2015].

35 K. Wade, 'A Settlement Site at Bonhunt Farm, Wicken Bonhunt, Essex', in David G. Buckley (ed.), *Archaeology in Essex to AD1500* (London : Council for British Archaeology, 1980), pp. 96–102; for discussion and analysis of the Winchester mill sites, see Alexander R. Rumble, *Property and Piety in Early Medieval Winchester*, Winchester Studies 4.3 (Oxford: Oxford University Press, 2002); for Abingdon, see C. J. Bond, 'The Reconstruction of the Medieval Landscape: The Estates of Abingdon Abbey', *Landscape History* 1 (1979), pp. 69–70.

36 Wilson and Hurst, 'Medieval Britain in 1957', pp. 183–85.

37 Wilson and Hurst, 'Medieval Britain in 1957', pp. 183–85.

38 I am most grateful to Brian Durham for obtaining information from the Old Windsor

site archive and sharing his analysis of the Old Windsor site with me.

39 See, for example, the Morett and Little Island structures illustrated in Rynne, 'Waterpower in Medieval Ireland', p. 42.

40 Philip Rahtz and Ken Sheridan, 'Fifth Report of Excavations at Tamworth, Staffs, 1971: A Saxon Water-Mill in Bolebridge Street: An Interim Note', *South Staffordshire Archaeological and Historical Society Transactions* 13 (1971–72), pp. 9–16; Philip Rahtz and Robert Meeson, *An Anglo-Saxon Watermill at Tamworth*, Council for British Archaeology Research Report 33 (London: Council for British Archaeology, 1992).

41 E.M. Trent, 'Examination of Bearing from Saxon Water Mill', *Journal of the Historical Metallurgy Society* 9.1 (1975), pp. 19–25.

42 Rynne, 'Waterpower in Medieval Ireland', pp. 30–35.

43 Colin Treen and Malcolm Atkin, *Wharram: A Study of Settlement on the Yorkshire Wolds*, vol. 10, *Water Resources and their Management*, York University Archaeological Publications 12 (York: York University Press, 2005); Andy Chapman, *West Cotton, Raunds: A Study of Medieval Settlement Dynamics AD 450–1450: Excavation of a Deserted Medieval Hamlet in Northamptonshire, 1985–1989* (Oxford: Oxbow, 2010).

44 A. Oswald, 'The Field Evidence', in Treen and Atkin, *Water Resources and their Management*, pp. 9–10.

45 Martin Watts, 'The Evidence for Milling Sites', in Treen and Atkin, *Water Resources and their Management*, pp. 222–25, reconsidered in Stuart Wrathmell (ed.), *A Study of Settlement on the Yorkshire Wolds, 13: A History of Wharram Percy and its Neighbours* (York: York University Press, 2012), pp. 206–07.

46 Chapman, *West Cotton*, p. 121.

47 Chapman, *West Cotton*, pp. 121–46.

48 Chapman, *West Cotton*, p. 132; for Morett, see A.T. Lucas, 'The Horizontal Mill in Ireland', *Journal of the Royal Society of Antiquaries of Ireland* 83 (1953), Fig. 4, where it was initially interpreted as a horizontal-wheeled mill, and Colin Rynne, 'The Introduction of the

Vertical Watermill into Ireland: Some Recent Archaeological Evidence', *Medieval Archaeology* 33 (1989), pp. 21–31.

49   Reconstructed in Chapman, *West Cotton*, Fig. 6.25. For Fullerton, see Barry Cunliffe and Bob Spain, 'The Canal and Mills', in Barry Cunliffe and Cynthia Poole (eds), *The Danebury Environs Roman Programme: A Wessex Landscape During the Roman Era*, vol. 2, Part 3, *Fullerton, Hants, 2000 and 2001* (Oxford: English Heritage and Oxford University School of Archaeology, 2008), pp. 73–100.

50   Kenneth MacGowan, 'Saxon Timber Structures from the Barking Abbey Excavations 1985–1986', *Essex Journal* 22.2 (1987), pp. 35–38; David Maynard, 'Excavations on a Pipeline near the River Frome, Worgret, Dorset', *Dorset Natural History and Archaeological Society (DNHAS) Proceedings* 110 (1988), pp. 77–98.

51   Damian Goodburn, personal communication.

52   David A. Hinton, 'Revised Dating of the Worgret Structure', *DNHAS Proceedings* 114 (1992), pp. 258–59.

53   Robin Jackson, 'Investigations by WHEAS in the Lower Lugg Valley', in Ian Bapty (ed.), *Lower Lugg Archaeology and Aggregates Resource Assessment* 2 (2007), pp. 84–112.

54   Margaret E. Snape, 'A Horizontal-Wheeled Watermill of the Anglo-Saxon Period at Corbridge, Northumberland, and its River Environment', *Archaeologia Aeliana* 32 (2003), pp. 37–72.

55   Alan Hardy, Martin Watts and Damian Goodburn, 'The Mid-Saxon Mill at Northfleet', in P. Andrews et al., *Settling the Ebbsfleet Valley*, vol. 1, *The Sites* (Oxford: Wessex Archaeology, 2011), pp. 307–49.

56   Wolfgang Czysz, *Die ältesten Wassermühlen. Archäologische Entdeckungen im Paartal bei Dasing* (Thierhaupten: Klostermühlenmuseum, 1998), p. 28.

57   Christopher K. Currie, 'Early Water Management on the Lower River Itchen in Hampshire', in Blair, *Waterways and Canal-Building*, p. 250.

58   Örjan Wikander, 'Mill-Channels, Weirs and Ponds: The Environment of Ancient Water-Mills', *Opuscula Romana* 15.13 (1985), pp. 151–52.

59   William Cunningham, *The Growth of English Industry and Commerce*, 5th edn (Cambridge: Cambridge University Press, 1915), pp. 572, 574.

60   A possible defensive function is suggested by Grenville Astill, *Historic Towns in Berkshire: An Archaeological Appraisal* (Reading: Berkshire Archaeological Committee, 1978), p. 70; Hooke, 'Uses of Waterways in Anglo-Saxon England', pp. 39–40.

61   Blair, 'Introduction', in Blair, *Waterways and Canal-Building*, pp. 4–5.

62   Bond, 'The Reconstruction of the Medieval Landscape', pp. 69–70.

63   Rumble, *Property and Piety*, pp. 140–43.

64   For Nendrum, see Thomas McErlean and Norman Crothers, *Harnessing the Tides: The Early Medieval Tide Mills at Nendrum Monastery, Strangford Lough* (Belfast: Stationery Office, 2007); for Little Island, see Colin Rynne, 'Milling in the 7th Century', *Archaeology Ireland* 6.2 (1992), pp. 22–24; a plan of the Little Island site is given in Rynne, 'Waterpower in Medieval Ireland', p. 42.

65   Rahtz and Bullough, 'Parts of an Anglo-Saxon Mill', p. 28.

66   Holt, *Mills of Medieval England*, p. 5; Colin Rynne, personal communication.

67   Anne Dodd (ed.), *Oxford before the University: The Late Saxon and Norman Archaeology of the Thames Crossing, the Defences and the Town* (Oxford: Oxford Archaeology, 2003), pp. 275–76; Brian Durham, personal communication.

68   Hardy et al., 'The Mid-Saxon Mill at Northfleet', p. 342; for a detailed discussion of early medieval waterwheel paddles, see Colin Rynne, 'The Technical Development of the Horizontal Water-Wheel in the First Millennium AD: Some Recent Archaeological Insights from Ireland', *International Journal for the History of Engineering and Technology* 85.1 (2015), pp. 70–93.

69   Holt, *Mills of Medieval England*, p. 118.

70   The paddles are in store at the Museum in the Park, Stroud, under reference numbers STGCM1967.170/1 and STGCM1967.170/2.

I am grateful to Alexia Clark for making them available for me to study.

71 Hardy et al., 'The Mid-Saxon Mill at Northfleet', p. 336.

72 Scott Gwara and David W. Porter, *Anglo-Saxon Conversations: The Colloquies of Ælfric Bata* (Woodbridge: Boydell, 1997), pp. 162–63.

73 Wilson and Hurst, 'Medieval Britain in 1957', p. 185; Rahtz and Meeson, *An Anglo-Saxon Watermill at Tamworth*, pp. 31–33; Hardy et al., 'The Mid-Saxon Mill at Northfleet', pp. 332–33.

74 Chapman, *West Cotton*, p. 142; Robin Jackson, personal communication.

75 Susan R. Watts, 'The Milling Stones', in Treen and Atkin, *Water Resources and their Management*, p. 126.

76 Shown on section drawings, as reference 34.

77 Robin Jackson, personal communication; Chris Salter, 'The Iron Working Slag from the River Frome Site', in Maynard, 'Excavations on a Pipeline near the River Frome', pp. 82–85.

78 Hagen, *Handbook of Anglo-Saxon Food*, pp. 3–15.

79 From *Anglo-Saxon Prose*, trans. and ed. Michael Swanton (London: Dent, 1993), pp. 169–77.

80 For a summary of the Irish laws relating to mills, see Rynne, 'Waterpower in Medieval Ireland', pp. 3–6; for Welsh laws, see Dafydd Jenkins, *The Laws of Hywel Dda* (Llandysul: Gomer, 2000).

81 *Laws of the Earliest English Kings*, trans. and ed. Frederick L. Attenborough (Cambridge: Cambridge University Press, 1922), p. 5.

82 *Laws of the Earliest English Kings*, pp. 58–59.

83 Hardy et al., 'The Mid-Saxon Mill at Northfleet', p. 348.

84 Dorothy Whitelock, *The Beginnings of English Society* (Harmondsworth: Penguin, 1982), p. 168.

85 Fergus Kelly, 'Water-Rights and Milling in Early Irish Law', *Mills and Millers of Ireland* 3 (2003), pp. 16–24.

86 Peter Herring and Della Hooke, 'Interrogating Anglo-Saxons in St Dennis', *Cornish Archaeology* 32 (1993), p. 73.

87 Martin Watts, 'The Mill and Dam Site at Wharram: Some Further Thoughts', in Stuart Wrathmell, *Wharram Percy and its Neighbours*, pp. 206–07.

88 Dorothy Whitelock, *The Will of Aethelgifu: A Tenth Century Anglo-Saxon Manuscript* (Oxford: Roxburghe Club, 1968), pp. 6–7.

89 Cunningham, *Growth of English Industry*, p. 572.

90 For the role of mills in the later medieval period, see John Langdon, *Mills in the Medieval Economy: England 1300–1540* (Oxford: Oxford University Press, 2004).

91 Wilson, *Archaeology of Anglo-Saxon England*, p. 276.

92 See, for example, Holt, *Mills of Medieval England*, pp. 17–21.

93 Agnes J. Robertson, *Anglo-Saxon Charters* (Cambridge: Cambridge University Press, 1939), pp. 254–55; Philip Rahtz, *The Saxon and Medieval Palaces at Cheddar* (Oxford: British Archaeological Reports, 1979), pp. 129–32.

Chapter 9: *Wics* and *Burhs*

1 *Bede's Ecclesiastical History of the English People*, ed. and trans. Bertram Colgrave, with an introduction by Judith McClure and Roger Collins (Oxford: Oxford University Press, 1994), ii.3.

2 Martin Biddle, 'Towns', in David M. Wilson (ed.), *The Archaeology of Anglo-Saxon England* (London: Methuen, 1976), pp. 99–150.

3 Daniel Russo, *Town Origins and Development in Early England*, c.400–950 AD (London: Greenwood, 1998).

4 John Wacher, *The Towns of Roman Britain*, 2nd edn (London: Routledge, 1997).

5 Russo, *Town Origins and Development*, pp. 231–32; see also Christopher Grocock, 'Enta geweorc: "The Ruin" and its Contexts Reconsidered', in Maren Clegg Hyer and Gale R. Owen-Crocker (eds), *The Material Culture of the Built Environment in the Anglo-Saxon*

World, The Material Culture of Daily Living in the Anglo-Saxon World 2 (Liverpool: University of Liverpool Press, 2015).

6   Robin Fleming, *Britain after Rome: The Fall and Rise, AD 400 to 1070* (London: Allen Lane, 2010), p. 185.

7   Grenville Astill, 'Overview: Trade, Exchange and Urbanization', in Helena Hamerow, David A. Hinton and Sally Crawford (eds), *The Oxford Handbook of Anglo-Saxon Archaeology* (Oxford: Oxford University Press, 2011), pp. 503–14.

8   The archaeological evidence from *Lundenwic* is summarized by Robert Cowie with Charlotte Harding, 'Saxon Settlement and Economy from the Dark Ages to Domesday', in Trevor Brigham et al. (eds), *The Archaeology of Greater London* (London: Museum of London Archaeological Service, 2000), pp. 171–206. Detailed excavation reports from sites in *wics* include: Gordon Malcolm, David Bowsher and Robert Cowie, *Middle Saxon London: Excavations at the Royal Opera House 1989–99*, MOLAS Monograph Series 15 (London: Museum of London Archaeological Service, 2003); Phil Andrews, *Excavations at Hamwic*, vol. 2, *Excavations at Six Dials*, Council for British Archaeology Research Report 109 (York: Council for British Archaeology, 1997); Richard Kemp, *Anglian Settlement at 46–54 Fishergate*, The Archaeology of York 7.1 (York: York Archaeological Trust, 1996).

9   Biddle, 'Towns', p. 114.

10   Tim Tatton-Brown, 'The Anglo-Saxon Towns of Kent', in Della Hooke (ed.), *Anglo-Saxon Settlements* (Oxford: Basil Blackwell, 1988), pp. 213–32.

11   Tim Pestell, 'Markets, Emporia, *Wics*, and "Productive" Sites: Pre-Viking Trade Centres in Anglo-Saxon England', in Hamerow, Hinton and Crawford, *The Oxford Handbook of Anglo-Saxon Archaeology*, pp. 556–79.

12   John Schofield and Heiko Steuer, 'Urban Settlement', in James Graham-Campbell with Magdalena Valor (eds), *The Archaeology of Medieval Europe*, vol. 1, *Eighth to Tenth Centuries AD* (Aarhus: Aarhus University Press, 2007), pp. 111–53.

13   Katrin Thier, 'Steep Vessel, High Horn-Ship: Water Transport', in Maren Clegg Hyer and Gale R. Owen-Crocker (eds), *The Material Culture of Daily Living in the Anglo-Saxon World* (Exeter: University of Exeter Press, 2011), pp. 49–72.

14   Ian Riddler and Nicola Trzaska-Nartowski, 'Chanting upon a Dunghill: Working Skeletal Materials', in Hyer and Owen-Crocker, *Material Culture of Daily Living*, pp. 116–41.

15   For a broader discussion, see Jeremy Haslam, 'The Landscape of Late Saxon *Burhs* and the Politics of Urban Foundation', in Maren Clegg Hyer and Gale R. Owen-Crocker (eds), *The Material Culture of the Built Environment in the Anglo-Saxon World*, The Material Culture of Daily Living in the Anglo-Saxon World 2 (Liverpool: Liverpool University Press, 2015).

16   Martin Ryan, 'The Anglo-Saxons and the Vikings, *c.*825–900', in Nicholas Higham and Martin Ryan (eds), *The Anglo-Saxon World* (London: Yale University Press, 2013), pp. 232–70; Richard Hall, '*Burhs* and Boroughs: Defended Places, Trade and Towns', in Hamerow, Hinton and Crawford, *The Oxford Handbook of Anglo-Saxon Archaeology*, pp. 600–21.

17   Alexander Rumble and David Hill (eds), *The Defence of Wessex: Burghal Hidage and Anglo-Saxon Fortifications* (Manchester: Manchester University Press, 1996).

18   Astill, 'Overview'.

19   Russo, *Town Origins and Development*, pp. 193–94.

20   Excavation reports and syntheses for individual *burhs* include: David Mason, *Excavations at Chester, 26–42 Lower Bridge Street: The Dark Age and Saxon Periods* (Chester: Chester City Council, 1985); Cowie and Harding, 'Saxon Settlement and Economy', pp. 171–206; Michael Jones, David Stocker and Alan Vince, *The City by the Pool: Assessing the Archaeology of the City of Lincoln* (Oxford: Oxbow, 2003); Ann Dodd (ed.), *Oxford before the University: The Late Saxon and Norman Archaeology of the Thames Crossing, the Defences and the Town* (Oxford: Oxford Archaeology, 2003); Martin Carver, *The Birth of a Borough: An Archaeological*

Study of Anglo-Saxon Stafford (Woodbridge: Boydell and Brewer, 2010); Neil Christie and Oliver Creighton with Matt Edgeworth and Helena Hamerow, *Transforming Townscapes: From Burh to Borough: The Archaeology of Wallingford, AD 800–1400*, Society for Medieval Archaeology Monographs 35 (London: The Society for Medieval Archaeology, 2013); Hal Dalwood and Rachel Edwards (eds), *Excavations at Deansway, Worcester, 1988–89: Romano-British Small Town to Late Medieval City* (York: Council for British Archaeology, 2004).

21　Biddle, 'Towns'.

22　Richard Hall, *Anglo-Scandinavian Occupation at 16–22 Coppergate: Defining a Townscape*, The Archaeology of York 8.5 (York: Council for British Archaeology, 2014).

23　David A. Hinton, *Archaeology, Economy and Society: England from the Fifth to the Fifteenth Century* (London: Seaby, 1990), pp. 82–85.

24　Hinton, *Archaeology, Economy and Society*, pp. 87–92.

25　Guy Halsall, *Warfare and Society in the Barbarian West, 450–900* (London: Routledge, 2003), pp. 215–27.

26　Cowie and Harding, 'Saxon Settlement and Economy', p. 183.

27　Halsall, *Warfare and Society*, p. 219.

28　Jeremy Haslam, 'King Alfred and the Vikings: Strategies and Tactics 876–886 AD', *Anglo-Saxon Studies in Archaeology and History* 13 (2005), pp. 136–37.

29　Richard Abels, *Lordship and Military Obligation in Anglo-Saxon England* (London: British Museum, 1988), pp. 43–57.

30　Halsall, *Warfare and Society*, p. 220.

31　Andrew Reynolds, *Later Anglo-Saxon England: Life and Landscape* (Stroud: Tempus, 1999), pp. 74–75.

32　Abels, *Lordship and Military Obligation*.

33　John Baker and Stuart Brookes, *Beyond the Burghal Hidage: Anglo-Saxon Civil Defence in the Viking Age* (Leiden: Brill, 2013), pp. 152–67.

34　Alan Cooper, *Bridges, Law and Power in Medieval England, 700–1400* (Woodbridge: Boydell and Brewer, 2006). For the Anglo-Saxon road network more generally, see Paul Hindle, 'Roads and Tracks in Anglo-Saxon England', in Hyer and Owen-Crocker, *The Material Culture of the Built Environment*.

35　Ann Dodd, 'Synthesis and Discussion', in Dodd, *Oxford before the University*, pp. 13–16, 32–35.

36　Duncan Garrow and Fraser Sturt, 'Grey Waters Bright with Neolithic Argonauts? Maritime Connections and Mesolithic-Neolithic Transition within the "Western Seaways" of Britain', *Antiquity* 85 (2011), pp. 59–72.

37　Gustav Milne, *The Port of Roman London* (London: Batsford, 1985).

38　Evan Jones, 'River Navigation in Medieval England', *Journal of Historical Geography* 26 (2000), pp. 60–82.

39　Valerie Fenwick, *The Graveney Boat: A Tenth-Century Find from Kent* (Oxford: British Archaeological Reports, 1978). See also Thier, 'Steep Vessel, High Horn-Ship', pp. 67–68.

40　Hinton, *Archaeology, Economy and Society*, pp. 21–23.

41　Henry Loyn, *Anglo-Saxon England and the Norman Conquest* (London: Longman, 1962), p. 80.

42　Cowie and Harding, 'Saxon Settlement and Economy', p. 187.

43　Paul Blinkhorn, *The Ipswich Ware Project: Ceramics, Trade and Society in Middle Saxon England*, Medieval Pottery Research Group Occasional Paper 7 (London: Medieval Pottery Research Group, 2012).

44　Ann Cole, *The Place-name Evidence for a Routeway Network in Early Medieval England*, British Archaeological Reports, British Series 589 (Oxford: Archaeopress, 2013), pp. 55–63.

45　David A. Hinton, *Gold, Gilt, Pots and Pins: Possessions and People in Medieval Britain* (Oxford: Oxford University Press, 2005).

46　Hinton, *Archaeology, Economy and Society*, pp. 39–40; Loyn, *Anglo-Saxon England*, pp. 86–89; Fleming, *Britain after Rome*, p. 209.

47　Cowie and Harding, 'Saxon Settlement and Economy', p. 183.

48　Adriaan Verhulst, *The Carolingian Economy* (Cambridge: Cambridge University Press, 2002), pp. 100–02.

49   John Maddicott, 'London and Droitwich, *c.*650–750: Trade, Industry and the Rise of Mercia', *Anglo-Saxon England* 34 (2005), pp. 14, 45.

50   Maddicott, 'London and Droitwich', p. 24.

51   Peter H. Sawyer, *Wealth of Anglo-Saxon England* (Oxford: Oxford University Press, 2013).

52   Fleming, *Britain after Rome*, pp. 191–93.

53   Hinton, *Gold, Gilt, Pots and Pins*, p. 88.

54   Hinton, *Archaeology, Economy and Society*, p. 56; Ben Jervis, 'Placing Pottery: An Actor-led Approach to the Use and Perception of Medieval Pottery in Southampton and its Region *c.*AD 700–1400' (unpublished doctoral thesis, University of Southampton, 2011), pp. 274–76. <http://eprints.soton.ac.uk/345132/1.hasCoversheetVersion/Ben_Jervis_EThesis.pdf> [accessed 1 December 2014].

55   Jervis, 'Placing Pottery', p. 306.

56   Sawyer, *Wealth of Anglo-Saxon England*, p. 106.

57   Fleming, *Britain after Rome*, p. 243.

58   Marianne Vedeler, *Silk for the Vikings* (Oxford: Oxbow, 2014), p. 40.

59   Loyn, *Anglo-Saxon England*, p. 90.

60   Sawyer, *Wealth of Anglo-Saxon England*, pp. 104–05.

61   Loyn, *Anglo-Saxon England*, p. 93–94.

62   John Blair, 'Introduction', in John Blair (ed.), *Waterways and Canal-Building in Medieval England* (Oxford: Oxford University Press, 2007), pp. 1–18.

63   Hindle, 'Roads and Tracks in Anglo-Saxon England'.

64   Blair, 'Introduction', in Blair, *Waterways and Canal-Building*, pp. 14–18, Figs 4 and 5.

65   Fleming, *Britain after Rome*, pp. 243–46.

66   Blair, 'Introduction', in Blair, *Waterways and Canal-Building*, p. 14.

67   James H. Barrett, Alison M. Locker and Callum M. Roberts, '"Dark Age Economics" Revisited: The English Fish Bone Evidence AD 600–1600', *Antiquity* 78 (2004), pp. 618–36.

68   Jonathan Parkhouse, 'The Distribution and Exchange of Mayen Lava Quernstones in Early Medieval Northwestern Europe', in Guy de Boe and Frans Verhaege (eds), *Environment and Subsistence in Medieval Europe: Papers of the 'Medieval Europe Brugge 1997' Conference* (Zellik: Instituut voor het Archeologisch Patrimonium, 1997), pp. 97–106.

69   Allen Frantzen, *Food, Eating and Identity in Early Medieval England* (Woodbridge: Boydell, 2014), pp. 86–88.

70   Hinton, *Gold, Gilt, Pots and Pins*, pp. 89–90.

71   David Peacock, 'Charlemagne's Black Stones: The Re-Use of Roman Columns in Early Medieval Europe', *Antiquity* 77 (1997), pp. 709–15.

72   Martyn Jope, 'The Saxon Building-Stone Industry in Southern and Midland England', *Medieval Archaeology* 8 (1964), pp. 91–117.

73   Robert Cowie, 'Mercian London', in Michelle Brown and Carol Farr (eds), *Mercia: An Anglo-Saxon Kingdom in Europe* (Leicester: Leicester University Press, 2001), pp. 200–01.

74   Peter H. Sawyer, *Anglo-Saxon Charters: An Annotated List and Bibliography* (London: Royal Historical Society, 1968), S 1628.

75   Cowie and Harding, 'Saxon Settlement and Economy', p. 193.

76   Cowie and Harding, 'Saxon Settlement and Economy', pp. 193–94; Fleming, *Britain after Rome*, pp. 254–58.

77   Alan Vince, 'The New Town: Lincoln in the High Medieval Era (*c.*900–*c.*1350)', in Michael Jones, David Stocker and Alan Vince (eds), *The City by the Pool: Assessing the Archaeology of the City of Lincoln* (Oxford: Oxbow, 2003), p. 238.

78   Ole Crumlin-Petersen, 'Ship Types and Sizes AD 800–1400', in Ole Crumlin-Pedersen (ed.), *Aspects of Maritime Scandinavia AD 200–1200* (Roskilde: Viking Ship Museum, 1991), pp. 69–82; Gareth Williams, *The Viking Ship* (London: British Museum, 2014), p. 80; Thier, 'Steep Vessel, High-Horn Ship', p. 67.

79   Benjamin Hudson, 'The Changing Economy of the Irish Sea Province: AD 900–1330', in Brendan Smith (ed.), *Britain and Ireland, 900–1300: Insular Responses to Medieval European Change* (Cambridge: Cambridge University Press, 1999), pp. 42–46.

80   David Mason, *Chester AD 400–1066: From Roman Fortress to Anglo-Saxon Town* (Stroud: Tempus, 2007), p. 133.

81   Michael Lapidge, 'Rome', in Michael Lapidge, John Blair, Simon Keynes and Donald Scragg (eds), *The Wiley Blackwell Encyclopedia of Anglo-Saxon England*, 2nd edn (Chichester: John Wiley, 2014), pp. 409–11.
82   Cowie and Harding, 'Saxon Settlement and Economy', p. 196.
83   John Cherry, 'Leather', in John Blair and Nigel Ramsey (eds), *English Medieval Industries: Craftsmen, Techniques, Products* (London: Hambledon, 1991), pp. 295–318.
84   Esther Cameron and Quita Mould, 'Devil's Crafts and Dragon's Skins? Sheaths, Shoes and Other Leatherwork', in Hyer and Owen-Crocker, *Material Culture of Daily Living*, pp. 93–115.
85   Derek Keene, 'Tanning', in Martin Biddle (ed.), *Object and Economy in Medieval Winchester*, Winchester Studies 7.2 (Oxford: Oxford University Press, 1990), vol. 1, pp. 243–45.
86   Dodd, 'Synthesis and Discussion', p. 42.
87   Cowie and Harding, 'Saxon Settlement and Economy', p. 196.
88   Philip Rahtz and Robert Meeson, *An Anglo-Saxon Watermill at Tamworth*, Council for British Archaeology Research Report 83 (London: Council for British Archaeology, 1992).
89   Natascha Mehler, 'Marine Trade and Transport-Related Crafts and their Actors – People without Archaeology?', in Gitte Hansen, Stephen Ashby and Irene Baug (eds), *Everyday Products in the Middle Ages: Crafts, Consumption and the Individual in Northern Europe c.AD 800–1600* (Oxford: Oxbow, 2015), pp. 360–74.
90   Peter Marsden, *Ships of the Port of London: First to Eleventh Centuries AD*,
English Heritage Archaeological Report 3 (London: English Heritage, 1996), pp. 163–74.
91   Della Hooke, 'Uses of Waterways in Anglo-Saxon England', in Blair, *Waterways and Canal-Building in Medieval England*, pp. 1–18.
92   Della Hooke, *The Anglo-Saxon Landscape: The Kingdom of the Hwicce* (Manchester: Manchester University Press, 1985), pp. 131–32.
93   Barrett et al., 'Dark Age Economics', pp. 623–30.
94   Barrett et al., 'Dark Age Economics', p. 628.
95   *Ælfric's Colloquy*, ed. and trans. George N. Garmonsway, rev. edn (Exeter: University of Exeter Press, 1978), pp. 26–30; British Museum Cotton MS, Tiberius A. iii, fols 60b–64b.
96   Malcolm et al., *Middle Saxon London: Excavations at the Royal Opera House 1989–99*.
97   Andrews, *Excavations at Hamwic 2*, pp. 188–97.
98   Vince, 'The New Town', p. 264, Fig. 9.84.
99   Keene, *Survey of Medieval Winchester*, Parts I, II and III (in two volumes), Winchester Studies 2 (Oxford: Oxford University Press, 1985), p. 56.
100   Allan Hall and Harry Kenward, 'Setting People in their Environment: Plant and Animal Remains from Anglo-Scandinavian York', in Richard Hall (ed.), *Aspects of Anglo-Scandinavian York*, The Archaeology of York 8.4 (York: Council for British Archaeology, 2004), pp. 391–94.
101   Hall and Kenward, 'Setting People in Their Environment', pp. 394–95, 401–03.
102   Dodd, 'Synthesis and Discussion', p. 45.
103   Cowie and Harding, 'Saxon Settlement and Economy', p. 190.
104   Cowie and Harding, 'Saxon Settlement and Economy', p. 190.

Suggested Reading

Chapter 1: Anglo-Saxon Poetry

Daniel Anlezark, *Water and Fire: The Myth of the Flood in Anglo-Saxon England*, Manchester Medieval Literature Series (Manchester and New York: Manchester University Press, 2006).

Sarah Foot, '"By Water in the Spirit": The Administration of Baptism in Early Anglo-Saxon England', in John Blair and Richard Sharpe (eds), *Pastoral Care Before the Parish* (Leicester and London: Leicester University Press, 1992), pp. 171–92.

Della Hooke, *The Landscape of Anglo-Saxon England* (London and New York: Leicester University Press, 1998).

Karen Jolly, 'Father God and Mother Earth: Nature-Mysticism in the Anglo-Saxon World', in Joyce E. Salisbury (ed.), *The Medieval World of Nature: A Book of Essays* (New York: Garland, 1993), pp. 221–25.

Jennifer Neville, *Representations of the Natural World in Old English Poetry* (Cambridge: Cambridge University Press, 1999).

Kelley M. Wickham-Crowley, 'Living on the *Ecg*: The Mutable Boundaries of Land and Water in Anglo-Saxon Contexts', in Clare A. Lees and Gillian R. Overing (eds), *A Place to Believe In: Locating Medieval Landscapes* (University Park: Pennsylvania State University Press, 2006), pp. 85–110.

Chapter 2: Charters, Laws and Place Names

Documentary evidence for the use of waterways is also discussed in Della Hooke, 'Uses of Waterways in Anglo-Saxon England', in John Blair (ed.), *Waterways and Canal-Building in Medieval England* (Oxford: Oxford University Press, 2007), pp. 37–54.

On river names, pioneering works such as Eilert Ekwall's *English River-Names* (Oxford: Clarendon Press, 1928) need to be consulted alongside more recent studies such as Victor Watts's *The Cambridgeshire Dictionary of English Place-Names* (Cambridge: Cambridge University Press, 2004) (*CDEPN*). Others may be covered in the county volumes of the English Place-Name Society and in specialist journals such as the *Journal of the English Place-Name Society* and *Nomina* (many referenced in Chapter 2).

On the interpretation of individual water terms, see Margaret Gelling and Ann Cole, *The Landscape of Place-Names* (Donington: Shaun Tyas, 2000; corrected reprint 2003; new edn 2014).

For the use of such names in a landscape context, see, among other similar works, Della Hooke, *Worcestershire Anglo-Saxon Charter-Bounds* (Woodbridge: Boydell, 1990) and Della Hooke, *The Anglo-Saxon Landscape: The Kingdom of the Hwicce* (Manchester: Manchester University Press, 1985).

Chapter 3: Fens and Frontiers

An English Fen, Dir. Ronald Haines, British Foundation Pictures. 1947. East Anglian Film Archive <www.eafa.org.uk/catalogue/390> [accessed 18 May 2015]. A short documentary depicting life in the fens, including making eel baskets, fishing for eels and turning wood products on a lathe.

Andy Crowson, Tom Lane, Kenneth Penn and Dale Trimble, *Anglo-Saxon Settlement on the Siltland of Eastern England*, Lincolnshire Archaeology and Heritage Reports Series 7 (Sleaford: Heritage Trust of Lincolnshire, 2005). See, especially, David Roffe, 'The Historical Context' (pp. 264–88).

Margaret Gelling and Ann Cole, *The Landscape of Place-Names* (Stamford: Shaun Tyas, 2000)

Hereward the Wake, trans. Michael Swanton, in Stephen Knight and Thomas Ohlgren (eds), *Robin Hood and Other Outlaw Tales*, TEAMS Middle English Texts Series (Kalamazoo: Medieval Institute Publications, 1997), unpaginated <http://d.lib.rochester.edu/teams/text/hereward-the-wake> [accessed 22 May 2015].

Liber Eliensis: A History of the Isle of Ely from the Seventh Century to the Twelfth, trans. Janet Fairweather (Woodbridge: Boydell, 2005).

Kelley M. Wickham-Crowley, 'Living on the *Ecg*: The Mutable Boundaries of Land and Water in Anglo-Saxon Contexts', in Clare A. Lees and Gillian R. Overing (eds), *A Place to Believe In: Locating Medieval Landscapes* (University Park: Pennsylvania State University Press, 2006), pp. 85–110.

Chapter 4: Marshlands and Other Wetlands

For a general introduction to the character, archaeology and history of land use on the coastal wetlands of southern Britain, see Stephen Rippon, *The Transformation of Coastal Wetlands* (London: The British Academy, 2000).

For the most extensive programme of survey, excavation and palaeoenvironmental analysis on early medieval marshland settlements, see Andy Crowson, Tom Lane, Ken Penn and Dale Trimble, *Anglo-Saxon Settlement on the Siltland of Eastern England*, Lincolnshire Archaeology and Heritage Reports Series 7 (Sleaford: Heritage Trust of Lincolnshire, 2005).

Another important marshland settlement excavation, with evidence for salt production: Paul Cope-Faulkner, *Clampgate Road, Fishtoft: Archaeology of a Middle Saxon Island Settlement in the Lincolnshire Fens*, Lincolnshire Archaeology and Heritage Reports

Series 10 (Sleaford: Heritage Trust of Lincolnshire, 2012).

For the fish weirs in Essex, and a summary of the evidence elsewhere, see Ellen M. Heppell, 'Saxon Fishtraps in the Blackwater Estuary, Essex: Monitoring Survey at Collin's Creek, Pewet Island and The Nass 2003–2007', *Transactions of the Essex Society for Archaeology and History* 2 (2011), pp. 76–97.

For the Norfolk fishtraps, see David Robertson and John Ames, 'Early Medieval Inter-Tidal Fishweirs at Holme Beach, Norfolk', *Medieval Archaeology* 54 (2010), pp. 329–46.

For the wider context of the increased intensification of landscape use around the eighth century, see Stephen Rippon, 'Landscape Change in the "Long Eighth Century"', in Nicholas Higham and Martin J. Ryan (eds), *The Landscape Archaeology of Anglo-Saxon England* (Woodbridge: Boydell, 2010), pp. 39–64.

Chapter 5: Sacred and Mystical Contexts

While many works refer to Anglo-Saxon votive offerings, holy wells etc., in passing (see references), few make this a major theme for discussion. Among the latter, referring to the English Anglo-Saxon evidence, see the following.

Graham Jones, *Saints in the Landscape* (Stroud: Tempus, 2007).

David Stocker and Paul Everson, 'The Straight and Narrow Way: Fenland Causeways and the Conversion of the Landscape in the Witham Valley, Lincolnshire', in Martin Carver (ed.), *The Cross Goes North: Processes of Conversion in Northern Europe, AD 300–1300* (Woodbridge: York Medieval Press, 2003), pp. 49–66.

James Rattue, *The Living Stream: Holy Wells in Historical Context* (Woodbridge: Boydell, 1995).

Chapter 6: Fishing

James H. Barrett, Alison M. Locker and Callum M. Roberts, '"Dark Age Economics" Revisted: The English Fish Bone Evidence AD 600–1600', *Antiquity* 78 (2004), pp. 618–36.

Otto Gabriel, Klaus Lange, Erdmann Dahm and Thomas Wendt, *Von Brandt's Fish Catching Methods of the World* (Oxford: Wiley, 2004).

David Orton, James Morris, Alison M. Locker and James H. Barrett, 'Fish for the City: Meta-analysis of Archaeological Cod Remains and the Growth of London's Northern Trade', *Antiquity* 88 (2014), pp. 516–30.

Chris R. Salisbury, 'Primitive British Fishweirs', in G.L. Good and R.H. Jones (eds), *Waterfront Archaeology: Proceedings of the Third International Conference, Bristol* (London: Council for British Archaeology, 1988), pp. 76–87.

Dale Serjeanston and Chris M. Woolgar, 'Fish Consumption in Medieval England', in Chris M. Woolgar, D. Serjeanston and T. Waldron (eds), *Food in Medieval England: Diet and Nutrition* (Oxford: Oxford University Press, 2006), pp. 102–30.

Aldwyn Wheeler and Andrew K.G. Jones, *Fishes* (Cambridge: Cambridge University Press, 2009).

Chapter 7: Landing Places, Canals and Bridges

Julian Ayre and Robin Wroe-Brown, 'The Post-Roman Foreshore and the Origins of the Late Anglo-Saxon Waterfront and Dock of Æthelred's Hithe: Excavations at Bull Wharf, City of London', *Archaeological Journal* 172 (2015), pp. 121–94.

John Blair (ed.), *Waterways and Canal-Building in Medieval England* (Oxford: Oxford University, 2007).

Alan Cooper, *Bridges, Law and Power in Medieval England, 700–1400* (Woodbridge: Boydell, 2006).

Valerie Fenwick, *The Graveney Boat: A Tenth-Century Find from Kent, British Archaeological Reports, British Series 53* (Oxford: British Archaeological Reports, 1978).

Mark Gardiner, 'Shipping and Trade between England and the Continent during the Eleventh Century', *Anglo-Norman Studies* 22 (2000), pp. 73–93.

Neil Middleton, 'Early Medieval Port Customs, Tolls and Controls on Foreign Trade', *Early Medieval Europe* 13 (2005), pp. 313–58.

Katrin Thier, 'Steep Vessel, High Horn-Ship: Water Transport', in Maren Clegg Hyer and Gale R. Owen-Crocker (eds), *The Material Culture of Daily Living in the Anglo-Saxon World* (Exeter: University of Exeter Press, 2011), pp. 48–72.

Chapter 8: Watermills and Waterwheels

John Blair (ed.), *Waterways and Canal-Building in Medieval England* (Oxford: Oxford University Press, 2007).

Richard Holt, *The Mills of Medieval England* (Oxford: Blackwell, 1988).

Philip Rahtz and Donald Bullough, 'The Parts of an Anglo-Saxon Mill', *Anglo-Saxon England* 6 (1977), pp. 15–31.

Colin Rynne, 'Waterpower in Medieval Ireland', in Paolo Squatriti (ed.), *Working with Water in Medieval Europe* (Leiden: Brill, 2000), pp. 1–50.

Martin Watts, *The Archaeology of Mills and Milling* (Stroud: Tempus, 2002).

Martin Watts, *Corn Milling* (Oxford: Shire, 2008).

Chapter 9: *Wics* and *Burh*s

John Blair (ed.), *Waterways and Canal-Building in Medieval England* (Oxford: Oxford University, 2007).

Robin Fleming, *Britain after Rome: The Fall and Rise, 400 to 1070* (London: Allen Lane, 2010).

Jeremy Haslam (ed.), *Anglo-Saxon Towns in Southern England* (Chichester: Phillimore, 1984). This volume is a wide-ranging survey, but is not up to date on more recent archaeological evidence.

Nicholas Higham, 'The Rebirth of Towns', in Nicholas Higham and Martin Ryan (eds), *The Anglo-Saxon World* (London: Yale University Press, 2013), pp. 277–83.

David Palliser (ed.), *The Cambridge Urban History of Britain*, vol. 1, *600–1540* (Cambridge: Cambridge University, 2000).

John Schofield and Heiko Steuer, 'Urban Settlement', in James Graham-Campbell with Magdalena Valor (eds), *The Archaeology of Medieval Europe*, vol. 1, *Eighth to Twelfth Centuries AD* (Aarhus: Aarhus University Press, 2007), pp. 111–53.

Index

(places given in modern counties; figures italicised)